2004 Supplement to the Accounting Desk Book

by Tom M. Plank, Lois Ruffner Plank, and Bryan R. Plank

Highlights

The *2004 Supplement to the Accounting Desk Book* is a practical working tool that provides quick, authoritative, and up-to-date answers for CPAs and Financial Services Professionals applying relevant accounting principles and standards as well as tax rules. It contains all of the important pronouncements from the FASB, GASB, and IASB; financial reporting presentation requirements; required and recommended disclosures; and specialized accounting topics needed to field a client's questions, brush up on the proper treatment of a transaction, or consider an engagement in a new area of practice.

Guidelines, illustrations, and step-by-step instructions simplify complex accounting issues and give public and private accountants quick answers to accounting application questions.

2004 Supplement

The 2004 Supplement to the Twelfth Edition of the *Accounting Desk Book* provides new and expanded coverage in these areas:

- Chapter 1, "Revenue and Expenses" — has been updated to include analysis of FASB 148, *Accounting for Stock-Based Compensation— Transition and Disclosure — An Amendment of FASB 123*. In addition, the chapter takes into consideration the decision the FASB is facing: whether the Board should undertake a more comprehensive reconsideration of the accounting for stock options, particularly in light of the IASB's proposals relating to them.

- Chapter 2, "Actions of the Financial Accounting Standards Board" — has been updated to include analysis of FASB 150, *Accounting for Certain Financial Instruments with Characteristics of Both Liabilities and Equity*. In addition to a well-stocked agenda of its own, it appears that the

Board is heeding the Sarbanes-Oxley Act and the SEC's suggestions to pursue the idea of convergence of GAAP and international standards.

- Chapter 3, "Consolidation of Variable Interest Entities" — this new chapter considers the details of FASB Interpretation (FIN) 46, *Consolidation of Variable Interest Entities*. The Interpretation addresses when a company should include the assets, liabilities, and activities of these entities in its financial statements.

- Chapter 4, "Governmental Accounting" — has been updated to provide the latest information on the GASB's efforts to effect smooth transitions and beginnings under GASB 34, *Basic Financial Statements — and Management's Discussion and Analysis — for State and Local Governments,* while systematically reviewing and updating some of the older standards.

- Chapter 5, "International Accounting" — has been updated to include information on the IASB's IFRS 1, *First-Time Adoption of International Financial Reporting Standards*. The standard explains how companies worldwide can make the transition to IFRSs from another basis of accounting.

- Chapter 6, "The International Federation of Accountants" — has been updated with discussions of IFAC's development of two additional International Public Sector Accounting Standards (IPSASs). Two special task forces have been formed to address current issues: rebuilding public confidence in financial reporting, and problems facing small and medium accounting practices and enterprises.

- Chapter 7, "The Sarbanes-Oxley Act of 2002" — has been updated with discussions of the key actions that have resulted in the past year from measures undertaken as required by this Act. Among the steps taken was the reaffirmation of the FASB as the preeminent accounting standard setter in the private sector.

- Chapter 8, "Public Company Accounting Oversight Board" — this new chapter details the responsibilities of this powerful overseer and reports on the continuing progress of this emerging organization in implementing the provisions of the Sarbanes-Oxley Act.

- Chapter 9, "Auditor Independence and the Audit Committee" — has been updated with discussions of the many new and revised rules aimed at addressing the auditor's independence in both fact and appearance.

- Chapter 10, "Foreign Currency Translations and Derivative Disclosure" — has been updated with analysis of FASB 149, *Amendment of Statement 133 on Derivative Instruments and Hedging Activities.* Affected are certain derivative instruments embedded in other contracts, and for certain hedging activities.

- Chapter 11, "Equity Strategies" — this new chapter explains the most basic aspects of equity investing and addresses some of the more advanced vehicles and approaches that the CPA/personal financial specialist (PFS) should be familiar with in the current environment.

- Chapter 12, "The Jobs and Growth Tax Relief Reconciliation Act of 2003" — this new chapter provides important information about the intermediate-duration tax laws that have been put in place to help stimulate a moribund economy. They are explained in a simple manner to provide both familiarity with the new laws and to address client questions and concerns that may arise.

- Chapter 13, "Saving for a Higher Education" — this new chapter explains education-related tax breaks, including deductions, credits, and income exclusions, and summarizes the extensive rules and regulations regarding eligibility requirements, qualified expenses, contribution and distribution rules, and advantages/disadvantages of various plans.

- Chapter 14, "Tip Income" — has been updated to include information on the IRS's EmTRAC (Employer's Tip Reporting Alternative Commitment), which allows those in the food and beverage industry to design their own program for reporting tips properly.

Accounting Research Manager™

Aspen Publishers' **Accounting Research Manager** is the most comprehensive, up-to-date, and objective online resource of financial reporting literature. It includes all authoritative and proposed accounting, auditing, and SEC literature, plus independent, expert-written interpretive guidance to assist you with your accounting and auditing research needs: accounting for public and nonpublic companies, auditing for public companies, and auditing for nonpublic companies.

Material is updated on a daily basis by our outstanding team of content experts, so you stay as current as possible. You'll learn of newly released literature and deliberations of current financial reporting projects as soon as they occur. You'll be kept up-to-date on the latest FASB, AICPA, SEC, EITF, and IASB authoritative and proposal-stage literature.

With Aspen's **Accounting Research Manager,** you maximize the efficiency of your research time, while enhancing your results. Learn more about our content, our experts, and how you can request a FREE trial by visiting us at **www.arm.aspenpublishers.com.**

11/03

For questions concerning this shipment, billing, or other customer service matters, call our Customer Service Department at 1-800-234-1660.

For toll-free ordering, please call 1-800-638-8437.

ACCOUNTING DESK BOOK

The Accountant's Everyday Instant Answer Book

TWELFTH EDITION
2004 SUPPLEMENT

TOM M. PLANK
LOIS RUFFNER PLANK
BRYAN R. PLANK

ΛSPEN

PUBLISHERS

1185 Avenue of the Americas, New York, NY 10036
www.aspenpublishers.com

© 2004 Aspen Publishers, Inc.
www.aspenpublishers.com
A Wolters Kluwer Company

Portions of this book were published in previous editions.

Printed in the United States of America
1 2 3 4 5 6 7 8 9 0

ISBN 0-7355-4321-6

About Aspen Publishers

Aspen Publishers, headquartered in New York City, is a leading information provider for attorneys, business professionals, and law students. Written by preeminent authorities, our products consist of analytical and practical information covering both U.S. and international topics. We publish in the full range of formats, including updated manuals, books, periodicals, CDs, and online products.

Our proprietary content is complemented by 2,500 legal databases, containing over 11 million documents, available through our Loislaw division. Aspen Publishers also offers a wide range of topical legal and business databases linked to Loislaw's primary material. Our mission is to provide accurate, timely, and authoritative content in easily accessible formats, supported by unmatched customer care.

To order any Aspen Publishers title, go to *www.aspenpublishers.com* or call 1-800-638-8437.

To reinstate your manual update service, call 1-800-638-8437.

For more information on Loislaw products, go to *www.loislaw.com* or call 1-800-364-2512.

For Customer Care issues, e-mail CustomerCare@aspenpublishers.com; call 1-800-234-1660; or fax 1-800-901-9075.

ASPEN PUBLISHERS
A Wolters Kluwer Company

About the Authors

Tom M. Plank is a specialist in SEC Accounting Rules and Regulations, new security issues registrations and annual reports and filings required by the SEC. He holds his degrees from the Graduate School of Management, University of California at Los Angeles.

Mr. Plank has served on the accounting, finance and economics faculties of various major universities in Chicago and Los Angeles. His business experience includes that of an officer and economist for a large commercial bank, a securities analyst for an investment banking firm, an account executive for a large securities firm and a consultant for various corporations for Securities and Exchange Commission filings.

Mr. Plank has published many articles in various journals and is the author of several business books: *SEC Accounting Rules and Regulations, The Age of Automation, The Science of Leadership,* and several editions and supplements to the *Accounting Desk Book.* He is also the co-editor of the *Encyclopedia of Accounting Systems.*

Lois Ruffner Plank received her B.A. degree in Public Administration and International Relations from Miami University in Oxford, Ohio, with additional work in investments at the University of California at Los Angeles and at the University of Illinois.

Mrs. Plank is the co-editor of the *Encyclopedia of Accounting Systems* and co-author of several of the supplements to the *Accounting Desk Book.* She has been involved in budgeting and financial management with a government agency in Washington, D.C., and instituted a public relations and marketing program for a suburban Chicago school district.

She is an editor of professional publications and books and is a public relations consultant. Additional experience includes newspaper reporting and chief copy consultant for a national magazine.

Bryan R. Plank is a senior financial advisor and vice president at a large international securities firm. In addition, he holds numerous licenses, certifications, and credentials in securities, insurance and real estate.

Mr. Plank has 20 years of experience in training and development in the securities industry and is a frequent guest speaker at many San Diego-area colleges and universities.

Mr. Plank earned university degrees from the University of Southern California and California State Polytechnic University, Pomona, with additional postgraduate work at Claremont Graduate School.

How to Use This Supplement

The objective of this 2004 *Supplement* is to furnish users of the *Accounting Desk Book*, Twelfth Edition, with recent developments in the financial accounting rules and regulations both in the United States and internationally. Since the *Desk Book* was published, the Financial Accounting Standards Board has continued wrestling with the serious problems created by entities ignoring or circumventing the existing standards. A new chapter considers the Financial Accounting Standards Board's FIN-46 on the consolidation of variable interest entities, a vital step in the approach to solving problems in this area.

In addition, the user of the 2004 *Supplement* should find the chapter on the rapid development of the Public Company Accounting Oversight Board in line with the requirements of the Sarbanes-Oxley Act useful in understanding the workings of this new regulatory body.

Now that the Governmental Accounting Standards Board Statement 34 has become effective for all levels of state and local governments, the Board is actively engaged in helping the accountants' auditors, and state and local officials, implement this comprehensive overhauling of their financial reporting. At the same time, the Board is systematically reviewing and updating some of the older standards with new standards and technical bulletins, which are discussed in this volume.

In a continuing effort to bring the CPA/personal finance specialist (PFS) up to speed with current investment trends, we have included a chapter on equity strategies that is both informative and timely. In the future, we plan to include chapters on advanced equity strategies and fixed income strategies. The chapter on saving for higher education will give the CPA/PFS a clear picture of alternatives available for any of their clients' educational planning needs.

Among the topics featured in the 2004 *Supplement* are:

- Strict new rules relating to Auditor Independence and the Audit Committee.
- Provisions of The Jobs and Growth Tax Relief Reconciliation Act of 2004.
- International Accounting with emphasis on preparing much of the business world to utilize international financial reporting standards.

The discussions in this Supplement are self-contained. All chapters included are either new or have been revised to include the most recent information that Supplement users need to remain current and advise their clients correctly and with confidence.

This supplement is meant to be used in conjunction with its larger, parent volume, the *Accounting Desk Book*, 2003 Edition, to provide complete coverage of the topics and questions the CPA/PFS must field day to day.

Supplement users will find the Index particularly helpful in locating all the major topics and minor subtopics covered in this Supplement.

ABOUT THE CD-ROM

Included with the 2004 *Supplement* is a companion CD-ROM that contains a searchable version of the Supplement.

ACCOUNTING RESEARCH MANAGER™

Aspen Publishers' **Accounting Research Manager** is the most comprehensive, up-to-date, and objective online resource of financial reporting literature. It includes all authoritative and proposed accounting, auditing, and SEC literature, plus independent, expert-written interpretive guidance to assist you with your accounting and auditing research needs: accounting for public and nonpublic companies, auditing for public companies, and auditing for nonpublic companies.

Material is updated on a daily basis by our outstanding team of content experts, so you stay as current as possible. You'll learn of newly released literature and deliberations of current financial reporting projects as soon as they occur. You'll be kept up-to-date on the latest FASB, AICPA, SEC, EITF, and IASB authoritative and proposal stage literature.

With Aspen's **Accounting Research Manager,** you maximize the efficiency of your research time, while enhancing your results. Learn more about our content, our experts, and how you can request a FREE trial by visiting us at **www.arm.aspenpublishers.com.**

ACKNOWLEDGMENT

Christie Plank Ciraulo has been the research editor for the *Accounting Desk Book* since 1997. Mrs. Ciraulo has a master's degree in Public Relations from the University of Southern California School of Journalism. She has contributed directly to the success of our book by her ability to edit, format, and systematize the book's presentation. In addition, she possesses the rare talent of reducing complicated topics into a series of simple sentences. Her efforts have the effect of making our book far more accessible to the reader than it would otherwise be.

Contents

xii Contents

Chapter 1
Revenue and Expenses

CONTENTS

It has been the Financial Accounting Standards Board's (FASB) intention for some time to develop a comprehensive statement on revenue recognition that is conceptually based and framed in terms of principles. This is being done in partnership with the International Accounting Standards Board (IASB). As a joint project, the FASB and the IASB are sharing staff resources and research and are working to coordinate the eventual issuance of Exposure Drafts and final standards. The Boards are also coordinating the timing of their deliberations of the issues within the joint project, but they deliberate and vote on those issues individually. As a result, at any given time there may be some issues for which the FASB has reached a tentative conclusion but for which the IASB has not yet deliberated, and vice-versa.

As conceived at present, the revenue recognition Statement will:

• Eliminate the inconsistencies in the existing authoritative literature and accepted practices.
• Fill the voids that have emerged in revenue recognition guidance in recent years.
• Provide guidance for addressing issues that arise in the future.

Although the FASB plans that a revenue recognition Statement should apply to business entities generally, it has been suggested that later it will decide to exclude certain transactions or industries requiring additional study. In developing this Statement, the FASB decided to reconsider the guidance pertinent to revenue recognition in its Concepts Statements. Conflicts can arise between the conceptual guidance on revenues in FASB Concepts Statement 5, *Recognition and Measurement in Financial Statements of Business Enterprises,* and FASB Concepts Statement 6, *Elements of Financial Statements.* Those conflicts can arise because revenues are defined in Concepts Statement 6 in terms of changes in assets and liabilities, but the revenue recognition criteria in Concepts Statement 5 do not focus on changes in assets and liabilities.

At an August 2003 Board meeting, the staff presented the FASB with an inventory of the existing guidance related to revenue recognition and described the various revenue recognition conventions that are used in practice. The staff also described a possible approach to addressing a comprehensive standard on revenue recognition. The Board is taking into consideration the following aspects of the suggested approach:

• Scope of the standard: possible removal of financial instruments from consideration.
• Balancing principles-based guidance and rules-based guidance: a standard incorporating broad principles with clear, concise implementation guidance.
• Transition from existing guidance: consideration of existing literature individually for retention, modification, or elimination.

Until such time as a new, comprehensive standard is issued by the FASB, the existing rules, regulations, staff bulletins, and other literature remain in effect.

REVENUE (INCOME)

The principles upon which net income is determined derive from the pervasive measurement principles, such as realization, and the modifying conventions, such as conservatism.

The entire process of income determination ("matching") consists of identifying, measuring, and relating revenue and expenses for an accounting period. Revenue is usually determined by applying the realization principle, with the changes in net asset value interrelated with the recognition of revenue. Revenue arises from three general activities:

1. Selling products;
2. Rendering services or letting others use owned resources, resulting in interest or rent;
3. Disposing of other resources (not products), such as equipment or investments.

Revenue does not include proceeds from stockholders, lenders, asset purchases or prior-period adjustments.

Revenue, in the balance sheet sense, is a gross increase in assets or a gross decrease in liabilities recognized and measured in conformity with generally accepted accounting principles (GAAP), which results from those profit-directed activities that can change owners' equity.

Revenue is considered *realized* when:

- The earning process is complete or virtually complete, and
- An exchange has taken place.

The objectives of accounting determination of income are not always the same as the objectives used for tax purposes.

There are various acceptable ways of determining income:

1. *Revenue* (see three general activities above):
   a. Accrual method—this is financial accounting and GAAP.
   b. Cash method—this is *not* considered financial accounting, and not GAAP, because one of the characteristics of GAAP is the *accrual* of appropriate items.
   c. Installment sales method—generally for retail stores.
   d. Completion of production method—used for precious metals.
   e. For long-term construction contracts:
      (1) Completed contract method.
      (2) Percentage-of-completion method.

    f. For leasing activities:
      (1) The direct financing method.
      (2) The operating method.
      (3) The sales method.
    g. The cost recovery method (used for installment sales).
    h. Consolidation method—for majority-owned subsidiaries (more than 50 percent).
    i. Equity method—for non-consolidated subsidiaries and for controlled non-subsidiaries.
2. *Other* types of income requiring special determination:
    a. Extraordinary items of income.
    b. Unrealized income arising from:
      (1) Foreign currency holdings or transactions.
      (2) Ownership of marketable securities shown as current assets.

A *shareholder* in a corporation does *not* have income when that corporation earns income (except for a Sub-S corporation). The shareholder has, and reports for tax purposes, income only upon *distribution* of that income in the form of dividends. Generally, distributions of stock—stock dividends and stock splits—are *not* income to the shareholder, but merely an adjustment of the number of shares he holds (for the same original cost plus token costs, if any). However, there are some situations which call for the stockholder to report stock dividends as income.

If a buyer has a right of return to the seller, revenue is recognized if *all* of the following criteria are met:

- Buyer is obligated to pay (and not contingent upon resale of the product) or has paid the seller;
- Buyer's obligation would not be changed by theft, damage, or destruction of the product;
- Seller does not have any significant obligation to buyer related to resale of the product by the buyer; and
- Buyer's business must have economic substance separate from the seller's business.

If these criteria are met, sales revenue and cost of sales reported in the income statement are reduced to reflect estimated returns; expected losses are accrued.

EXPENSES

Expenses are one of the six basic elements of financial accounting, along with assets, liabilities, owners' equity, revenue and net income. Expenses are determined by applying the expense recognition principles on the basis of relationships, between acquisition costs [the term "cost" is commonly used to refer to the amount at which assets are initially recorded, regardless of how determined], and either the independently determined revenue or accounting periods. Since the point in time at which revenue and expenses are recognized is also the time at which changes in amounts of net assets are recorded, income determination is interrelated with asset valuation.

All costs are not expenses. Some costs are related to later periods, will provide benefits for later periods, and are carried forward as assets on the balance sheet. Other costs are incurred and provide no future benefit, having expired in terms of usefulness or applicability—these expired costs are called "expenses." All expenses, therefore, are part of the broader term "cost." These expired costs are not assets and are shown as deductions from revenue to determine net income.

Expenses are gross decreases in assets or gross increases in liabilities recognized and measured in conformity with GAAP that result from those types of profit-directed activities that can change an owner's equity.

Recognizing Expenses

Three pervasive principles form the basis for recognizing expenses to be deducted from revenue to arrive at net income or loss:

1. Associating cause and effect ("matching")—For example, manufacturing cost of goods sold is measured and matched to the *sale* of the product. Assumptions must be made as to how these costs attach to the product— whether on machine hours, space used, or labor expended. Assumptions must also be made as to how the costs flow out (LIFO, FIFO, average costs).

2. Systematic and rational allocation—When there is no direct way to associate cause and effect and certain costs are known (or presumed) to have provided benefits during the accounting period, these costs are allocated to that period in a systematic and rational manner and to appear so to an unbiased observer. The methods of allocation should be consistent and systematic, though methods may vary for different types of costs. Examples are depreciation of fixed assets, amortization of intangibles and interperiod allocation of rent or interest. The allocation referred to here is not the allocation of expired manufacturing costs with the "cost" area to determine unit or job costs; it is rather the broader area of allocation to the manufacturing area from the unexpired asset account: Depreciation on factory building, rather than overhead-depreciation on Product A, B, or C.

3. Immediate recognition (period expenses)—Costs are expensed during an accounting period because:
   a. They cannot be associated on a cause-and-effect basis with revenue, yet no useful purpose would be achieved by delaying recognition to a future period,
   b. They provide no discernible future benefits, or
   c. They were recorded as assets in a prior period and now no longer provide discernible future benefits.

Examples are officer salaries, most selling expenses, legal fees, and most general and administrative expenses.

OTHER EXPENSES (AND REVENUE)

Gains and Losses.   Expenses and revenue from *other* than sales of products, merchandise or services may be separated from (operating) revenue and disclosed net separately.

Unusual Items.   Unusual items of expense or income not meeting the criteria of "extraordinary" should be shown as a separate component of income from continuing operations.

Extraordinary Items.   Extraordinary items are discussed elsewhere in this book. They should be shown separately—net of applicable taxes—*after* net income from continuing operations. Any disposals of business segments should be shown immediately prior to extraordinary items—also with tax effect.

IMPUTED INTEREST ON NOTES RECEIVABLE OR PAYABLE

Accounting Considerations

The American Institute of Certified Public Accountants (AICPA) sets forth the appropriate accounting when the face amount of certain receivables or payables ("notes") does not reasonably represent the present value of the consideration given or received in certain exchanges. The objective of these rules is to prevent the form of the transaction from prevailing over its economic substance. (*Present value* is the sum of future payments, discounted to the present date at an appropriate rate of interest.)

Accounting Principles Board (APB) Opinion 21 states that:

1. When a note is received or issued solely for cash, the note is presumed to have a present value equal to the cash received. If it is issued for cash equal to its face amount, it is presumed to earn the stated rate of interest.

2. When a note is received for cash and some other rights or privileges, the value of the rights or privileges should be given accounting recognition by establishing a note discount or premium account, with the offsetting amount treated as appropriate. An example is a five-year noninterest-bearing loan made to a supplier in partial consideration for a purchase of products at lower than prevailing market prices. Under such circumstances, the difference between the present value of the receivable and the cash lent to the supplier is regarded as (a) an additional cost of the purchased goods, and (b) interest income, amortized over the life of the note.

3. When a note is exchanged for property, goods, or services and (a) interest is not stated, or (b) it is stated but is unreasonable, or (c) the stated face amount of the note is materially different from the current cash sale price of goods (or services), the note, the sales price, and the cost of the property (goods or services) should be recorded at their fair value, or at an amount that reasonably approximates the market value of the note, whichever is more clearly determinable.

Any resulting discount or premium should be regarded as interest expense or income and be amortized over the life of the note, in such a way as to result in a constant effective rate of interest when applied to the amount outstanding at the beginning of any given period.

Opinion 21 also provides some general guides for determining an "appropriate" interest rate and the manner of amortization for financial reporting purposes.

IMPUTED INTEREST: When a sale is made for an amount that is collectible at a future time giving rise to an account receivable, the amount is regarded as consisting of a sales price *and* a charge for interest for the period of the payment deferral. APB Opinion 21 requires that in the absence of a stated rate of interest, the present value of the receivable should be determined by reducing the face amount of the receivable by an interest rate that is approximated under the circumstances for the period that payment is deferred.

This rate is the *imputed rate.* It is determined by approximating the rate the supplier pays for financing receivables, or by determining the buyer's credit standing and applying the rate the borrower would have to pay if borrowing the sum from, say, a bank.

The process of arriving at the present value of the receivable is referred to as *discounting* the sum. If the total present value of the receivable (face amount plus the imputed interest) is less than the face amount, the difference between the face value of the receivable and its present value is recognized as a discount. If the present value exceeds the face amount of the receivable, the difference is recognized as a premium.

The sale is recorded as a debit to a receivable account, a credit to a discount on the receivable, and a credit to sales at the present value as reported for the receivable. The discount is amortized as a credit to interest income over the life of the receivable. On the balance sheet any unamortized discount at the end of the accounting period is reported as a direct subtraction from the *face amount* of the receivable.

Example: A seller ships merchandise totaling $10,000 to a customer with payment deferred for five years. Seller and customer agree to impute an interest charge of 10 percent for the $10,000. The journal entries follow.

Accounts Receivable	10,000	
Sales (Present value at 10%)		6,209
Unamortized Discount		3,791
(To record the sale of merchandise at the present value of the receivable)		

The *interest method* is applied to amortize the discount.

End of Year 1		
Unamortized Discount	620.90	
Interest Income		620.90
(10% of $6,209.00)		
End of Year 2		
Unamortized Discount	682.99	
Interest Income		682.99
(10% of $6,829.90)		
End of Year 3		
Unamortized Discount	751.29	
Interest Income		751.29
(10% of $7,512.89)		
End of Year 4		
Unamortized Discount	826.42	
Interest Income		826.42
(10% of $8,264.18)		
Unamortized Discount	909.06	
End of Year 5		
Unamortized Discount	909.06	
Interest Income		909.06
(10% of $9,090.60)		

At the end of five years full amortization of the discount has been recorded and the face amount of the receivable results. (*Note:* Opinion 21 does not require the imputed interest method when ". . . receivables and payables arising from transactions with customers or suppliers in the normal course of business which are due in customary trade terms not exceeding approximately one year.")

CLASSIFYING AND REPORTING EXTRAORDINARY ITEMS

Income statement presentation requires that the results of *ordinary operations* be reported first, and applicable provision for income taxes provided for.
In order, the following should then be shown:

1. Results of discontinued operations:
   a. Income or loss from the operations discontinued for the portion of the period until discontinuance—shown net of tax, with the tax shown parenthetically;
   b. Loss (or gain) on disposal of the business segments, including provision for phase-out operating losses—also shown net of tax parenthetically.
2. Extraordinary items—Should be segregated and shown as the last factor used in arriving at net income for the period. Here, the caption is shown net of applicable income taxes, which are shown parenthetically. Note that extraordinary items do *not* include disposal of business segments as such, because they are segregated and shown separately prior thereto (as above).

An example of the reporting of the above:

	2002		2001
Income from continuing operations			
before income taxes	$ xxx		$ xxx
Provision for income taxes	xx		xx
Income from continuing operations		$ xxx	xxx
Discontinued operations (Note):			
Income from operations of discontinued			
Division B (less applicable taxes of $xx)	$ xx		
	2002		2001
Loss on disposal of Division B, including			
provision for phase-out operating losses of			
$xx (less applicable income taxes of $xx)	xx	xx	
Income before extraordinary items		xxx	
Extraordinary items (less applicable			
income taxes of $xx)			
(Note)		xx	
Net Income		$ xxx	$ xxx
Earnings per share:			
Income from continuing operations		$ x.00	$ x.00
Discontinued operations		x.00	x.00
Extraordinary items		x.00	x.00
Net Income		$ x.00	$ x.00

Note that earnings per share should be broken out separately for the factors of discontinued operations and extraordinary items, as well as for income from (continuing) operations.

The criteria for classifying a transaction or event as an "extraordinary item" are as follows:

Extraordinary items are events and transactions that are distinguished by their unusual nature *and* by the infrequency of their occurrence. Thus, *both* of the following criteria should be met to classify an event or transaction as an extraordinary item:

1. *Unusual nature.* The underlying event or transaction should possess a high degree of abnormality and be of a type clearly unrelated to, or only incidentally related to, the ordinary and typical activities of the entity, taking into account the environment in which the entity operates.
2. *Infrequency of occurrence.* The underlying event or transaction should be of a type that would not reasonably be expected to recur in the foreseeable future, taking into account the environment in which the entity operates.

Items that are *not* to be reported as extraordinary, because they may recur or are not unusual, are:

- Write-downs of receivables, inventories, intangibles, or leased equipment.
- Effects of strikes.
- Gains or losses on foreign currency translations.
- Adjustment of accruals on long-term contracts.
- Gains or losses on disposal of business segments.
- Gains or losses from abandonment or sale of property, plant or equipment used in the business.

Note that some highly unusual occurrence might cause one of the above types of gains or losses and should be considered extraordinary, such as those resulting from major casualties (earthquake), expropriations and legal restrictions. Disposals of business segments, though not extraordinary in classification, should be shown separately on the income statement, just prior to extraordinary items, but after operations from continuing business.

Miscellaneous data pertaining to extraordinary items:

- Bargain sales of stock to stockholders are *not* extraordinary items, but they should be shown separately.
- A gain or a loss on sale of coin collections by a bank is *not* an extraordinary item.

PRESENT VALUE COMPUTATION AND APPLICATION

The procedure of computing interest on principal *and interest on interest* under-lies the concept of *compounding*. There are a number of accounting procedures (accounting for bonds, accounts receivable, accounts payable, and leases, for example) to which the compound interest formula (and variations) can be applied:

- The *future value* of a sum of money. If $1,000 (the principal *P*) is deposited in a bank today, what will be the balance (*S*) in the account in *n years* (or *periods*) if the bank accumulates interest at the rate of *i* percent per year?
- The *present value* of a sum of money due at the end of a period of time. What is the value *today* of the amount owed if $1,000 has to be paid, say to a creditor, *n* years from today?
- The *future value of an annuity,* which is a series of *equal* payments made at *equal* intervals. If $1,000 a year is deposited for *n* years, how much will have accumulated at the end of the *n*-years period if the deposits earn interest at the rate of *i* percent per year?
- The *present value of an annuity,* which is a series of *equal* payments made at *equal* intervals. If we are to be paid $1,000 a year for *n* years, how much is this annuity worth today, given *i* percent rate of interest?

The formula for the future value of a sum of money is the familiar compound interest formula. In the four examples to follow, let:

S = The future worth of a sum of money invested today.

P = Principal, or the sum of money that will accumulate to S amount of money.

i = The rate of interest (r may be substituted).

n = Number of periods of time.

It is important to understand that a "period of time" is not necessarily one year, even though rates of interest in the United States are always understood to mean the rate for a period of one year. A period can be any length of time (e.g., day, week, month, year, second, minute, hour). Time is a *continuous,* not a *discrete,* function.

With compound interest the total amount accumulated (S in the formula) at the end of one period earns interest during the subsequent period, or "interest on interest." The formula is:

$$S = P(1 + i)^n$$

At this point, it should be emphasized that the user no longer must do the arithmetic. Not only can the problem types be solved by the use of tables, but now inexpensive hand calculators will perform the computations and give the answers. The user has simply only to enter the numbers that represent the letters in the formula. Users with computers can, of course, program the formulas for permanent storage and simply "call out" whichever formula applies to the problem at hand. With respect to the arithmetic, however, three of the variables in the equation are always known quantities; therefore, finding the value of the fourth and *un*known variable follows.

A Word of Caution. Computational errors caused by entering the wrong value for *n* are not uncommon. If *i* = 12% and the compounding period is every six months, *n* in the formula is 6. If the compounding period is quarterly *n* is 3. If the compounding period is daily (as is the case in many financial institutions savings policies) *n* becomes *i*/360 — 360 days in the year are applied in this country for interest calculations instead of 365. This is because the smaller the denominator, the bit more interest the *lender* collects. However, if the formula applies to a problem involving U.S. Government bonds, a 365-day year must be assumed because it enables the government to borrow a bit cheaper, relatively.

Annuities

The previous discussion considers the accumulation of interest on a *single* payment, however the single payment may be invested. *Annuities* apply to problems that involve a series of *equal payments* (or investments or savings) made at *equal intervals* of time. The period of time between payments is called the *payment period*. The period of time between computation of the interest accumulation is called the *interest-conversion period*. When the payment period exactly equals the interest-conversion period, the annuity is an *ordinary annuity*. The equal payments are termed rents, which are spread over equal periods of time, the first rent payment made at the *start* of the annuity, and the last payment made at the *end* of the annuity.

The *future worth* of the annuity is the sum of the future worths of each of the separate rents. Assuming $100 invested we have $100 at time 1. At time 2 we have the $100 invested that day, plus the $100 invested at time 1, plus the interest earned during the period between time 1 and time 2. At time 3 another $100 is deposited; we now have the $100 deposited that day, the $100 deposited at time 2 plus the interest earned for one period, and the $100 deposited at time 1 plus the interest earned during the period between time 1 and time 2.

The formula for the future worth of an annuity of $1 is:

$$S = \frac{(1 + i)^n - 1}{i}$$

Note that the formula for the accumulation of interest on an ordinary annuity has the same variables as the compounding formula for a single payment.

To obtain S for any amount more than $1, multiply both sides of the equation by the amount invested, by P. In this case multiply both sides of the equation by 100. As above the amount for $1 can be found in tables (or by the use of a hand calculator).

The *present worth* of an annuity concerns the same question as the present worth of a single payment for *n years at i rate of interest.* How much would we pay today for an annuity in order to receive a given number of equal payments at equal intervals for a given number of periods in the future? The formula for $1 is:

$$S = \frac{1 - (1 + i)^{-n}}{i}$$

The method for accounting for the premium or discount on bonds payable are compound interest procedures. The resultant interest charges are the product of the net balance of bonds payable and the effective interest rate at the time the bonds were issued. For bonds issued at a premium, the computed interest charges will *decrease* each year as the bonds approach maturity because the net balance of the liability decreases each year due to the amortization of the premium. Conversely, for bonds issued at a discount, the computed interest charges will *increase* each year as the bonds approach maturity because of the accumulation of the discount.

A straight-line method is used for the amortization of premiums or accumulation of discounts which involves simply dividing the original premium or discount by the number of years until maturity to determine the constant annual amount of amortization or accumulation.

The most frequent application of the above formula for accounting procedures is the present value formula. For example, when a company issues bonds, cash is debited for the proceeds of the bond issue and a liability account is credited for the amount. The entries will be the present value of the bonds. Assume a bond issue sold at a premium, or for more than the typical $1,000 par value, the present value of which we assume to be $1,200. The entries at the time of the sale of the bonds are:

Cash	$1,200	
Bonds Payable		$1,200

An alternative treatment is permissible by rule:

Cash	$1,200	
Bonds Payable		$1,000 (par)
Premium on Bonds		200

The Premium Account is an adjunct account (an addition) to Bonds Payable. The interest charge each year is computed by multiplying the bond liability *at the end of each year* by the effective rate of interest (see the definition). The adjunct account at the end of each period is debited for the amount of interest which reduces the liability each period. *The interest charge calculation is computed on the reduced amount of the liability that occurs each year as the adjunct account is debited.* At maturity the Premium Account has a zero balance and the liability will be reduced to the maturity, or face amount (the par value of $1,000) of the bond.

Assume the bond is sold at a $200 *discount,* that is, $200 less than the $1,000 par value. The journal entry is:

Cash	$800	
Bond Discount	200	
Bonds Payable		$1,000

The Bond Discount account is a *contra* account to bonds payable with the liability at time of issue $800. Again, for an amount deposited for the annuity of more than $1 multiply both sides of the equation by that amount. Also, again note the same variables as in the compound interest formula.

FASB's PLANS FOR ACCOUNTING FOR EMPLOYEE STOCK OPTIONS

The accounting for employee stock options has received renewed attention. In July 2002, important developments related to accounting for employee stock options arose from the general concern over the recognition of revenue and expenses and/or skullduggery involved therein.

Several major U.S. companies have announced their intentions to change their method of accounting for employee stock options to an approach that *recognizes an expense* for the fair value of the options granted in arriving at reported earnings. Evidently, a number of other companies also are getting on the bandwagon. The FASB is naturally quite pleased by the fact that, at long last, somebody is actually paying attention to what it had wanted done several years ago.

Forced Compromise in FASB 123

Recognizing compensation expense relating to the fair value of employee stock options granted was what the Board was trying to accomplish in FASB 123, *Accounting for Stock-Based Compensation.* At that time, to get *anything* adopted, Board members were forced to agree to an either/or compromise.

Obviously, very few companies selected the "fair value" method; in fact, many as it turns out did not even play fair in the "or" method. As a result of the recent accounting fiascoes, the fair value method is the treatment advocated by an increasing number of investors and other users of financial statements.

When the FASB developed FASB 123 in the mid-1990s, the Board proposed requiring that treatment because it believed that this was the best way to report the *actual effect* of employee stock options in a company's financial statements. The FASB modification of that proposal was in the face of strong opposition by many in the business community and in Congress that directly threatened the very existence of the FASB as an independent standard setter.

Thus, while FASB 123 provides that expense recognition for the fair value of employee stock options granted is the *preferable* approach, it permitted the continued use of existing methods. The existing (APB 25) method was modified only to the extent of requiring disclosure in the footnotes to the financial statements. This was to show the pro forma effect on net income and earnings per share as if the preferable, expense recognition method had been applied. Until now, only a handful of companies elected to follow the preferable method.

IASB PROPOSAL ON ACCOUNTING FOR SHARE-BASED PAYMENT

The International Accounting Standards Board, in November 2002, published proposals in Exposure Draft (ED) 2, *Share-Based Payment,* on how entities should account for share-based payment transactions, including grants of share options to employees. There is no existing International Financial Reporting Standard (IFRS) on share-based payment. The proposals in ED 2 replace the disclosure requirements in IAS 19, *Employee Benefits,* dealing with equity compensation benefits.

This gap in international accounting standards has become a cause for concern with the extensive use of share-based payment in recent years. The objective of the proposals in ED 2 is to ensure that entities recognize share-based payment transactions in their financial statements in order to provide high-quality, transparent, and comparable information to users of financial statements.

In developing its proposals, the IASB concluded that there is no valid reason that share-based payment transactions involving grants of shares or share options to employees should not be accounted for in the same way as other transactions in which an entity receives resources as consideration for its equity instruments. Therefore, the proposals include recognizing an expense for the consumption of the resources received, whether in the form of employee services, other services, or goods.

The Board believes that the proposals are timely, given the demand for greater transparency in financial reporting, particularly with regard to employee share options. Typically, transactions in which share options are granted to employees are not recognized in an entity's financial statements. As a result, the entity's expenses have been understated and its profits often vastly overstated. The Board feels that this measure will close an obvious gap in accounting standards. The IASB has spearheaded the effort to develop an accounting standard that will provide a basis for international convergence of standards in this area. In this endeavor, it has had support from its partner national standard setters, including the FASB.

Basic Provisions

The Exposure Draft covers six main principles:

1. All share-based payment transactions should be recognized in the financial statements, using a fair value measurement basis. An expense should be recognized when the goods or services received are consumed. There are no proposed exemptions from these requirements.
2. In principle, transactions in which goods or services are received as consideration for equity instruments of the entity should be measured at the fair value of the goods or services received or the fair value of the equity instruments granted, whichever is more readily determinable.

   For transactions measured at the fair value of the equity instruments granted (e.g., transactions with employees), fair value should be estimated at grant date. For transactions measured at the fair value of the goods or services received, fair value should be estimated at the date of receipt of those goods or services.
3. To estimate the fair value of a share option, where an observable market price does not exist, an option pricing model should be used. The Exposure Draft does not specify which particular model should be used. The entity should disclose the model used, the inputs to that model, and other information about how fair value was measured.
4. The Exposure Draft contains various proposals on estimating the fair value of employee share options, to allow for differences between employee share options and traded options. For example, the valuation should take into account all types of vesting conditions, including service conditions and performance conditions. The grant date valuation should be reduced to allow for the possibility of forfeiture because of failure to satisfy vesting conditions.
5. Repricing of options (and other changes in terms and conditions), should be accounted for by recognizing additional remuneration expense based on the incremental value given on repricing — that is, additional to expenses recognized in respect of the original option grant.

6. The Exposure Draft also contains proposals on accounting for cancellation of share or option plans, share-based payment transactions settled in cash, and transactions in which either the entity or the counterparty may choose whether the entity settles in cash or by issuing equity instruments.

Scope

The ISAB's proposal applies to all share-based compensation, with some narrow exceptions. By law, European Union companies must comply with IASB standards by 2007; Australian companies by 2005. Canada has indicated it will also require compliance with IASB standards. The proposal would apply to both listed and unlisted companies.

Problems with Measurement

Companies would be required to measure the value of options as of the date of grant using a formula designed to estimate their fair value. Therein lies the problem. Finding a formula that will produce reasonably accurate estimates has met with little success. The IASB did not specify a particular option pricing model, although it mentioned Black-Scholes or binomial models as examples. Regardless of the formula used, it must include the following elements:

- Exercise price of the option
- Life of the option
- Current price of the underlying shares
- Expected volatility of the share price
- Dividends expected on the shares, to be adjusted to take into account whether the optionee or shareholder actually has a right to interim dividends before any restrictions on the awards lapse
- Risk-free interest rate (such as T-bills) for the life of the option

If this all sounds familiar, it may be because these are the same elements as those now required by the FASB for U.S. companies expensing options on their income statements or in their footnotes. Thus, convergence would not be a big problem if the FASB does follow through on mandatory expensing of options.

Disclosure Requirements

In much the same vein as the SEC's Plain English Disclosure rule, the IASB's disclosure requirements in ED 2 are aimed at helping the user more readily understand the effect of the provisions. Thus, the proposal requires extensive disclosures, governed by three sets of principles:

1. User's should be able to understand the nature and extent of share-based payment arrangements during the accounting period.
2. Users should be able to understand how the fair values of the services received and the equity awards granted were determined.
3. Users should be able to understand the effect expenses based on share-based payments will have on projected income for the period.

Corporate entities must disclose myriad details, which have previously been glossed over, if even mentioned. Among the required items are:

- Awards broken down by employee class.
- Who is getting how many awards.
- Option terms.
- Weighted exercise prices.
- Grant dates.

Expected Effective Date

If adopted as planned before the end of 2003, the proposal would become effective for annual financial statements for periods beginning on or after January 1, 2004. Earlier adoption would be encouraged. For unvested options or shares outstanding as of the effective date, a company would have to apply the accounting principles of the proposal retroactively to November 7, 2002, the date that ED 2 was published.

SAB 101, *Revenue Recognition in Financial Statements*

This Staff Accounting Bulletin (SAB) summarizes certain of the Securities and Exchange Commission staff's views in applying GAAP to revenue recognition in financial statements. The staff is providing this guidance due, in part, to the large number of revenue recognition issues that registrants encounter. For example, a March, 1999 report entitled *Fraudulent Financial Reporting 1987–1997: An Analysis of U. S. Public Companies,* sponsored by the Committee of Sponsoring Organizations (COSO) of the Treadway Commission, indicated that more than half of financial reporting frauds in the study involved overstating revenue. At this point, it would be almost impossible to "fix" a figure for the number of fraudulent cases of overstated revenue.

During the upcoming 10-K season, the SEC appears to be planning to investigate cases, particularly high-profile ones, of improper accounting for premature and excessive revenue recognition.

Because the SEC believes the revenue recognition accounting rules do not cover a number of areas, it is expecting companies to voluntarily correct their improper accounting in anticipation of additional revenue recognition requirements from the FASB. They will then not be subject to enforcement action as long as they have not violated existing generally accepted accounting principles. This correction in most cases will be reported by companies as a one-time accounting change item.

Corrections Required

The following corrections have been outlined by the SEC:

- Those collections previously included in revenue that were made when acting as an agent for a third party.
- Revenue recorded in reciprocal barter transactions of similar products or services that do not represent the culmination of the earnings process.
- Sales recorded before receipt of a written sales agreement.
- Sales recorded in consignment-like arrangements.
- Sales where the customer has not taken title and assumed the risks and rewards of ownership.
- Bill-and-hold sales that do not have a customer business purpose.
- Sales in situations where returns cannot be reliably estimated, such as "channel stuffing."

Conditions for Recognition

The SEC has stated that a bill-and-hold sale transaction must meet all six of the following conditions to qualify for revenue recognition:

1. The risks of ownership must have been passed to the buyer;
2. The customer must commit to purchase the goods;
3. The buyer must substantiate a business purpose for the bill-and-sale transaction;
4. A fixed delivery date must be set;
5. The seller must not have any material performance obligations; and
6. The goods must be ready for shipment and not available to meet other orders.

The Effect of SAB 101

Among other responses to the SEC's SAB 101, some companies will find it necessary to:

1. Exclude from revenues and/or improve the disclosure of amounts collected by the company acting as an agent. One facet of this will involve assessing whether revenue (if recognized) should be reported gross with separate display of cost of sales to arrive at gross profit or on a net basis. In their appraisal, the SEC staff considers whether the registrant:

    a. Acts as principal in the transaction.

    b. Takes title to the products.

    c. Has risks and rewards of ownership, such as the risk of loss for collection, delivery, or returns.

    d. Acts as an agent or broker (including performing services, in substance, as an agent or broker) with compensation on a commission or fee basis.

    If the company performs as an agent or broker without assuming the risks and rewards of ownership of the goods, sales should be reported on a net basis.

2. Not recognize revenue from "channel stuffing" and other transactions that make it difficult to estimate product returns.

    Registrants and their auditors should carefully analyze all factors, including trends in historical data, that may affect registrants' ability to make reasonable and reliable estimates of product returns.

    The staff believes that the following additional factors, among others, may affect or preclude the ability to make reasonable and reliable estimates of product returns:

    a. Significant increases in or excess levels of inventory in a distribution channel (sometimes referred to as "channel stuffing").

    b. Lack of "visibility" into, or the inability to determine or observe the levels of inventory in, a distribution channel and the current level of sales to end users.

    c. Expected introductions of new products that may result in the technological obsolescence of and larger than expected returns of current products.

    d. The significance of a particular distributor to the registrant's business, sales and marketing.

    e. The newness of a product.

    f. The introduction of competitors' products with superior technology or greater expected market acceptance, and other factors that affect

market demand and changing trends in that demand for the registrant's products.

3. Exclude from revenue consignment-like transactions. Products delivered
    to a consignee pursuant to a consignment arrangement are not sales and
    do not qualify for revenue recognition until a sale occurs. The staff be-
    lieves that revenue recognition is not appropriate because the seller re-
    tains the risks and rewards of ownership of the product and title usually
    does not pass to the consignee.

    Other situations may exist where title to delivered products passes to a
    buyer, but the substance of the transaction is that of a *consignment or a*
    financing. Such arrangements require a careful analysis of the facts and
    circumstances of the transaction, as well as an understanding of the rights
    and obligations of the parties, and the seller's customary business prac-
    tices in such arrangements.

    The staff believes that the presence of one or more of the following char-
    acteristics in a transaction precludes revenue recognition even if title to
    the product has passed to the buyer, but the buyer has the right to return
    the product and:

    a. The buyer does not pay the seller at the time of sale, nor is the buyer
        obligated to pay the seller at a specified date or dates.

    b. The buyer does not pay the seller at the time of sale but rather is obli-
        gated to pay at a specified date or dates, but the buyer's obligation to
        pay is contractually or implicitly excused until the buyer resells the
        product or subsequently consumes or uses the product.

    c. The buyer's obligation to the seller would be changed (e.g., the seller
        would forgive the obligation or grant a refund) in the event of theft or
        physical destruction or damage of the product.

    d. The buyer acquiring the product for resale does not have economic
        substance apart from that provided by the seller.

    e. The seller has significant obligations for future performance to
        directly bring about resale of the product by the buyer.

4. Only include in revenue those sales backed up by a *binding* written sales
    agreement. (See item 3.)

5. Exclude from sales all shipments where the customer has not taken title
    to the goods and thereby not assumed the risks and rewards of owner-
    ship. (See item 3.)

6. Defer revenue recognition of up-front fees until the related earnings pro-
    cess is completed. The staff believes that up-front fees, even if nonre-
    fundable, are normally earned as the products and services are delivered
    or performed over the term of the arrangement or the expected period of

performance. Therefore, they should generally be deferred and recognized systematically over the periods that the fees are earned.

7. Defer recognition of revenue from refundable membership sales until the end of the refund period, except in limited circumstances when certain rigorous and demanding criteria have been met.

Because reasonable people hold different views about the application of the accounting literature in this regard, pending further action in this area by the FASB, the SEC staff will not object to the recognition of refundable membership fees, net of estimated refunds, as earned revenue over the membership term in the limited circumstances where *all* of the following criteria have been met:

a. The estimates of terminations or cancellations and refunded revenues are being made for a large pool of homogeneous items (e.g., membership or other service transactions with the same characteristics, such as terms, periods, class of customers, or nature of service).

b. Reliable estimates of the expected refunds can be made on a timely basis.

c. There is a sufficient company-specific historical basis upon which to estimate the refunds, and the company believes that such experience is predictive of future events.

d. The amount of the membership fee specified agreement at the outset of the arrangement is fixed, other customer's right to request a refund.

8. End the practice of including the fair value of free services included as part of a sale transaction as revenue.

The new materiality test is the standard the SEC will use for enforcement purposes in regard to revenue recognition.

Revenue Recognition Accounting Literature

The accounting literature on revenue recognition includes both broad conceptual discussions as well as certain industry-specific guidance. Examples of existing literature on revenue recognition in December 1999, when SAB 101 was issued, included:

- FASB Statements of Financial Accounting Standards: 13, Accounting for Leases; 45, *Accounting for Franchise Fee Revenue;* 48, *Revenue Recognition When Right of Return Exists;* 49, *Accounting for Product Financing Arrangements;* 50, *Financial Reporting in the Record and Music Industry;* 51, *Financial Reporting by Cable Television Companies,* and 66, *Accounting for Sales of Real Estate.*
- APB Opinion 10, *Omnibus Opinion—1966.*

- Accounting Research Bulletins (ARB) 43 and 45, *Long-Term Construction-Type Contracts.*
- AICPA Statements of Position (SOP) 81-1, *Accounting for Performance of Construction-Type and Certain Production-Type Contracts,* and 97-2, *Software Revenue Recognition.*
- Emerging Issues Task Force (EITF) Issue 88-18, *Sales of Future Revenues;* 91-9, *Revenue and Expense Recognition for Freight Services in Process;* 95-1, *Revenue Recognition on Sales with a Guaranteed Minimum Resale Value,* and 95-4, *Revenue Recognition on Equipment Sold and Subsequently Repurchased Subject to an Operating Lease.*
- FASB Statement of Financial Accounting Concepts (SFAC) 5, *Recognition and Measurement in Financial Statements of Business Enterprises.*

If a transaction is within the scope of specific authoritative literature that provides revenue recognition guidance, that literature should be applied. However, in the absence of authoritative literature addressing a specific arrangement or a specific industry, the staff will consider the existing authoritative accounting standards as well as the broad revenue recognition criteria specified in the FASB's conceptual framework that contain basic guidelines for revenue recognition.

Based on these guidelines, revenue should not be recognized until it is realized or realizable and earned. SFAC 5 states that "an entity's revenue-earning activities involve delivering or producing goods, rendering services, or other activities that constitute its ongoing major or central operations, and revenues are considered to have been earned when the entity has substantially accomplished what it must do to be entitled to the benefits represented by the revenues." It continues "the two conditions (being realized or realizable and being earned) are usually met by the time product or merchandise is delivered or services are rendered to customers, and revenues from manufacturing and selling activities and gains and losses from sales of other assets are commonly recognized at time of sale (usually meaning delivery)."

If services are rendered or rights to use assets extend continuously over time (for example, interest or rent), reliable measures based on contractual prices established in advance are commonly available, and revenues may be recognized as earned as time passes.

The staff believes that revenue generally is realized or realizable and earned when all of the following criteria are met:

- Persuasive evidence of an arrangement exists.
- Delivery has occurred or services have been rendered.
- The seller's price to the buyer is fixed or determinable.
- Collectibility is reasonably assured.

Disclosures for Revenue Recognition

Disclosures relating to the recognition of revenue are covered in several different areas of the accounting literature:

- A registrant should disclose its accounting policy for the recognition of revenue in line with APB Opinion 22, *Disclosure of Accounting Policies,* which states, ". . . the disclosure should encompass important judgments as to appropriateness of principles relating to recognition of revenue . . ." Because revenue recognition generally involves some level of judgment, the staff believes that a registrant should always disclose its revenue recognition policy. If a company has different policies for different types of revenue transactions, including barter sales, the policy for each material type of transaction should be disclosed.
- If sales transactions have multiple elements, such as a product *and* service, the accounting policy should clearly state the accounting policy for each element as well as how multiple elements are determined and valued. In addition, the staff believes that changes in estimated returns recognized in accordance with FASB 48 should be disclosed, if material (e.g., a change in estimate from 2% of sales to 1% of sales).
- Regulation S-X requires that revenue from the sales of products, services, and other products each be separately disclosed on the face of the income statement. The SEC staff believes that costs relating to each type of revenue similarly should be reported separately on the face of the income statement.
- Management's Discussion and Analysis (MD&A) requires a discussion of liquidity, capital resources, results of operations and other information necessary to an understanding of a registrant's financial condition, changes in financial condition, and results of operations.

Changes in revenue should not be evaluated solely in terms of volume and price changes, but should also include an analysis of the reasons and factors contributing to the increase or decrease. To go beyond evaluation in terms of volume and price changes, the Commission stated in Financial Reporting Release (FRR) 36 that MD&A should "give investors an opportunity to look at the registrant through the eyes of management by providing a historical and prospective analysis of the registrant's financial condition and results of operations, with a particular emphasis on the registrant's prospects for the future."

Examples of such revenue transactions or events that the staff has asked to be disclosed and discussed in accordance with FRR 36 are:

- Shipments of product at the end of a reporting period that significantly reduce customer backlog and might be expected to result in lower shipments and revenue in the next period.

- Granting of extended payment terms that will result in a longer collection period for accounts receivable and slower cash inflows from operations, and the effect on liquidity and capital resources.
- Changing trends in shipments into, and sales from, a sales channel or separate class of customer that could be expected to have a significant effect on future sales or sales returns.
- An increasing trend toward sales to a different class of customer, such as a reseller distribution channel with a lower gross profit margin than existing sales to end users.
- Increasing service revenue that has a higher profit margin than product sales.
- Seasonal trends or variations in sales.
- Gain or loss from the sale of an asset(s).

FASB 148, ACCOUNTING FOR STOCK-BASED COMPENSATION — TRANSITION AND DISCLOSURE — AN AMENDMENT OF FASB STATEMENT 123

This Statement, adopted in December 2002, amends FASB 123, *Accounting for Stock-Based Compensation,* to provide alternative methods of transition for a voluntary change to the fair value method of accounting for stock-based employee compensation. In addition, FASB 148 amends the disclosure requirements of Statement 123 to require prominent disclosures in both annual and interim financial statements about the method of accounting for stock-based employee compensation and the effect of the method used on reported results.

Reasons for Issuing the Statement

FASB 123 required prospective application of the fair value recognition provisions to new awards granted after the beginning of the period of adoption. When Statement 123 was issued in 1995, the Board recognized the potential for misleading implications caused by the ramp-up effect on reported compensation cost from prospective application of the fair value method of accounting for stock-based employee compensation to new grants only after the date of adoption. However, the Board was concerned that retroactive application would be excessively burdensome to financial statement preparers because the historical assumptions required to determine the fair value of awards of stock-based compensation for periods prior to the issuance of Statement 123 were not readily available. This is no longer a problem. FASB 123 required disclosure of the pro forma effect of applying the fair value method of accounting for those entities that continued to use the intrinsic value method of accounting; therefore, historical information about the fair value of awards granted since the original effective date of Statement 123 is now readily available.

In light of all the scandals and lack of openness in financial reporting, a number of companies have recently adopted or announced their intention to adopt the fair value method of accounting for stock-based employee compensation. To respond to concerns raised by constituents (including financial statement preparers' concerns about the ramp-up effect arising from the transition method prescribed by FASB 123 as well as financial statement users' concerns about the lack of consistency and comparability in reported results caused by that transition method) FASB 148 requires new disclosures about the effect of stock-based employee compensation on reported results. The Statement also requires that those effects be disclosed more prominently by specifying the form, content, and location of those disclosures.

Improvement in Financial Reporting

FASB 148 permits two additional transition methods for entities that adopt the preferable method of accounting for stock-based employee compensation. Both methods avoid the ramp-up effect arising from prospective application of the fair value method. In addition, to address concerns raised by some constituents about the lack of comparability caused by multiple transition methods, the Statement does not permit the use of the original Statement 123's prospective method of transition for changes to the fair value method made in fiscal years beginning after December 15, 2003. In addition, in the absence of a single accounting method for stock-based employee compensation, FASB 148 requires disclosure of comparable information for *all* companies, regardless of whether, when, or how an entity adopts the preferable fair value method of accounting. This Statement improves the prominence and clarity of the pro forma disclosures required by Statement 123 by prescribing a specific tabular format and by requiring disclosure in the "Summary of Significant Accounting Policies" or its equivalent. In addition, this Statement improves the timeliness of those disclosures by requiring their inclusion in financial reports for interim periods as well as the annual report.

FASB Delays Recognition and Measurement Considerations

The Board did not reconsider the recognition and measurement provisions of Statement 123 in FASB 148 because of the ongoing International Accounting Standards Board project on share-based payment. The IASB concluded its deliberations on the accounting for share-based payments, including employee stock options, and issued an exposure draft for public comment in November 2002. That proposal would require companies using IASB standards to recognize as an expense, starting in 2004, the fair value of employee stock options granted. Despite some important differences between the recognition and measurement provisions in the IASB proposal and those contained in FASB 123, the basic approach is the same: *fair value measurement of stock-based employee compensation at the date of grant with expense recognition over the vesting period.*

The Board has been actively working with the IASB and other major national standard setters to bring about convergence of accounting standards across the major world capital markets. In particular, the Board and the FASB staff have been monitoring the IASB's deliberations on share-based payments and, in November 2002, issued an Invitation to Comment summarizing the IASB's proposal and explaining the key similarities of and differences between its provisions and current U.S. accounting standards. In the near future, the Board plans to consider whether it should propose changes to the U.S. standards on accounting for stock-based compensation.

The transition guidance and annual disclosure provisions of FASB 148 are effective for fiscal years ending after December 15, 2002. Earlier application was permitted in certain circumstances. The interim disclosure provisions were effective for financial reports containing financial statements for interim periods beginning after December 15, 2002.

Consideration of Stock Option Disclosure to Continue

As previously mentioned, the FASB requested comments from its constituents on the accounting for stock-based compensation in the Invitation to Comment, *Accounting for Stock-Based Compensation: A Comparison of FASB Statement No. 123, Accounting for Stock-Based Compensation, and Its Related Interpretations, and IASB Proposed IFRS, Share-Based Payment.* The FASB is considering, in accordance with its objectives of improving U.S. financial accounting and reporting standards and promoting international convergence of high-quality accounting standards, whether it should propose any changes to the U.S. accounting standards on stock-based compensation. The Board believes the Invitation to Comment will also be useful to constituents that are planning to respond to the IASB's proposed IFRS, *Share-Based Payment.*

The request explains the similarities of, and differences between, the two approaches. The question has been that, perhaps because many Fortune 500 companies have decided that the safest way to avoid trouble with options is to be as open as possible, the Board will take advantage of the moment and require the full disclosure and expensing of options that it has wanted from the very beginning.

After considering the responses to the Invitation to Comment, the Board will decide whether it should undertake a more comprehensive reconsideration of the accounting for stock options. As part of that process, the Board may revisit its 1995 decision permitting companies to disclose the pro forma effects of the fair value method rather than require all companies to recognize the fair value of employee stock options as an expense in the income statement. Under the provisions of FASB 123 that remain unaffected by FASB 148, companies may either recognize expenses on a fair value method in the income statement or disclose the pro forma effects of that method in the footnotes to the financial statements.

FASB 123, *Accounting for Stock-Based Compensation*

Passage of FASB 123 in 1995 was not so much a compromise measure as an apparent agreement to get on to something else. In the final (at that time) analysis, it offered an alternative approach to the method of using APB Opinion 25, *Accounting for Stock Issued to Employees,* to account for stock options.

The Statement set forth a preferred method for accounting for stock-based employee compensation. Companies, however, were not required to follow the new guidelines and were permitted to continue in the same accounting practice with only slight modification. The alternative approaches were:

1. The fair value method.
2. The intrinsic value method.

Fair Value Method

In line with the effort to bring a greater degree of uniformity and understanding to financial reporting, the FASB premised the preferred method on fair value. Using this procedure, stock-based compensation cost was to be measured at the grant date based on the value of the award and to be recognized over the employee's entire service period, which is also normally the vesting period.

For stock options granted by a public entity, the fair value is determined using an option-pricing model that considers several factors on the grant date:

- The exercise price and expected life of the option.
- The current price of the underlying stock and its expected volatility.
- Expected dividends on the stock with specified exception.
- The risk-free interest rate for the expected term of the option.

The text suggests the Black-Scholes or a binomial model. When the fair value of the option has been determined at the grant date, it is not later adjusted for:

1. Changes in the price of the underlying stock
2. Its volatility
3. The life of the option
4. Dividends on the stock
5. The risk-free interest rate

For a nonpublic enterprise, the procedure is the same, except that expected volatility need not be considered in estimating the option's fair value. Exclusion of the volatility factor in the estimation results in what is termed *minimum value*.

The Board felt, at the time, that it should be possible to reach a reasonably accurate estimate of the fair value of most stock options and other equity instruments when they are granted. However, if complicated features make this extremely difficult—even impossible—alternatives are suggested. If all else fails in finding a satisfactory estimate for the grant date, the Statement provides that the final measure of compensation cost is to be the value based on the stock price and any other pertinent information available on the first date that it is possible to reach a reasonable estimate of the value (generally, the date when the number of shares to which an employee is entitled and the exercise price are both determinable).

For nonvested or restricted stock awarded to an employee, the fair value is measured at the market price—or estimated market price, if the stock is not publicly traded—of a share of nonrestricted stock at the grant date.

Intrinsic Value Method

Stock-based compensation standards had been based on APB 25 and continued to be so for most companies. Using the intrinsic value method, compensation cost is the excess (if there is any) of the quoted market price of the particular stock over the employee's exercise price at the grant date, or at another specified measurement date, perhaps the service date.

There actually is no intrinsic value or excess of exercise price over market price of the stock at the grant date for most fixed stock option plans. Therefore, the current accounting requirements generally do not result in an expense charge for most options, and no compensation cost is recognized. On the other hand, normally a compensation cost is recognized for other types of stock compensation plans under the intrinsic value method. They are usually plans with variable, often performance-based, features.

Exceptions

Compensation costs need not be recognized for employee stock purchase plan discounts under FASB 123 if the following three conditions exist:

1. The discount is relatively small.
2. Substantially all full-time employees participate on an equitable basis.
3. Provisions in the plan do not include any stock option features.

The compensation cost of stock awards required to be settled in cash is the amount of the change in the stock price in the periods in which the changes occur.

Additional Requirements

Although FASB 123 is effective for calendar year 1996 and information about options granted in 1995 must be included in the 1996 financial statements, the decade-long consideration of the controversial issue only encourages companies to account for stock compensation awards based on their fair value at the date the awards are granted with the compensation cost shown as an expense on the income statement.

Companies continuing to use the APB 25 intrinsic value method will be required to disclose—but only in a note to the financial statements—what the net income and earnings would have been had they followed the new accounting method.

Controversy

The Board had long hoped to require full-scale fair-value-type measurement and accounting for employee stock compensation using a generally accepted options pricing model; however, those outside the Board were not ready to accept a mandate. After rather overwhelming pressure for more than a year from Congress, other politicians, other government agencies, business, and CPAs in public practice as well as those with commercial and industrial companies, a majority of the Board decided to emphasize improving disclosure rather than hold out for requiring an expense charge for all options.

Many who were on the "winning side" in that tug-of-war are now in the front line of those calling for reform of the accounting for revenue recognition and expense charges.

Chapter 2

Actions of the Financial Accounting Standards Board

CONTENTS

All sectors of the accounting and auditing world have come under attack as a result of Enron. Rather uncharacteristically, this attack has included the Financial Accounting Standards Board (FASB) and its vaunted due process. There appear to be those who consider the FASB's work "due," but, far too often and for too long, having no "process" in place.

With the reaffirmation of their status as a Designated Private-Sector Standard Setter by the Securities and Exchange Commission (SEC) in April 2003, the Financial Accounting Standards Board has gone about its business of setting standards for the accounting profession. The Commission determined that the FASB and its parent organization, the Financial Accounting Foundation (FAF), satisfy the criteria in section 108 of the Sarbanes-Oxley Act of 2002 and, accordingly, FASB's financial accounting and reporting standards are recognized as "generally accepted" for purposes of the federal securities laws.

With this matter taken care of, the Board promptly issued a minimum of two new Standards and two Exposure Drafts, and undertook work on numerous other projects.

FASB 150, *Accounting for Financial Instruments with Characteristics of Both Liabilities and Equity*

The FASB issued Statement 150 in May 2003 to improve the accounting for certain financial instruments that, under previous guidance, issuers could account for as equity. The Statement requires that those instruments now be classified as liabilities in statements of financial position.

FASB 150 affects the issuer's accounting for three types of freestanding financial instruments:

1. Mandatorily redeemable shares, which the issuing company is obligated to buy back in exchange for cash or other assets. This is an unconditional obligation requiring the issuer to redeem it by transferring its assets at a specified or determinable date (or dates) or upon an event that is certain to occur.

2. Put options and forward purchase contracts, which involve instruments that do or may require the issuer to buy back some of its shares in exchange for cash or other assets. This is an instrument, other than an outstanding share, that from the very beginning embodies an obligation to repurchase the issuer's equity shares, or is indexed to such an obligation. It requires, or may require, the issuer to settle the obligation by a transfer of assets (e.g., a forward purchase contract or written put option on the issuer's equity shares that is to be physically settled or net cash settled).

3. A financial instrument that embodies an unconditional obligation, or a financial instrument other than an outstanding share that embodies a conditional obligation, that the issuer must or may settle by issuing a variable number of its equity shares, if, at inception, the monetary value of the obligation is based solely or predominantly on any of the following:

   a. A fixed monetary amount known at inception (e.g., a payable that can be settled with a variable number of the issuer's equity shares).

   b. Variations in something other than the fair value of the issuer's equity shares (e.g., a financial instrument indexed to the S&P 500 and that can be settled with a variable number of the issuer's equity shares).

   c. Variations inversely related to changes in the fair value of the issuer's equity shares (e.g., a written put option that could be settled with net share).

FASB 150 does not apply to features embedded in a financial instrument that is not a derivative in its entirety.

Financial instruments involving the potential issuance of common stock classified as liabilities under SFAS 150 are excluded from the computation of basic and diluted earnings per share.

Most of the provisions of the Statement are consistent with the existing definition of *liabilities* in FASB Concepts Statement 6, *Elements of Financial Statements*. The remaining provisions are consistent with the Board's proposal to revise that definition to encompass certain obligations that a reporting entity can or must settle by issuing its own equity shares, depending on the nature of the relationship established between holder and issuer. That revision is scheduled as part of a second phase of the Board's project on liabilities and equity that is planned to begin late in 2003. In that phase, the plans are to address the accounting for convertible bonds, putable stock, and other instruments with embedded features characteristic of both liability and equity that are not in the scope of FASB 150.

In addition to its requirements for the classification and measurement of financial instruments in its scope, this subsequent Statement also requires disclosures about alternative ways of settling the instruments and the capital structure of entities, all of whose shares are mandatorily redeemable.

Effective Dates for Application

Most of the guidance is effective for all financial instruments entered into or modified after May 31, 2003, and otherwise is effective at the beginning of the first interim period beginning after June 15, 2003. For private companies, mandatorily redeemable financial instruments are subject to the provisions of this Statement for the fiscal period beginning after December 15, 2003.

This Statement is effective for contracts entered into or modified after June 30, 2003, except as stated below and for hedging relationships designated after June 30, 2003. The guidance should be applied prospectively.

The provisions of this Statement that relate to the Implementation Issues of FASB 133, *Accounting for Derivative Instruments and Hedging Activities,* that have been effective for fiscal quarters that began prior to June 15, 2003, should continue to be applied in accordance with their respective effective dates. In addition, certain provisions relating to forward purchases or sales of *when-issued* securities or other securities that do not yet exist should be applied to existing contracts as well as new contracts entered into after June 30, 2003. Restatement is not permitted. A cumulative effect of a change in accounting principle for financial instruments existing at the beginning of the transition interim period must be recognized.

Phase 2 of the Project Under Way

With the issuance of FASB 150, the Board will continue with phase 2 of the liabilities and equity project. In this phase, the Board will consider the following issues:

- Separating compound financial instruments with characteristics of both liabilities and equity (including convertible debt, conditionally redeemable stock, and dual-indexed obligations to issue shares) into their liability and equity components.

- The definition of ownership relationship.
- The definition of liabilities in Concepts Statement 6.

FASB 149, AMENDMENT OF STATEMENT 133 ON DERIVATIVE INSTRUMENTS AND HEDGING ACTIVITIES

The FASB issued Statement 149 to amend and clarify accounting for derivatives, including certain derivative instruments embedded in other contracts, and for hedging activities under Statement 133 in April 2003.

The new guidance amends FASB 133 for decisions made:

- As part of the Derivatives Implementation Group process that effectively requires amendments to Statement 133.
- In connection with other Board projects dealing with financial instruments.
- Regarding implementation issues raised in relation to the application of the definition of a derivative. This is particularly in regard to the meaning of an underlying instrument and the characteristics of a derivative that contains financing components. The language now conforms to that used in the definition of an underlying instrument in FASB Interpretation 45, *Guarantor's Accounting and Disclosure Requirements for Guarantees, Including Indirect Guarantees of Indebtedness of Others*.

The amendments set forth in FASB 149 improve financial reporting by requiring that contracts with comparable characteristics be accounted for similarly. It clarifies under what circumstances a contract with an initial net investment meets the characteristic of a derivative described in Statement 133. In addition, it clarifies *when* a derivative contains a financing component that calls for special reporting in the statement of cash flows.

Statement 149 also amends certain other existing pronouncements. Those changes will result in more consistent reporting of contracts that are derivatives in their entirety or that contain embedded derivatives that warrant separate accounting.

Effective Dates

This Statement was effective for contracts entered into or modified after June 30, 2003, except as stated below, and for hedging relationships designated after June 30, 2003. The guidance should be applied prospectively.

The provisions of this Statement that relate to Statement 133 Implementation Issues that have been effective for fiscal quarters that began prior to June 15, 2003, should continue to be applied in accordance with their respective effective dates. In addition, certain provisions relating to forward purchases or sales of *when-issued* securities or other securities that do not yet exist should be applied to existing contracts as well as new contracts entered into after June 30, 2003.

FASB 148, Accounting for Stock–Based Compensation — Transition and Disclosure — An Amendment of FASB 123

This Statement, adopted in December 2002, amends FASB 123, *Accounting for Stock-Based Compensation,* to provide alternative methods of transition for a voluntary change to the fair value method of accounting for stock-based employee compensation. In addition, FASB 148 amends the disclosure requirements of Statement 123 to require prominent disclosures in both annual and interim financial statements about the method of accounting for stock-based employee compensation and the effect of the method used on reported results.

Reasons for Issuing the Statement

Statement 123 required prospective application of the fair value recognition provisions to new awards granted after the beginning of the period of adoption. When Statement 123 was issued in 1995, the Board recognized the potential for misleading implications caused by the "ramp-up" effect on reported compensation cost from prospective application of the fair value method of accounting for stock-based employee compensation to new grants only after the date of adoption. However, the Board was concerned that retroactive application would be excessively burdensome to financial statement preparers because the historical assumptions required to determine the fair value of awards of stock-based compensation for periods prior to the issuance of Statement 123 were not readily available.

This is no longer a problem. FASB 123 required disclosure of the pro forma effect of applying the fair value method of accounting for those entities that continued to use the intrinsic value method of accounting; therefore, historical information about the fair value of awards granted since the original effective date of Statement 123 is now readily available.

In light of all the scandals and lack of openness in financial reporting, a number of companies have recently adopted or announced their intention to adopt the fair value method of accounting for stock-based employee compensation. To respond to concerns raised by constituents (including financial statement preparers' concerns about the ramp-up effect arising from the transition method prescribed by FASB 123, as well as financial statement users' concerns about the lack of consistency and comparability in reported results caused by that transition method), this Statement requires new disclosures about the effect of stock-based employee compensation on reported results. The Statement also requires that those effects be disclosed more prominently by specifying the form, content, and location of those disclosures.

Improvement in Financial Reporting

This Statement permits two additional transition methods for entities that adopt the preferable method of accounting for stock-based employee compensation. Both of those methods avoid the ramp-up effect arising from prospective application of the fair value method. In addition, to address concerns raised by some constituents about the lack of comparability caused by multiple transition methods, the Statement does not permit the use of the original Statement 123 prospective method of transition for changes to the fair value method made in fiscal years beginning after December 15, 2003.

Further, in the absence of a single accounting method for stock-based employee compensation, this Statement requires disclosure of comparable information for *all* companies, regardless of whether, when, or how an entity adopts the preferable, fair value method of accounting. This Statement improves the prominence and clarity of the pro forma disclosures required by Statement 123 by prescribing a specific tabular format and by requiring disclosure in the "Summary of Significant Accounting Policies" or its equivalent. In addition, this Statement improves the timeliness of those disclosures by requiring their inclusion in financial reports for interim periods as well as the annual report.

FASB Delays Recognition and Measurement Considerations

The Board did not reconsider the recognition and measurement provisions of Statement 123 in this Statement because of the ongoing International Accounting Standards Board (IASB) project on share-based payment. The IASB concluded its deliberations on the accounting for share-based payments, including employee stock options, and issued an Exposure Draft for public comment in November 2002. That proposal would require companies using IASB standards to recognize as an expense, starting in 2004, the fair value of employee stock options granted. Despite important differences between the recognition and measurement provisions in the IASB proposal and those contained in FASB 123, the basic approach is the same: *fair value measurement of stock-based employee compensation at the date of grant with expense recognition over the vesting period.*

The FASB has been actively working with the IASB and other major national standard setters to bring about convergence of accounting standards across the major world capital markets. In particular, the FASB and its staff have been monitoring the IASB's deliberations on share-based payments, and in November 2002 the FASB issued an Invitation to Comment summarizing the IASB's proposal and explaining the key similarities of and differences between its provisions and current U.S. accounting standards. In the near future, the Board plans to consider whether it should propose changes to the U.S. standards on accounting for stock-based compensation.

The transition guidance and annual disclosure provisions of Statement 148 are effective for fiscal years ending after December 15, 2002. Earlier application was permitted in certain circumstances. The interim disclosure provisions were effective for financial reports containing financial statements for interim periods beginning after December 15, 2002.

Consideration of Stock Option Disclosure to Continue

The FASB requested comments from its constituents on the accounting for stock-based compensation in an Invitation to Comment on *Accounting for Stock-Based Compensation: A Comparison of FASB Statement No. 123, Accounting for Stock-Based Compensation, and Its Related Interpretations, and IASB Proposed IFRS, Share-Based Payment*. The FASB is considering, in accordance with its objectives of improving U.S. financial accounting and reporting standards and promoting international convergence of high-quality accounting standards, whether it should propose any changes to the U.S. accounting standards on stock-based compensation. The Board believes the Invitation to Comment will also be useful to constituents that are planning to respond to the IASB's proposed International Financial Reporting Standard (IFRS), *Share-Based Payment*.

The request explains the similarities of, and differences between, the two approaches. The question has been that, perhaps because many Fortune 500 companies have decided that the safest way to avoid trouble with options is to be as open as possible, will the Board will take advantage of the moment and require the full disclosure and expensing of options that they have wanted from the very beginning.

After considering the responses to the Invitation to Comment, the Board plans to decide whether it should undertake a more comprehensive reconsideration of the accounting for stock options. As part of that process, the Board may revisit its 1995 decision permitting companies to disclose the pro forma effects of the fair value method, rather than require all companies to recognize the fair value of employee stock options as an expense in the income statement. Under the provisions of Statement 123 that remain unaffected by Statement 148, companies may either recognize expenses on a fair value method in the income statement or disclose the pro forma effects of that method in the footnotes to the financial statements.

Short-Term International Convergence

The FASB and IASB have agreed that convergence of their standards is a primary objective of both standard setters. In line with this goal, the Board has reached certain conclusions:

1. To agree with the IASB position that a voluntary change in accounting principle should be accounted for retrospectively. Prior periods should be restated as if this accounting policy had always been used, except when retroactive application is impracticable. This occurs only when:

   a. The effects of retroactive application are indeterminable.

   b. Retroactive application requires assumptions about management's intent in a prior period.

   c. Retroactive application requires significant management estimates as of a prior period.

2. A change in accounting resulting from a new pronouncement would be reported using the guidance for voluntary changes in accounting principles, unless the transition provisions require a different method.

3. Nonmonetary exchanges of productive assets should be accounted for at fair value unless:

   a. Neither the asset received nor that surrendered has a fair value determinable within reasonable limits.

   b. The transaction lacks commercial substance.

4. To adopt the IASB position that a long-term financial liability to be settled within 12 months of the balance sheet date should be classified as a current liability, unless an agreement to refinance the liability on a long-term basis is completed on or before the balance sheet date. It would no longer be permissible to classify as current a financing agreement completed after the balance sheet date but before the financial statements are authorized for issue.

5. That a long-term financial liability that is payable on demand at the balance sheet date because the entity breached a condition of its loan agreement should be classified as current, unless:

   a. The lender has agreed on or before the balance sheet date to demand payment as a consequence of the breach (convergent with the IASB position), or

   b. The lender has agreed on or before the balance sheet date not to provide a period of grace during which the obligation is not callable, and within which an entity can rectify the breach, and either:

      (1) The entity rectifies the breach within the period of grace, or

(2) At the time that the financial statements are issued, it is probable that the breach will be rectified within the period of grace. (This is consistent with U.S. GAAP.)

6. To converge with the IASB position that a change in depreciation method is a change in accounting estimate that is affected by a change in accounting principle. As a result, a change in depreciation method would be accounted for in:

   a. The period of change if the change affects that period only.

   b. The period of change and also the future periods if the change affects both.

If the FASB and the IASB can continue their flexibility along the convergence route, the idea of one set of global accounting rules should not be dismissed lightly. Both Boards have much to gain, and lose. U.S. Standards can certainly not be considered inviolate; however, they are the most complete and have been the basis of an economy that is second to none. Possibly this present accord is just an early step in a successful attack on the short-term convergence project launched by the two standard setters. Among other projects in about 20 areas relative to which they hope to achieve convergence are accounting for research and development, interim financial reporting, proportionate consolidation, construction contracts, financial performance, pension plan disclosure, and income taxes.

FASB Issues ED on Financial Statement Disclosure of Pension Information

The FASB issued an ED, *Employers' Disclosures about Pensions and Other Postretirement Benefits,* in September 2003, that would improve financial statement disclosures for defined benefit plans. The FASB began work on this earlier in the year in response to concerns raised by investors and other users of financial statements regarding the need for greater transparency of pension information. The proposed changes are to replace existing FASB accounting guidance.

To provide the public with better and more complete information, the FASB plans to require that companies provide more details about:

- Plan assets.
- Benefit obligations.
- Cash flows.
- Benefit costs.
- Other relevant information.

The Board believes that the proposed disclosures will provide investors with better information about plan assets and a clearer picture of cash requirements for benefit payments, contributions to fund pension and other postretirement benefit plans. The desire for information of this type comes in the wake of the discovery that many plans are definitely underfunded. Along with this is also the realization that things will only get worse unless something is done about the situation.

For the first time, companies would be required to provide financial statement users with a breakdown of plan assets by category, such as equity, debt, and real estate. The expected rates of return and target allocation percentages, or target ranges, for these asset categories also would be required in financial statements.

Cash flows would include projections of future benefit payments and an estimate of contributions to be made in the next year to fund the pension and other postretirement benefit plans.

In addition to expanded annual disclosures, the FASB seeks to improve the information available to investors in interim financial statements; therefore, companies would be required to report the various elements of pension and other benefit costs on a quarterly basis.

The proposed guidance would be effective for fiscal years ending after December 15, 2003, and for the first fiscal quarter of the year following initial application of the annual disclosure requirements.

FASB Issues ED on Improved Accounting for QSPEs

In June 2003, the FASB issued an Exposure Draft, *Qualifying Special-Purpose Entities and Isolation of Transferred Assets,* that would amend FASB Statement 140, *Accounting for Transfers and Servicing of Financial Assets and Extinguishments of Liabilities.* The purpose of the proposal is to provide more specific guidance on the accounting for transfers of financial assets from a company to an off-balance-sheet structure known as a qualifying special-purpose entity (QSPE).

The proposal would change the requirements that an entity must meet to be considered a QSPE, a structure often used by companies to make financial assets into securities and to clarify certain other requirements of Statement 140. It proposes changing these qualifications and is significant because these entities, which are frequently used to scrutinize financial assets, do not have to be consolidated by the transferor.

The guidance is aimed at improving the accounting for QSPEs in several key respects:

- It prohibits an entity from being a QSPE if a company that transfers assets to the entity enters into a commitment (such as a financial guarantee, liquidity commitment, or total return swap) to provide additional cash or other assets to fulfill the QSPE's obligations to its beneficial interest holders.

- The proposal would prohibit classification of an entity as a QSPE if the entity can reissue beneficial interests and if any party involved with the entity has certain risks or combinations of risks and decision-making abilities, unless none of these parties, including affiliates or agents, provides a commitment:
    - That has a fair value equaling more than half the aggregate fair value of all such commitments.
    - That makes decisions about reissuing beneficial interests.
    - That holds beneficial interests that are not the most senior in priority.
- The proposed Statement prohibits an entity from being a QSPE if it holds equity instruments such as shares or partnership interests.
- The proposed Statement clarifies certain of the requirements in Statement 140 related to legally isolating assets and surrendering control of assets.

Existing accounting standards do not mention the powers of a QSPE to reissue beneficial interests. The FASB is concerned that this lack might create an incentive to convert certain entities to QSPEs to avoid consolidation. This Exposure Draft is intended to close this loophole.

FASB Issues ED on Accounting for Real Estate Time-Sharing Transactions

Concurrent with the issuance of a Proposed Statement of Position, *Accounting for Real Estate Time-Sharing Transactions* by the Accounting Standards Executive Committee (AcSEC) of the American Institute of Certified Public Accountants in February 2003, the FASB issued an Exposure Draft, *Accounting for Real Estate Time-Sharing Transactions,* an amendment of FASB Statements 66 and 67. FASB 66, *Accounting for Sales of Real Estate,* was issued in 1982 and adopted the specialized profit recognition principles in certain AICPA Industry Accounting Guides and Statements of Position. This Statement provides limited guidance for time-sharing transactions.

Subsequent to the issuance of Statement 66, extensive changes in the methods used by the time-sharing industry to offer its products resulted in divergent accounting practices. Those divergent practices centered on revenue recognition, recording of credit losses, and the treatment of selling costs. In response, AcSEC developed the proposed SOP, which applies to all time-sharing transactions in financial statements prepared in conformity with GAAP. The proposed FASB Statement would amend FASBs 66 and 67 to exclude time-sharing transactions from the scope of those Statements, should the proposed SOP be issued as final. It would also amend other authoritative pronouncements.

Both proposals would be effective for financial statements issued for fiscal years beginning after June 15, 2004. Earlier application would be encouraged.

POTPOURRI OF BOARD PROJECTS

The current Board appears not only to be a very active one with a well-stocked agenda, but also one that is heeding the Sarbanes-Oxley Act and the SEC's suggestions to pursue the idea of convergence of GAAP and international standards as well as to do all things in a timely manner.

The nature of many of the changes and plans appears to stem from the failures of U.S. GAAP, highlighted by the collapse of Enron Corporation and the abusive accounting practices employed by certain telecommunications and high-tech companies. A few of the many projects under way are mentioned below.

Principle-Based Standards

The FASB had earlier initiated an evaluation of whether or not and, if so, how to adopt a *principles-based approach to standard setting.* The Sarbanes-Oxley Act *requires* the Securities and Exchange Commission to study the adoption of a principles-based accounting system by the U.S. financial reporting system. The FASB and SEC are working together on this effort.

The principles-based accounting standards with emphasis on detailed rules has obviously not worked too well in recent years, perhaps because the U.S. approach has:

- Been too complex for many financial report users to understand.
- Been difficult and sometimes costly to implement causing rules to be ignored, overlooked, or subverted.
- Failed to reveal the economic substance of transactions, even when the preparer "followed" the detailed rules.
- Allowed Enron (and other companies) to use the "specifics" of GAAP and various rules and regulations as a starting point for figuring out just what they could get away with, despite knowing full well the principle behind the rule.

To date, the FASB has stated its support for a principles-based approach and has issued for public comment a proposal discussing a possible approach to principle-based standards. As this proposal indicates, standards developed under this approach would:

- Apply broadly to transactions other than the events covered by the standards; accounting principles would continue to be developed from the FASB's conceptual framework.
- Contain few, if any, exceptions to the principles.
- Provide less interpretive and implementation guidance for applying standards.

The FASB is exploring the International Accounting Standard Board's principle-based approach to standard setting inasmuch as many countries will be adopting the IASB's Standards.

There are some who question whether it is wise to expect the necessary degree of good judgment and moral fortitude required of CEOs, CFOs, auditors, and other decision makers in light of recent financial reporting scandals. Those holding this view believe a principles-based approach to standard setting may not be workable. On the other hand, the prescriptive type seems not to have worked in quite a number of cases, either.

Financial Performance Reporting

The FASB's Financial Performance Reporting by Business Enterprises project may change the form and content, classifications and aggregations, and display of specified items and summarized amounts on the face of all basic financial statements. The important result of this project could well be the elimination of net income as an income statement item. It would be replaced by *comprehensive income.* Currently, comprehensive income plays little, if any, role in equity valuations.

The project's goal is twofold:

1. Improve the quality of information displayed in financial statements so statement users can better evaluate an enterprise's performance.
2. Ensure that sufficient information is contained in financial statements to permit calculation of key financial measures used by investors and creditors.

The FASB is working closely on the project with the IASB, which has a similar project under way with the United Kingdom's Accounting Standards Board.

Comprehensive Income Defined.   The FASB's Concept Statement No. 6 defines comprehensive income as the change in equity of a business enterprise during a period from transactions and other events and circumstances from nonowner sources. It includes all changes in equity during a period except those resulting from investments by owners and distributions to owners.

FASB 130, *Comprehensive Income,* required companies to display in their financial statements total comprehensive income and its components in either an income statement-type format or in a changes in equity format. Most companies chose to use the changes in equity format.

The operational definition of comprehensive income in FASB 130 is net income plus other comprehensive income. Other comprehensive income is made up of the accounting items that are direct debits or credits to owners' equity in U.S. GAAP that do not involve transactions with owners, such as foreign currency translation gains and losses and unrealized gains or losses on marketable securities classified as available-for-sale.

Revenue Recognition

The FASB continues to discuss a possible new comprehensive accounting standard on revenue recognition. Its current focus is on two possible approaches:

1. Liability extinguishment view.
2. Broad performance view.

Under the liability extinguishment view, revenues arise from extinguishment of obligations to the reporting entity's customer for which it is primarily liable. Under the broad performance view, revenues arise from the reporting entity's output of assets in the form of its goods and services that it ultimately sacrifices by transferring them to customers. It is expected that a new revenue recognition rule based on one or a combination of these views will replace the current general rule that revenue needs to be earned and realized before it is recognized.

Purchase Method Procedures

The purchase method procedures project is reconsidering many aspects of the purchase method of accounting for business combinations. It is a joint effort with the IASB. Work on this project is nearing completion.

THE FAF CONSIDERS CHANGES TO STREAMLINE THE FASB PROCESS

In light of the criticism leveled at the FASB and accountants and auditors in general, the Financial Accounting Foundation, the body that oversees, appoints members and funds the activities of the FASB, has determined to strengthen its commitment to a strong, transparent, and rigorous system of financial accounting standards for America's capital markets.

FAF Trustees have admitted that in the minds of some investors the system of accounting standards along with the audited financial statements that must comply with them are being questioned. The FAF has announced it plans to do everything within its power both to review and improve the procedures and policies within its official mandate and to participate, where appropriate, in the larger debate about how to strengthen all parts of the evolving regulatory environment.

Trustees agree that there is a need for the FASB to be more flexible in responding to change and to increase the efficiency of its standard-setting process. By doing so, financial reporting standards would be enhanced.

Chairman Points to Accomplishments

In defense of the FASB, the Chairman pointed out that despite significant resistance from some of those affected, the FASB has made substantial improvements to financial reporting that have resulted in greater transparency of financial information. These include requiring:

- That reporting entities recognize liabilities for retirement benefits when those entities promise them to employees rather than when they later pay them.

- Significant disclosures about the separate operating segments of an entity's business so that investors can evaluate the differing risks in the diverse operations.

- That derivative instruments and hedging transactions be reflected in financial statements. Previously they were not reflected.

- That the acquisition of one company by another is accounted for in the same way for all entities and that the total amount paid for the acquisition is reflected in the financial statements. In the past, that was not often the case. (FASBs 141 and 142 cover this topic. To clarify purchase accounting rules, practices, and requirements, the Board is working with the International Accounting Standards Board as explained below. The Board believes such a project is necessary since current rules do not provide transparent information to users and are sometimes inconsistent with the FASB's Conceptual Framework.)

The FAF Changes FASB Voting to Increase Efficiency

In following up on its earlier proposals to increase the efficiency of the FASB's process, the Financial Accounting Foundation changed the FASB's voting process from a supermajority to a simple majority vote. The decision, which received unanimous support, was made by the FAF Trustees at its quarterly meeting held in April 2002, in Washington, D.C. The change in voting of the seven-member FASB was effective immediately.

As part of its commitment to a strong, transparent, and rigorous accounting standard-setting system, the FAF considered several other options. Proposed changes included a reduction in the size of the FASB from seven to five members, a simple majority versus a supermajority vote and shortened comment periods.

After full discussion of those recommendations and a review of comment letters, the Trustees determined that the change from a 5-to-2 to a 4-to-3 member voting requirement would make for a more efficient process without compromising the quality of the FASB's standard-setting process. The FAF recognized the need for the FASB to accelerate its standard-setting process and believes that this change should help to do so. At the same time, it should also reduce the lead time before an exposure draft can be published for comment or a new standard can be implemented.

FASB Reorganizes Research and Technical Activities

The FAF also discussed the FASB's reorganization of its research and technical activities to address increasing demands on staff and other resources. A study, commissioned by the FASB in the latter part of 2001, determined that the Board would be best served by reallocating its research and technical activities functions across three distinct sections rather than just one that covered all areas.

The three sections report to the Chairman of the FASB. The new directorships and their responsibilities cover the following areas:

1. Major projects and technical activities.
2. Technical application and implementation activities.
3. Planning, development and support activities.

FASB 147, ACQUISITIONS OF CERTAIN FINANCIAL INSTITUTIONS

The FASB issued Statement 147, *Acquisitions of Certain Financial Institutions,* on October 1, 2002. The Statement provides guidance on the accounting for the acquisition of a financial institution. It applies to all acquisitions except those between two or more mutual enterprises. (The Board has a separate project on its agenda that will provide this guidance.)

Statement 147 contains the following provisions:

- The excess of the fair value of liabilities assumed over the fair value of tangible and identifiable intangible assets acquired in a business combination represents goodwill that should be accounted for under FASB 142, *Goodwill and Other Intangible Assets.*
- The specialized accounting guidance in paragraph 5 of FASB 72, *Accounting for Certain Acquisitions of Banking or Thrift Institutions,* does not apply after September 30, 2002. If certain criteria in Statement 147 are met, the amount of the unidentifiable intangible asset will be reclassified to goodwill upon adoption of the new Statement.
- Financial institutions meeting conditions outlined in FASB 147 are required to restate previously issued financial statements. The objective of the restatement requirement is to present the balance sheet and income statement as if the amount accounted for under FASB 72 as an unidentifiable intangible asset had been reclassified to goodwill as of the date FASB 142 was initially applied. The transition provisions were effective on October 1, 2002.
- The scope of FASB 144, *Accounting for the Impairment or Disposal of Long-Lived Assets,* has been amended to include long-term customer-relationship intangible assets, such as depositor- and borrower-relationship intangible assets and credit cardholder intangible assets.

FASB 146, ACCOUNTING FOR COSTS ASSOCIATED WITH EXIT OR DISPOSAL ACTIVITIES

In July 2002, the FASB issued Statement 146, *Accounting for Costs Associated with Exit or Disposal Activities.* The Standard requires companies to recognize costs associated with exit or disposal activities *when they are incurred* rather than at the date of a commitment to an exit or disposal plan. Examples of costs covered by the standard include lease termination costs and certain employee severance costs that are associated with a restructuring, discontinued operation, plant closing, or other exit or disposal activity.

Guidance had been provided by EITF 94-3, *Liability Recognition for Certain Employee Termination Benefits and Other Costs to Exit an Activity (including Certain Costs Incurred in a Restructuring).* FASB 146 replaces it and completes work begun in FASB 144 as discussed below.

Commenting on the standard, the FASB stated that liabilities represent present obligations to others. Because a commitment to a plan, by itself, does not create a present obligation to others, the principal effect of applying Statement 146 will be on the *timing of recognition of costs* associated with exit or disposal activities. In many cases, those costs will be recognized as liabilities in periods following a commitment to a plan, not at the date of the commitment.

FASB 146 is to be applied prospectively to exit or disposal activities initiated after December 31, 2002.

FASB 144, ACCOUNTING FOR THE IMPAIRMENT OR DISPOSAL OF LONG–LIVED ASSETS

The FASB issued Standard 144, in August 2000, governing the financial accounting and reporting for the impairment or disposal of long-lived assets individually or as asset groups that include long-lived assets. An impaired long-lived asset or asset group is one whose carrying amount exceeds its fair value. This Statement:

- Supersedes FASB 121, *Accounting for the Impairment of Long-Lived Assets and for Long-Lived Assets to Be Disposed Of.*
- Supersedes the accounting and reporting provisions of Accounting Principles Board (APB) Opinion 30, *Reporting the Results of Operations— Reporting the Effects of Disposal of a Segment of a Business, and Extraordinary, Unusual and Infrequently Occurring Events and Transactions,* for the disposal of a segment of a business (as previously defined in that Opinion).
- Amends ARB 51, *Consolidated Financial Statements,* to eliminate the exception to consolidation for a subsidiary for which control is likely to be temporary.

Caution from the Securities and Exchange Commission

The Securities and Exchange Commission warned companies that it expects impaired assets to be written down to their *net realizable value.* The SEC's warning was motivated by the economic slowdown and the historical reluctance of managers to recognize asset impairment losses in a timely manner.

It was mandatory that the anticipated impact of the new standard on 2002 balance sheets and income statements be disclosed in 2001 financial reports as well as in subsequent reports.

Reasons for Issuing This Statement

Because FASB 121 did not address the accounting for a segment of a business accounted for as a discontinued operation under ARB 30, two accounting models were in use for long-lived assets to be disposed of. The Board decided to establish a single accounting model, based on the framework established in FASB 121, for long-lived assets to be disposed of by sale. The Board also decided to resolve significant implementation issues related to it.

Long-Lived Assets to Be Held and Used

FASB 144 retains the requirements of FASB 121 relating to when an impairment loss must be recognized for a long-lived asset or asset group to be held and used. Two test conditions apply. First, an impairment loss is recognized only if the carrying amount of the long-lived asset is *not recoverable* from its undiscounted cash flows. A long-lived asset or asset group's carrying amount is not recoverable if it exceeds the sum of the undiscounted cash flows expected to result from the use and eventual disposal of the long-lived asset or asset group. The estimates of future cash flows should be based on the existing service potential of the long-lived asset or asset group and include only those cash flows necessary to maintain the existing service potential. Second, an impairment loss is measured as the difference between the carrying amount and fair value of the asset when the carrying amount exceeds its fair value. A long-lived asset's cash flows should be based on the existing service potential of the long-lived asset or asset group and include only those cash flows necessary to maintain the existing service potential.

If a long-lived asset or asset group fails the first test, its fair value must be determined using the best information available. Suggested procedures include:

- Using quoted market prices to determine fair value. The wording of FASB 144 expresses a preference for this technique but also recognizes that these may not always be available.
- Using a present-value-based valuation technique based on assumptions marketplace participants would consider an acceptable alternative. This is the next choice the Standard suggests.
- If market-based assumptions are unavailable, management can use its own assumptions.

To resolve implementation issues, FASB 144:

- Removes goodwill from its scope and therefore eliminates the requirement of FASB 121 to allocate goodwill to long-lived assets to be tested for impairment.
- Describes a probability-weighted cash flow estimation approach to deal with situations in which alternative courses of action to recover the carrying amount of a long-lived asset are under consideration or a range is estimated for the amount of possible future cash flows.

• Establishes a primary-asset approach to determine the cash flow estimation period for a group of assets and liabilities that represents the unit of accounting for a long-lived asset to be held and used.

Long-Lived Assets to Be Disposed of by Sale

The accounting model for long-lived assets to be disposed of by sale is used for all long-lived assets, whether previously held and used or newly acquired. That accounting model retains the requirement of Statement 121 to measure a long-lived asset classified as held for sale at the lower of its carrying amount or fair value less cost to sell and to cease depreciation (amortization). *Therefore, discontinued operations are no longer measured on a net realizable value basis, and future operating losses are no longer recognized before they occur.*

If the fair value less cost to sell of an asset or asset group held for sale is lower than its carrying amount, the carrying amount is written down to its fair value less cost to sell and an operating loss is recognized for the write-down. The loss is included in the measurement of operating income, unless the long-lived asset or asset group is deemed for the purpose of the new standard to be a component of an entity.

If subsequently the fair value less cost to sell increases, the carrying amount is increased by the increase in fair value less cost to sell to the extent of previously recognized write-downs and a gain is recognized in operating income. (Any loss or gain adjustments are made only to the carrying amount of the long-lived asset whether classified as held for sale individually or as part of a group of assets.)

Long-lived assets held for sale should not be depreciated or amortized; however, interest on liabilities attributable to an asset or asset group held for sale must continue to be accrued.

Long-lived assets or asset groups held for sale should be presented separately on the balance sheet or in the notes on a gross basis. (Any gain or loss resulting from the eventual sale is recognized at the time of sale.)

In such cases, this Statement retains the basic provisions of *Opinion 30* for the presentation of discontinued operations in the income statement but broadens that presentation to include *a component of an entity* rather than *a segment of a business.*

A component of an entity comprises operations and cash flows that can be clearly distinguished, operationally and for financial reporting purposes, from the rest of the entity. A component of an entity that is classified as held for sale or that has been disposed of is presented as a discontinued operation *if* the operations and cash flows of the component will be (or have been) eliminated from the ongoing operations of the entity and the entity will not have any significant continuing involvement in the operations of the component.

Important Features of Implementation. To resolve implementation issues, FASB 144:

1. Establishes criteria beyond that previously specified in Statement 121 to determine when a long-lived asset is held for sale, including a group of assets and liabilities that represents the unit of accounting for a long-lived asset classified as held for sale. Among other things, those criteria specify that:

    a. The asset must be available for immediate sale in its present condition subject only to terms that are usual and customary for sales of such assets.

    b. The sale of the asset must be probable, and its transfer expected to qualify for recognition as a completed sale, within one year, with certain exceptions.

2. Provides guidance on the accounting for a long-lived asset if the criteria for classification as held for sale is met *after* the balance sheet date but *before* issuance of the financial statements. That guidance prohibits retroactive reclassification of the asset as held for sale at the balance sheet date. Therefore, the guidance in EITF Issue 95-18, *Accounting and Reporting for a Discontinued Business Segment When the Measurement Date Occurs after the Balance Sheet Date but before the Issuance of Financial Statements,* is superseded.

3. Provides guidance on the accounting for a long-lived asset classified as held for sale if the asset is reclassified as held and used. The reclassified asset is measured at the *lower* of its:

    a. Carrying amount before being classified as held for sale, adjusted for any depreciation (amortization) expense that would have been recognized had the asset been continuously classified as held and used.

    b. Fair value at the date the asset is reclassified as held and used.

Long-Lived Assets to Be Disposed of Other Than by Sale

Long-lived assets or asset groups to be disposed of other than by sale, such as by abandonment, should be classified as *held for use* until the disposal date. When the disposal date is earlier than the asset's previously estimated useful life, future depreciation estimates are to be revised to reflect the new shorter useful life.

If long-lived assets or asset groups are to be exchanged for similar productive assets, or if distributed to owners in a spin-off are tested for recoverability before the exchange or distribution date, the cash flows used in the recoverability test should be based on the assumption that the exchange or disposal will not occur. At the exchange or disposal date, a loss should be recognized for any excess of carrying amount over the fair value of the long-lived asset or asset group exchanged or disposed of.

In summary, FASB 144 applies to a long-lived asset that is scheduled to be:

- Abandoned.
- Exchanged for a similar productive asset.
- Distributed to owners in a spin-off. (In such a case, it must then be considered held and used until it is disposed of.)

The effects from other literature upon these portions of the Statement are twofold. The requirement that the depreciable life of a long-lived asset to be abandoned is revised in accordance with APB Opinion 20, *Accounting Changes.* In addition, the amendment of APB Opinion 29, *Accounting for Nonmonetary Transactions,* to require that an impairment loss be recognized at the date a long-lived asset, as mentioned above, is exchanged for a similar productive asset or distributed to owners in a spin-off when the carrying amount of the asset exceeds its fair value.

Discontinued Operations

If long-lived assets or asset groups are disposed of and are deemed for the purposes of FASB 144 to be a component of an entity, they should be reported in financial statements as discontinued operations. A component of an entity consists of those operations and cash flows that for financial reporting purposes are clearly distinguishable from the rest of the entity. In practice, a component of an entity may be:

- A reportable or operating segment presented in the business segment disclosures included in financial statements.
- A reporting unit to which goodwill has been assigned for goodwill testing purposes.
- A subsidiary, or the lowest level of a group of long-lived assets and their related other assets and liabilities for which associated identifiable cash flows are largely independent of the cash flows of other groups of assets and liabilities.

The results of operations of a component of an entity either disposed of or classified as held for sale should be classified as discontinued operations if after the disposal transaction:

- The component's cash flows and operations have been or will be eliminated from the ongoing cash flows of the company.

- The company will not have any significant continuing involvement in the component.

Changes Should Result in Improved Financial Reporting

Prior to the issuance of FASB 144, there were a number of inconsistencies in accounting for long-lived assets or asset groups to be held for use or disposed of. These inconsistencies were confusing to investors and creditors—in fact, to all users of the financial statement information. The new standard eliminates these inconsistencies. The changes improve financial reporting by requiring that one accounting model be used for long-lived assets to be disposed of by sale, whether previously held and used or newly acquired. It also broadens the presentation of discontinued operations to include more disposal transactions. Therefore, the accounting for similar events and circumstances will be the same. Additionally, the information value of reported financial information should be improved. Finally, resolving significant implementation issues should make compliance with the requirements of the Statement easier.

Relation to FASB Conceptual Framework

In reconsidering the use of a measurement approach based on net realizable value, and the accrual of future operating losses required under that approach, the Financial Accounting Standards Board used the definition of a liability in FASB Concepts Statement 6, *Elements of Financial Statements*. The Board determined that *future operating losses* do not meet the definition of a liability.

In considering changes to FASB 121, the Board focused on the qualitative characteristics discussed in FASB Concepts Statement 2, *Qualitative Characteristics of Accounting Information*. In particular, the Board determined that:

- Broadening the presentation of discontinued operations to include more disposal transactions provides investors, creditors, and others with decision-useful information that is relevant in assessing the effects of disposal transactions on the ongoing operations of an entity.
- Eliminating inconsistencies resulting from two accounting models for long-lived assets to be disposed of by sale improves comparability in financial reporting among entities. Thus, it enables users to identify similarities in and differences between two sets of economic events.

FASB 144 also incorporates the guidance in FASB Concepts Statement 7, *Using Cash Flow Information and Present Value in Accounting Measurements,* for using present value techniques to measure fair value.

Later Standard Covers Other Aspects

The new standard did not address the accounting for obligations often associated with the disposal of long-lived assets or asset groups, such as employee termination benefits, restructuring charges, and lease terminations. The FASB addressed the accounting for these obligations at a later date.

Effective Date of Statement 144

The provisions of this Statement were effective for financial statements issued for fiscal years beginning after December 15, 2001.

FASB 145, *Rescission of FASB Statements 4, 44, and 64, Amendment of FASB Statement 13, and Technical Corrections*

In April 2002, the FASB issued Statement 145, *Rescission of FASB Statements No. 4, 44, and 64, Amendment of FASB Statement No. 13, and Technical Corrections,* which updates, clarifies and simplifies existing accounting pronouncements.

The Board added this project to its agenda in August 2001 in response to constituent requests to examine the accounting for gains and losses from the extinguishment of debt.

This request was particularly important to those operating in the secondary lending market because the use of debt extinguishment is a part of their day-to-day risk management activities and Statement 4, issued in 1975, no longer addressed the needs of a changed marketplace.

FASB 145 rescinds FASB 4, which required all gains and losses from extinguishment of debt to be aggregated and, if material, classified as an extraordinary item, net of related income tax effect. As a result, the criteria in APB Opinion 30 will now be used to classify those gains and losses.

FASB 64 amended FASB 4, and is no longer necessary since FASB 4 is no more.

FASB 44 was issued to establish accounting requirements for the effects of transition to the provisions of the Motor Carrier Act of 1980. Because the transition has been completed, Statement 44 is no longer necessary.

FASB 145 amends FASB 13 to require that certain lease modifications that have economic effects similar to sale-leaseback transactions is accounted for in the same manner as sale-leaseback transactions. This amendment is consistent with the FASB's goal of requiring similar accounting treatment for transactions that have similar economic effects.

This Statement also makes technical corrections to existing pronouncements. While those corrections are not substantive in nature, in some instances, they may change accounting practice. Thus, FASB 145 appears to have taken care of a multitude of housekeeping chores.

BUSINESS COMBINATIONS: PURCHASE METHOD PROCEDURES

The Board initially added this project to its agenda as a broad reconsideration of existing purchase accounting guidance, including that issued by the FASB, its predecessor the Accounting Principles Board and the Emerging Issues Task Force (EITF), as well as other accepted practices. Now that the purchase method of accounting for business combination is the only one permitted since the elimination of the pooling-of-interests method, it is important to get it right.

The Board believes the project is necessary, since some current purchase accounting rules and practices do not provide transparent information to users and are sometimes inconsistent with the Conceptual Framework.

The Board is joining with the International Accounting Standards Board on the project. As a joint project, the FASB and IASB will share staff resources and research and work toward issuance of exposure drafts and final standards. Although the Boards will also coordinate the timing of deliberation on issues within the joint project, each will individually deliberate (and vote) on the issues.

The joint project broadly reconsiders aspects of the purchase method of accounting, excluding most areas deliberated by the Board in FASBs 141, *Business Combinations,* and 142, *Goodwill and Other Intangible Assets.* These areas include:

- Measuring the value of the business combination.
- Recognition and measurement of identifiable assets and liabilities (including such issues and contingencies and liabilities for terminating activities of an acquired entity).

Summary of Tentative Decisions

FASB members reached a tentative agreement on the following working principles for recording a business combination. The accounting for a business combination is based on the assumption that the transaction is an exchange of equal values; the total amount to be recognized should be measured based on the fair value of the consideration paid or the fair value of the net assets acquired, whichever is more clearly evident. If the consideration paid is cash or other assets (or liabilities incurred) of the acquiring entity, the fair value of the consideration paid determines the total amount to be recognized in the financial statements of the acquiring entity. If the consideration is in the form of equity instruments, the fair value of the equity instruments ordinarily is more clearly evident than the fair value of the net assets acquired and, thus, will determine the total amount to be recognized by the acquiring entity.

In a business combination, the acquiring entity obtains control over the acquired entity and is, therefore, responsible for the assets and liabilities of the acquired entity. An amount equal to the fair value, on the date control is obtained, should be assigned to the identifiable assets acquired and liabilities assumed. If the total fair value exchanged in the purchase transaction exceeds the amounts recognized for identifiable net assets, that amount is the *implied fair value* of goodwill. If the total fair value exchanged in the purchase transaction is less than the amounts recognized for identifiable net assets, that amount should be recognized as a gain in the income statement.

Other decisions reached are discussed below.

Contingent Consideration in a Business Combination

Contingent consideration issued in a business combination is an obligation of the acquirer as of the acquisition date and, therefore, should be recognized as part of the purchase price on that date. Consistent with the working principle, the initial measurement of contingent consideration should be at fair value.

Some contingent consideration arrangements obligate the acquirer to deliver its equity securities if specified future events occur. Classification of these instruments as either equity or as a liability depends on existing U.S. GAAP. Presuming that the Board issues a standard on accounting for financial instruments with the characteristics of liabilities, equity, or both, prior to the issuance of guidance in this project, the guidance in that standard would apply to contingent consideration arrangements.

An exception in FASB 133, *Accounting for Derivative Instruments and Hedging Activities,* should be eliminated in order that contingent consideration arrangements that otherwise meet the definition of a derivative would be subject to the requirements of Statement 133.

Subsequent remeasurement (after the acquisition date) of contingent consideration liabilities does not result in a change to the purchase price of the business combination. These amounts, therefore, should be recorded in the income statement.

Other Measurement Issues Related to the Acquired Business

Equity securities issued, as consideration in a business combination, should be measured on the acquisition date. The description of the acquisition date in FASB 141 should be modified to clarify that the acquisition date is the date that the acquirer gains control over the target entity.

Recognition and Measurement of Identifiable Assets and Liabilities

In the acquisition of less than 100 percent of the acquired entity, the identifiable assets and liabilities of the acquired entity should be recorded at full fair value. The current practice of considering the subsidiaries' carryover basis to the extent of the noncontrolling interest should be eliminated.

If negative goodwill is present in a business combination, the acquiring entity should review the procedures used to identify and measure the net assets of the subsidiary; however, no asset acquired should be measured at an amount that is known to be less than its fair value, nor should any liability assumed or incurred be measured at an amount known to be higher than its fair value. If negative goodwill remains, the acquiring entity should recognize the amount in the income statement (recognized as an extraordinary item under FASB 141).

Preacquisition contingencies of the acquired entity that are assets or liabilities should be recognized and should be initially measured at fair value. The Board agreed to eliminate the alternative described in Statement 141 that allows for recognition under an approach consistent with FASB 5, *Accounting for Contingencies*. The issue of measuring preacquisition contingencies subsequent to the acquisition date will be addressed in the project at a later date.

The period of time permitted to recognize and measure all assets acquired and liabilities assumed (referred to as the "allocation period") ends at the earlier of one year from the acquisition date or when the acquiring entity is no longer waiting for information that it has arranged to obtain and that is known to be available or obtainable. The objective of obtaining information during the allocation period is to measure the assets acquired and liabilities assumed at their fair values as of the acquisition date. Therefore, the only information that should be considered in recording assets acquired and liabilities assumed in a business combination is information that would affect the determination of their fair values as of the acquisition date. For example, discovery during the allocation period of the need for an adjustment to the measurement of an acquired asset for an event that had not occurred as of the acquisition date would not be reflected in the purchase price allocation but would result in a *charge to earnings*.

BUSINESS COMBINATIONS: NEW BASIS ACCOUNTING

In August 1996, the Board added to its agenda a project on business combinations to reconsider APB Opinions 16, *Business Combinations*, and 17, *Intangible Assets*. In June 2001, this phase of the project was completed when

FASB 141, *Business Combinations*, and FASB 142, *Goodwill and Other Intangible Assets*, were issued.

This project is a portion of the Business Combinations: Phase 2, and focuses on new basis accounting issues. The IASB has added the project to its agenda to make the new basis accounting project a joint undertaking between the IASB and the FASB.

Fresh-Start Recognition and Measurement

The project focuses on those situations in which fresh-start (a new basis at fair value) recognition and measurement of all of an entity's assets and liabilities would be appropriate. Identified conditions for application of this accounting treatment are:

- A multiparty business combination or other new entity formation in which no single preexisting entity obtains majority ownership and control of the resulting new entity.
- Joint venture formations.
- Related issues, including the recognition and measurement of goodwill and other intangibles in combinations or other transactions accounted for by the fresh-start method.

In September 2000, the FASB formally approved the initial focus of Business Combinations: Phase 2 on new-basis accounting issues. The Board also approved a draft working principle for use in determining the appropriateness of recognizing a new basis of accounting. The Board decided that the scope of the project should include the issue of gain recognition in the financial statements of the entity that has transferred control over net assets to a joint venture.

During the fourth quarter in 2000, the Board discussed the recognition of a new basis of accounting in connection with the formation of a joint venture. The Board decided that a change in control over net assets from unilateral control by one entity to joint or shared control by that entity and one or more other entities should result in a new basis of accounting for those net assets in the financial statements of the jointly controlled entity. The Board also discussed gain recognition, as of the date of formation of a joint venture, in the financial statements of an investor that transfers an appreciated (or previously unrecognized) asset to the joint venture. The Board decided that an entity that exchanges appreciated (or previously unrecognized) assets for an equity interest in a joint venture should recognize a gain on the assets exchanged.

Immediate Plans

During the first quarter of 2002, the FASB staff continued working with the IASB staff in developing the joint project scope and plan, which will be subject to review by both the FASB and IASB prior to further Board deliberations on fresh-start (new-basis) issues. And, as a matter of fact, as a result of more immediate pressures on both Boards, the project is temporarily on hold.

NEW PROJECTS TO CONSIDER STANDARDS OVERLOAD

The term "standards overload" is one that has been used off and on over the years by the FASB's various constituent groups to describe concerns about:

- The volume of accounting rules.
- The level of complexity and detail of those rules.
- The resulting profusion of footnote disclosures.
- The difficulty of finding all the accounting rules on a particular subject.

Those concerns surfaced in the responses to the 2001 Annual Financial Accounting Standards Advisory Council (FASAC) Survey—with respondents suggesting that the Board places a high priority (in the form of resources) on finding ways to codify and simplify the accounting literature.

In early 2002, the Board agreed to commit staff resources to a variety of projects that have a common goal of improving the usability and the effectiveness of the accounting literature. Those projects are described below.

Simplification

The Board agreed to evaluate the feasibility of issuing standards that emphasize *basic principles and objectives* rather than issue standards that include detailed rules, exceptions, and alternatives to the underlying principles. A shift to less detailed standards would place the focus on accounting for the *substance* of a transaction *rather than the form*. Such an approach would encourage those applying an accounting standard to comply not only with the letter of the law, but, more important, with the *objective* and *intent*—the spirit—of that law. Much of the rest of the accounting world including the IASB standards adhere to this principle.

The success of this project and the possible future direction of U.S. accounting standards depend upon the willingness of all those involved—preparers, practitioners, and regulators to support this framework. For example, if the

FASB is to issue standards that focus on underlying principles and objectives, it feels that much of the chance for improvement lies with others as well as with itself:

- The SEC should be willing to accept some divergence in application.
- Preparers would need to adhere to the *spirit* of a standard and not look for the all-too-easy-to-find loopholes.
- The auditing profession would need to enforce that spirit diligently and unquestioningly.
- Constituents would need to accept the absence of specific guidance for many transactions. (Their reward for transparency and openness should be regaining their advantage in the capital markets.)
- The Board must be prepared to resist requests for detailed guidance and remember that it has been impossible to codify ethical conduct.

The initial plans are to draft the framework, which will include guidelines for deciding the types of issues that should and should not be addressed in FASB standards.

The Board also plans to draft illustrations of how several existing standards might look if that framework had been applied while the standard was being developed. Once Board members have agreed in principle with the draft framework, a discussion paper explaining the framework and the illustrative standards will be distributed to, and discussed with, various constituent groups. The Board planned to begin the discussions in the summer of 2002.

Once agreed to by all parties, the framework would be applied to current and future Board agenda projects. The hope is that application of that framework would decrease the amount of time taken to issue a standard and result in standards that are easier to understand and, therefore, apply.

If future FASB standards are less detailed, the potential exists for similar transactions to be accounted for differently from entity to entity. If that different accounting produces diverse results that diminish comparability (and the relevance and reliability of financial reporting), they feel there will be a need for an authoritative body to provide implementation and interpretive guidance on those standards.

Thus, concurrent with developing a framework for more general standards, Board members plan to evaluate—in collaboration with others—how the current standard-setting structure might be modified to adapt to issuance of standards following that framework. One objective of that effort will be to make the U.S. process of issuing authoritative literature more efficient. A second objective will be to clarify the scope of each rule-making body's activities.

The initial plans are to work with a small group of representatives from the EITF, American Institute of Certified Public Accountants (AICPA), and SEC to develop a model for deciding when additional authoritative literature is necessary on a given topic and then determine the most effective segregation of duties among those bodies with respect to issuing pronouncements and providing supplemental guidance. Once that group has agreed in principle to that model, the Board plans to seek input from various constituent groups.

Cost / Benefit Analysis

Another project aimed at simplifying FASB standards will focus on improving the quality of the cost/benefit analysis performed on proposed standards by more actively engaging constituents in that analysis. The aim is to determine the costs of applying a new standard and to minimize those costs without decreasing the benefits to financial reporting. The hope is that the result will be simplified standards that are easier to understand and apply.

The FASB has always made a point of adopting a standard only when the expected benefits exceed the perceived costs. Thus, the Board currently weighs the cost/benefit relationship of each standard before issuing it. A cost/benefit section is included in the basis for conclusions of each proposed and final standard.

CODIFICATION AND RETRIEVABILITY

In response to the concerns about the ever-increasing volume of authoritative literature and the various places to research to find information on a particular topic, the Board agreed to consider a number of projects aimed at improving the retrievability and usability of the accounting literature.

The staff is in the process of developing due process procedures to be followed in current and future FASB agenda projects to ensure that future standards do not further complicate the whole process. The goal is for the Board to identify, and where possible, resolve all potential conflicts with other accounting literature—EITF, Accounting Standards Executive Committee, and SEC—before issuing a standard and either incorporate or refer to any existing relevant authoritative literature.

The FASB has attempted to incorporate existing ARB, APB, and FASB literature in recent standards (e.g., FASBs 141 and 144); however, it is imperative to broaden the effort to encompass all authoritative literature.

Formally adopting this all-inclusive approach to setting standards should reduce the number of places necessary to search for guidance on a particular topic and reduce the volume of the literature. Because the Board will need to address inconsistencies that arise between a new standard and existing rulings (including AcSEC and SEC literature), the earlier in the process those inconsistencies are identified and addressed, the better.

The Board is planning to include references to all of the applicable U.S.

accounting literature in the FASB's *Current Text* (a compilation of all FASB accounting standards categorized by subject). The next step of this project is to partner with others in developing a comprehensive *searchable online database* that will include all of the U.S. accounting requirements. It would include not only FASB and EITF literature but also AICPA and SEC literature.

Consistent with the objective of making the accounting literature easier to retrieve, the Board has agreed to consider (on an ad hoc basis) issuing documents codifying specific accounting topics. Currently, they plan to combine all of the EITF issues related to APB Opinion 25, *Accounting for Stock Issued to Employees,* in one EITF issue and then include that Issue with the rest of the APB 25 literature in a codified document. That and all future codified documents will include references to AICPA and SEC literature.

FASB and SEC Combine Efforts to Solve Disclosure Overload

In response to disclosure overload concerns, the Board has assigned a FASB staff member to work with the SEC staff on its initiative to:

- Simplify financial disclosures.
- Make financial statements useful for all who need to access them.
- Produce rulings and statements that are easily understood by the ordinary investor.

FASB Issues FIN 45 to Expand Disclosure Requirements for Guarantees

In the hope of improving disclosures about loan guarantees, the FASB issued Interpretation 45, *Guarantor's Accounting and Disclosure Requirements for Guarantees, Including Indirect Guarantees of Indebtedness of Others, in November 2002.*

The Interpretation clarifies and expands existing disclosure requirements for guarantees, including loan guarantees. It also requires that when a company issues a guarantee, the company must recognize a liability for the fair value, or market value, of its obligations under that guarantee. An improved disclosure and accounting treatment should provide a more faithful picture of a company's financial position and the risk it has assumed.

The Interpretation does not address the subsequent measurement of the guarantor's recognized liability over the term of the guarantee. It also incorporates, without change, the guidance in FASB Interpretation 34, *Disclosure of Indirect Guarantees of Indebtedness of Others.*

This guidance would not apply to:

- Guarantee contracts issued by insurance companies.
- A lessee's residual value guarantee embedded in a capital lease.
- Contingent rents and price rebates.

The provisions related to recognizing a liability at inception for the fair value of the guarantor's obligations would not apply to product warranties or to guarantees accounted for as derivatives.

The initial recognition and initial measurement provisions apply on a prospective basis to guarantees issued or modified after December 31, 2002, regardless of the guarantor's fiscal year-end. The disclosure requirements in the Interpretation are effective for financial statements of interim or annual periods ending after December 15, 2002.

FASB Adds Revenue Recognition Project

In a very busy May 2002, the FASB officially added a project on revenue recognition to its agenda. The purpose is to provide more comprehensive guidance regarding when companies should record revenues.

Revenue is normally the largest item in financial statements; revenue recognition issues top the list of reasons given for financial reporting restatements. It is also responsible for about 50 percent of all SEC enforcement cases that involve financial accounting and reporting cases, according to a former chief accountant at the SEC. And that was before the recent rash of restatements. The FASB's proposed project would address such matters by developing one accounting standard that would apply to a broad range of industries.

As part of its project on revenue recognition, the FASB will seek to:

- Eliminate inconsistencies in the existing accounting literature and accepted practices.
- Fill voids in the guidance that have recently emerged.
- Provide further guidance for addressing issues that arise in the future.

The Board decided that while the standard is being developed, the EITF should continue to provide guidance on issues of revenue recognition based on the existing authoritative literature.

In developing the revenue recognition standard, the Board has decided to reconsider, as necessary, the guidance pertinent to revenue recognition in its Concepts Statements, particularly that in FASB Concepts Statement 5, *Recognition and Measurement in Financial Statements of Business Enterprises.*

Because of the interrelationships and interdependencies of the issues to be addressed, the Board decided that the project would be addressed in two parts being developed simultaneously. One part will take a bottom-up approach that provides an inventory of existing revenue recognition guidance and accepted practices; that inventory will help identify inconsistencies and gaps in the literature that need to be resolved. The other part will take a top-down approach that focuses on the conceptual guidance. This involves the process of developing guidance at the concepts level and standards level. The Board will test its tentative conclusions about the conceptual guidance by applying it to specific revenue recognition issues identified in the inventory. This might highlight the need for further improvements in the concepts. The simultaneous pursuit of the two parts will expedite completion of the project.

In the meantime, the SEC's Staff Accounting Bulletin (SAB) 101, *Revenue Recognition in Financial Statements,* would appear to be a good model to follow. It is discussed in Chapter 1, "Revenue and Expenses."

FASB 139, RESCISSION OF FASB STATEMENT 53 AND AMENDMENTS TO FASB STATEMENTS 63, 89, AND 121

The Statement rescinds FASB 53, *Financial Reporting by Producers and Distributors of Motion Picture Films.* The Statement defers to a Statement of Position developed by the American Institute of CPAs.

A business that is a producer or distributor of films and that previously applied FASB 53 is now required to follow the guidance in the AICPA's Statement of Position 00-2, *Accounting by Producers or Distributors of Films.* This Statement and the AICPA's SOP were effective for fiscal years beginning after December 15, 2000.

When Statement 53 was issued in 1981, the majority of a film's revenue resulted from distribution to movie theaters and free television. Since that time, extensive changes have occurred in the film industry. Home video, satellite and cable television, and pay-per-view television have come into existence, and international revenue has increased in significance. Because of these changes, considerable variations in the application of Statement 53 arose.

The SOP's purpose is to eradicate variations in accounting practices between producers and distributors of films and applies to all types of films and to producers or distributors who own or hold rights to them.

The SOP requires that:

1. Revenue should be recognized only when all of the following requirements are met:
   a. There is persuasive evidence that a customer sale or licensing arrangement exists.
   b. The film has been delivered or is ready for delivery and unconditional exploitation by the customer.
   c. The licensing period has begun.

d. The revenue receivable is fixed or determinable.

e. Collection of the revenue is reasonably assured.

2. If the above requirements are not met, revenue recognition should be deferred until they are met.

3. Licensing fee revenue recognized should be the present value of the license fee as of the time it is first recognized.

4. A flat fee covering a single film licensing arrangement should be recognized immediately when the above revenue recognition requirements are met.

5. A fee based on customer revenues should be recognized as the customer earns those revenues, and the above requirements for revenue recognition are met.

6. Film costs should be listed as a separate asset. Capitalized film costs include those costs required to bring the film to market.

7. Film cost assets should be amortized using the individual-film-forecast computation method, beginning when the film is released and revenue recognition begins. The individual-film-forecast computation method amortizes capitalized film costs in the same ratio as the current period's revenue bears to the film's estimated ultimate revenues.

8. If the fair value of a film falls below its unamortized film costs, the shortfall should be charged to income and the film's carrying amount reduced to its fair value. Any subsequent increases in fair value should not be recognized.

9. All marketing and related exploitation costs, except those direct advertising costs that qualify under existing accounting for capitalization, should be expensed as incurred.

10. Manufacturing and duplication costs should be recorded on a unit-specific basis and charged to income when the related unit's revenue is recognized.

FASB 139 also amends FASB Statement 63, *Financial Reporting by Broadcasters,* to indicate that a broadcaster is required to apply the guidance in SOP 00-2 if it owns the film (program material) that is shown on its cable, network, or local television outlets. It also amends FASB Statements 89, *Financial Reporting and Changing Prices,* and 121, *Accounting for the Impairment of Long-Lived Assets and Long-Lived Assets to Be Disposed Of.*

FASB Statement 140, Accounting for Transfers and Servicing of Financial Assets and Extinguishments of Liabilities—A Replacement of FASB Statement 125

FASB 140 replaces FASB 125, *Accounting for Transfers and Servicing of Financial Assets and Extinguishments of Liabilities,* and revises the standards for accounting for securitizations and other transfers of financial assets and collateral. It also requires certain disclosures, but it carries over most of Statement 125's provisions without reconsideration.

It provides accounting and reporting standards for transfers and servicing of financial assets and extinguishments of liabilities. Those standards are based on consistent application of a *financial-components approach* that focuses on control. Under that approach, after a transfer of financial assets, an entity:

- Recognizes the financial and servicing assets it controls and the liabilities it has incurred.
- Derecognizes financial assets when control has been surrendered.
- Derecognizes liabilities when extinguished.

The Statement provides consistent standards for distinguishing transfers of financial assets that are sales from transfers that are secured borrowings.

Assets Accounted for as a Sale

A transfer of financial assets in which the transferor surrenders control over those assets is accounted for as a sale to the extent that consideration other than beneficial interests in the transferred assets is received in exchange. The transferor has surrendered control over transferred assets if and only if all three of the following conditions are met:

1. The transferred assets have been isolated from the transferor—put presumptively beyond the reach of the transferor and its creditors, even in bankruptcy or other receivership.
2. Each transferee (or, if the transferee is a qualifying special-purpose entity [SPE], each holder of its beneficial interests) has the right to pledge or exchange the assets (or beneficial interests) it received. In addition, nothing prevents the transferee (or holder) from taking advantage of its right to pledge or exchange or provide more than a trivial benefit to the transferor.
3. The transferor does not maintain effective control over the transferred assets through either:
   a. An agreement that both entitles and obligates the transferor to repurchase or redeem them before their maturity, or
   b. The ability to unilaterally cause the holder to return specific assets, other than through a cleanup call.

Measurement of Assets and Liabilities

This Statement requires that liabilities and derivatives incurred or obtained by transferors as part of a transfer of financial assets be initially measured at fair value, if practicable. It also requires that servicing assets and other retained interests in the transferred assets be measured by allocating the previous carrying amount between the assets sold, if any, and retained interests, if any, based on their relative fair values at the date of the transfer.

This Statement requires that servicing assets and liabilities be subsequently measured by:

- Amortization in proportion to and over the period of estimated net servicing income or loss.
- Assessment for asset impairment or increased obligation based on their fair values.

FASB 140 requires that a liability be derecognized if and only if either:

- The debtor pays the creditor and is relieved of its obligation for the liability, or
- The debtor is legally released from being the primary obligor under the liability either judicially or by the creditor. Therefore, a liability is not considered extinguished by an in-substance defeasance.

Implementation Guidance Provided

FASB 140 provides implementation guidance for:

- Assessing isolation of transferred assets.
- Conditions that constrain a transferee.
- Conditions for an entity to be a qualifying SPE.
- Accounting for transfers of partial interests.
- Measurement of retained interests.
- Servicing of financial assets.
- Securitizations.
- Transfers of sales-type and direct financing lease receivables.
- Securities lending transactions.
- Repurchase agreements including "dollar rolls," "wash sales," loan syndications, and participations.
- Risk participations in bankers' acceptances.
- Factoring arrangements.
- Transfers of receivables with recourse.
- Extinguishments of liabilities.

In addition to all of that, the Statement also provides guidance about whether a transferor has retained effective control over assets transferred to qualifying SPEs through removal-of-accounts provisions, liquidation provisions, or other arrangements.

It requires a debtor to:

1. Reclassify financial assets pledged as collateral and report those assets in its statement of financial position separately from other assets not so encumbered, if the secured party has the right by contract or custom to sell or repledge the collateral.
2. Disclose assets pledged as collateral that have not been reclassified and separately reported in the statement of financial position.

Additional Disclosures

FASB 140 also requires a secured party to disclose information about collateral that it has accepted and is permitted by contract or custom to sell or repledge. The required disclosure includes the fair value at the end of the period of that collateral, and of the portion of that collateral that it has sold or repledged, and information about the sources and uses of that collateral.

The Statement requires an entity that has securitized financial assets to disclose information about accounting policies, volume, cash flows, key assumptions made in determining fair values of retained interests, and sensitivity of those fair values to changes in key assumptions.

It also requires that entities that securitize assets disclose for the securitized assets and any other financial assets it manages together with them:

- The total principal amount outstanding, the portion that has been derecognized, and the portion that continues to be recognized in each category reported in the statement of financial position, at the end of the period.
- Delinquencies at the end of the period.
- Credit losses during the period.

Effect upon Earlier Standards

The new Statement replaces Statement 125 and rescinds FASB Statement 127, *Deferral of the Effective Date of Certain Provisions of FASB Statement 125*. It also carries forward the actions taken by FASB 125.

Statement 125 had superseded FASB Statements 76, *Extinguishment of Debt*, and 77, *Reporting by Transferors for Transfers of Receivables with Recourse*. It amended FASB Statement 115, *Accounting for Certain Investments in Debt and Equity Securities*, to clarify that a debt security may not be classified as held-to-maturity if it can be prepaid or otherwise settled in such a way that the holder of the security would not recover substantially all of its recorded investment.

Statement 125 amended and extended to all servicing assets and liabilities the accounting standards for mortgage servicing rights now in FASB Statement 65, *Accounting for Certain Mortgage Banking Activities,* and superseded FASB Statement 122, *Accounting for Mortgage Servicing Rights.*

Statement 125 also superseded FASB Technical Bulletins 84-4, *In-Substance Defeasance of Debt,* and 85-2, *Accounting for Collateralized Mortgage Obligations (CMOs),* and amended FASB Technical Bulletin 87-3, *Accounting for Mortgage Servicing Fees and Rights.*

Special Report on FASB 140.   In addition to the rather comprehensive guidance provided in the Standard, the FASB published a special report covering the most frequently asked questions about FASB 140.

The Special Report is a cumulative document, incorporating new questions and answers as well as those that have been updated and reworked from the first, second, and third editions of the FASB Special Report, *A Guide to Implementation of Statement 125 on Accounting for Transfers and Servicing of Financial Assets and Extinguishments of Liabilities.*

Most of the questions are unchanged from the previous Special Report, but many of the answers are newly updated, reflecting changes made by Statement 140. The new questions focus on the effects of various kinds of call options on sale treatment and the application of the expected cash flow technique to the measurement of the fair value of retained interests in securitizations.

Effective Dates

FASB 140 is effective for transfers and servicing of financial assets and extinguishments of liabilities occurring after March 31, 2001. It is effective for recognition and reclassification of collateral and for disclosures relating to securitization transactions and collateral for fiscal years ending after December 15, 2000. Disclosures about securitization and collateral accepted need not be reported for periods ending on or before December 15, 2000, for which financial statements are presented for comparative purposes.

FASB 141 AND 142, BUSINESS COMBINATIONS AND GOODWILL AND OTHER INTANGIBLE ASSETS

In August, 1996, the Board added to its agenda a project on business combinations to reconsider APB Opinions 16, *Business Combinations,* and 17, *Intangible Assets.* The project was an attempt to improve the transparency of the accounting for business combinations presumably to give the user of the financial statement a clearer picture of the financial health of the new entity.

The project focused on the accounting for goodwill and other purchased intangible assets and the fundamental issues related to the methods of accounting for business combinations, including whether there is a need for two separate and distinct methods (purchase method and pooling-of-interests method).

The project did not address how to account for in-process research and development (IPR&D) costs.

FASBs 141 and 142 Approved

And, indeed, the FASB did conclude the voting process on its business combinations project after Board members submitted final ballots on June 29, 2001. The Board members unanimously voted in favor of the two measures: Statement 141, *Business Combinations,* and Statement 142, *Goodwill and Other Intangible Assets.*

As expected, the Statements change the accounting for business combinations and goodwill in two significant ways. Statement 141 requires that the purchase method of accounting be used for all business combinations initiated after June 30, 2001. Use of the pooling-of-interest method is prohibited.

Application of the purchase method requires identification of the acquiring enterprise. To determine which enterprise is the acquiring enterprise, all pertinent facts need to be considered, particularly the relative voting rights in the combined enterprise after the combination, the composition of the board of directors, the senior management of the combined enterprise, and which enterprise received a premium.

FASB 142 changes the accounting for goodwill from an amortization method to an impairment-only approach. Thus, amortization of goodwill, including goodwill recorded in past business combinations, ceases upon adoption of that Statement, which for companies with calendar year ends is January 1, 2002.

The Board decided that the definition of financial asset used in FASB Statement 141, *Business Combinations,* should be based on the definition of financial instrument in FASB Statement 107, *Disclosures about Fair Value of Financial Instruments.*

The Statement requires that an impairment loss recognized in the year of initial application for nonamortized intangible assets should be recognized in the same manner as goodwill; that is, as the effect of a change in accounting principle. Intangible assets that will no longer be amortized should be tested for impairment in the first interim period in which the Statement is initially applied.

Acquired intangibles other than goodwill will be amortized over their useful life, which may extend beyond the current 40-year maximum amortization period. An intangible asset that is being amortized and is subsequently determined to have an indefinite useful life should stop being amortized and be accounted for in the same manner as other intangible assets deemed to have an indefinite useful life.

But this is still not the end of the business combinations project. In January 2000, the Board began discussions on a closely related project to consider purchase method procedures and new basis accounting.

The Board believes that comment letters received in the first phase of the business combinations project indicated the necessity to address the purchase method procedures. The project will reconsider purchase method guidance that was not reconsidered as part of Statements 141 and 142.

Tentatively, the project is focusing on purchase method guidance in the following areas:

1. Accounting for noncontrolling interests.
2. Determining the cost of an acquisition, and accounting for contingent consideration.
3. Recognizing assets acquired and liabilities assumed.
4. Accounting for pre-acquisition contingencies.

The Canadian Accounting Standards Board is adopting identical Standards to those adopted by the FASB with the goal of converging North American accounting standards related to business combinations.

FASB 143, *ACCOUNTING FOR ASSET RETIREMENT OBLIGATIONS*

The Board concluded deliberations and unanimously voted to issue Statement 143, *Accounting for Asset Retirement Obligations*. Initiated in 1994 as a project to account for the costs of nuclear decommissioning, the Board soon expanded the scope to include similar closure or removal-type costs in other industries. These include oil and gas production facilities, landfills, mines, and environmental cleanups. The existing financial reporting practices had been inconsistent and, in some cases, misleading.

The new Standard requires entities to record the fair value of a liability for an asset retirement obligation in the period in which it is incurred. When the liability is initially recorded, the entity capitalizes a cost by increasing the carrying amount of the related long-lived asset. Over time, the liability is accreted to its present value each period, and the capitalized cost is depreciated over the useful life of the related asset. Upon settlement of the liability, an entity either settles the obligation for its recorded amount or incurs a gain or loss upon settlement.

The standard is effective for fiscal years beginning after June 15, 2002, with earlier application encouraged.

Objective of the Project

The aim of the asset retirement obligations (ARO) project has been to provide accounting requirements for retirement obligations associated with these tangible long-lived assets. The obligations included within the scope of the project are those that an entity cannot avoid as a result of either the acquisition, construction, or normal operation of a long-lived asset.

The obligation must result from a long-lived asset's acquisition, construction, or normal use. The "asset" may be a functional group of assets or a component part of a group of long-lived assets for which there are separable, identifiable asset retirement obligations.

In the case of leased long-lived assets, the standard applies to a lessee's long-lived leased assets accounted for as a capital lease. It applies to the lessor if the lease is an operating lease.

Capitalization

The Board decided that an asset retirement cost should be capitalized as part of the cost of the related long-lived asset. That capitalized asset retirement cost should then be allocated to expense by using a systematic and rational method. An entity is not precluded from using an allocation method that would have the effect of capitalizing and allocating to expense the same amount of cost in the same accounting period.

Requirements

The new standard requires:

- Recognition of a long-lived tangible asset retirement obligation liability and an offsetting increase in the amount of the related long-lived asset.
- The obligation be measured at its fair value.
- Allocation of the asset retirement cost in the form of additional depreciation to expense over the related asset's useful life.
- Changes in the amount of the obligation liability subsequent to initial recognition be recognized if they arise from the passage of time and revisions to either the timing or amount of the related estimated cash flows.
- Recognition of an interest-type charge related to the obligation.

Change in Fair Value Methodology

The Board decided that the objective for initial measurement of an ARO liability should be use of the fair value method using a valuation technique, such as expected present value, to estimate fair value.

The methodology to determine fair value under the new Standard represents a departure from past practice. The FASB now believes when the timing or amount of estimated cash flow related to an obligation is uncertain and in the absence of quoted market prices in active markets or prices for similar liabilities, fair value should be determined using an expected present value technique.

"Expected present value" refers to the sum of probability-weighted present values in a range of estimated cash flows, all discounted using the same interest rate convention. For purposes of measuring an ARO liability, an entity is required to use a discount rate that equates to a risk-free rate adjusted for the effect of its credit standing (credit-adjusted risk-free rate).

FASB's traditional present value approach used a single estimate of future cash flows, and the Board still believes the traditional approach is appropriate for measuring the fair value of assets and liabilities with contractual cash flows.

Recognition

An asset retirement obligation must be recognized when three requirements are met:

1. The obligation meets the definition of a liability.
2. A future transfer of assets associated with the obligation is probable.
3. The amount of the liability can be reasonably measured.

In order to meet the definition of a liability—the first test—the three characteristics of a liability must be satisfied:

1. The company has a present duty or responsibility to one or more other entities that entails settlement by probable future transfer or use of assets.
2. The company has little or no discretion to avoid a future transfer of use of assets.
3. An obligating event has already happened.

Obligating Events

The Standard deals with obligations arising under three circumstances:

1. Obligations incurred upon acquisition, construction, or development of an asset.

2. Obligations incurred during the operating life of an asset, either ratably or nonratably.
3. Obligations incurred any time during the life of an asset because of a newly enacted law or statute, or a change in contract provisions, or because an entity has otherwise incurred a duty or responsibility to one or more other entities.

Obligations incurred upon acquisition, construction, or development of an asset should be recognized when the cost of the long-lived asset is recognized. Those incurred during the operating life of an asset should be recognized concurrent with the events creating the obligation.

Subsequent Measurement of an ARO Liability

The Board decided that an entity should be required to use an allocation approach for subsequent measurement of an ARO liability. Under that approach, an entity is not required to remeasure an ARO liability at fair value each period. Instead, it is required to recognize changes in an ARO liability resulting from the passage of time and revisions in cash flow estimates. Those changes are then incorporated into a remeasurement of an ARO liability. The rate used to record accretion of the liability and revisions in cash flow estimates is the credit-adjusted risk-free rate applied when an ARO liability was initially measured.

Disclosures

An entity should disclose the following information in its financial statements:

- A general description of the asset retirement obligations and of the associated long-lived assets.
- The fair value of assets that are legally restricted for purposes of settling asset retirement liabilities.
- If any significant change occurs in the components of an asset retirement obligation, a reconciliation of the beginning and ending aggregate carrying amount of the liability showing separately the changes attributable to:
  — The liability incurred in the current period.
  — The liability settled in the current period.
  — Accretion expense.
  — Revisions in expected cash flows.

Transition

When the Standard is first applied, the company must recognize the following on its balance sheet as if the Standard had been in effect when an asset retirement obligation was incurred:

- A liability for any existing asset retirement obligations adjusted for cumulative interest to the date of adoption of the new standard.
- An asset retirement cost capitalized as an increase to the carrying amount of the associated long-lived asset.
- Accumulated depreciation on the capitalized cost.

Amounts resulting from initial application should be measured using current (as of the date of adoption) information, current assumptions, and current interest rates.

FIN 44, ACCOUNTING FOR CERTAIN TRANSACTIONS INVOLVING STOCK COMPENSATION

This FASB stock option ruling in Interpretation 44, *Accounting for Certain Transactions Involving Stock Compensation,* is an interpretation of APB Opinion 25, *Accounting for Stock Issued to Employees.*

Accounting for stock options is governed by FASB 123, *Accounting for Stock-Based Compensation,* which allows companies to select one of two approaches to accounting and reporting of stock-based employee compensation plans. It was this "compromise" from requirements of a *fair value method only* standard that finally led to the adoption of FASB 123. Now, it is either intrinsic value method or fair value method.

The FASB encourages companies to adopt the fair value method, but it is not required. It is acceptable to use the intrinsic value method prescribed in APB Opinion 25, *Accounting for Stock Issued to Employees,* which is the pre-FASB 123 Standard dealing with stock-based compensation plans. If a company continues to use the Opinion 25 approach, the entity must disclose the pro forma impact on income and earnings per share of using the fair value method.

In the case of stock options, the fair value is determined using an option pricing model. Once the fair value is determined at the grant date, it is not subsequently adjusted for:

- Changes in the price of the underlying stock.
- The volatility of the stock.

- The life of the option.
- Dividends on the stock.
- The risk free interest rate.

Delineation of Requirements

The Interpretation requires the following:

1. Compensation in the form of stock options granted to independent contractors or other providers of services and goods, who are not employees, are to be accounted for using the *fair value method*. The principal consequence of this Interpretation is that the granting company must record a stock compensation cost based on the option's fair value at the grant date over the option's life for a transaction. Previously, this may not have resulted in a stock compensation cost.

2. Nonemployee board members are considered to be employees for stock option compensation accounting purposes. As a result, under the stock option plans of most companies, the practice will continue that no compensation cost will be recognized for stock options granted to nonemployee directors.

3. If the exercise price of a fixed option award is reduced or repriced, the modified stock options must be accounted for as a variable option plan from the date of modification to the date the award is exercised, forfeited, or expires unexercised. The consequence for the grantor is:

   a. Very few fixed option plans will lead to a stock compensation cost.

   b. If the company's stock price exceeds the option's strike price during the stock option's life, variable option plans may result in a stock compensation cost.

4. A modification to a fixed stock option to add a reload feature requires the modified award be accounted for as a variable plan award regardless of the method used to determine the terms of the reload grant. Therefore, a reload feature provides for the automatic grant of a new option at the current market price in exchange for each previously owned share tendered by an employee in a stock-for-stock exercise.

   Most reload grants awarded as modifications of a fixed plan will now result in a compensation cost if the company's stock price exceeds the reload option's strike price during the stock option's life.

5. There is no accounting consequence for changes in the exercise price or the number of shares of a stock option award as the result of an exchange of fixed stock option awards in a business combination accounted for as a pooling of interests as long as two criteria are met:

a. The aggregate intrinsic value of the options immediately *after* the exchange is no greater than the aggregate intrinsic value of the options immediately *before* the exchange.

b. The ratio of the exercise price per option to the market value per share is not reduced.

(This is a very important facet of the requirements. If these two criteria are not met, a new measurement of compensation is *required.*)

6. A modification to a fixed stock option award that does *not* affect the life of the award, the exercise price, or the number of shares to be issued does not have an accounting consequence.

7. A modification that either renews a fixed award or extends the award's life requires a new measurement of compensation cost as if the award were newly granted. As a result, a compensation cost would be recognized in the case of:

a. An employee fixed plan award over the life of the award for any significant difference between the current stock price and the stock price at the modification date.

b. A nonemployee stock grant at the fair value of the stock option at the modification date.

8. Any modification increasing the number of shares to be issued under a fixed stock option plan requires that the award be accounted for as a variable plan award from the modification date to the date the award is exercised, forfeited, or expires. The accounting consequence is that if the stock price exceeds the award's strike price during the stock option's life, after the award date a stock compensation cost will be recognized.

A fixed option award that is canceled and replaced with a new award that results in a lower option price must be accounted for as a variable plan if the replacement award is made within six months of the cancellation date.

Possible Results of the Interpretation

Repercussions of FIN may lead to the following:

- It potentially increases the cost of acquiring nonemployee services paid for with stock options.
- It discourages the repricing of options.
- It encourages companies, as an alternative to repricing, to grant new stock option awards at the current market price to employees whose existing stock option award's strike prices are below the current market price.

IMPROVING BUSINESS REPORTING: INSIGHTS INTO ENHANCING VOLUNTARY DISCLOSURES

The purpose of this report is to demonstrate that companies can markedly improve their business reporting by voluntarily disclosing more available information about which the investment community and shareholders have a keen interest.
These matters include:

- Identifying factors important to the financial success of the company.
- Delineating management's plans and strategies for managing those factors in the past and future.
- Specifying measurements used by management to assess its effectiveness in implementing those plans and strategies.

These were key recommendations in a broad report entitled *Improving Business Reporting: Insights into Enhancing Voluntary Disclosures.*
The recommendations resulted from a two-year project supervised by a 14-member Steering Committee of FASB constituents. The Steering Committee guided and directed the activities of a group of more than 50 professionals representing the preparer, financial statement user, auditing, and academic communities who worked on the project.
In addition to this report on voluntary disclosures, two other reports that resulted from the Business Reporting Research Project address the electronic distribution of business information and redundancies between the Securities and Exchange Commission's and the FASB's reporting requirements.
The objective of this report on voluntary disclosures is to help companies improve their business reporting by providing evidence that many leading companies are making extensive voluntary disclosures and by listing examples of those disclosures. The examples serve to provide companies with useful ideas on how to describe and explain their investment potential to investors. The basic premise underlying the Business Reporting Research Project is that improving disclosures makes the capital allocation process more efficient and reduces the average cost of capital. (And, not incidentally, avoid undue attention from the Securities and Exchange Commission.)
This project could very well be a reaction to the SEC's obviously being disillusioned by the fact that too many companies are trying to "cook the books" or resort to "creative" accounting to paint a rosier picture than the dark one that would otherwise be projected. If voluntary disclosure does not disclose enough, more stringent requirements will undoubtedly result.
The project studied the present practices for the voluntary disclosure of business information by six to nine companies in each of eight industries:

automobiles, chemicals, computer systems, foods, oil-integrated domestic, pharmaceuticals, regional banks, and textile-apparel. The companies provided the project with copies of all materials that had been available to the public over the course of a year—materials such as annual and quarterly reports, SEC filings, press releases, fact books, and transcripts of presentations to shareholders, analysts, and potential investors. Corporate Web sites were also reviewed.

Some of the findings and recommendations noted in the report include:

1. The importance of voluntary disclosures is expected to increase in the future because of the fast pace of change in the business environment.

2. Voluntary disclosures related to matters that are important to the success of individual companies are very useful, particularly disclosures of management's view of the company's "critical success factors" and trends surrounding those factors.

3. Although some disclosures were found about unrecognized intangible assets, additional data about those assets would be beneficial because of the importance of intangibles to a company's value.

4. Voluntary disclosure should cover not only good news but also disappointments. Disclosures are most useful if they report on previously disclosed plans and goals and the results achieved in meeting those plans and goals.

5. The metrics used by companies to manage their operations and drive their business strategies often are very useful voluntary disclosures. Those metrics should be explained and consistently disclosed from period-to-period to the extent they continue to be relevant to a company's success.

BUSINESS AND FINANCIAL REPORTING, CHALLENGES FROM THE NEW ECONOMY

The FASB decided to find out if there really is a "disconnect" between the information provided in today's financial statements and the information needs of investors and creditors. In examining this issue, observers have complained about the widening gap existing between information needs of "New Economy" companies and "Old Economy" financial reporting.

Therefore, after some investigation, FASB has published a special report, *Business and Financial Reporting, Challenges from the New Economy,* that examines the relationship between the new economy and business and financial reporting.

The report reviews a range of studies and articles that compare accounting treatments for traditional assets and the challenges of new economy notions of intangible assets. The report concludes that the debate over "new" versus "old" is of very little value. The FASB appears to believe that a more important question is whether business financial reporting should change and, if so, how.

The report also concludes that the perceived shortcomings of business and financial reporting do not easily lend themselves to a simplistic and single solution.

The Board decided that there is no simple financial reporting solution to the issues raised in the report. The best set of solutions will come from national and international standard setters working together. The issues are not limited to a specific country and probably do not lend themselves to an answer developed by one accounting standard setter acting in isolation. Any standard setter (foreign, domestic, or international), any SEC staff member, any preparer of financial statements, and the like, would certainly agree with all of the above.

Conclusions of Combined Effort

The report describes important contributions by groups in several nations, including the United States, the United Kingdom, Canada, Denmark, Sweden, the Netherlands, and the Organization for Economic Cooperation and Development (OECD).

The report concludes that standard setters should focus their attention on:

- Examination of the conceptual and practical issues surrounding recognition of internally generated intangible assets and measurement of those assets.
- Expanded and systematic use of nonfinancial performance metrics.
- Expanded use of forward-looking information.

An appendix to the report describes four projects that standard setters might consider in addressing the financial reporting challenges that are a part of the new economy (in an international setting).

As the Board begins to consider whether it should add new projects to its agenda, the FASB hopes constituents will view this report as an opportunity to offer their insights on the subjects covered.

Chapter 3
Consolidation of Variable Interest Entities

CONTENTS

Just as derivatives received much of the blame for questionable accounting practices during the 1990s, special-purpose entities (SPEs) appear now to be getting much of the blame for the accounting profession's fall from grace. Yet both of these vehicles can serve, and have served, a useful and legitimate purpose. However, as is often suggested, as long as there is someone who is determined to show a profit regardless of what is right or wrong, a way will be found. The more legitimate appearing, the better to subvert! Measures have been taken to see that derivatives are properly regulated; the ones used to sort out special-purpose entities are variable interest entities (VIEs), and assorted off-balance-sheet vehicles.

IMPROVING FINANCIAL REPORTING FOR VARIOUS ENTITIES

In an effort to end the abusive accounting for, to restore the legitimacy of, and to expand upon and strengthen existing accounting guidance on special-purpose entities, the Financial Accounting Standards Board (FASB) issued Interpretation 46 (FIN 46), *Consolidation of Variable Interest Entities*. The Interpretation addresses when a company should include the assets, liabilities, and activities of these entities in its financial statements.

Although many variable interest entities have commonly been referred to as special-purpose entities or off-balance-sheet structures, the guidance applies to a *larger group* of entities. The FASB explains that, in general, a variable interest entity is a corporation, partnership, trust, or any other *legal* structure used for business purposes that either:

- Does not have equity investors with voting rights; or
- Has equity investors that do not provide sufficient financial resources for the entity to support its activities.

A variable interest entity often holds financial assets, including loans or receivables, real estate, or other property. A VIE may be essentially passive or it may engage in research and development or other activities on behalf of another company. As pointed out, these types of entities can be put to perfectly legitimate use. Therefore, the Board's objective in FIN 46 is not to restrict the use of variable interest entities, but to improve financial reporting by companies involved with them.

Until now, one company generally has included another entity in its consolidated financial statements *only* if it controlled the entity through voting interests. However, the Board believes that if a business enterprise actually has a controlling *financial* interest (regardless of method of determination) in a variable interest entity, the assets, liabilities, and results of the activities of that variable interest entity should be included in consolidated financial statements with those of the business enterprise. Thus, FIN 46 changes present use by requiring a variable interest entity to be consolidated by a company if that company is subject to a majority of the risk of loss from the variable interest entity's activities or entitled to receive a majority of the entity's residual returns, or both.

Impetus for FIN 46

According to various reports, the failure of Enron was due largely to losses it incurred in connection with its financial guarantees and interests in off-balance-sheet partnerships (or SPEs). In Enron's case, the company's significant interests and obligations relating to those partnerships were not fairly or adequately reported in its financial statements. Therefore, this rule was drafted primarily in response to the financial failure of Enron with the hope that such disasters could be prevented in the future.

In a project begun early in 2002 to clarify the rules regarding the circumstances in which a business enterprise must consolidate an off-balance-sheet entity, the Board acknowledged that very little accounting literature addressed the topic. It also acknowledged that the need for such guidance had become critical because transactions involving SPEs (which had previously raised concerns) had become increasingly common in recent years. But, what is the cause of the current number of references to VIEs when so much of the Enron debacle was blamed on the part played by SPEs?

FASB Coins a New Term

Leading up to FIN 46's final form, the FASB made several significant changes to the draft rule relating to the Interpretation. During a meeting in mid-October 2002, the Board agreed to discontinue the use of the term "special-purpose entities" in favor of the term "variable interest entities." The new term coined by the FASB includes many, but not all, of the entities that were referred to in the past as special-purpose entities or off-balance-sheet structures, as well as additional entities.

FIN 46 began as an interpretation of FASB Accounting Research Bulletin (ARB) 51, *Consolidated Financial Statements,* which addresses consolidation by business enterprises of variable interest entities. (The Exposure Draft that preceded this Interpretation referred to the entities being covered by its requirements as special-purpose entities. Because some entities that have been commonly referred to as SPEs may not be subject to this Interpretation, and other entities that have not commonly been referred to as SPEs may be subject to the Interpretation, the FASB decided to use the term "variable interest entity."

VIEs and Exceptions Defined

The new term is used for those entities having at least one of the following characteristics:

- The equity investment at risk is not sufficient to permit the entity to finance its activities without additional subordinated financial support from other parties. This is provided through other interests that are to absorb some or all of the expected losses of the entity.

- The equity investors lack one or more of the following essential characteristics of a controlling financial interest:
  - The direct or indirect ability to make decisions about the entity's activities through voting rights or similar rights.
  - The obligation to absorb the expected losses of the entity if they occur, which makes it possible for the entity to finance its activities.
  - The right to receive the expected residual returns of the entity if they occur, which is the compensation for the risk of absorbing the expected losses.

Exceptions. With only a few exceptions, the Interpretation applies to any business enterprise that has an ownership interest, contractual relationship, or other relationship to a VIE. Those that should not consolidate include:

- Not-for-profit organizations, unless they are used by business enterprises in an attempt to circumvent the provisions of the Interpretation. The FASB explains that the Interpretation generally applies to business enterprises and the arrangements used by them. ARB 51 refers to "companies," and FASB 94, *Consolidation of All Majority-Owned Subsidiaries,* which amends ARB 51, refers only to "business enterprises." The Board considered it inappropriate to extend the requirements of this Interpretation to not-for-profit organizations because the document being interpreted does not apply specifically to them. The Board is aware that some of the requirements in ARB 51 are applied in modified forms to certain not-for-profit organizations and does not intend this Interpretation to cause a change in those practices.
- Employee benefit plans covered by the provisions of FASB 87, *Employers' Accounting for Pensions;* FASB 106, *Employers' Accounting for Postretirement Benefits Other Than Pensions;* and FASB 112, *Employers' Accounting for Postemployment Benefits.*
- Registered investment companies subject to the Investment Company Act of 1940.
- Separate accounts of life insurance enterprises covered in the *AICPA Auditing and Accounting Guide: Life and Health Insurance Entities.* Existing accounting standards specifically require life insurance enterprises to recognize these accounts and the Board considered it unwise to change them without more extensive reconsideration of insurance accounting.
- An enterprise subject to SEC Regulation S-X Rule 6-03(c)(1) should not consolidate any entity that is not also subject to that same rule.
- A transferor of financial assets or their affiliates should not consolidate a qualifying SPE or grandfathered qualifying SPE covered by FASB 140,

Accounting for Transfers and Servicing of Financial Assets and Extinguishments of Liabilities. They are not required to consolidate those entities used to transfer assets, as long as the transferor of assets has no rights or obligations that would prevent it under existing accounting rules from derecognizing the assets. The transferor is, however, required to report its rights and obligations related to the particular qualifying special-purpose entity according to the requirements of FASB 140.

This prohibition was specifically intended to exclude those special-purpose entities from ongoing and future Board decisions about consolidations. The derecognition requirements in Statement 140 are based on control of assets. Reporting of an enterprise's rights and obligations related to financial assets that have been transferred and derecognized is based on a *financial components approach.* Because a qualifying SPE has such limited decision-making abilities, the Board decided that retention of the financial components approach for parties involved with a qualifying SPE entity was more appropriate than consolidation based on variable interests. Therefore, this Interpretation does not change that requirement.

Importance of Exempting Transferors of Assets from Consolidating SPEs Covered by FASB 140.   This is an important exemption, because many asset-backed security issuance structures involve a qualifying SPE. FASB 140 defines a qualifying SPE as a trust or other legal vehicle that meets certain conditions. The principal conditions are:

1. It is demonstrably distinct from the transferor.
2. Its permitted activities:
   a. Are significantly limited.
   b. Were entirely specified in the legal documents that established the SPE or created the beneficial interests in the transferred assets that it holds.
   c. May be significantly changed only with the approval of the holders of at least a majority of the beneficial interests held by entities other than any transferor, its affiliates, and its agents.
3. It may hold only:
   a. Financial assets transferred to it that are passive in nature.
   b. Passive derivative financial instruments that pertain to beneficial interests.
   c. Financial assets that would reimburse it if others were to fail to adequately service financial assets transferred to it or to timely pay obligations due to it and that it entered into at one of these points:
      (1) When it was established.
      (2) When assets were transferred to it.

(3) When beneficial interests (other than derivative financial instruments) were issued by the SPE.

d. Servicing rights related to financial assets that it holds.

e. Temporarily, nonfinancial assets obtained in connection with the collection of financial assets that it holds.

f. Cash collected from assets that it holds and investments purchased with that cash pending distribution to holders of beneficial interests that are appropriate for that purpose (that is, money-market or other relatively risk-free instruments without options and with maturities no later than the expected distribution date).

4. If it can sell or otherwise dispose of noncash financial assets, it can do so in automatic response to conditions specified in FASB 140.

In the case of nonqualifying SPEs, a transferor that holds a subordinated retained interest in the transferred assets may be considered to be a variable interest holder.

Specific Provisions of FIN 46

The FASB divided entities into two classes in the determination of which entities should be consolidated in the financial statements of another entity:

1. Those for which the consolidation decision is based on the controlling equity interests in the entity.

2. Those where the consolidation decision is based on interests *other than* controlling equity interests. (These are the interests now referred to as variable interests. Thus, these are the entities in which consolidation is subject to the nature of these variable interests. It is these, in particular, that are the subject of the Interpretation.)

FIN 46 addresses consolidation by business enterprises where equity investors do *not* bear the residual economic risks and rewards. These entities have been commonly referred to as special-purpose entities.

The underlying principle behind the new Interpretation is that, if a business enterprise has the majority financial interest in an entity (defined in the guidance as a variable interest entity), the assets, liabilities, and results of the activities of the variable interest entity should be included in consolidated financial statements with those of the business enterprise.

Majority-owned subsidiaries are entities separate from their parents that are subject to this Interpretation and may be VIEs.

The Interpretation explains how to identify variable interest entities. It also explains how an enterprise should assess its interest in an entity when deciding whether or not to consolidate that entity and include the assets, liabilities, noncontrolling interests, cash flows, and results of operations of a particular VIE in its consolidated financial statements.

Determination of Status

The initial determination of whether an entity is a VIE and thus subject to the Interpretation is made at the time when an enterprise becomes involved with the entity through ownership, a contractual interest, or other pecuniary interest (i.e., the determination date). These interests can change with the entity's net asset value and may take a variety of forms, including but not limited to guarantees, options to acquire assets, purchase contracts, management or other service contracts, credit enhancements, leases, or subordinated loans. Equity interests with or without voting rights are considered variable interests if the entity is a VIE.

Also at the determination date, the enterprise should determine whether its investments or other interests will absorb any portions of the VIE's expected losses or receive any portions of the entity's expected residual returns. If so, they are indeed variable interests and subject to the Interpretation. VIEs whose variable interests effectively disperse risk among the parties involved need not be consolidated by any of the parties.

A company that consolidates a VIE is called the *primary beneficiary* of that entity. The FASB believes consolidation by a primary beneficiary of the assets, liabilities, and results of activities of VIEs will provide more complete information about the resources, obligations, risks, and opportunities of the consolidated company. To further assist financial statement users in assessing a company's risks, FIN 46 also requires disclosures about VIEs that a company is *not* required to consolidate but in which it has a significant variable interest.

Difference between FIN 46 and Previous Practice

In the past, two enterprises generally have been included in consolidated financial statements because one enterprise controlled the other through voting interests. FIN 46 explains other methods of identifying variable interest entities and then indicates how an enterprise assesses its particular interests in a VIE to decide whether or not to consolidate that entity. FIN 46 requires existing unconsolidated variable interest entities to be consolidated by their *primary beneficiaries* if the entities do not effectively disperse risks among parties involved. The variable interest entities that do effectively disperse risks will not be consolidated, unless a single party holds an interest or combination of interests that effectively recombines risks that had previously been dispersed.

The ability to make decisions is not a variable interest, but it is an indication that the decision maker should carefully consider whether it holds sufficient variable interests to be the primary beneficiary. An enterprise with a variable interest in a VIE must consider variable interests of related parties and de facto agents as its own in determining whether it is the primary beneficiary of the entity.

Measurement

Assets, liabilities, and noncontrolling interests of newly consolidated VIEs generally will be initially measured at their fair values except for assets and liabilities transferred to a variable interest entity by its primary beneficiary, which will continue to be measured as if they had not been transferred. If recognizing those assets, liabilities, and noncontrolling interests at their fair values results in a *loss* to the consolidated enterprise, that loss will be reported immediately as an extraordinary item. On the other hand, if recognizing those assets, liabilities, and noncontrolling interests at their fair values results in a *gain* to the consolidated enterprise, that amount will be allocated to reduce the amounts assigned to assets in the same manner as if consolidation resulted from a business combination.

However, assets, liabilities, and noncontrolling interests of newly consolidated variable interest entities that are under common control with the primary beneficiary are measured at the amounts at which they are carried in the consolidated financial statements of the enterprise that controls them (or would be carried if the controlling entity prepared financial statements) at the date the enterprise becomes the primary beneficiary. After initial measurement, the assets, liabilities, and noncontrolling interests of a consolidated variable interest entity will be accounted for as if the entity were consolidated based on voting interests. In some circumstances, earnings of the variable interest entity attributed to the primary beneficiary arise from sources other than investments in equity of the entity.

Disclosure Requirements

An enterprise that holds significant variable interests in a variable interest entity but *is not the primary beneficiary* is required to disclose:

- The nature, purpose, size, and activities of the variable interest entity.
- The nature of its involvement with the entity and date when the involvement began.
- Its maximum exposure to loss as a result of involvement with the VIE.

The *primary beneficiary* of a variable interest entity is required to disclose the following, unless it also holds a majority voting interest in the VIE:

- The nature, purpose, size, and activities of the variable interest entity.
- The carrying amount and classification of consolidated assets that are collateral for the variable interest entity's obligations.
- Any lack of recourse by creditors (or beneficial interest holders) of a consolidated variable interest entity to the general credit of the primary beneficiary.

The primary beneficiary must, in addition, disclose all information that may be required by other standards. It is also important for a primary beneficiary to reconsider its status from time to time, particularly if:

- The VIE's governing documents or contractual arrangements among the involved parties change.
- The primary beneficiary sells or otherwise disposes of all or part of its interest to other parties.

A holder of beneficial interests that is *not a primary beneficiary* should also reconsider its status if the enterprise acquires newly issued interests in the entity or part of the primary beneficiary's interest in the VIE.

A cautionary note about disclosure: disclosures required by FASB 140 about a variable interest entity must be included in the same note to the financial statements as the information required by FIN 46. Information about VIEs may be reported in the aggregate for similar entities if separate reporting would not add material information.

WHAT CONSTITUTES A VARIABLE INTEREST?

An entity is a VIE and, therefore, subject to consolidation according to the provisions of FIN 46 if, by the way it is structured, either of two conditions exists:

1. The total equity investment as reported as equity in the entity's statements at risk is not sufficient to permit the entity to finance its activities without additional subordinated financial support from other parties. That is, the equity investment at risk is not greater than the expected losses of the entity. For this purpose, the total equity investment at risk:
   a. Includes only equity investments in the entity that participate significantly in profits and losses, even if those investments do not carry voting rights.
   b. Does not include equity interests that the entity issued in exchange for subordinated interests in other VIEs.

    c. Does not include amounts provided to the equity investor by the entity or other parties involved with the entity (such as fees, charitable contributions, or other payments), unless the provider is a parent, subsidiary, or affiliate of the investor required to be included in the same set of consolidated financial statements as the investor.

    d. Does not include amounts financed for the equity investor (for example, by loans or guarantees of loans) directly by the entity or by other parties involved with the entity, unless that party is a parent, subsidiary, or affiliate of the investor that is required to be included in the same set of financial statements of the investor.

2. As a group, the holders of the equity investment at risk lack any one of the following three characteristics of a controlling financial interest:

    a. The direct or indirect ability to make decisions about an entity's activities through voting rights or similar rights. The investors do not have that ability through voting rights or similar rights if no owners hold voting rights or similar rights (such as those of a common shareholder in a corporation or a general partner in a partnership). In addition, the equity investors as a group also are considered to lack the characteristic of this condition if:

        (1) The voting rights of some investors are not proportional to their obligations to absorb the expected losses of the entity, to receive the expected residual returns of the entity, or both.

        (2) Substantially all of the entity's activities (for example, providing financing or buying assets) either involve or are conducted on behalf of an investor and any related parties of the investor that have disproportionately few voting rights. According to FIN 46, this provision is necessary to prevent a primary beneficiary from avoiding consolidation of a VIE by organizing the entity with non-substantive voting interests.

    b. The obligation to absorb the expected losses of the entity if they occur. Investor or investors do not have that obligation if they are directly or indirectly protected from the expected losses or are guaranteed a return by the entity itself or by other parties involved with the entity.

    c. The right to receive the expected residual returns of the entity if they occur. The investors do not have that right if their return is capped by the entity's governing documents or arrangements with other variable interest holders or with the entity.

Several of these provisions have been included in an attempt to forestall methods of circumventing the intent of the various rulings to provide a true financial picture for the benefit of the financial statement user in general and the investor in particular.

Equity Investment at Risk

The determination of the total amount of equity investment at risk that is necessary to permit an entity to finance its activities is a matter of judgment. FIN 46 offers guidance, but each case must be determined based on its facts and circumstances. A VIE's expected losses and expected residual returns include:

- The expected variability in the entity's net income or loss.
- The expected variability in the fair value of the entity's assets (except as explained below in "Specified Assets"), if it is not included in net income or loss.
- Fees to the decision maker (if there is one).
- Fees to providers of guarantees of the values of all or substantially all of the entity's assets (including writers of put options and other instruments with similar results) and providers of guarantees that all or substantially all of the entity's liabilities will be paid.

Ten Percent Guideline

An equity investment of *less than 10 percent* of the entity's total assets is *not* to be considered sufficient to permit the entity to finance its activities without subordinated financial support in addition to the equity investment *unless* the equity investment can be demonstrated to be sufficient in at least one of three ways:

1. The entity has demonstrated that it can actually finance its activities without additional subordinated financial support.
2. The entity has at least as much equity invested as other entities that hold only similar assets of similar quality in similar amounts and operate with no additional subordinated financial support. (This comparison should be very carefully researched and considered, not merely an attempt to validate a questionable decision.)
3. The amount of equity invested in the entity exceeds the estimate of the entity's expected losses based on reasonable quantitative evidence.

FIN 46 points out that some entities may require an equity investment greater than 10 percent of their assets to finance their activities. This is particularly true if they engage in high-risk activities, hold high-risk assets, or have exposure to risks that has not been adequately shown in the reported amounts of their assets or liabilities. It is unquestionably the responsibility of the enterprise to determine whether a particular entity with which it is involved needs an equity investment *greater than 10 percent* of its assets in order to finance its activities without subordinated financial support in addition to the equity investment. At the time of the Enron fiasco, the guideline was only 3 percent, and even this was not observed. Auditors and management must move very cautiously when deciding whether or not an entity must be consolidated.

Specfied Assets

A variable interest can be in the VIE or specified assets of the VIE, such as a guarantee or subordinated residual value.

A variable interest in specific assets of a VIE are considered to be a variable interest in the VIE only if:

- The fair value of the specific asset is more than 50 percent of the fair value of the VIE's total assets.
- The holder has another variable interest in the VIE as a whole, except where those other interests are insignificant or have little or no variability.

If an enterprise has a variable interest in specified assets that are essentially the only source of payment for specified liabilities or other specified interests of the VIE, the enterprise should treat that portion of the entity as a separate VIE. If this is the case and the holder is required to consolidate only this discrete piece of the VIE, the holders of other variable interests need not consider that portion to be part of the larger VIE.

WHO SHOULD CONSOLIDATE WHOM AND WHEN?

The consolidation policy rule appears on the surface, and from all the provisos, to be very complicated. However, once everything has been considered, it is relatively simple. An enterprise must consolidate a VIE if that enterprise has a variable interest (or a combination of variable interests) that will:

- Absorb a majority of the VIE's expected losses, if they occur.
- Receive a majority of the VIE's expected residual returns if they occur.
- Both.

In the situation where one enterprise will absorb the majority of the expected losses and another enterprise will absorb the majority of the expected residual returns, the enterprise absorbing the losses must consolidate the VIE.

The consolidating entity is called the primary beneficiary in the Interpretation. The determination of primary beneficiary status is made at the time the enterprise becomes involved in the VIE.

Decisions Relating to Variable Interests

The initial determination of whether an entity is a variable interest entity needs to be *reconsidered* only if one or more of the following occur:

- The entity's governing documents or the contractual arrangements among the parties involved change.
- The equity investment or some part thereof is returned to the investors, and other parties become exposed to expected losses.
- The entity undertakes additional activities or acquires additional assets that increase the entity's expected losses.

Determination Date

The initial determination of whether an entity is a variable interest entity is to be made on the date at which an enterprise becomes involved with the entity through ownership, a contractual interest, or other pecuniary interest. Such determination should be based on the circumstances occurring on that date, including future changes that are required in existing governing documents and existing contractual arrangements. An enterprise is not required to determine whether an entity with which it is involved is a variable interest entity if it is apparent that the enterprise's interest would not be a significant variable interest and if the enterprise, its related parties, and its de facto agents were not involved in forming the entity.

Any entity that previously did not require consolidation does not become subject to the Interpretation because it loses more than its "expected losses," resulting in a reduction of the equity investment.

Related Parties

An enterprise's variable interest in a VIE includes the variable interests of any related parties in the same VIE. For the purposes of the Interpretation, related parties as identified in FASB 57, *Related Parties,* and certain other de facto agents of the variable interest holder are considered to be related parties. FASB 57 identifies related parties as:

- A parent company and its subsidiaries.
- Subsidiaries of a common parent.
- An enterprise or trust for the benefit of employees that is managed by or under the trusteeship of the enterprise's management.

- An enterprise and its principal owners, management, or members of their immediate families.
- Affiliates.

FIN 46 considers the following to be de facto agents of an enterprise:

- A party that cannot finance its operations without subordinated financial support from the enterprise (e.g., another VIE of which the enterprise is the primary beneficiary).
- A party that received its interests as a contribution or loan from the enterprise.
- An officer, employee, or member of the governing board of the enterprise.
- A party that has:
  - An agreement that it cannot sell, transfer, or encumber its interests in the entity without the prior approval of the enterprise.
  - A close business relationship like that between a professional service provider and one of its significant clients.

If two or more related parties hold variable interests in the same VIE, the following guidelines should be used to determine which is the primary beneficiary:

- If two or more parties with variable interests have an agency relationship, the principal is the primary beneficiary.
- If the relationship is not that of a principal and an agent, the party with activities that are most closely associated with the entity is the primary beneficiary.

Fair Value Measurement

A primary beneficiary initially measures the assets, liabilities, and non-consolidated interests in a VIE at their *fair value* upon consolidation. There are two exceptions to this rule. Assets and liabilities transferred by a primary beneficiary to a newly consolidated VIE are measured at the same amount they would have been measured at if no transfer had occurred. If the primary beneficiary and the VIE are under common control, assets and liabilities transferred to the VIE are measured at their carrying amounts on the financial statements of the enterprise that controls the VIE. After the initial measurement, the assets, liabilities, and noncontrolling interests of a consolidated VIE are accounted for based on voting interests.

EXPECTED RESULTS OF FIN 46 IMPLEMENTATION

The effects of FIN 46 could hasten possibly more significant changes in consolidation policy. In November 2001, the FASB decided to defer consideration of changes in the consolidation policy rules, including its proposal requiring consolidation of all controlled entities, irrespective of the level of equity ownership, to concentrate effort on developing the VIE Interpretation. With this project completed, the FASB is again considering the broader consolidation issues. Indications from the earlier proposals are that the changes in consolidation accounting could be far more encompassing than those resulting from the new *rulings.*

FIN 46 is a reaction to the flouting of honest accounting for off-balance-sheet entities by Enron and others. FASB's earlier proposal, on the other hand, is a proactive initiative to improve the relevance, comparability, consistency, and completeness of consolidated statements. The proposals would also bring U.S. consolidation practices more in line with non-U.S. accounting practices and International Accounting Standards. Both the Sarbanes-Oxley Act and the Securities and Exchange Commission indicate the growing desire to close the gaps between FASB and the International Accounting Standards Board standards.

EFFECTIVE DATE AND TRANSITION

FIN 46 applies immediately to variable interest entities created after January 31, 2003, and to variable interest entities in which an enterprise obtains an interest after that date. It applies in the first fiscal year or interim period beginning after June 15, 2003, to variable interest entities in which an enterprise holds a variable interest that it acquired before February 1, 2003. It applies to public enterprises as of the beginning of the applicable interim or annual period, and to nonpublic enterprises as of the end of the applicable annual period.

This Interpretation may be applied prospectively with a cumulative-effect adjustment as of the date on which it is first applied or by restating previously issued financial statements for one or more years with a cumulative-effect adjustment as of the beginning of the first year restated.

FASB Defers Implementation Date

At its October 2003 Board meeting, the FASB decided to defer to the fourth quarter from the third quarter the implementation date for FIN 46. This deferral applies only to variable interest entities that existed prior to February 1, 2003. The FASB believes that additional time is needed for companies and their auditors to complete the evaluation of existing variable interest entities and to determine which of those entities must be included in their consolidated financial statements.

The requirements of Interpretation 46 applied immediately to any and all variable interest entities created after January 31, 2003. The Board emphasized that those situations are not subject to the deferral.

This deferral means that public companies must now complete their evaluations of variable interest entities that existed prior to February 1, 2003, and the consolidation of those for which they are the primary beneficiary for financial statements issued for the first interim or annual period ending after December 15, 2003. For calendar year companies, consolidation of previously existing variable interest entities will be required in their December 31, 2003, financial statements. While many companies may need the additional time being allotted, others may have already implemented the provisions of FIN 46 because early application of the Interpretation has been encouraged.

INTERPRETATION AND GUIDANCE FOR FIN 46

In March 2003, the Board decided that the appropriate way to provide implementation guidance for FIN 46, as needed, was through FASB Staff Positions and routine technical inquiries. The Board also directed the staff to begin work on other aspects of the consolidations project. The four issues to be addressed are:

1. Consolidation without a majority voting interest.
2. Effect on consolidation of minority shareholder rights.
3. Possible consolidation because of ownership of convertible debt, options, or other means of obtaining a voting interest.
4. Related parties and de facto agents.

Guidance Provided on Questions Raised by Users

Guidance in several areas was provided in July 2003 through five FASB Staff Positions (FSPs). The guidance in each of the FSPs was effective immediately for VIEs to which the requirements of the Interpretation had already been applied. The guidance is applied to other variable interest entities as a part of the adoption of FIN 46. If the guidance results in changes to previously reported information, the cumulative effect of the accounting change should be reported in the first period ending after July 24, 2003.

These FSPs may be applied by restating previously issued financial statements for one or more years with a cumulative-effect adjustment as of the beginning of the first year restated.

Regardless of specific language used in FIN 46 that caused some readers to question whether a distinction was being drawn regarding certain types of health care organizations, this was not the intention. All not-for-profit organizations as defined in FASB 117, *Financial Statements of Not-for-Profit Organizations,* including health care organizations subject to the AICPA *Audit Guide,* are included within the scope of the exemption for not-for-profits. To make this perfectly clear, the Board has agreed that the not-for-profit organization scope exception to Interpretation 46 will be clarified in a forthcoming technical amendment to the Interpretation. However, FIN 46 does point out that not-for-profit organizations may be related parties for purposes of applying certain portions of the Interpretation. In addition, as emphasized earlier in this chapter, a not-for-profit entity used by a business enterprise in a manner similar to a VIE in an effort to circumvent the provisions of Interpretation 46 is subject to the Interpretation.

A specified asset (or group of assets) of a variable interest entity and a related liability secured only by the specified asset or group are not treated as a separate VIE if other parties have rights or obligations related to the specified asset or to residual cash flows from the specified asset. The FSP explains that this is considered so because a separate VIE is deemed to exist for accounting purposes only if essentially all of the assets, liabilities, and equity of the deemed entity are separate from the overall entity and specifically identifiable. It is further explained that, essentially none of the returns of the assets of the deemed entity can be used by the remaining variable interest entity, and essentially none of the liabilities of the deemed entity are payable from the assets of the remaining VIE.

Transition requirements for initial application of FIN 46 provide that both of the following determinations should be made as of the date the enterprise became involved with the entity unless events requiring reconsideration of the entity's status or the status of its variable interest holders have occurred:

1. Whether an entity is a VIE.
2. Which enterprise, if any, is a VIE's primary beneficiary.

If a reconsideration event has occurred, each determination should be made as of the most recent date at which the Interpretation would have required consideration. However, if, at transition, it is impracticable for an enterprise to obtain the information necessary to make such a determination (as of the date the enterprise became involved with an entity or at the most recent reconsideration date), the enterprise should make the determination as of the date on which FIN 46 is first applied. If the VIE and primary beneficiary determinations are made in accordance with these conditions, then the primary beneficiary must measure the assets, liabilities, and noncontrolling interests of the VIE at fair value as of the date on which the Interpretation is first applied.

The two remaining June 2003 FSPs deal with the term "expected losses". The phrase "expected losses of the entity" as used in the Interpretation, is based on the variability in the entity's net income or loss and not on the amount of the net income or loss. Procedures in FIN 46 and Appendix A require that the outcomes used to calculate expected losses include (1) the expected unfavorable variability in the entity's net income or loss and (2) expected unfavorable variability in the fair value of the entity's assets, if it is not included in the net income or loss. (Even an entity that expects to be profitable will have expected losses when this criterion for determining expected losses is considered.) Detailed instructions for calculating expected losses are also provided.

Chapter 4
Governmental Accounting

CONTENTS

Phase 3 governments, those with annual revenues of less than $10 million, are applying the requirements of GASB 34 in their financial statements from June 15, 2003. All levels of government have now begun functioning under that all-encompassing Standard. The Governmental Accounting Standards Board (GASB) continues to do everything it can to make the transition of all state and local governments to this "new" governmental accounting model as painless and error-free as possible by providing implementation guides and how-to manuals. At the same time, the Board is systematically reviewing and updating some of the older Standards.

GASB 41 Provides Guidance on Budgetary Comparisons

The GASB issued Statement 41, *Budgetary Comparison Schedule—Perspective Differences,* in May 2003 to clarify existing guidance on budgetary comparisons in GASB 34, *Basic Financial Statements—and Management's Discussion and Analysis—for State and Local Governments.* This amendment applies to governments whose budgetary structures (for example, certain program-based budgets) prevent them from presenting budgetary comparison information for their general funds and major special revenue funds, as currently required by GASB 34. Under GASB 41, these governments will present their budgetary comparison schedules as required supplementary information (RSI) based on the fund, organization, or program structure that that particular government uses for its legally adopted budget. Generally, governments should present budgetary comparisons for the activities that are reported in the general fund and each major special revenue fund.

The requirements were effective for financial statements for periods beginning after June 15, 2002. Unless otherwise specified, pronouncements of the GASB apply to financial reports of all state and local governmental entities, including general-purpose governments; public benefit corporations and authorities; public employee retirement systems; public utilities, hospitals, and other health care providers; and colleges and universities.

GASB 40, DEPOSIT AND INVESTMENT RISK DISCLOSURES— AN AMENDMENT OF GASB STATEMENT NO. 3

In March 2003, the GASB issued GASB 40, *Deposit and Investment Risk Disclosures—an Amendment of GASB Statement No. 3*, to consider the deposits and investments of state and local governments that are exposed to risks that have the potential to result in losses. This Statement addresses common deposit and investment risks related to credit risk, concentration of credit risk, interest rate risk, and foreign currency risk. As an element of interest rate risk, this Statement requires certain disclosures of investments that have fair values that are highly sensitive to changes in interest rates. Deposit and investment policies related to the risks identified in this Statement should also be disclosed.

The Board reconsidered the disclosures required by GASB 3, *Deposits with Financial Institutions, Investments (including Repurchase Agreements), and Reverse Repurchase Agreements*. Portions of that Statement are modified or eliminated. The custodial credit risk disclosures of GASB 3 are modified to limit required disclosures to:

- Deposits that are not covered by depository insurance and are:
  - Uncollateralized.
  - Collateralized with securities held by the pledging financial institution.
  - Collateralized with securities held by the pledging financial institution's trust department or agent but not in the depositor-government's name.
- Uninsured investment securities that are not registered in the name of the government and are held by either:

—The counterparty.
—The counterparty's trust department or agent but not in the government's name.

GASB 3 disclosures generally referred to as category 1 and 2 deposits and investments are eliminated. However, GASB 40 does not change the required disclosure of authorized investments or the requirements for reporting certain repurchase agreements and reverse repurchase agreements, and it maintains, with modification, the level-of-detail disclosure requirements of GASB 3.

The provisions of GASB 40 are effective for financial statements for periods beginning after June 15, 2004. Earlier application is encouraged.

How the Changes in This Statement Improve Financial Reporting

Deposit and investment resources often represent significant assets of governmental, proprietary, and fiduciary funds. These resources are necessary for the delivery of governmental services and programs or to carry out fiduciary responsibilities. GASB 40 is designed to inform financial statement users about deposit and investment risks that could affect a government's ability to provide services and meet its obligations as they become due. The Board believes that there are risks inherent in all deposits and investments, and it believes that the disclosures required by this Statement provide users of governmental financial statements with information to assess common risks inherent in deposit and investment transactions.

The Board adopted fair value accounting for most investments in GASB 31, *Accounting and Financial Reporting for Certain Investments and for External Investment Pools*. Fair value portrays the market's estimate of the net future cash flows of investments, discounted to reflect both time value and risk. In order to understand the measurement of investments at fair value, the timing of cash flows (including investment time horizons) and investment risks need to be communicated.

In the Exposure Draft (ED), the Board had pointed out that all investments carry some form of risk and the public should be made aware of any risks in financial statements. Deposit and investment resources often represent the largest assets of governmental and fiduciary funds. Proprietary funds also report significant deposit and investment balances. These resources are critical to delivering governmental services and programs.

Financial statement disclosures would cover deposit and investment risks. Among these would be:

• Credit risk disclosures, including credit quality information issued by rating agencies.

- Interest rate disclosures, including investment maturity information, such as weighted average maturities or specification identification of the securities.
- For investments that are highly sensitive to changes in interest rates (e.g., inverse floaters, enhanced variable-rate investments, and certain asset-backed securities), disclosures that indicate the basis for their sensitivity.
- Disclosure of foreign investment disclosures would indicate the foreign investment's denomination.
- Deposit and investment policies related to risks.

GASB 40 results from the Board's formal reviews of its existing standards. These reviews—part of the Board's strategic plan—are designed to evaluate the continuing usefulness of current requirements. The reduction of existing custodial credit risk disclosures follows from federal banking reforms adopted since the release of GASB 3.

Technical Bulletin to Improve Disclosures About Derivatives

In an effort to improve disclosures about the risks associated with derivative contracts, the GASB issued accounting guidance in June 2003 that provides more consistent and comprehensive reporting by state and local governments. The Technical Bulletin, *Disclosure Requirements for Derivatives Not Presented at Fair Value on the Statement of Net Assets,* is designed to increase the public's understanding of the significance of derivatives to a government's net assets and to provide key information about the potential effects on future cash flows. It will also provide the users of financial statements with better information about the risks assumed in derivative contracts. Derivatives are often used by governments as a means to potentially reduce borrowing costs. Although derivatives may support financing needs, the lower costs come with additional risks. The objectives and terms of derivative contracts, their risk, and the fair value of the contracts had generally not been specified in financial reports.

This Technical Bulletin is designed to increase the public's understanding of the significance of derivatives to a government's financial position and provide key information about their potential effects on future cash flows.

GASB pointed out that even estimating the notional amounts of outstanding derivatives in this market based on information that has been readily available is difficult. Estimates of notional value range from $200 billion to $400 billion. Under this guidance, state and local governments are *required* to disclose such information.

One GASB official agreed that GASB's own research indicated that it often has been difficult to understand how governments have been accounting for derivatives. These disclosures should clear up the mystery surrounding the transactions. It should now be possible to see what a government has done, why it has done it, the fair value of the derivative, and the risks that have been assumed. Governments will be required to disclose information in their financial statements about risks that relate to credit, interest rates, basis, termination dates, rollovers, and market access.

Whereas state and local governments use an array of increasingly complex derivative instruments to manage debt and investments, they may, at the same time, be assuming significant risks. Governments are expected to communicate those risks to financial statement users and the public. The proposed Technical Bulletin's purpose is to clarify existing accounting guidance so that more consistent disclosures can be made across all governments.

The GASB is aware that the market for derivative instruments has expanded for state and local governments, which find themselves in a dismal budgetary environment. Some derivative contracts may pose substantial risks; therefore, the Board's aim is to help officials better explain those risks in their financial statements.

This Technical Bulletin requires that governments disclose the derivative's:

- Objectives,
- Terms,
- Fair value, and
- Risks.

The proposed accounting guidance requires the governments to disclose in their financial statements what is faced in terms of:

- Credit risk,
- Interest rate risk,
- Basis risk,
- Termination risk,
- Rollover risk, and
- Market access risk.

This Technical Bulletin became effective for periods ending after June 15, 2003.

REPORT ON COMMUNICATING PERFORMANCE INFORMATION

In October 2003, the GASB published a Special Report, Reporting Performance Information: Suggested Criteria for Effective Communication, presenting a set of suggested criteria for use in developing external reports on performance information. The report is the result of work performed as part of the continuing GASB research project on service efforts and accomplishments (SEA) reporting, funded, in part, through a Sloan Foundation grant. The purpose of this SEA research project is multi-faceted. The purpose is to:

* To encourage state and local governments to experiment with reporting
* performance information.
* To provide nonauthoritative guidance for the communication of performance
* information.
* To assess how successful the guidance has been in assisting governments to communicate effectively the results of these efforts and accomplishments.

This is not an altogether new venture; the GASB has issued research reports in the past that emphasized current practice in SEA reporting. Some governmental units have begun experimenting with reporting SEA information based on examples from current practice. Emphasis in this report describes what governments can do to produce effective reports on performance. The 16 suggested criteria discussed in the document provide guidance that should result in external reports on performance that communicate relevant, reliable information about the performance of government programs and services to elected officials, citizens and other users of financial reports.

The development of the criteria reflects lessons gained from:

* Studying state and local governments' use of performance measures for budgeting, management, and external reporting.
* Discussions with groups of citizens.
* Information received for the GASB's SEA task force.
* Discussions with preparers.
* Analysis of criteria used by other types of organizations and in other countries.

ED ON REPORTING MORE INFORMATION IN FINANCIAL STATEMENTS

The GASB issued an ED, *Economic Condition Reporting: The Statistical Section,* in September 2003. The proposal revises the statistical section that accompanies a state or local government's basic financial statements to include more comprehensive government-wide financial information. It is designed to enhance and update the supporting information that governments present with their annual financial statements.

The statistical section comprises schedules presenting trend information about:

- Revenues and expenses.
- Outstanding debt.
- Economics and demographics.
- Various other topics.

The schedule's intended purpose is to provide financial statement users with contextual information to aid them in assessing a governmental body's financial health better.

The section is aimed at updating the significant changes that have taken place in government finance. For instance, governments are scheduled to report the broader array of debt they now issue in addition to the more usual general obligation bonds. The proposal would, in effect, replace current Standards that are oriented toward general purpose local governments. The ED provides clearer guidelines that can be implemented by any type of governmental entity.

Although the statistical section is a required part of a comprehensive annual financial report (CAFR), state and local governments are not required to prepare a statistical section if they present their basic financial statements in a report other than a CAFR. The proposed standard would not change this situation. The proposal would, however, govern any statistical section accompanying a government's basic financial statements, whether presented in a CAFR or not.

The proposed Standard would become effective for periods beginning after June 15, 2005.

ED ON OTHER POSTEMPLOYMENT BENEFITS TO INCREASE TRANSPARENCY

After issuing two Exposure Drafts in mid-December 2002, the GASB published two more Exposure Drafts in February 2003. These proposed Statements are on financial reporting of postemployment benefits. They consider *Accounting and Financial Reporting by Employers for Postemployment Benefits Other Than Pensions* and *Financial Reporting for Postemployment Benefit Plans Other Than Pension Plans.* The proposed guidance is expected to produce greater transparency for decision makers who rely on state and local governments' financial statements.

In addition to pensions, many state and local governmental employers provide other postemployment benefits (OPEB) as part of the total compensation offered to attract and retain the services of qualified employees. OPEB include postemployment health care as well as other forms of postemployment benefits, such as life insurance, when provided separately from a pension plan. The proposed Statement on employer reporting would establish standards for the measurement, recognition, and display of OPEB expense or expenditures and related liabilities in the financial reports of state and local governments. Currently, most governmental employers finance OPEB plans on a pay-as-you-go basis, and financial statements generally do not report financial effects of OPEB until the promised benefits are paid, often many years after the related employee services are received.

Under the proposed accounting change, governments would:

- Measure the cost of benefits, and recognize OPEB expense, on the accrual basis of accounting in periods that approximate employees' years of service.
- Provide information about the actuarial accrued liabilities for promised benefits associated with past services and whether, or to what extent, those benefits have been funded.
- Provide information useful in assessing potential demands on the employer's future cash flows.

The companion Exposure Draft would establish uniform financial reporting standards for OPEB plans and would supersede the previously issued interim guidance. The proposed overall approach to reporting of OPEB generally is consistent with that adopted by the GASB for pension reporting.

ED on Asset Impairment and Insurance Recoveries

In December 2002, GASB published an Exposure Draft, *Accounting and Financial Reporting for Impairment of Capital Assets and for Insurance Recoveries,* that would require governments to report the effects of capital asset impairment in their financial statements when they occur. The proposed guidance also enhances comparability of financial statements between governments by requiring all governments to account for insurance recoveries in the same manner.

The impact of the proposed accounting Statement is in relation to capital assets, which represent the largest category of assets on the statement of net assets of most governments. The public has long expressed concern about the condition of those capital assets, especially roads and bridges, sewer and water systems, and schools. This change will ensure that government financial statements reflect the reduction in service capacity when impairment of capital assets occurs.

The proposed Statement would require governments to evaluate major events affecting capital assets to determine whether they are impaired. Those events include:

- Physical damage.
- Changes in legal or environmental factors.
- Technological changes or obsolescence.
- Changes in manner or duration of usage.
- Construction stoppage.

Impairment would be measured using the method that best reflects the value-in-use for that particular capital asset. The measurement methods in the proposed Statement include the restoration cost approach, the service units approach, and deflated depreciated replacement cost. These measurement methods are designed to isolate the historical cost of the capital asset's service capacity that has been rendered unusable by impairment.

The proposed guidance includes several disclosure requirements that would assist users of financial statements in understanding the nature and impact of impairment of capital assets. Disclosures would be required for impairment losses that are not evident from the face of the financial statements, for impaired capital assets that are idle, and for insurance recoveries that are not evident from the face of the financial statements.

The effective date of the standard would be for fiscal years beginning after December 15, 2004.

ED ON BUDGETARY COMPARISONS THAT IMPROVE TRANSPARENCY

The GASB has published an Exposure Draft, *Budgetary Comparison Schedules—Perspective Differences,* that clarifies existing guidance on budgetary comparisons in GASB 34, *Basic Financial Statements—and Management's Discussion and Analysis—for State and Local Governments* in December 2003. This amendment applies to governments with budgetary structures that prevent them from being able to present budgetary comparison information for their general funds and major special revenue funds, as currently required by Statement 34.

The proposed Statement mandates that governments present budgetary comparison schedules as required supplementary information based on the fund, organization, or program structure that the government uses for its legally adopted budget. By and large, governments should present budgetary comparisons for the activities that are reported in the general fund and each major special revenue fund.

The accounting changes were effective for periods beginning after June 15, 2002.

GASB 37, BASIC FINANCIAL STATEMENTS—AND MANAGEMENT'S DISCUSSION AND ANALYSIS—FOR STATE AND LOCAL GOVERNMENTS: OMNIBUS—AN AMENDMENT OF GASB STATEMENTS 21 AND 34

GASB 37, which was adopted in June 2001, amends GASB 21, *Accounting for Escheat Property*, and GASB 34, *Basic Financial Statements—and Management's Discussion and Analysis—for State and Local Governments*.

The amendments to Statement 21 are necessary because of the changes to the fiduciary fund structure required by Statement 34. Generally, escheat property that was previously reported in an *expendable trust fund* should now be reported in a *private-purpose trust fund* under Statement 34. Statement 37 explains the effects of that change.

The amendments to GASB 34 either:

1. Clarify certain provisions that, in retrospect, may not be sufficiently clear for consistent application, or
2. Modify other provisions that the Board believes may have unintended consequences in some circumstances.

The provisions aimed at *clarifying* previous provisions are not new but may have been unclear or confusing for the user. They include:

1. *Management's Discussion and Analysis (MD&A) requirements*—Governments should confine the topics discussed in MD&A to those listed in Statement 34 rather than consider those topics as "minimum requirements."
2. *Modified approach*—Adopting the modified approach for infrastructure assets that have previously been depreciated is considered a change in an *accounting estimate*. The effect of the change is accounted for prospectively rather than as a restatement of prior periods.
3. *Program revenue classifications*—Fines and forfeitures should be included in the broad *charges for services* category. Also, additional guidance is provided to aid in determining to which function certain program revenues pertain.
4. *Major fund criteria*—Major fund reporting requirements apply to a governmental or enterprise fund if the *same* element (for example, revenues) exceeds *both* the 10 percent *and* 5 percent criteria.

The provisions, which are modifications of the requirements of Statement 34, include:

1. Eliminating the requirement to capitalize construction-period interest for governmental activities.
2. Changing the minimum level of detail required for business-type activities in the statement of activities from *segments* to *different identifiable activities*.

The Board believed that GASB 37 would help governments implement Statement 34 and improve the usefulness of state and local governments' financial statements under the far-reaching new reporting model. Statement 38 (below) was implemented to provide users with new information and eliminate some disclosures that the Board found were no longer needed.

The provisions of Statement 37 were to be simultaneously implemented with Statement 34. For governments that had already implemented GASB 34 prior to the issuance of GASB 37, the requirements were effective for financial statements for periods beginning after June 15, 2000.

GASB 38, *CERTAIN FINANCIAL STATEMENT NOTE DISCLOSURES*

Statement 38 modifies, adds, and deletes various note disclosure requirements. The requirements cover such areas as:

1. Revenue recognition policies.
2. Actions taken in response to legal violations.
3. Debt service requirements.
4. Variable-rate debt.
5. Receivable and payable balances.
6. Interfund transfers and balances.
7. Short-term debt.

The new requirements are an additional attempt to address the needs of users of financial statements as determined through ongoing Board research. In discussing the benefits to users, the Board considered that with respect to interfund transfers, users of financial statements will, for the first time, be able to trace transfers from the source fund to the receiving fund and to understand why the government uses transfers.

Now users will also be able to see the purpose and extent of the use of short-term debt, which is especially important for debt issued and redeemed within the government's fiscal year.

Statement 38 is the result of the GASB's intention to ensure the continuing effectiveness of existing standards. The Board reaffirmed that most note disclosure requirements are still relevant.

The requirements of this Statement issued in June 2001 are effective in three phases based on a government's total annual revenues in the first fiscal year ending after June 15, 1999:

1. *Phase 1 governments*—The large governmental organizations with annual revenues of $100 million or more, were required to implement portions of GASB 38 for fiscal periods beginning after June 15, 2001. These governments implemented the remaining portions for fiscal periods beginning after June 15, 2002.

2. *Phase 2 governments*—Those with total annual revenues of $10 million or more but less than $100 million, applied the requirements of the Statement in financial statements for periods beginning after June 15, 2002.

3. *Phase 3 governments*—The small entities with total annual revenues of less than $10 million should apply the requirements in financial statements for periods beginning after June 15, 2003. Thus, the effective date coincides with the effective date of GASB Statement 34 for the reporting government.

FINANCIAL REPORTING GUIDANCE FOR FUND-RAISING FOUNDATIONS AND SIMILAR ORGANIZATIONS UNDER GASB 39

In May 2002, the GASB issued Statement 39, *Determining Whether Certain Organizations Are Component Units, an Amendment of GASB Statement 14,* which clarifies existing accounting guidance and provides greater consistency in accounting for organizations that are closely related to a primary government. The standard provides criteria for determining whether certain organizations, such as not-for-profit foundations related to public universities and school districts, should be reported as component units based on the nature and significance of their relationship to a state or local government.

Under this ruling, state and local governments that have qualifying fund-raising foundations would be required to include, through discrete presentations, the financial activities of those foundations in their financial statements. Previously, there was no consistency in dealing with their financial matters:

1. Some entities had included the balances and transactions of their related fund-raising organizations in their financial statements.
2. Others disclosed limited information in the notes.
3. Still others provided no information at all.

GASB 39 should bring a greater level of comparability to state and local financial reporting. It amends Statement 14 to provide additional guidance to determine whether certain organizations for which the primary government is not financially accountable should be reported as component units based on the nature and significance of their relationship with a primary government.

The standard sets forth criteria on which a government is required to provide a discrete presentation that includes financial information about its own activities as well as those of the affiliated organization.

Generally, a legally separate, tax-exempt, fund-raising organization whose primary purpose is to raise or hold significant resources for the benefit of a specific governmental unit should be included as a component unit of that governmental unit's financial reporting entity.

SMOOTHING THE TRANSITION TO GASB 34

After the adoption of Governmental Accounting Standard Board Statement 34, *Basic Financial Statements—and Management's Discussion and Analysis—for State and Local Governments,* in June, 1999, it is understandable that the Board appeared to be much more concerned about helping the accountants, auditors, and state and local officials "get it right" than about adopting any more new rules and regulations. Because GASB 34 is such a comprehensive overhauling of state and local government financial reporting, those involved needed time as well as helpful input to meet the requirements.

Acknowledgement of this is demonstrated by the Board's publication of:

1. An *Implementation Guide* for accountants.
2. Two *What You Should Know* guides.
3. A more sophisticated analyst's guide.
4. Three *Quick Guides.*

A GUIDE FOR IMPLEMENTING NEW FINANCIAL STATEMENTS

For those accountants faced with the daunting task of putting Statement 34 into practice, the GASB issued an *Implementation Guide* to help the preparers and auditors of state and local government financial statements understand and apply the provisions. The provisions are detailed later in this chapter.

The guide includes nearly 300 questions and answers developed by the GASB staff with the assistance of a 36-member advisory group. In addition to the question-and-answer section, the guide also includes:

1. More than 50 illustrative financial statement exhibits.
2. How-to exercises on ten of the more difficult requirements.

3. The complete standards section of Statement 34.
4. A sample financial statement for a state government.
5. A sample financial statement for a municipal government, including a complete illustrative MD&A and selected note disclosures.
6. A sample financial statement for an independent school district.

In-Depth Instructions for Compliance

The "Exercises" section furnishes step-by-step suggestions on how to comply with some of the requirements of Statement 34, including:

1. Calculating composite depreciation rates.
2. Applying group depreciation to infrastructure assets at transition and in subsequent years.
3. Calculating net asset balances for governmental activities.
4. Reporting internal service fund balances and results.
5. Determining major funds.
6. Reconciling fund financial statements to government-wide financial statements.
7. Indirectly determining direct-method cash flows.
8. Estimating historical cost using current replacement cost.
9. Calculating weighted-average age of infrastructure assets at transition.
10. Determining major general infrastructure assets.

A GUIDE TO LOCAL GOVERNMENT FINANCIAL STATEMENTS

The guide, *What You Should Know About Your Local Government's Finances: A Guide to Financial Statements,* is the GASB's first publication written specifically for citizens, taxpayers, legislators, researchers, and other people who use government financial information. The specific purpose is to highlight for financial statement users the information contained in the annual reports of local governments.

The guide is intended not only for those accustomed to using financial statements but also as a resource for auditors and government finance officers who need to explain financial statements to elected officials, citizens, and clients.

Providing a Pathway to Information

The guide emphasizes how information in the financial statements of counties, cities, and other local governments may be used to aid in the decision-making process. This publication should be of value to a varied group of people including:

1. Entrepreneurs considering where to locate a business.
2. Investors deciding whether to buy a particular government's bonds.
3. Real estate agents developing information for a "sales pitch."
4. Developers determining a viable location for construction of a shopping mall or condominium complex.

The guide is designed to be suitable for use by a newcomer to the world of government finance as well as by the the long-time government manager or official.

It contains graphics as well as text to enhance its readability and usefulness, such as:

1. Figures and tables, including an annotated set of illustrative financial statements (complete with management's discussion and analysis) for a local government.
2. A running story that makes it easier for the reader to understand the concepts by relating them to personal financial decisions.
3. Boxes and sidebars that:

   a. Explore the issues raised in the text.

   b. Provide more detailed definitions and explanations.

   c. Offer tips on using financial statement information.
4. Easy identification of key terms that are defined in a glossary that accompanies the text.
5. An appendix containing an overview of the basics of governmental accounting and financial reporting.
6. A second appendix that explains some basic financial ratios that may be used to analyze government financial statements.

The guide covers the history-making changes in the preparation of state and local government financial statements brought about by the issuance of GASB Statement 34.

In line with the provisions of the Statement, some governments have already begun to implement these new requirements in their financial statements and others will begin complying with them over the next few years. This guide should give the preparer as well as the user of financial statements an overview of governmental accounting with particular emphasis on GASB 34's new "business" approach to accountability.

A GUIDE TO A SCHOOL DISTRICT'S FINANCIAL STATEMENTS

What You Should Know About Your School District's Finances: A Guide to Financial Statements is the second in the series of guides developed specifically for persons who use public sector financial information. It is aimed at educating readers about the information that can be found in the financial statements that public school districts will prepare under the historic changes in accounting standards that were adopted in mid-1999.

The new school district guide is designed to help anyone from public finance novices to long-time public sector managers understand school district financial statements. For the users of public school financial information (school board members, parents, taxpayers, financial analysts, and others) the guide provides insight into how the information in financial statements can be used to as a basis for decision making. The guide is also a handy reference for school district finance officers and certified public accountants seeking to understand the usefulness of the new financial statements and to explain them to citizens, elected officials, and clients.

Unlocking the Key to a School District's Fiscal Condition

Those charged with or interested in the fiscal health of public school systems should be able to use this guide to learn something about how to judge a school district's fiscal health. The GASB believes that this guide serve a double purpose: it may help the public use financial statements to hold school districts accountable; on the other hand, it may assist the districts in demonstrating their accountability to the public they serve.

The guide provides important insights into a broad range of issues, including:

1. The comparative fiscal health of a given school district in relation to previous years, as well as to similarly situated districts.
2. The reasons for a district's improved or degenerating financial condition.
3. What a school district owns and how much it owes.
4. Whether a school system will be able to pay its bills and repay its debts.
5. Looming issues that may affect a district's future finances.

Among the features contained in the school guide, which encompasses the sweeping changes the Board made to state and local government financial statements with the issuance of GASB 34, are:

1. Nearly two dozen figures and tables, including a set of annotated sample financial statements for a fictional school district.

2. Boxes and sidebars that help to explain and simplify financial statement information.
3. Clear identification of important terms and an extensive glossary.
4. Two appendices that introduce the basics of financial statement analysis and school district accounting.

A GUIDE FOR FINANCIAL ANALYSTS

The GASB has also published a guide intended to assist analysts as they incorporate the new state and local government financial statements into their work. The new publication, *An Analyst's Guide to Government Financial Statements,* introduces the financial statements that governments are beginning to prepare under GASB Statement 34.

The analyst's guide was developed specifically for regular and intensive users of public sector financial statements, including:

1. Mutual fund analysts.
2. Rating agencies.
3. Institutional investors.
4. Bond insurers.
5. Research organizations.
6. Taxpayer groups.

The Greater Depth of Information in the New Statements

This historic Standard was actually developed to provide analysts as well as other financial statement users with the more comprehensive and comprehensible data they require to assess government finances. The Board's goal in developing this guide is to help analysts more effectively assimilate the information from the new and expanded governmental financial statements into their analytical and decision-making processes.

For years the complaint about any given level of government has been, "Why can't they run it more like a business?" With the Statement, *Basic Financial Statements—and Management's Discussion and Analysis—for State and Local Governments,* establishing new requirements for state and local governments, this may happen. These requirements appear to be headed in the direction of a more businesslike approach, at least from an accountant's point of view. Governmental units must now prepare their financial reports according to GAAP. The new rules substantially change the appearance and content of government financial statements, which had previously been solely involved with fund accounts.

An Analyst's Guide to Government Financial Statements is written in an easy-to-understand style, but is more comprehensive in coverage than the two *What You Should Know* guides. It presents nearly 80 illustrations of financial statements for states, localities, school districts, public colleges and universities, and other special-purpose types of governments.

"CLIFFIES" FOR GOVERNMENT FINANCIAL STATEMENTS

The GASB has also published three *Quick Guides* — one each for state governments, local governments, and school districts. In an attempt to reach more of its constituents, the GASB has issued this series of "pocket" guides to assist users in understanding the financial statements that state and local governments prepare once they have fully implemented GASB Statement 34. The *Quick Guides* provide a summarized overview of the thorough introduction to government financial statements presented in the GASB's first three user guides.

They provide "need-to-know" information in brief and easy-to-read style delineating the major features of the new financial statements. They also highlight the ways in which government financial statement information may be useful to decision makers such as legislators, taxpayers, citizen groups, parents, public employees, financial analysts-even interested, involved citizens and voters.

The *Quick Guides* are directed toward school board members, legislators, and other elected officials who need a short and understandable explanation of government financial statements-and don't have the time or inclination for an in-depth indoctrination.

They are the perfect companion to the larger user guides, which are useful resources to government finance officers, accountants, and auditors who need to understand how financial statement information is used and are looking for help in explaining the new financial statements to their elected officials or clients.

INTERPRETATION RELATING TO MODIFIED ACCRUAL STANDARDS

The Board decided this Interpretation was necessary to shore up usage of modified accrual accounting used in governmental fund accounting retained by GASB 34.

Interpretation 6, *Recognition and Measurement of Certain Liabilities and Expenditures in Governmental Fund Financial Statements,* addresses concerns about the interpretation and application of existing *modified accrual standards.* The purpose of modified accrual accounting is to measure flows of current financial resources in governmental *fund financial statements.*

This Interpretation clarifies the application of existing standards for distinguishing between the portions of certain types of liabilities that should be reported as:

1. Governmental fund liabilities and expenditures.
2. General long-term liabilities of the government.

GASB 34, *Basic Financial Statements—and Management's Discussion and Analysis—for State and Local Governments,* carried forward the requirement that governmental fund financial statements be prepared using the existing financial resources measurement focus and the modified accrual basis of accounting. This traditional measurement focus and basis of accounting provides useful information related to a government's fiscal accountability, as part of the new financial reporting model. In addition, the new model provides useful information related to a government's operational accountability, including government-wide financial statements prepared on the *accrual basis* of accounting.

Concerns had been raised, however, about the interpretation and application of *existing modified accrual standards.* These concerns included:

1. Lack of comparability in the application of standards for recognition of certain fund liabilities and expenditures.
2. Perceived subjectivity of some interpretations and applications.
3. Potential circularity of the criteria for recognition of revenues and expenditures.

The objective of Interpretation 6 is to improve the comparability, consistency, and objectivity of financial reporting in governmental fund financial statements by providing a common, internally consistent interpretation of standards in areas where practice differences have occurred or could occur.

The effective date of this Interpretation was designed to coincide with the effective date of Statement 34 for the particular reporting government. Earlier application was encouraged, provided that the Interpretation and Statement 34 would be implemented simultaneously.

REVIEW OF EXISTING STANDARDS

The GASB has begun a comprehensive review of existing accounting standards. One of the first results of this forward-looking activity was the redeliberation of its revised exposure draft, *The Financial Reporting Entity-Affiliated Organizations, an Amendment of GASB Statement 14.*

GASB 39, *Determining Whether Certain Organizations Are Component Units* (discussed above), resulted from this redeliberation. The Standard amends GASB 14 to provide additional guidance to determine whether certain organizations for which the primary government is not financially accountable should be reported as component units based on the nature and significance of their relationship with a primary government.

Another project in this effort was the reconsideration of the existing requirements in GASB 3, evaluating the ongoing usefulness of current requirements by taking into consideration recent federal banking reforms. This resulted in the Exposure Draft titled *Deposit and Investment Risk Disclosures,* which became GASB 40 discussed earlier in this chapter. The need for a new Statement is to provide the public with better information about the risks that could potentially impact a government's ability to provide services and pay its debts.

Other projects are outlined below.

Asset Impairment / Preservation Method

The objective of this project is twofold:

1. To develop criteria for when asset impairment should be recognized in the financial statements.
2. To determine whether reported changes in asset condition levels (associated with the modified approach of accounting for infrastructure assets) can be measured in monetary terms that meet the qualitative characteristics for financial reporting.

An exposure draft is planned in the near future. The preservation method portion of this project is on the Board's long-term agenda.

Conceptual Framework—Communication Methods

The objectives of this project are to:

1. Clarify the definition of general-purpose external financial reporting (GPEFR).
2. Identify and provide definitions of various methods of communicating financial and finance-related information to users.
3. Develop criteria for using each method.

During 2001, the Board continued discussions of the scope of GPEFR. They compared the tentative definitions of economic condition and its components with the objectives of GPEFR and the types of information needed to meet those objectives, according to Concepts Statement No. 1, *Objectives of Financial Reporting.*

The Board tentatively agreed that the definition of GPEFR encompasses both economic condition and service results. Further deliberations on this issue as well as the tentative definition of economic condition continued through April 2002. An exposure draft is tentatively scheduled for the first quarter of 2003.

Economic Condition

The objective of this project is to determine whether additional information on the elements of *economic condition* should be *required* in or with basic financial statements or *encouraged* to be provided in other forms of financial reporting. This project builds on the Board's tentative definitions of *economic condition* and its underlying elements of *financial position, fiscal capacity, and service capacity,* which are being developed in the Board's conceptual framework project on methods of communication in financial reporting.

This project has been tentatively divided into four phases:

1. Basic research to establish the frame of reference.
2. Board deliberations focused on the comprehensive annual financial report's (CAFR's) current statistical section, to begin in the third quarter of 2002.
3. An exposure draft is anticipated for the third quarter of 2003. The third phase of this project is on the Board's long-term agenda.
4. The fourth phase is on the Board's research agenda.

Environmental Liabilities

The objective of this project is to determine whether additional guidance is needed to account properly for, and report liabilities associated with, environmental laws and regulations (e.g., clean water, clean air, and superfund activities).

Board deliberations were held in 2002, and an exposure draft is planned for the third quarter of 2003.

Other Postemployment Benefits (OPEB)

The final standards from this project will address accounting and financial reporting of postemployment benefits other than pensions by employers and plans or the entities that administer them (e.g., pension plans and public employee retirement systems that administer OPEB plans).

In the final third of 2001, the Board tentatively agreed to apply to OPEB the requirements of Statement 25, *Financial Reporting for Defined Benefit Pension Plans and Note Disclosures for Defined Contribution Plans,* with respect to:

1. Measurement focus, basis of accounting and display of financial information in the basic financial statements of fiduciary funds and similar component units.

2. Measurement and recognition criteria pertaining to specific financial statement accounts. In addition, the Board discussed several potential disclosure requirements for employers and plans. An exposure draft is planned.

BUSINESS-LIKE ACCOUNTING COMES TO STATE AND LOCAL GOVERNMENT

The Governmental Accounting Standards Board unanimously adopted the long-awaited comprehensive changes for state and local government financial reporting throughout the country in June 1999. GASB 34, *Basic Financial Statements—and Management's Discussion and Analysis—for State and Local Governments,* provides a new look and focus in reporting public finance in the U.S. The Board's action may be a response to the oft-voiced complaint, ". . . if only they'd run the government more like a business!" Now "they" must, at least from an accounting standpoint. Many big "businesses" and even more mid-size and small "businesses"—states, cities, counties, towns—adding up to a total of 87,000 in 1999, according to the GASB, are adopting the new measures.

THE GASB GAINS STATURE

This Statement can certainly be considered the most significant change in the history of governmental accounting and should signal the "coming of age" of the GASB. It represents a dramatic shift in the manner and comprehensiveness in which state and local governments present financial information to the public. When fully implemented, it will create new information and will restructure much of the fund information that governments have presented in the past.

The new requirements were developed to make annual reports more comprehensive and easier to understand and use. Now, anyone with an interest (vested or otherwise) in public finance—citizens, the media, bond raters, creditors, investors, legislators, investment bankers and others—will have readily available information about the respective governmental bodies.

Thousands of preparers, auditors, academics, and users of governmental financial statements participated during a decade and a half in the research, consideration, and deliberations that preceded the publication of GASB 34. Members of various task forces began work on this and related projects as early as 1985.

PROVISIONS OF GASB 34

Among the major innovations of Statement 34, governments are required to:

1. Report on the *overall* state of the government's financial health, not just its individual funds as has been the case.
2. Provide the most complete information ever made available about the cost of providing services to the citizens.
3. Prepare an introductory narrative section (the Management's Discussion and Analysis—MD&A) to the basic report analyzing the government's financial performance.
4. Provide enhanced fund reporting.
5. Include information about the government's public infrastructure assets. The Statement explains these assets as long-lived assets that are normally stationary and capable of being preserved longer than most capital assets. Bridges, roads, storm sewers, tunnels, drainage systems, dams, lighting systems, and swimming pools are among those mentioned. (This is certainly the most innovative requirement introduced to governmental financial reporting.)

BACKGROUND INFORMATION

The GASB's first concepts Statement, *Objectives of Financial Reporting,* issued in 1987, identified what the Board believes are the most important objectives of financial reporting by governments. Some of those objectives reaffirm the importance of information that governmental units have historically included in their annual reports. To cover more of the original objectives, the Board felt it necessary to provide for a much broader range of information.

As a result, Statement 34 is a dual-perspective report requiring governmental bodies to retain much of the information they currently report, but also requiring them to go further in revealing their operations. The first perspective focuses on the traditional funds with some additional information required for major funds. The second perspective is government-wide to provide an entirely new look at a government's financial activities.

The Board feels that adding new material will result in reports that accomplish more of the objectives emphasized in the original concepts Statement.

THE TIME FOR ACCOUNTABILITY IS NOW

According to the GASB, state and local governments in the U.S. invest approximately $140–$150 billion annually in the construction, improvement, and rehabilitation of capital assets, including infrastructure assets like bridges, highways, and sewers. Since these expenditures represent more than 10% of the monies spent by those governments, it would appear quite natural for them to be accounted for in financial documents readily available to the public.

The majority of this infrastructure investment is financed by borrowing— selling municipal bonds and using the proceeds to pay for construction. (Enter the investor.)

The need for public accountability arises when such sums are spent and when current and future generations are committed to repay such debts. The public should know how much governments spend on infrastructure construction and how much they borrow to finance it. (Enter the taxpayer.)

The public also wants to know if government officials subsequently are caring for the infrastructure they have built with public resources. (Enter the voter.)

Although the need for information about infrastructure should be fairly obvious, the primary instruments for demonstrating fiscal accountability (the government's annual financial statements) have not previously been required to provide this information. The accounting method for preparing state and local government financial statements has focused on short-term financial resources like cash and investments. Infrastructures have been left off the balance sheet and no charge was included on the income statement for the cost of using the infrastructure assets to provide services. Because of the significant share of government spending devoted to capital assets, this has been a major omission. But with the advent of GASB 34, all of that is changing.

Opportunities for Government Consulting

Considering the number of affected governmental bodies—regardless of the considerable lead time provided—the present supply of government accountants is certainly being stretched to the limit. In addition, many have had little experience in the required more "corporate-style" accounting. Even though the smaller governments have the longest time to make the necessary changes, they face a rather daunting task as they have few, if any, accounting professionals on their staff.

Thus, the Statement opens up business opportunities for interested accountants. It should be fairly obvious that many governments need help in complying with requirements that mandate the dramatic shift in the way state and local governments present their financial information.

RETENTION OF FUND ACCOUNTING

Annual reports currently provide information about funds. Most funds are established by governing bodies (such as state legislatures, city councils, or school boards) to show restrictions on the planned use of resources or to measure, *in the short term,* the revenues and expenditures arising from certain activities. GASB 1 noted that annual reports should allow users to assess a government's accountability by assisting them in determining compliance with finance-related laws, rules, and regulations.

This new Statement requires governments to continue to present financial statements that provide fund information. The focus of these statements has been sharpened to require governments to report information about their major funds, including the general fund. In previous annual reports, fund information was reported in the aggregate by fund type. This often made it difficult for users to assess accountability of any "public servants."

Fund statements continue to measure and report the "operating results" of many funds by measuring cash on hand and other assets that can be easily converted to cash. These statements show the performance, in the short term, of individual funds using the same measures that many governments use when financing their current operations. The Board points out that if a government issues fifteen-year debt to build a school, it does not collect taxes in the first year sufficient to repay the *entire* debt; it levies and collects what is needed to make that year's required payments. On the other hand, when governments charge a fee to users for services—as is done for most water or electric utilities—fund information continues to be based on accrual accounting to ensure all costs of providing services are being measured.

THE ALL-IMPORTANT GOVERNMENTAL BUDGET

Showing budgetary compliance is an important component of government's accountability. (At the national level, with which GASB 34 has no connection, of course, THE BUDGET is undoubtedly the most widely recognized financial document.) At the state and local levels, diverse citizen groups, special interest groups, and individuals participate in the process of establishing the original annual operating budgets of the particular body.

Governments will be required to continue to provide budgetary comparison information in their annual reports. An important change that should certainly make the comparison more meaningful is the requirement to add the government's *original* budget to that comparison. Many governments revise their original budgets during the year for various reasons. Requiring governments to report that original document in addition to their *revised* budget adds a new analytical dimension and should increase the usefulness of the budgetary comparison.

Presumably, the original budget was the "best thought" of the adopting body at the time. Subsequent "revised" budgets could be the result of political pressures or personal preferences. The GASB concedes that budgetary changes are not necessarily undesirable. However, the Board decided that in the interest of accountability to those who were aware of, and may have made decisions based upon the original budget, inclusion of its contents could deter ill-considered changes. The comparison also gives the user a look at any changes that have been made. The Board suggested that this is an additional method of assessing the governmental body's ability to estimate and manage its general resources—without too many detours.

Thus, the original budget, the final appropriated budgets and the actual inflows, outflows and balances stated on the government's budgetary basis are mandated as required supplemental information (RSI) for the general fund and for each major special revenue fund that has a legally adopted annual budget. Rather than include this information in RSI, a government may elect to report these comparisons in a budgetary comparison statement as part of the basic financial statements.

NEW INFORMATION IS READILY AVAILABLE

For the first time, government financial managers are required to introduce the financial report by sharing their attitude toward and understanding of the transactions, events, and conditions reflected in the government's report and of the fiscal policies that govern its operations. The required MD&A should give the users an easily readable analysis of the government's *financial* performance for the year. Users thus have information they need to help them gauge the government's state of financial health as a result of the year's operations.

Additionally, financial managers themselves are in a better position to provide this analysis because, for the first time, the annual report also includes new government-wide financial statements prepared using accrual accounting for all of the government's activities. Most governmental utilities and private-sector companies use accrual accounting. With GASB 34, state and local governments join most of the rest of the world in using it. The reason for the change is that accrual accounting measures not just current assets and liabilities, but also long-term assets and liabilities (such as capital assets, including infrastructure, and general obligation debt). It also reports all revenues and *all* costs of providing services each year, not just those received or paid in the current year or soon after year-end. After all, government is an ongoing endeavor; officials elected or appointed come and go.

Users Benefit

These governmentwide financial statements undoubtedly will help users:

1. Assess the finances of a government in its entirety, including the year's operating results.

2. Determine whether a government's overall financial position improved or deteriorated.

3. Evaluate whether a government's current-year revenues were sufficient to pay for current-year services.

4. Be aware of the cost of providing services to the citizenry.

5. Become cognizant of the way in which a government finances its programs—through user fees and other program revenues, or general tax revenues.

6. Understand the extent to which a government has invested in capital assets, including roads, bridges, and other infrastructure assets.

7. Make better comparisons between governments.

REQUIRED INFORMATION AND FORMAT

GASB 34 sets financial reporting standards for state and local governments, including states, cities, towns, villages, and special-purpose governments such as school districts and public utilities. It establishes that the basic financial statements and required supplementary information for general purpose governments should consist of:

1. *Management's Discussion and Analysis.* MD&A introduces the basic financial statements and provides an analytical overview of the government's financial activities. Although it is required supplementary information and one would expect to find it in the final portion of the report, governments are required to present MD&A *before* the basic financial statements. Presumably the belief is that a clearly written—plain English, perhaps—introduction provides a link between the two perspectives (fund and government-wide) to prepare the reader for a better understanding of the financial statements.

2. *Basic Financial Statements.* The basic financial statements must include:

   a. *Government-wide financial statements,* consisting of a statement of net assets and a statement of activities. Prepared using the economic resources measurement focus and the accrual basis of accounting, these statements should report all of the assets, liabilities, revenues, expenses, and gains and losses of the government. Each statement should distinguish between the *governmental* and *business-type activities* of the primary government and between the total primary government and the separately presented component units by reporting each in separate columns. (*Fiduciary activities,* with resources not available to finance the government's programs, are not included in the government-wide statements.)

b. *Fund financial statements* consisting of a series of statements that focus on information about the government's major governmental and enterprise funds, including blended component units. Fund financial statements also should report information about a government's fiduciary funds and component units that are fiduciary in nature.

c. *Governmental* fund financial statements (including financial data for the general fund and special revenue, capital projects, debt service, and permanent funds). These are to be prepared using the current financial resources measurement focus and the modified accrual basis of accounting.

d. *Proprietary* fund financial statements (including financial data for enterprise and internal service funds) and *fiduciary* fund financial statements (including financial data for fiduciary funds and similar component units). This group is to be prepared using the economic resources measurement focus and the accrual basis of accounting.

e. *Notes to the financial statements* are notes and explanations that provide information which is *essential* to a user's understanding of the basic financial statements.

3. ***Required Supplementary Information (RSI).*** In addition to MD&A, this Statement requires *budgetary comparison schedules* to be presented as RSI along with other types of data as required by previous GASB pronouncements. This Statement also requires RSI for governments that use the modified approach for reporting infrastructure assets.

Special-purpose governments engaged in only governmental activities (such as some library districts) or engaged in both governmental and business-type activities (such as some school districts) should normally be reported in the same manner as general purpose governments. Special-purpose governments engaged only in business-type activities (such as utilities) should present the financial statements required for enterprise funds, including MD&A and other RSI.

CONTENT OF MD&A

MD&A should provide an objective and easily readable analysis of the government's financial activities based on currently known facts, decisions, or conditions. It should be emphasized that this section is a preparation for the casual reader who is less skilled in reading financial statements as well as for the more experienced "user" to understand fully the implications of the basic report.

MD&A should include:

1. Comparisons of the current year to the prior year based on the governmentwide information.
2. An analysis of the government's overall financial position and results of operations to assist users in assessing whether that financial position has improved or deteriorated as a result of the year's activities.
3. An analysis of balances and transactions of individual funds and significant budget variances.
4. A description of capital asset and long-term debt activity during the period.
5. A conclusion with a description of currently known facts, decisions, or conditions that could be expected to have a significant effect upon the financial position or results of operations.

GOVERNMENT-WIDE FINANCIAL STATEMENTS

The new annual reports contain much more comprehensive financial information. Government-wide statements now display information about the reporting government as a whole, except for its fiduciary activities. These statements include separate columns for the governmental and business-type activities of the primary government and its component parts. Government-wide statements are prepared using the economic resources measurement focus and the accrual basis of accounting. This latter requirement is a fairly dramatic step forward since heretofore governmental accounting followed only the modified-accrual basis. The statement must include a statement of net assets as well as all of the government's activities, not just those that cover costs by charging a fee for services, as currently required.

Governments should report all *capital assets,* including infrastructure assets, in the government-wide statement of net assets and generally should report depreciation expenses in the statement of activities. Infrastructure assets that are part of a network or subsystem of a network are not required to be depreciated as long as the government manages those assets using an asset management system that has certain characteristics and the government can document that the assets are being preserved approximately at (or above) a condition level established and disclosed by the government in the RSI.

To qualify for a qualified asset management system, the government must:

1. Have an up-to-date inventory of the eligible infrastructure assets.
2. Perform condition assessments of the eligible assets and summarize the results using a measurement scale.

3. Estimate each year the annual amounts necessary to maintain and preserve the assets at the established and disclosed condition level. Condition assessments are to be documented so that they can be replicated. The assessments may be performed by the government itself or by contract with an outside source.

The net assets of a government should be reported in three categories— *invested in capital assets net of related debt, restricted, and unrestricted.* Net assets are considered "restricted" when constraints are placed on their use by:

1. External sources such as creditors, grantors or contributors.
2. Laws or regulations of other governments.
3. Legal or constitutional provisions or enabling legislation.

Permanent endowments or permanent fund principal amounts included in restricted net assets should be displayed in two additional components— *expendable and nonexpendable.*

The government-wide *statement of activities* should be presented in a format that reports expenses minus program revenues, to obtain a measurement of "net (expense) revenue" for each of the government's functions. Program expenses should include all direct expenses. General revenues, such as taxes, and special and extraordinary items should be reported separately to arrive at the change in net assets for the period.

Special and extraordinary items are both significant transactions or other events, either unusual or infrequent, over which management has control. Both types should be reported separately at the bottom of the statement of activities with special items listed prior to any extraordinary items. These types of transactions or events over which a government does not have control should be disclosed in the notes to financial statements.

FUND FINANCIAL STATEMENTS

To report additional and detailed information about the primary government, separate fund financial statements should be presented for each fund category: governmental, proprietary and fiduciary.

1. *Governmental funds* report on the basic activities of the government, including general fund accounts and special revenue, capital projects, debt service, and permanent funds.
2. *Proprietary funds* cover activities that are generally financed and operated like private businesses such as enterprise (fees charged to outside users) and internal service funds.

3. *Fiduciary funds* include pension and other employee benefit and private purpose trust funds that cannot be used to support the government's own programs.

Required *governmental fund* statements are:

1. A balance sheet.
2. A statement of revenues, expenditures, and changes in fund balances.

Required *proprietary fund* statements are:

1. A statement of net assets.
2. A statement of revenues, expenses, and changes in fund net assets.
3. A statement of cash flows.

To allow users to assess the relationship between fund and government-wide financial statements, governments should present a summary reconciliation to the government-wide financial statements at the bottom of the fund financial statements or in an accompanying schedule.

Each of the fund statements should report separate columns for the *general fund* and for *other major governmental and enterprise funds.*

1. *Major funds* are funds in which revenues, expenditures/expenses, assets, or liabilities (excluding extraordinary items) are at least 10% of corresponding totals for all governmental or enterprise funds and at least 5% of the aggregate amount for all governmental and enterprise funds. Any other fund may be reported as a major fund if the government's officials consider it to be particularly important to financial statement users.
2. *Nonmajor funds* should be reported in the aggregate in a separate column.
3. *Internal service funds* also should be reported in the aggregate in a separate column on the proprietary fund statements.

Fund balances for governmental funds should also be segregated into *reserved* and *unreserved* categories. Proprietary fund net assets should be reported in the same categories required for the government-wide financial statements. Proprietary fund statements of net assets should distinguish between current and noncurrent assets and liabilities and should display restricted assets.

Proprietary fund statements of revenues, expenses, and changes in fund net assets should distinguish between operating and nonoperating revenues and expenses. These statements should also report capital contributions, contributions to permanent and term endowments, special and extraordinary items, and transfers separately at the bottom of the statement to arrive at the all-inclusive change in fund net assets. Cash flow statements should be prepared using the direct method.

Separate fiduciary fund statements (including component units that are fiduciary in nature) also should be presented as part of the fund financial statements. Fiduciary funds should be used to report assets that are held in a trustee or agency capacity for others and that cannot be used to support the government's own programs.

Required *fiduciary fund* statements are:

1. A statement of fiduciary net assets.
2. A statement of changes in fiduciary net assets.

Interfund activity includes interfund loans, interfund services provided and used, and interfund transfers. This activity should be reported separately in the fund financial statements and generally should be eliminated in the aggregated government-wide financial statements.

REQUIRED SUPPLEMENTARY INFORMATION

To demonstrate whether resources were obtained and used in accordance with the government's legally adopted budget, RSI should include budgetary comparison schedules for the general fund and for each major special revenue fund that has a legally adopted annual budget.

The budgetary comparison schedules should include:

1. The original budget.
2. The final appropriated budgets for the reporting period.
3. Actual inflows, outflows, and balances, stated on the government's budgetary basis.

As pointed out above, the Statement also requires certain disclosures in RSI for governments that use the modified approach for reporting infrastructure assets and data currently required by earlier Statements.

EFFECTIVE DATE AND TRANSITION

The requirements of this Statement were effective in three phases based on a government's total annual revenues in the first fiscal year ending after June 15,

1999. Governments with total annual revenues (excluding extraordinary items) of $100 million or more (phase 1) should apply this Statement for fiscal years beginning after June 15, 2001. Medium-size governments with at least $10 million but less than $100 million in revenues (phase 2) should apply this Statement for fiscal years beginning after June 15, 2002. Smaller governments with less than $10 million in revenues (phase 3) should apply this Statement for periods beginning after June 15, 2003. Earlier application is encouraged.

Governments that elected early implementation of this Statement for periods beginning before June 15, 2000, also implemented GASB Statement 33, *Accounting and Financial Reporting for Nonexchange Transactions,* at the same time. (See below.)

REQUIREMENTS FOR PROSPECTIVE AND RETROSPECTIVE REPORTING

Prospective reporting of general infrastructure assets is required at the effective dates of this Statement. Retroactive reporting of all existing major general governmental infrastructure assets is encouraged at that date.

For phase 1 and phase 2 governments, retroactive reporting is *required four years after* the effective date on the basic provisions for all major general infrastructure assets that were acquired or significantly reconstructed, or that received significant improvements, in fiscal years ending after June 30, 1980. Thus, larger governments will have to report retroactively all major general infrastructure assets for all fiscal years beginning after June 15, 2005 and medium-size governments have until fiscal years beginning after June 15, 2006.

Phase 3 governments are encouraged to report infrastructure retroactively, but may elect to report general infrastructure prospectively only.

GUIDANCE ON MODIFIED ACCRUAL STANDARDS

The Governmental Accounting Standards Board issued Interpretation 6, *Recognition and Measurement of Certain Liabilities and Expenditures in Governmental Fund Financial Statements.* This Interpretation clarifies the application of standards for modified accrual recognition of fund liabilities and expenditures in governmental fund financial statements.

In GASB 34, the Board concluded that traditional governmental fund financial statements continue to provide useful information for assessing a government's fiscal accountability and should continue to be prepared with a current financial resources measurement focus and modified accrual basis of accounting. This Interpretation clarifies undefined terms and reduces differences in the ways that financial statement preparers, auditors, and others interpret and apply the standard.

The goal is to provide an interpretation that will promote more consistent and comparable reporting. The Board pointed out that the effect of the Interpretation may include both increases and decreases in accruals for governments that have applied the standards differently.

The effective date of the proposed Interpretation coincides with the effective date of Statement 34 for the reporting government.

GASB 35 FOR PUBLIC COLLEGES AND UNIVERSITIES

After an earlier decision by the Governmental Accounting Standards Board not to require a separate financial reporting model for public colleges and universities in order to make it easier for state and local governments to include these institutions in their financial statements, the GASB issued a proposal in July, 1999 to provide accounting and financial reporting guidance for public colleges and universities in their separately issued financial statements. That proposal became GASB 35.

This Statement amends GASB 34, *Basic Financial Statements—and Management's Discussion and Analysis—for State and Local Governments,* to include public colleges and universities within its guidance for general purpose external financial reporting.

It is anticipated that this step will make it easier to compare public institutions and their private counterparts. Such a step had been requested by GASB constituents.

Under the new guidance, public colleges and universities can report their finances as public institutions:

1. Engaged only in business-type activities.
2. Engaged only in governmental activities.
3. Engaged in both governmental and business-type activities.

A public institution is also required to include the following in separately issued financial reports, regardless of whether or not they are legally separate entities:

1. Management's discussion and analysis (MD&A).
2. Basic financial statements, as appropriate for the category of special-purpose government reporting.
3. Notes to the financial statements.
4. Required supplementary information other than MD&A.

The requirements of the Statement are effective in three phases for public institutions that are not part of another reporting entity, beginning with fiscal years beginning after June 15, 2001. All public institutions that are part of (or are component units of) a primary government are required to implement this standard at least by the same time as its primary government, regardless of the phase-in guidance contained in GASB 34.

Public colleges and universities are required to report infrastructure assets as follows:

1. Public institutions that are not part of another primary government and report as either special-purpose governments engaged only in governmental activities or engaged in both governmental and business-type activities must report infrastructure in accordance with the phase-in guidance of GASB 34 beginning with fiscal years ending after June 15, 2005.

2. Public institutions that report as special-purpose governments engaged only in business-type activities are required to report infrastructure upon implementation, without regard to the phase-in periods included in Statement 34.

GASB 33 ON NONEXCHANGE TRANSACTIONS

Late in 1998, the Governmental Accounting Standards Board issued GASB Statement 33, *Accounting and Financial Reporting for Nonexchange Transactions,* which specifies the accounting and reporting for nonexchange transactions involving financial or capital resources. These transactions include most taxes, grants, and donations. The Statement is effective for periods beginning after June 15, 2000.

In a nonexchange transaction, the government gives or receives value without directly receiving or giving equal value in exchange. When there isn't an exchange, it can be difficult to decide *when* a transaction should be recognized in the financial statements. Statement 33 attempts to simplify the problem.

The timing of financial statement recognition will depend on the nature of the nonexchange transaction as well as the basis of accounting (accrual or modified accrual). The GASB has identified four classes of nonexchange transactions:

1. Derived tax revenues, such as sales and income taxes. These will be recognized when the underlying exchange on which the government imposes the tax actually occurs. An example would be when a customer buys a washing machine or refrigerator that is subject to a sales tax.

2. Imposed nonexchange revenues, such as property taxes and fines. These are to be recognized as assets when the government has an enforceable

legal claim. For example, property taxes receivable generally will be recognized on the lien date, even though a lien may not be formally placed on the property at that date. Revenues will be recognized in the period in which the resources are required to be used.

3. Government-mandated nonexchange transactions, such as federal or state programs that state or local governments are required to provide. These will be recognized when all eligibility requirements are met, as specified in Statement 33. For example, when a recipient is required to incur allowable costs before reimbursement is made, the incurring of allowable costs is an eligibility requirement.

4. Voluntary nonexchange transactions, such as most grants, appropriations, donations, and endowments. These will also be recognized when the Statement 33 eligibility requirements are met. These requirements include contingencies. For example, to qualify for a grant, a recipient may be required to provide matching resources.

For revenue recognition on the modified accrual basis, resources also should be "available," as defined in existing standards. Statement 33 goes hand in hand with the Board's standards on the governmental and the college and university financial reporting models under GASB 34. The Board feels that GASB 33 will improve consistency in how governments report nonexchange transactions.

GASB 36 ON SYMMETRY BETWEEN RECIPIENTS AND PROVIDERS IN ACCOUNTING FOR CERTAIN SHARED REVENUES

GASB 36 amends GASB 33, *Accounting and Financial Reporting for Nonexchange Transactions,* which required recipients of shared derived tax or imposed nonexchange revenue to account for it differently from the provider government. This practice could have resulted in the two governments recognizing the sharing at different times.

The new Statement provides symmetrical accounting treatment for both the giver and receiver of the shared revenue. Statement 36 eliminates the timing difference by requiring recipients to account for the sharing in the same way as provider governments.

It was to be implemented simultaneously with Statement 33, which became mandatory for periods beginning after June 15, 2000.

Chapter 5
International Accounting

CONTENTS

The use of International Accounting Standards (IASs) and International Financial Reporting Standards (IFRSs), starting January 1, 2005, by listed public companies in the European Union (EU) is considered by U.S. regulators to be an important move toward global uniformity in standards for cross-border securities offerings. A representative of the SEC, testifying before a congressional committee, viewed Europe's shift from many national accounting standards of varying quality and completeness to a single EU standard that was developed in an independent and transparent manner as an important development for both issuers and investors. It also appears to be a natural progression from the adoption of a common currency.

END OF THE EUROPEAN FINANCIAL STATEMENT TOWER OF BABEL?

Many European companies that offer securities in the United States must reconcile their own country's standards to U.S. generally accepted accounting principles (GAAP), others use IASs. However, many prepare their financial statements in U.S. GAAP in the first place. Much of the current reporting complexities that arise from this approach would be reduced under a common EU standard.

IASs and IFRSs applied correctly and consistently and enforced effectively would provide a higher degree of quality and transparency in financial statements than the individual systems in the EU countries at present.

The effects of accounting standards uniformity in Europe will also be generally favorable for U.S. companies doing business abroad because it is expected that U.S. companies will continue to be able to list in the EU using U.S. GAAP.

The benefits of IAS/IFRS adoption in the EU may take on even greater significance if the FASB and the International Accounting Standards Board (IASB) make substantial progress toward achieving convergence of accounting principles.

THE IASB AGENDA FOR IMPROVING EXISTING STANDARDS

The goal of a global convergence of accounting standards moved closer to reality in May 2002, when the International Accounting Standards Board (IASB) unveiled plans for a series of key improvements in the current standards that govern cross-border securities offerings.

Those changes, advanced in the form of an exposure draft, seek to foster convergence of international accounting standards by establishing uniformity in a number of murky areas of financial reporting.

In addition to eliminating accounting loopholes, such as the use of a narrow definition of "related parties" by some countries, the exposure draft also seeks to prohibit accountants from labeling items of income or expense as "extraordinary items," either in the income statement or in the notes.

The plan also eliminates certain options for accountants using IASs, including the LIFO (last-in, first-out) inventory valuation method that is used here, as well as in several other countries.

Calling the exposure draft a first step toward establishing a globally accepted set of accounting standards, IASB officials pledged to press forward to "promote convergence on high-quality solutions" in other areas where cross-border differences exist.

A Closer Look at Problems to Be Faced

While the Board is actively working on global GAAP convergence, its members as well as others in the standard-setting arena are aware of problems. Politically, the issue is sensitive, as was brought out at the 2002 Accounting Standards and Financial Reporting conference of the New York Society of Security Analysts (NYSSA). There is little question that convergence is likely to take the form of moving IAS GAAP closer to U.S. GAAP. The United States has the most developed capital markets in the world, but at times the accounting standards have been unnecessarily complicated. This fact was admitted and corrected in the cooperative endeavor when the IASB and the FASB worked on developing their earnings-per-share (EPS) Standards.

The conference brought out the fact that the IASB realizes that although European companies being required to use IASs by 2005 is a giant leap forward, convergence will not be without problems. Impediments to convergence include:

- General resistance to change.
- The cynical, but undeniable, conviction that convergence inevitably results in a move to the lowest common denominator.
- Recent revelations of accounting and auditing wrongdoing by some high-profile U.S. companies could slow down the process of convergence.
- Each country or group of countries questioning whether or not their own systems would prove more effective.
- The complexity of the U.S. accounting provisions being seen as another barrier, although some European systems, such as Germany's, have been even more convoluted. The consensus in Europe now is that simplification is essential.
- The U.S. system provides a great deal of explicit and transparent data but is widely seen as more open to manipulation than the European.
- The perceived role of the U.S. auditor. European auditors are mandated to define "true and fair" value. Europe tends to see the United States as heavily dependent on the principle "buyer beware." Can the auditor be trusted?

STEADY GROWTH TO PREEMINENCE IN GLOBAL STANDARD SETTING

There is no question but that the IASB has enjoyed a steady growth in influence, and acceptance of its right to be the body to bring a reasonable degree of conformity to global financial accounting standards. Admittedly, this has not always been easy. Early gains in providing a base for an accounting system for developing nations and economies validated their efforts then. Gradually, countries like the United States, the United Kingdom and the now dissolved G4+1, at least worked together to try to bring conformity to some of the more difficult standards.

The reorganization after the acceptance of the core set of accounting standards by the International Organization of Securities Commissions (IOSCO) and the inclusion of the Standards Advisory Council has given the IASB further legitimacy. But the real validation stamp has been the decision by the EU requiring that all listed companies adopt the IASs and IFRSs by 2005.

European Union Plans to Adopt IASs and IFRSs

In June 2002, the European Union did, indeed, adopt the European Commission's (EC's) International Accounting Standards Regulation, which require publicly traded companies to use IASs and IFRSs in their consolidated accounts by January 1, 2005, after a formal EU endorsement process. There will be a temporary exception for companies that are currently traded in the United States and use U.S. GAAP and for companies that have issued debt instruments but not equity instruments. Those companies will be required to comply with international standards by January 1, 2007.

Endorsement of International Accounting and Financial Reporting Standards

After adopting the European Commission's International Accounting Standards Regulation in June 2002, the next step toward the application of IASs and IFRSs by listed companies (including banks and insurance companies) in the EU from 2005 onward was the endorsement of those IASs already in existence. The EU points out that companies should already be preparing for the changeover. The European Commission followed through and adopted a Regulation at the end of September 2003, endorsing International Accounting Standards (IASs), including related interpretations (SICs). This, in effect, confirms the requirement for their compulsory use from 2005 under the terms of the general IAS Regulation adopted by the European Parliament and the Council in 2002.

The Commission's adoption of this implementing Regulation follows the Accounting Regulatory Committee's unanimous endorsement of IASs in July. It includes all existing IASs and SICs, except for IASs 32 and 39 and related SICs 5, 16 and 17. IAS 32 and 39. These items, dealing with the accounting and disclosure of financial instruments, are not included because they are currently in the process of being revised by the IASB, in co-operation with European accounting experts.

It is generally felt that adoption by the Commission of this Regulation, endorsing most of the existing International Accounting Standards and publishing them in the EU's official languages, will help the 7000 or so listed EU companies affected to get ready for 2005, when their consolidated accounts are required to be in line with IAS. Expectations are that this will put an end to the current Tower of Babel in financial reporting, improve competition and transparency and make the free movement of capital much easier in Europe.

Before the IASs and IFRSs become legally binding under the Regulation, they had to be endorsed by the Commission, following consultation with Member States in the Accounting Regulatory Committee and receiving the views of the European Financial Reporting Advisory Group (EFRAG). This endorsement is precisely what the Commission has now done, in the case of all IASs (except 32 and 39), with the adoption of this latest Regulation.

To contribute towards the consistent application of IASs across the EU, the endorsed IAS will shortly be published in the official EU languages in the Official Journal of the EU. The first endorsement process was delayed in order to produce high quality translations. In total, there are at present 34 existing

IASs (including IASs 32 and 39) and 31 existing SICs (including SICs 5, 16 and 17), which cover about 1,500 pages.

To ensure appropriate political oversight, the Regulation established a new EU mechanism for assessing the quality of the IAS translations adopted by the IASB. On the basis of the opinion of the newly established Accounting Regulatory Committee, composed of representatives of the Member States, and with the technical advice of the European Financial Reporting Advisory Group (EFRAG), the European Commission makes the decisions relating to the endorsement of IASs and IFRSs. The Commission actively works with the Accounting Regulatory Committee on the examination of completed translations.

EU Parliament Updates Financial Reporting Rules in Line with the IAS Regulation

In May 2003, the European Union's Council of Ministers approved the definitive adoption of the Directive amending the European Union's Accounting Directives. This, in effect, adopts changes approved by the European Parliament in January 2003, bringing existing EU rules into line with current best practice. They complement the International Accounting Standards Regulation, adopted in June 2002, that requires all EU companies listed on a regulated market to use IASs and IFRSs from 2005 onward and allows Member States to extend this Regulation to all companies. These amendments allow Member States that do not apply the requirement to all companies to move toward similar, high-quality financial reporting. They allow appropriate accounting for special-purpose vehicles, improve the disclosure of risks and uncertainties, and increase the consistency of audit reports across the EU.

The Commission's view is that Parliament's support for the proposal sends a strong political signal not only that the European Union is serious about achieving an integrated capital market by 2005 but also that it is committed to improving financial reporting and auditing for *all* EU companies, whether listed or not. High-quality financial reporting is essential so that investors and customers can make informed decisions about these companies.

As stated the IAS Regulation requires all EU companies listed on a regulated market to prepare their consolidated accounts in accordance with endorsed IASs and IFRSs from 2005 onward. Member States may extend this requirement to unlisted companies and to annual accounts. Where endorsed IASs and IFRSs are not applied, the detailed provisions of the Fourth and Seventh Accounting Directives will continue to act as the basis of EU accounting requirements. These Directives may, therefore, continue to be applicable to as many as 5 million companies in Europe.

Moreover, as pointed out, the proposed amendments would bring EU accounting requirements into line with modern accounting theory and practice.

In doing so, all inconsistencies with IASs and IFRSs are removed. Notably, it makes it more difficult for a company to hide liabilities by setting up artificial structures (i.e., special-purpose vehicles) that, in substance, it controls but that, considering only the shareholdings, appear to be largely unrelated. This is considered a vital step in the proper treatment of off-balance-sheet financing.

Given the link, in some Member States, between annual accounts and taxation, it is important that each Member State align with IASs and IFRSs at a pace appropriate to that individual country. Accordingly, most changes are implemented as Member State options allowing gradual alignment of national accounting requirements with these standards.

Besides modernizing accounting requirements, the proposed amendments make clear that, in the annual report, the analysis of risks and uncertainties facing the company should not be restricted to only the financial aspects of its business. This is in order to encourage disclosure of key social and environmental aspects where relevant. The proposed amendments also move toward a more harmonized presentation of statutory audit reports by outlining the necessary content of such reports, which are a valuable assurance that accounts are reliable. The new requirements are consistent with those of International Standards on Auditing issued by the International Auditing and Assurance Standards Board.

Directive Exempts Some SMEs from Financial Reporting Rules

The EU's Council of Ministers adopted a wide-ranging Directive in May 2003, amending the Accounting Directives to bring existing EU rules into line with current best practices. These amendments will complement the International Accounting Standards Regulation adopted in June 2002. Adoption of the May 2003 Directive allows thousands of small and medium-sized enterprises (SMEs) to be exempted from certain accounting requirements. The Directive amends the existing Accounting Directives by raising by about 17 percent the thresholds for turnover and balance sheet total under which Member States can apply the exemptions. This action is expected to lessen the regulatory burden on thousands of smaller and medium-sized companies in the EU while maintaining sufficient transparency and protection against fraud. The Council of Ministers believes that allowing small and medium-sized businesses to spend more time on creating wealth and less on administration will also give the European economy as a whole a much needed boost.

Under the Fourth and Seventh Company Law Directives, also known as the Accounting Directives, Member States have the option of granting SMEs exemptions from certain financial reporting and disclosure requirements usually imposed on limited liability companies. For example, Member States may allow them to publish only an:

- Abridged balance sheet.
- Abridged notes to the accounts.
- Abridged profit and loss account.

In addition, Member States may exempt small, but *not* medium-sized companies, from:

- Publishing a profit and loss account or an annual report.
- Disclosing certain types of information in their accounts.
- Having their accounts audited.

The definitions of SMEs in the Fourth Company Law Directive and the thresholds are for accounting purposes only. To qualify under the Directive as either a small company or a medium-sized one, companies must meet at least two of three criteria:

1. They may not have more than a certain number of employees.
2. Their balance sheet total (the value of the company's main assets defined as the total of subscribed capital unpaid, formation expenses, fixed assets, current assets prepayments, and accrued income) must be below a specified figure.
3. Their net turnover (income from sales after deduction of rebates, value added tax, and other turnover taxes) must be below a specified figure.

Under EU law, these thresholds are revised every five years to take into account economic and monetary trends. On the basis of these trends since the last revision, the new Directive, which follows a Commission proposal in January 2003, increases the thresholds for balance sheet total and net turnover by 16.8 percent as follows:

- Small companies: Balance sheet total — old, €3.125 million; new, €3.65 million.
- Net turnover — old, €6.25 million; new, €7.30 million.
- Medium-sized: Balance sheet total — old, €12.5 million; new, €14.6 million.
- Net turnover — old, €25 million; new, €29.2 million.

The Directive leaves the "employees" threshold unchanged, at 50 to qualify as a small company and 250 for medium-sized enterprises.

These definitions of SMEs in the Accounting Directives differ from the definitions in Commission Recommendations that are used by Member States, the Commission, and the European Investment Bank, among others, for defining SMEs eligible for support programs and loans. These were also recently modified.

The EFRAG Recommends Endorsement of IASB Standards

The European Financial Reporting Advisory Group, a group composed of accounting experts from the private sector in several countries, was requested by the European Commission to review the IASB standards. The Group was asked to confirm that there were no remaining incompatibilities between International Financial Reporting Standards (from IAS 1 to 41 with related Standing Interpretations Committee [SIC] interpretations) and the Fourth and Seventh Directives as modified under proposals (dated November 13, 2001) still under discussion.

EFRAG reviewed IASs 1 to 41 (inclusive) and the related SIC interpretations 1 to 33 inclusive (the current standards) as of March 1, 2002. The evaluation of the current standards was based on:

- A general review of those standards;
- EFRAG's experience of the application of those standards in practice by various companies within Europe;
- The Group's general knowledge of discussions surrounding those standards; and
- Input from standard setters and market participants.

Based on this review, EFRAG was of the opinion that the current standards met the requirements of the Regulation of the European Parliament and of the Council on the application of International Accounting Standards and International Financial Reporting Standards by EU-listed companies from 2005 onward in two respects:

1. They were not contrary to the true and fair principle set out in Article 2(3) of the Fourth Directive and Article 16(3) of the Seventh Directive.
2. They met the criteria of understandability, relevance, reliability and comparability required of the financial information needed for making economic decisions and assessing the stewardship of management.

For those reasons, the accounting experts of EFRAG thought that it was in the European interest that the process of adopting the current standards should be set in motion. Accordingly, they recommended endorsement of the current standards *en bloc.*

EFRAG noted that the IASB was actively reviewing a number of the current standards, and changes and improvements were expected to result from this review. The Group will give its advice on those changes when the changes are promulgated. However, this did not in any way affect the recommendation that the current standards should be endorsed.

Expect Agreement on IASs to Help Investors and Business in the EU

The European Commission has welcomed the Council's adoption, in a single reading, of the Regulation requiring listed companies, including banks and insurance companies, to prepare their consolidated accounts in accordance with IASs and IFRSs from 2005 onward. The Regulation will help eliminate barriers to cross-border trading in securities by ensuring that company accounts throughout the EU are more reliable and transparent and that they can be more easily compared.

The Commission believes that this should increase market efficiency and reduce the cost of raising capital for companies, ultimately improving competitiveness and helping boost growth. The Regulation was proposed by the European Commission in February 2001. It is a key measure in the Financial Services Action Plan, on which significant progress has been made recently. Unlike Directives, EU Regulations have the force of law without requiring transposition into national legislation. Member States have the option of extending the requirements of this Regulation to unlisted companies and to the production of individual accounts.

The Commission points out that it had put forward the IAS proposal long before Enron et al., but that the Regulation is one of a series of measures that will help protect the EU from such problems. Others include the Commission's recent Recommendation on Auditor Independence and its proposal to amend the Accounting Directives.

European officials think that the adoption will mean that:

- Investors and other stakeholders will be able to compare like with like.
- It will help European firms compete on equal terms when raising capital in world markets.
- The U.S. will be inclined to work even more actively with the EU toward full convergence of accounting standards.

CSA Proposals Affecting Foreign Issuers in Canada

The Canadian Securities Administrators (CSA), the body that coordinates certain activities of the various provincial and territorial securities regulators in Canada, has issued a request for comment on proposed nationally harmonized continuous disclosure requirements for reporting issuers as well as exemptions for eligible foreign issuers. Comments were requested by September 19, 2002, however, no further action has been taken. Highlights, from an accounting perspective include:

- Permission for Securities Exchange Commission (SEC) issuers to file financial statements prepared in accordance with U.S. GAAP, provided that for a two-year period after starting to use U.S. GAAP, their statements will have to be reconciled to Canadian GAAP. SEC foreign issuers may file without reconciliation to Canadian GAAP. Eligible foreign issuers (as defined) may file financial statements prepared in accordance with International Financial Reporting Standards, *without reconciliation.* Certain designated foreign issuers may file financial statements in accordance with principles in designated foreign jurisdiction. Others must reconcile.
- Removal of any size exemption for filing of management's discussion and analysis (MD&A) of financial position and results of operations and inclusion of a requirement for Board of Directors to review MD&A.
- The MD&A must include discussion of the outcome of previously disclosed forward-looking information, disclosures about off-balance-sheet arrangements and critical accounting policies.
- Shortened filing deadlines for annual and interim financial statements.

AcSB of Canada Attitude Toward Convergence. The Accounting Standards Board (AcSB) of Canada states that its international activities have become increasingly important to its mission. It believes that in the absence of any clearly demonstrated, unique Canadian circumstances, it is unlikely that the AcSB will adopt a new accounting standard in Canada that differs from those of its international colleagues. Consequently, the activities of such international groups as the IASB and FASB significantly affect Canadian standard setting.

The AcSB's international program currently has two fundamental points of focus:

1. Harmonization with U.S. GAAP—that is, elimination of significant unjustifiable differences with FASB standards. Particularly, in light of the numerous cross-border transactions between Canada and the U.S., the AcSB is working to eliminate existing differences between Canadian and U.S. GAAP and to ensure that new differences are not created.
2. Convergence with the highest quality of U.S. and international accounting standards—that is, working with the FASB, IASB, and other national standard-setting bodies to agree on much needed improvements to existing standards and the development of new standards.

New Zealand FRSB/ASRB Adopts International Standards

The Financial Reporting Standards Board (FRSB) has agreed to implement the decision by the Accounting Standards Review Board (ASRB) that New Zealand reporting entities should apply international financial reporting standards in general-purpose financial reporting on periods beginning on or after January 1, 2007 (or, from January 1, 2005).

The Board indicated that it uses the term "international financial reporting standards" to refer to the IASB's standards and the *Framework for the Preparation and Presentation of Financial Statements.* The Board specified that this includes the original IASs inherited by the IASB from its predecessor body, the IASC, and the interpretations of these standards (SICs), issued by the IASC's Standing Interpretations Committee. In addition, New Zealand's FRSB, of course, will adopt the IFRSs, the new standards being issued by the IASB, and the interpretations of these standards (IFRICs) issued by the IASB's International Financial Reporting Interpretations Committee.

The ASRB is aware of the need to ensure that adoption of IFRSs do not result in compliance costs that exceed the benefits of the reports produced. IFRSs are therefore required to be adopted only by reporting entities. The ASRB points out that the term "reporting entity" is used by it only in the conceptual sense and has yet to be defined operationally.

The FRSB developed for consideration by the ASRB a new financial reporting structure that is intended to make the reporting entity concept operational. The FRSB's proposed structure was reviewed by the ASRB, and in turn proposed to the Ministry of Economic Development. The Ministry is expected to issue, around late August 2003, a discussion paper seeking public comment on the structure. The general approach in the structure, as proposed by the FRSB/ASRB, is similar to that currently followed in Australia and is intended to replace the relevant requirements of the Financial Reporting Act of 1993 on exempt companies as well as the Institute of Chartered Accountants of New Zealand's Framework for Differential Reporting.

The proposed structure extends legal requirements on financial reporting to a wider set of entities—in particular, partnerships, charities, and trusts. However, because of the higher thresholds, fewer entities will be subject to legal requirements than is currently the case.

The question of which entities are reporting entities is unlikely to be resolved before late 2003. However, preparation for early adoption of IFRS cannot wait for resolution of this question and therefore the issue of exposure drafts of new standards will have to proceed while the scope of application of the standards remains uncertain, at least at the margins.

One Set of Standards.   The ASRB has decided that there should continue to be one set of standards for application by all reporting entities. However, IFRSs are developed for application by profit-oriented entities; therefore, in order for IFRSs to also be applied by public benefit entities, it will be necessary in the case of some IFRSs to introduce additional requirements on measurement and recognition applicable to only public benefit entities. Furthermore, it may be appropriate to add disclosure requirements, and these could in some cases be applicable to all reporting entities. Thus, the intended overall effect of introducing additional requirements is to make the resulting standards more relevant and appropriate to New Zealand reporting entities, in particular, public benefit entities.

New Zealand defines *public benefit reporting entities* as reporting entities whose primary objective is to provide goods or services for a community or a social benefit and where any risk capital has been provided with a view to supporting that primary objective rather than for the financial return to equity shareholders. Most central government, local government, and not-for-profit entities are public benefit entities.

Application Date. New Zealand IFRSs (NZ IFRSs) will apply to reporting periods beginning on or after January 1, 2007. However, reporting entities electing to adopt IFRSs for reporting periods beginning on or after January 1, 2005, will apply the standards early.

Reporting entities adopting IFRSs from 2005 are required to apply the following standards:

- NZ IASs, based on the revised IASs.
- NZ IFRS 1, *First-Time Adoption of International Financial Reporting Standards,* and other new NZ IFRSs that are applicable from 2005.

It is expected that the IASB's revision of IASs and development of the new IFRSs will be completed by March 2004 and that these standards will have been reviewed, gone through due process, and been approved as NZ IFRSs by the ASRB by June 2004.

Reporting entities adopting IFRSs from 2007 will apply NZ IFRSs then in effect. However, until 2007, these entities will continue to apply IFRSs currently in effect. When a reporting entity first applies IFRSs, whether from 2007 or early from 2005, it must apply NZ IFRS 1, *First-Time Adoption of International Financial Reporting Standards.* The key principle underlying first-time adoption is that the entity's accounting policies must comply with each IFRS applicable to the entity and effective at the reporting date, and IFRS must be applied throughout all periods presented in the financial statements and in the opening IFRS statement of financial position.

Australian Board Considering International Standards

In July 2002, the Financial Reporting Council (FRC) of Australia determined to endorse formally the adoption of IASs and IFRSs for Australian reporting entities by January 1, 2005. The FRC's decision is in line with Australian government policy and legislation calling for the international convergence of accounting standards.

The IASB believes that the FRC's announcement demonstrates growing support for the development and implementation of a single set of high-quality global accounting standards by 2005. Australia's adoption of international accounting standards closely followed the European Union's decision in June 2002 to adopt international standards for publicly traded companies within the EU. The addition of highly developed economies to the list of countries embracing the IASs adds validity to the international body.

Also in June, the Canadian Securities Administrators proposed for public comment that certain foreign listed companies in Canada be able to use the IASB's standards without reconciliation to Canadian generally accepted accounting principles, beginning in 2005.

The Board considers the decision of Australia's FRC a sign of increased momentum behind the IASB's efforts. The Board believes that this vote of confidence will increase momentum for convergence toward high-quality international standards. The input and active participation of interested parties in Australia and the Australian Accounting Standards Board (AASB) are and will remain a vital element in ensuring the IASB's success. It is through national standard setters, such as the AASB, and the members of various committees that the IASB is able jointly to:

- Develop high-quality solutions to accounting issues.
- Leverage resources to research topics not yet on the international agenda so as to expedite conclusions.
- Reach interested parties throughout the world.
- Better understand differences in operating environments, thus fulfilling the role as a global standard setter.

UK Board Considers Amending Standards

The Accounting Standards Board (ASB) in the United Kingdom has made a start toward implementing international standards in order to ease the transition to International Financial Reporting Standards in 2005. Six proposals to amend existing UK standards were issued in mid-2002. Included are changes to the standards dealing with:

1. The effects of changes in foreign exchange rates.
2. Financial reporting in hyperinflationary economies.
3. Related-party disclosures.

4. Events after the balance sheet date.
5. Inventories and long-term contracts.
6. Property, plant, and equipment.

The ASB expects to issue an exposure draft on hedge accounting soon.

THE IASB ANNOUNCES NEW WORK PROGRAM

After extensive consultation with its Standards Advisory Council, national accounting standard setters, regulators, and other interested parties, the IASB announced its new program of technical projects. These build on and carry forward the IASB's initial agenda, announced in July 2001.

The main program is made up of three elements. It is probably not too surprising that these topics are also at the top of the FASB's list of things to do:

1. Consolidations (including special-purpose entities).
2. Revenue — definition, recognition, and related aspects of liabilities.
3. Convergence of standards on topics on which the IASB believes that a high-quality solution is available from existing international and national standards:
   a. Pension accounting.
   b. Income taxes.
   c. Segment reporting.
   d. Revaluations.

In addition, the IASB proposes to embark on active research, often in collaboration with others, on:

• The application of international accounting standards to small and medium-sized entities and in emerging economies (the small and medium economies project).
• Lease accounting.
• Accounting concepts, including a strategic review of the basic elements of accounting and design work on measurement, focusing initially on impairments.
• Aspects of accounting for financial instruments.

The intention is that, when preparatory work on these topics is concluded, they should be moved to the IASB's main agenda.

Longer-Range Plans

Looking further forward, the IASB will encourage the national standard setters and others to carry out initial work on projects that may in time be included in the IASB's main agenda. These projects include:

- Management reporting in relation to financial reports (loosely termed MD&A reporting).
- Accounting for extractive industries.
- Accounting for public and other concessions (e.g., public to private arrangements for transport, health and other infrastructure activities).

The IASB announced that this wide-ranging program has been drawn up in consultation with representatives of the world's business community and reflects the consensus on priorities for the next stage of the IASB's work. The IASB has been working hard on its initial agenda (after rising from the ashes of the IASC). The chairman points to its accomplishments:

- It has issued its Preface to International Financial Reporting Standards.
- It has published extensive proposals for improvements to 12 standards as well as the 2 standards on financial instruments.
- It has published its proposals on the first-time application of international standards.
- It will soon publish phase 1 of the business combinations project.
- As resources become available, the IASB will phase in the new projects alongside the remaining projects from the initial agenda.

The IASB is well aware that the development of such a program must rely on the strength of its liaison relationship with national standard setters. Board members are committed to pooling resources, monitoring each others' work, sharing research findings, and developing new standards together to meet the legitimate expectations of the global business community.

Moving Ahead on New Business Combination Standard

The IASB is in the process of drafting its new business combination standard (which sounds very much like the FASB's provisions in Statements 141 and 142). The major decisions thus far include:

- Pooling-of-interests accounting (merger accounting) would be prohibited.
- Goodwill should not be amortized. Instead, it should be carried on the balance sheet indefinitely, subject to an impairment test.

- Intangible assets acquired in a business combination before the effective date of the new standard and recognized separately from goodwill at the effective date should be reclassified as goodwill if they are:
  - Not separable and do not arise from contractual or legal rights.
  - An assembled work force.
- At the adoption date, the useful life of intangible assets should be reassessed and intangible assets reclassified as having finite or indefinite lives.
- The existing 20-year useful life rebuttable presumption for finite lived intangible assets will not be carried forward to the new standard.

Accounting for Share-Based Payment

The IASB, in November 2002, published proposals in Exposure Draft (ED) 2, *Share-Based Payment,* on how entities should account for share-based payment transactions, including grants of share options to employees. The proposals in ED 2 replace the disclosure requirements in IAS 19, *Employee Benefits,* dealing with equity compensation benefits. In developing its proposals, the IASB concluded that there was no valid reason that share-based payment transactions involving grants of shares or share options to employees should not be accounted for in the same way as other transactions in which an entity receives resources as consideration for its equity instruments. Therefore, the proposals include recognizing an expense for the consumption of the resources received, whether in the form of employee services, other services, or goods.

Typically, transactions in which share options are granted to employees are not recognized in an entity's financial statements. As a result, the entity's expenses have been understated and its profits often vastly overstated. The Board feels that this measure will close an obvious gap in accounting standards.

Basic Provisions.   The Exposure Draft covers six main principles:

1. All share-based payment transactions should be recognized in the financial statements, using a fair value measurement basis. An expense should be recognized when the goods or services received are consumed. There are no proposed exemptions from these requirements.

2. In principle, transactions in which goods or services are received as consideration for equity instruments of the entity should be measured at the fair value of the goods or services received or the fair value of the equity instruments granted, whichever is more readily determinable.

   For transactions measured at the fair value of the equity instruments granted (e.g., transactions with employees), fair value should be estimated at grant date. For transactions measured at the fair value of the goods or services received, fair value should be estimated at the date of receipt of those goods or services.

3. To estimate the fair value of a share option, where an observable market price does not exist, an option pricing model should be used. The Exposure Draft does not specify which particular model should be used. The entity should disclose the model used, the inputs to that model, and other information about how fair value was measured.

4. The Exposure Draft contains various proposals on estimating the fair value of employee share options, to allow for differences between employee share options and traded options. For example, the valuation should take into account all types of vesting conditions, including service conditions and performance conditions. The grant date valuation should be reduced to allow for the possibility of forfeiture because of failure to satisfy vesting conditions.

5. Repricing of options (and other changes in terms and conditions), should be accounted for by recognizing additional remuneration expense based on the incremental value given on repricing—that is, additional to expenses recognized in respect of the original option grant.

6. The Exposure Draft also contains proposals on accounting for cancellation of share or option plans, share-based payment transactions settled in cash, and transactions in which either the entity or the counterparty may choose whether the entity settles in cash or by issuing equity instruments.

Scope. The ISAB's proposal applies to all share-based compensation, with some narrow exceptions. By law, European Union companies must comply with IASB standards by 2007, and Australian companies by 2005. Canada has indicated it will also require compliance with IASB standards. The proposal would apply to both listed and unlisted companies.

Problems with Measurement. Companies would be required to measure the value of options as of the date of grant using a formula designed to estimate their fair value. Therein lies the problem. Finding a formula that will produce reasonably accurate estimates has met with little success. The IASB did not specify a particular option pricing model, although it mentioned Black-Scholes or binomial models as examples. Regardless of the formula used, it must include the following elements:

- Exercise price of the option.
- Life of the option.
- Current price of the underlying shares.

- Expected volatility of the share price.
- Dividends expected on the shares, to be adjusted to take into account whether the optionee or shareholder actually has a right to interim dividends before any restrictions on the awards lapse.
- Risk-free interest rate (such as T-bills) for the life of the option.

If this all sounds familiar, it may be because these are the same elements as those now required by the FASB for U.S. companies expensing options on their income statements or in their footnotes. Thus, convergence would not be a big problem if the FASB does follow through on mandatory expensing of options.

Disclosure Requirements. In much the same vein as the SEC's Plain English Disclosure rule, the IASB's disclosure requirements in ED 2 are aimed at helping the user more readily understand the effect of the provisions. Thus, the proposal requires extensive disclosures, governed by three sets of principles:

1. Users should be able to understand the nature and extent of share-based payment arrangements during the accounting period.
2. Users should be able to understand how the fair values of the services received and the equity awards granted were determined.
3. Users should be able to understand the effect expenses based on share-based payments will have on projected income for the period.

Corporate entities must disclose myriad details, which have previously been glossed over, if even mentioned. Among the required items are:

- Awards broken down by employee class.
- Who is getting how many awards.
- Option terms.
- Weighted exercise prices.
- Grant dates.

Expected Effective Date. If adopted as planned before the end of 2003, the proposal would become effective for annual financial statements for periods beginning on or after January 1, 2004. Earlier adoption would be encouraged. For unvested options or shares outstanding as of the effective date, a company would have to apply the accounting principles of the proposal retroactively to November 7, 2002, the date that ED2 was published.

The IASB Proposes Improvement of Financial Instrument Standards

In June 2002, the IASB published for public comment proposals to improve the two International Accounting Standards related to accounting for financial instruments—IAS 32, *Financial Instruments: Disclosures and Presentation,* and IAS 39, *Financial Instruments: Recognition and Measurement.* The proposals are in the form of an exposure draft.

The IASB has focused in the near term on improving the existing standards, which are closely modeled on the approach of U.S. GAAP. Although the Board has signaled its desire ultimately to develop a principles-based approach for the accounting for financial instruments, the proposed improvements are aimed at removing inconsistencies in the existing standards, providing additional guidance and easing implementation.

The IASB recognizes that to undertake a complete overhaul would require time for a comprehensive reexamination of the complex issues involved and would prolong uncertainty for the many companies required to make the transition to international standards under the new European Union regulation. Furthermore, having usable standards for financial instruments is increasingly important for investors as the use of derivatives and other financial instruments grows.

The IASB pointed out that since thousands of companies are required to implement international standards in the next few years, there is an urgent need to remove uncertainty and to make it easier to implement the standards on the reporting of financial instruments.

The Board considers that these exposure drafts offer a practical and timely solution to the immediate problem. The Board is continuing its consideration of issues related to the accounting for financial instruments. However, it expects that the basic principles in the improved IAS 32 and IAS 39, once finalized, will be in place for a considerable period.

Proposals on Macro Hedging.   In August 2003, the IASB published an Exposure Draft of additional proposed amendments to further improve the implementation of IAS 39. If adopted, the proposals will enable fair value hedge accounting to be used more readily for a portfolio hedge of interest rate risk (sometimes referred to as "macro hedging"). The Exposure Draft retains the basic principles behind IAS 39 while aiming to reduce the cost of compliance.

The June 2002 Exposure Draft included only limited proposals on the requirements for hedge accounting, as was brought out in numerous comment letters and a series of roundtable discussions. The main issue raised in the letters and discussions related to hedge accounting for a portfolio hedge of interest rate risk (i.e., macro hedging). The concern was that it is very difficult under IAS 39 to achieve fair value hedge accounting for such a hedge.

In the light of these representations, the IASB decided to explore whether and how IAS 39 might be amended to enable fair value hedge accounting to be used more readily for a portfolio hedge of interest rate risk. The IASB's aim was to develop an approach that complied with the principles that underlie IAS 39 and was workable in practice for entities that manage interest rate risk on a portfolio basis.

The IASB believes that the further amendments to IAS 39 proposed in this Exposure Draft meet these objectives. It decided to limit any amendments to applying fair value hedge accounting to a hedge of interest rate risk on a portfolio of items.

The Board's plan is to publish IAS 32 by the end of 2003 and finalize IAS 39 by March 2004, at the latest.

Basic Points Covered. The Exposure Draft proposes the following:

1. In a fair value hedge of the interest rate risk associated with a portion of a portfolio of financial assets (or financial liabilities), the hedged item may be designated in terms of an amount of assets (or liabilities) in an expected maturity time period, rather than as individual assets or liabilities or the overall net position. It also proposes that the entity may hedge a portion of the interest rate risk associated with this designated amount.

2. That all of the assets (or liabilities) from which the hedged amount is drawn must be items that could have qualified for fair value hedge accounting if they had been designated individually. In the case of financial liabilities included in the balance sheet that a counterparty can redeem on demand (i.e., demand deposits and some time deposits), the IASB concluded that the fair value of such liabilities is not less than the amount payable on demand and does not change with changes in the interest rate. Including such liabilities (i.e., demand deposits and some time deposits) in a fair value hedge would imply that its fair value changes with interest rates, which is inconsistent with the IASB's decision. It follows that a financial liability that the counterparty can redeem on demand cannot qualify for fair value hedge accounting for any time period beyond the shortest period in which the counterparty can demand payment.

3. The amount of the assets (or liabilities) designated as the hedged item in a maturity time period determines the percentage measure that is used to evaluate hedge effectiveness. Any ineffectiveness is recognized in the profit and loss account.

4. For qualifying fair value hedges, the adjustment arising from the gain or loss attributable to the hedged item because of a change in the hedged risk may be presented in the following manner:

   a. In a separate line item within assets, if the hedged item for a particular maturity time period is an asset, or

b. In a separate line item within liabilities, if the hedged item for a particular maturity time period is a liability.

The separate line items referred to in (a) and (b) above are to be presented in the financial statements next to financial assets or financial liabilities. Amounts contained in these line items will be removed from the balance sheet when the assets or liabilities to which they relate are derecognized.

THE IASC FOUNDATION ASSESSMENT AND CERTIFICATION PROGRAM

With the European Union's decision to require all EU-listed companies to prepare their financial statements according to IASs and IFRSs by 2005, and with other developed economies following close behind, first-time users will need to have attained a high level of knowledge about and understanding of the application of these standards.

To satisfy the demand for high-quality learning materials and training programs and to ensure that they are available quickly, the International Accounting Standards Committee Foundation (IASC Foundation) Trustees have decided that assessment and certification programs to examine financial reporting under IAS and IFRSs should be established.

As an initial step, the Foundation has invited those experienced in providing learning materials and training programs to submit proposals for materials and programs to teach and test the understanding of financial reporting requirements under IASs and IFRSs. Once a determination of the quality of the training and materials is assessed, those approved would carry the certificate "IASC Foundation Approved Training."

The Foundation Trustees believe that, as a consequence of the EU decision as well as the increased use of IASs and IFRSs worldwide, there will be a demand to satisfy the public interest and professional requirements by demonstrating that an individual has attained a certain level of proficiency in being able to apply them. For this reason, the Trustees are considering the introduction of a two-tiered assessment program:

1. *Application Level.* Those who qualify at this level would receive a certification in IAS and IFRSs. The application level would cover basic knowledge of the Standards. The treatments and disclosures required would be examined using computer-based assessment.
2. *Advanced Level.* Those who qualify at this level would receive a diploma in IAS and IFRSs. The advanced level would cover:
   a. Application of the Standards.
   b. The concepts involved in the thinking behind the Standards.

c. The exercise of judgment in achieving a fair presentation. Suggestions relating to how this level could be assessed are currently being sought.

An independent board to oversee education and assessment for expertise in IAS and IFRSs will be established by the IASC Foundation Trustees.

PREFACE TO IFRSs

The IASB issued its *Preface to International Financial Reporting Standards* to set out the objectives and procedures for due process, reflecting the IASB's new structure. The Preface also explains the scope, authority and timing of application of International Financial Reporting Standards. These standards are designed to apply to the general-purpose financial statements and other financial reporting of all profit-oriented entities.

The Preface provides a brief description of the purpose and function of the main structures of the new arrangements for setting global standards. As such, it is a short but essential introduction to the context within which the Board will frame its standards. It states that:

1. The IASB, based in London, began operations in 2001. It is funded by contributions from the major accounting firms, private financial institutions and industrial companies throughout the world, central and development banks, and other international and professional organizations. The 14 Board members (12 of whom are full-time) reside in 9 countries and have a variety of functional backgrounds.

    The IASB emphasizes that it is committed to developing, in the public interest, a single set of high-quality, global accounting standards that require transparent and comparable information in general-purpose financial statements. In pursuit of this objective, the IASB cooperates with national accounting standard setters to achieve convergence in accounting standards around the world.

2. Upon its inception, the IASB adopted the body of IASs issued by its predecessor, the International Accounting Standards Committee.

IASB ISSUES TRANSITION STANDARD, IFRS 1

Following recent decisions by several additional jurisdictions to adopt International Financial Reporting Standards, more than 90 countries plan to either require or permit the use of IFRSs during the next five years. Thousands of companies worldwide are making a transition in financial reporting by breaking away from national practices and changing to accounting standards set by the IASB. To help companies make this change as smoothly as possible, and to enable users of company reports to understand the effect of applying a new (in some cases, completely new) set of accounting standards, the IASB issued IFRS 1, *First-Time Adoption of International Financial Reporting Standards,* in June 2003. The standard explains how the transition is made to IFRSs from another basis of accounting.

Through IFRS 1, the IASB has sought to address the demand of investors to have transparent information that is comparable over all periods presented. IFRS 1 is also fashioned to give reporting entities a suitable starting point for their accounting under IFRSs. In developing the standard, the IASB consulted interested parties throughout the world and paid particular attention to the necessity of ensuring that the cost of compliance with the new requirements did not exceed the benefits to users of the financial information. The standard is based on the proposals published as Exposure Draft 1 (ED 1) in July 2002, modified by changes that the IASB made after consideration of suggestions in the 83 comment letters it received.

IFRS 1 requires an entity to comply with every IASB standard in force in the first year when the entity first adopts IFRSs, with some targeted and specific exceptions after consideration of the cost of full compliance. Under IFRS 1, entities must explain how the transition to IASB standards affects their reported financial position, financial performance, and cash flows.

The IASB explains that IFRS 1 is timely because demand is growing for high-quality international standards set by the IASB. Thousands of companies throughout the world must adopt IFRSs in the coming years. The requirements in IFRS 1 are designed to ease the transition for all concerned and to ensure that users of financial statements are provided high-quality information. This is the IASB's first completely new standard—several more are scheduled for adoption.

The IASB pointed out that it benefited greatly from input by the French Conseil National de la Comptabilité (CNC), which participated actively and made a significant contribution in the development of IFRS 1.

Summary of IFRS 1

IFRS 1 outlines the procedures that an entity must follow when it adopts IFRS for the first time as the basis for preparing its general-purpose financial statements.

Definition of First-Time Adoption.   A first-time adopter is an entity that, for the first time, makes an explicit and unreserved statement that its general-purpose financial statements comply with IFRS.

An entity is considered to be a first-time adopter if, in the preceding year, it prepared IFRS financial statements for internal management use, as long as those IAS financial statements were not given to owners or external parties, such as investors or creditors. If a set of IFRSs was, for any reason, given to an external party in the preceding year, the entity is considered to already be on IFRS, and IFRS 1 does not apply.

An entity can also be a first-time adopter if, in the preceding year, its published financial statement:

- Was in compliance with some, but not all, IFRSs.
- Included a reconciliation of selected figures from previous GAAP to IFRS. (Previous GAAP being the GAAP an entity followed immediately before adopting IFRSs.)

However, an entity is *not* a first-time adopter if, in the preceding year, its published financial statements asserted:

- Compliance with IFRSs, but the auditor's report contained a qualification with respect to conformity with IFRSs.
- Compliance with both previous GAAP and IFRSs.

Entities Need to Plan Ahead for First-Time Adoption. It is necessary for entities to begin considering their preparation for the 2005 adoption of the international standards. As outlined below, preparation will take some thought and planning. Following are some of the necessary steps:

1. IFRS 1 applies when an entity adopts IFRSs for the first time, by an explicit and unreserved statement of compliance with IFRSs.
2. To create a starting point for its later accounting under IFRSs, an entity adopting IFRSs for the first time (a *first-time adopter*) needs to prepare an *opening IFRS balance sheet* at the *date of transition to IFRSs* (the beginning of the earliest period for which it presents full comparative information under IFRSs in its first IFRS financial statements). For example, if an entity's first IFRS financial statements are for the year ended December 31, 2005, it will need to prepare an opening IFRS balance sheet at January 1, 2004.
3. In general, IFRS 1 requires a first-time adopter to comply with each IFRS that has come into effect at the reporting date for its first IFRS financial statements (December 31, 2005, in the preceding example). In particular, it requires a first-time adopter to do the following in its opening IFRS balance sheet:
   a. Recognize all assets and liabilities whose recognition is required by IFRSs.

b. Not recognize items as assets or liabilities if IFRSs do not permit such recognition.

c. Classify all recognized assets and liabilities in accordance with IFRSs.

d. Apply IFRSs in measuring all recognized assets and liabilities.

4. IFRS 1 grants a first-time adopter limited exemptions from these requirements in specified areas where the cost of complying with them would likely exceed the benefits to users of financial statements.

5. IFRS 1 applies if an entity's first IFRS financial statements are for a period beginning on or after January 1, 2004, although earlier application is encouraged. It replaces SIC-8, *First-Time Application of IASs as the Primary Basis of Accounting.* Like SIC-8, the IFRS requires retrospective application of IFRSs in most areas. Unlike SIC-8, the IFRS:

a. Includes some targeted exemptions.

b. Clarifies that an entity applies the latest version of IFRSs and specifies that the transitional provisions in other IFRSs do not apply to a first-time adopter, except for transitional provisions in IAS 39, *Financial Instruments: Recognition and Measurement,* on hedge accounting and derecognition.

c. Clarifies how a first-time adopter's estimates under IFRSs relate to its estimates for the same date under previous GAAP.

d. Requires enhanced disclosure to explain how the transition to IFRSs affected the entity's reported financial position, financial performance, and cash flows.

6. The IASB has published IFRS 1 together with two separate booklets. The first contains the IASB's *Basis for Conclusions,* which sets out the IASB's reasoning for the requirements in the IFRS; the second consists of implementation guidance.

PROPOSED INTERPRETATION ON GREENHOUSE GAS EMISSIONS

The International Financial Reporting Interpretations Committee (IFRIC), in May 2003, proposed accounting requirements for companies participating in government schemes aimed at reducing greenhouse gas emissions. The Draft Interpretation D1, *Emission Rights,* is aimed at preventing further development of divergent accounting practices in this new area. The proposals focus on the common features of the new schemes and may go further as practice develops. At present, some companies are not accounting for the assets, liabilities, or government grants involved, or at least are very uncertain about the appropriate accounting treatment.

The IASB points out that it is vital that the IFRIC respond to emerging issues, such as the gas emission schemes. The accounting matters involved in such schemes are challenging and may need consideration beyond the current proposals. The Committee feels that industries affected by these schemes need to take an active part in the IFRIC exposure process.

Background of the Proposals

As businesses, technologies, and activities move into new areas, so do the financial arrangements — and the accounting for them, as in the case of dealing with "the greenhouse effect." Thus, a little background information may be helpful. In light of the Kyoto agreement, several governments have, or are in the process of developing, schemes to encourage reductions in greenhouse gas emissions. The Draft Interpretation focuses on the accounting to be adopted by participants in a cap-and-trade scheme, although its requirements also apply to other schemes that share one or more of the features of a cap-and-trade scheme. Typically in cap-and-trade schemes, a government (or government agency) allocates to participating entities the rights (allowances) to emit a specified level of pollutant. The allowances may be allocated free of charge to the participant or the participant may be required to pay for them. Participants in the scheme are able to buy and sell allowances; therefore, in many schemes, there is a liquid market for the allowances. At the end of a specified period, participants are required to deliver allowances equal to their actual emissions or incur a penalty.

The main proposals in the Draft Interpretation are:

- Rights (allowances) to emit pollutant are intangible assets that should be recognized in the financial statements in accordance with IAS 38, *Intangible Assets.*
- When allowances are allocated to a participant by government (or government agency) for less than their fair value, the difference between the amount paid (if any) and the fair value of the allowance is a government grant that is accounted for under IAS 20, *Accounting for Government Grants and Disclosure of Government Assistance.*
- As a participant emits pollutant, it recognizes a provision for its obligation to deliver allowances or pay a penalty in accordance with IAS 37, *Provisions, Contingent Liabilities and Contingent Assets.* This provision is normally measured at the market value of the allowances needed to settle it.

Work on Other IFRSs Under Way.   The IASB expects to also complete or amend in 2004 (or early 2005) IASs/IFRSs dealing with:

- Business combination procedures (including accounting for noncontrolling interests).

- Performance reporting.
- Postemployment benefits.
- Revenue and liabilities.
- Consolidations (including special-purpose entities).
- Segment reporting.
- Financial institutions (deposit taking, lending, and securities activities).

These, and possibly other, IFRSs are expected to have an effective date some time after 2005.

PROPOSED INTERPRETATION, CHANGES IN DECOMMISSIONING, RESTORATION AND SIMILAR LIABILITIES

The IFRIC released IFRIC Draft Interpretation D2, *Changes in Decommissioning, Restoration and Similar Liabilities,* in September 2003. The proposed Interpretation contains guidance on accounting for certain changes in decommissioning, restoration and similar liabilities that are recognized both as:

- Part of the cost of an item of property, plant and equipment in accordance with IAS 16, *Property, Plant and Equipment;* and
- Liability in accordance with IAS 37, *Provisions, Contingent Liabilities and Contingent Assets.*

Specifically, the proposal addresses accounting for changes in:

- The estimated outflow of resources embodying economic benefits (e.g., cash flows).
- The current market-assessed discount rate.
- An increase that reflects the passage of time (also referred to as the unwinding of the discount).

The IFRIC discovered that differing views and potentially divergent practices exist in accounting for changes in decommissioning, restoration and similar liabilities; therefore, they agreed that guidance should be developed.

The proposed Interpretation would require companies to capitalize only the portion of a change in an estimated decommissioning liability that relates to the future use of the related asset. The remaining amount would be recognized in current period profit or loss. Basic points and considerations include:

- Addressing the accounting for certain changes in estimated costs to dismantle, restore and remove items of property, plant and equipment that fall within the scope of IAS 16 and are recognized as a provision under IAS 37.
- Dealing with changes that arise from:
  - The revision of estimated outflows of resources embodying economic benefits;
  - Revisions to the current market-assessed discount rate.

Under the proposed Interpretation, these two changes are accounted for in the same manner as the initial estimated cost. Therefore, amounts relating to the depreciation of the asset that would have been recognized to date are reflected in current period income or expense; amounts relating to future depreciation are capitalized. This approach views the asset, from the time the liability for decommissioning is initially incurred until the end of the asset's useful life, as the unit of account to which decommissioning costs relate.

Keeping in mind the spirit of convergence, the IFRIC considered the U.S. GAAP approach in FASB 143, *Accounting for Asset Retirement Obligations,* in which changes in estimated cash flows are capitalized as part of the cost of the asset and depreciated prospectively; the decommissioning obligation is not required to be revised to reflect the effect of a change in the current market-assessed discount rate. The IFRIC did not choose this approach because IAS 37, unlike FASB 143, requires a decommissioning obligation to reflect the effect of a change in the current market-assessed discount rate. The IFRIC agreed that it was important that any Interpretation it developed should deal consistently with changes in estimated cash flows and changes in the discount rate.

THE IASB PROPOSES IMPROVEMENTS

The International Accounting Standards Board, in May 2002, published for public comment proposals to revise 12 of its 34 active standards. The proposals are in the form of an Exposure Draft, *Improvements to International Accounting Standards,* on which comments were invited by September 2002.

The ED was the first product of the IASB's Improvements project. The aim is to raise the quality and consistency of financial reporting by drawing on best practices from around the world, and removing options in international standards. (This matter of options and either/or possibilities was one of the FASB's early objections to the IASC's stance on some topics. The FASB now finds itself in the position of being criticized for having attempted to be too specific about the "hows, whys and wherefores" in many instances. As a result, too little was done too late, and there were so many loopholes that often the investor was not protected.)

Stepped-Up Efforts to Improve International Standards

The Improvements project is a first step by the new IASB to promote convergence on high-quality solutions in its objective to establish a globally accepted set of accounting standards.

The release of the Exposure Draft marks the IASB's initial response to the demand for the continued development and rapid improvement of international standards by market participants: regulators through IOSCO, national standard setters, the IASB's Standards Advisory Council, international corporations and others.

The project has been given added impetus by the European Union's requirement that publicly listed companies use international standards beginning on or before January 2005.

The IASB believes that investors, businesses, and policy makers worldwide are looking to the Board as the international standard setter, in partnership with national standard setters, to lead the global drive toward better financial reporting, based on convergence of standards toward high-quality solutions.

Need to Improve Existing Standards

The IASB points out that its new accounting standards will take time to develop, and in the meantime, it plans to:

1. Fix problems with existing standards now if an acceptable solution is readily available.
2. Follow up with the publication of proposals to revise the two standards on financial instruments.
3. Draft guidance for those adopting international standards for the first time.
4. Publish proposals to overhaul the reporting of business combinations, including reforms to accounting for goodwill.

Examples of the improvements to IASs proposed in the Exposure Draft are:

- Those relating to *convergence*:
  - The definition of related parties will be extended to cover further parties (e.g., joint ventures and pension plans) and further information (e.g., amounts of transactions and balances, terms and conditions, details of guarantees).

—It will no longer be permissible to label items of income or expense as extraordinary items either in the income statement or in the notes.

—Guidance on the calculation of earnings per share will be expanded and will conform to practice in a number of countries.

Among the *options* that had been permitted, the following are slated for elimination:

- LIFO (last in, first out—an inventory valuation method sometimes used in the United States and elsewhere) will be prohibited.
- Corrections of errors now must be accounted for retrospectively, not either through current income or retrospectively.
- Similarly, voluntary changes in accounting policies will also have to be accounted for retrospectively and not either through current income or retrospectively.

Other planned improvements are:

- Requirements are introduced to ensure that compliance with standards does not lead to misleading results in jurisdictions where compliance is mandatory irrespective of circumstance.
- Disclosure is required of the critical judgments made by management in applying accounting policies.
- Disclosure is required of the key assumptions about uncertainties made by management that could cause material adjustment of the carrying amounts of assets and liabilities in financial statements.
- Separate disclosure is required of the amounts by which inventories have been written down.

THE IFRIC ISSUES INTERPRETATION ON WEB SITE COSTS

In March 2002, the IASB's Standing Interpretations Committee was renamed the International Financial Reporting Interpretations Committee (IFRIC). Under its new name, the committee issued an Interpretation to clarify the accounting for Web site costs under IAS.

The Interpretation, SIC-32, *Intangible Assets—Web Site Costs,* was submitted to the IASB for approval before the Committee's name was changed and was therefore published as an SIC Interpretation and approved by the IASB at the meeting in March.

All Interpretations issued by IFRIC are part of the binding International Accounting Standards literature. SIC-32 became effective on March 25, 2002, and is aimed at clarifying the existing requirements of IAS 38, *Intangible Assets,* as it applies to expenditure on internally developing and operating a Web site. If an enterprise applies the Interpretation and the outcome is to recognize the Web site as an intangible asset, then unless the Web site has an active market and its carrying amount is revalued regularly, the enterprise will need to amortize the expenditure over a short period.

Some of the interpretive groups sponsored by the IASB's liaison national standard setters have already issued guidance on this topic. The Committee considered those rulings when developing the Interpretation in order to ensure convergence. (The FASB, EITF, and SEC have all been working for several years to figure out just how to handle accounting matters related to Web sites and Internet transactions.)

In addition, the Committee addressed the accounting treatment of expenditure on developing content that is included in a Web site. This facet was not addressed by all of those groups. Because IAS 38 applies equally to such expenditure, it was necessary to include it within the Interpretation.

Specific Provisions

The Interpretation agreed that a Web site developed by an enterprise from internal expenditure for internal or external access is an internally generated intangible asset that is subject to the requirements of IAS 38, and pointed to various paragraphs within the Standard as verification.

The Interpretation also addresses the appropriate accounting treatment for internal expenditure on the development and operation of an enterprise's own Web site for internal or external access. The Committee agreed that:

- A Web site arising from development should be recognized as an intangible asset if, and only if, in addition to complying with the general requirements described in IAS 38 for recognition and initial measurement, an enterprise could satisfy the requirements in that IAS. In particular, an enterprise may be able to satisfy the requirement to demonstrate how its Web site will generate probable future economic benefits.
- Any internal expenditure on the development and operation of an enterprise's own Web site should be accounted for in accordance with IAS 38:
  — The Planning stage is similar in nature to the research phase in IAS 38. Expenditure incurred in this stage should be recognized as an expense when it is incurred.
  — The Application and Infrastructure Development stage, the Graphical Design stage, and the Content Development stage, to the extent that content is developed for purposes other than to advertise and promote

an enterprise's own products and services, are similar in nature to the development phase in IAS 38.

—Expenditure incurred in the Content Development stage, to the extent that content is developed to advertise and promote an enterprise's own products and services (e.g., digital photographs of products) should be recognized as an expense when incurred in accordance with a different paragraph in IAS 38.

—The Operating stage begins once development of a Web site is complete. Expenditure incurred in this stage should be recognized as an expense when it is incurred unless it meets the criteria in yet another section of IAS 38.

• A Web site that is recognized as an intangible asset under this Interpretation should be measured after initial recognition by applying the requirements of IAS 38. The best estimate of a Web site's useful life should be short.

THE IASB PROPOSES AMENDMENT TO IAS 19, EMPLOYEE BENEFITS

The IASB published an Exposure Draft in February 2002 of a limited amendment to the pension accounting provisions of the standard, "Amendment to IAS 19, *Employee Benefits*: The Asset Ceiling."

Reflecting the recent fall in global equity markets, many pension plans have suffered actuarial losses. The IASB considered advice from the accounting profession that IAS 19 would have an unintended effect in some situations. The problem was produced by the interaction of two aspects of IAS 19:

1. The option to defer gains and losses in the pension fund.

2. The limit on the amount that can be recognized as an asset (the asset ceiling).

The combination of the asset ceiling and the option for an entity to defer losses can in certain circumstances require the entity to report an *increase in profit*. Equally perversely, the combination of the asset ceiling and the option for an entity to defer gains can require the entity to report a *decrease in profit*. The IASB concluded that reporting gains and losses in these circumstances is wholly inappropriate. The limited amendment would prevent their recognition.

At the same time, rather than merely fix problems as they arise, the Board decided upon a general reexamination of IAS 19 (which was adopted in 1998) with a view to the convergence of pension accounting standards worldwide.

THE SIC ISSUES SIX NEW INTERPRETATIONS

The Standing Interpretations Committee published six new Interpretations on Christmas Eve, 2001, to clarify accounting issues under the International Accounting Standards. (SIC-32 was issued in March 2002, as mentioned in the previous section, "IFRIC Issues Interpretation on Web Site Costs.") The new Interpretations follow.

SIC-27: Evaluating the Substance of Transactions in the Legal Form of a Lease. A discussion on this topic had been on the agenda for some time. It went through a number of changes, but the Committee considers the final document to be of wider application and more useful than it was at earlier stages. It highlights the significance of determining the *substance* of a transaction to determine whether that arrangement is actually a lease.

SIC-28: Business Combinations— "Date of Exchange" and Fair Value of Equity Instruments. The Interpretation dealing with the date of exchange and the fair value of equity instruments issued in a business combination clarifies the existing requirements of IAS 22.

When an acquisition is achieved in a single step, the fair value of equity instruments issued is determined at the date when the acquirer obtains control over the acquiree. The published price of a quoted equity instrument is the best evidence of its fair value; therefore, that price is used when measuring fair value. No adjustments are made for block premiums or discounts to the published price.

When approving SIC-28, the Board noted that it is considering in phase 1 of its business combinations project the date on which equity instruments issued as consideration should be measured. Any possible change to the existing requirements *as a result of that project* would be effective only after the Board has completed its due process.

SIC-29: Disclosure—Service Concession Arrangements. The disclosures required by SIC-29 should significantly improve the transparency of financial statements of enterprises that are a party to a service concession arrangement.

SIC-30: Reporting Currency—Translation from Measurement Currency to Presentation Currency. This SIC resolves the method of translating from a measurement currency determined under SIC-19 to a presentation currency. Also, during the Board's discussion of SIC-30, it noted that the Interpretation is consistent with its tentative decision in November 2001 to require translation of financial statements into a presentation currency using the method set out in IAS 21.

SIC-31: Revenue—Barter Transactions Involving Advertising Services. The Interpretation addresses the circumstances when a Seller can reliably measure revenue at the fair value of advertising services received or provided in a barter transaction. The SIC agreed that revenue from a barter transaction involving advertising cannot be measured reliably at the fair value of advertising services received. However, a Seller can reliably measure revenue at the fair value of the advertising services it provides in a barter transaction, by reference only to non-barter transactions that:

- Involve advertising similar to the advertising in the barter transaction.
- Occur frequently.
- Represent a predominant number of transactions and amount when compared to all transactions to provide advertising that is similar to the advertising in the barter transaction.
- Involve cash and/or another form of consideration (e.g., marketable securities, non-monetary assets, and other services) that has a reliably measurable fair value.
- Do not involve the same counterparty as in the barter transaction.

SIC-33: Consolidation and Equity Method—Potential Voting Rights and Allocation of Ownership Interests. This action clarifies that share call options and other similar instruments that have the potential to give an enterprise voting power, can affect an assessment of control and significant influence.

The Interpretation addresses whether the existence and effect of potential voting rights should be considered when assessing whether an enterprise controls or significantly influences another enterprise according to IAS 27 and IAS 28 respectively.

It also addresses whether any other facts and circumstances related to potential voting rights should be assessed. The Committee agreed that all facts and circumstances that affect potential voting rights should be examined, except the intention of management and the financial capability to exercise or convert.

Effective Dates

These Interpretations were approved by the IASB at its meeting in December 2001, except SIC-32, which was adopted in March 2002. All Interpretations issued by SIC are part of the binding International Accounting Standards literature. Their effective dates are:

- SIC-27, 29, and 31 became effective on December 31, 2001.
- SIC-30 and 33 became effective for annual financial periods beginning on or after January 1, 2002.

- SIC-28 became effective for acquisitions given initial accounting recognition on or after December 31, 2001.
- SIC-32 became effective on March 25, 2002.

FOUNDATION TRUSTEES NAME STANDARDS ADVISORY COUNCIL TO PROVIDE ADVICE TO IASB

The Trustees of the International Accounting Standards Committee Foundation announced the appointment of the Standards Advisory Council (SAC) in June 2001. The members of the SAC will be asked to provide advice to the IASB on priorities in setting standards. It will also inform the Board of implications of proposed standards for both users and producers of financial accounts.

The 49-member body includes chief financial and accounting officers from some of the world's largest corporations and international organizations, leading financial analysts and academics, regulators, accounting standard setters and partners from leading accounting firms. The members of the SAC are drawn from 6 continents, 29 countries, and 5 international organizations. Additionally, the European Commission, the U.S. Securities and Exchange Commission, and the Financial Services Agency of Japan will participate as observers.

Unquestionably, this new arm of the IASC will be of the utmost importance in the quest for a globally acceptable set of accounting standards. The only question will be whether the advisors can remember that the ultimate aim is to provide the users of the finished product with the information that they need to make informed decisions.

REVISED ORGANIZATION LAUNCHED

When the Board of the International Accounting Standards Commission (IASC) unanimously approved a new Constitution in 2000, they created an organization with two main bodies. These two are the IASC Trustees, an oversight body, and the IASB, the new group of experienced accounting professionals appointed by the Trustees. This Board has the responsibility of working to develop "a single set of high-quality accounting standards that national bodies around the world can broadly support."

Additionally, the SIC was to continue as it had in the past. However, the name was subsequently changed to the International Financial Reporting Interpretations Committee (IFRIC). A new Standards Advisory Council is expected to be the key vehicle for obtaining advice and injecting fresh thinking into the standard-making process.

Putting the New Constitution in Place

On March 8, 2001, the Trustees activated the new Constitution, effective immediately. In doing so, they established a not-for-profit Delaware corporation, the International Accounting Standards Committee Foundation, to oversee the London-based IASB. The 14-member IASB began full-time operations in April 2001, and held its first public meetings in London. In effect, the IASB is the professional standard-setting body taking up its task of attempting to create a single-set of high-quality global accounting standards.

IASC Foundation.   The governance of the IASB organization is ultimately in the hands of the Trustees of the IASC Foundation. There are 19 Trustees. The IASC Foundation Constitution provides that the Trustees must:

• Show a firm commitment to the IASC Foundation and the IASB as a high-quality global standard setter.
• Be financially knowledgeable.
• Have an ability to meet the time commitment.
• Have an understanding of, and be sensitive to, international issues relevant to the success of an international organization responsible for the development of high-quality global accounting standards for use in the world's capital markets and by other users.

The Trustees appoint the members of the IASB, the International Financial Reporting Interpretations Committee and the Standards Advisory Council. In addition they:

• Review annually the strategy of IASB and its effectiveness.
• Approve annually the budget of IASB and determine the basis for funding.
• Review broad strategic issues affecting accounting standards, promote IASB and its work and promote the objective of rigorous application of International Accounting Standards (however, they are excluded from involvement in technical matters relating to accounting standards).
• Establish and amend operating procedures for the IASB, the Standing Interpretations Committee (now the International Standards Advisory Council).
• Approve amendments to this Constitution after following a due process, including consultation with the Standards Advisory Council and publication of an Exposure Draft for public comment.

- Exercise all powers of the IASC Foundation except those expressly reserved to the IASB, the Standing Interpretations Committee (now IFRIC) and the Standards Advisory Council.

The Trustees are not responsible for setting International Financial Reporting Standards. That responsibility rests *solely* with the International Accounting Standards Board.

Distribution of Trustees. The distribution of Trustees, required by paragraph 9 of the IASB Constitution, is as follows:

- *North America* — 6 (5 from the United States and 1 from Canada).
- *Europe* — 6 (1 each from Denmark, France, Germany, Italy, Netherlands and the United Kingdom).
- *Asia-Pacific* — 4 (1 each from Australia and China-Hong Kong, and 2 from Japan).
- *Other* — 3 from any area, as long as balance is maintained (1 each from Brazil, South Africa and an International Organization [the Bank for International Settlements based in Switzerland]).

The Board. The previous Board was replaced by a new Board of fourteen individuals — twelve full-time members and two part-time members. Because the Board has sole responsibility for setting accounting standards, the foremost qualification for Board membership is technical expertise.

The Trustees reviewed more than 200 candidates for Board positions. The IASC Constitution mandated that the Board comprise individuals who represent "the best available combination of technical skills and experience of relevant business and market conditions." Further, in their selection of members, the Trustees are expected to exercise their best judgment to ensure that the Board is not dominated by any particular constituency or regional interest.

To achieve a balance of perspectives and experience, a minimum of five Board members must have a backgrounds as practicing auditors; a minimum of three, a background in the preparation of financial statements; a minimum of three must be users of financial statements; and at least one member must be from academia. The publication of a Standard, an Exposure Draft, or a final SIC Interpretation requires approval by eight of the Board's fourteen members.

In order to encourage cooperation among the new Board and national standard setters, the Trustees appointed seven of the Board members as official liaisons to national bodies. These liaison Board members will maintain close contact with their respective national standard setters, and will be responsible for coordinating agendas and ensuring that the new IASB and national bodies are working toward the goal of global convergence on the single set of high-quality standards.

Countries with formal liaisons are Australia and New Zealand together; Canada; France; Germany; Japan; the United States; and the United Kingdom. In addition, Board members will have frequent contacts with financial regulators and central banks, private industry, analysts, and academics throughout the world.

The International Financial Reporting Interpretations Committee. As mentioned earlier, the SIC was to continue in its form and function as previously. Its name, however, has changed as noted above. Its primary function is to review, on a timely basis within the context of existing International Accounting Standards, issues that are likely to receive divergent or unacceptable treatment where authoritative guidance is lacking. When consensus is reached on appropriate accounting treatment, the IFRIC publishes pronouncements on the application of the relevant IAS. It also recommends solutions for situations not covered by existing standards. The Committee's function is similar to that of the FASB's Emerging Issues Task Force (EITF).

The IFRIC has 12 voting members from various countries, including individuals from the accounting profession, preparer groups, and user groups. The International Organization of Securities Commissions (IOSCO) and the European Commission are nonvoting observers. To ensure adequate liaison with the Board, two Board representatives may attend IFRIC meetings as nonvoting members.

Setting Up the Advisory Council. This new part of the organization was initiated in the revised Constitution to provide a formal vehicle for other groups and individuals having diverse geographic and functional backgrounds to give advice to the Board and the Trustees.

At the April meeting, the Trustees reiterated their commitment to achieving a broad and representative balance of perspectives, both professionally and geographically, through the creation of this Advisory Council. It will meet regularly with the IASB to advise the Board Members on priorities, and to inform them of ramifications of proposed standards for particular users and producers of financial accounts. Specifically, this new group must represent the diverse interests involved in the standard setting process to ensure that the result is usable, relevant information.

The Relationship of the IASC with Other International Groups. The IASC previously had important relationships with many other international groups; for example, IOSCO, the Basel Committee, the International Federation of Accountants, and the European Commission.

The new Constitution lessens the formal ties between IASC and IFAC. They no longer have a common membership, and the IFAC Council will no longer be responsible for appointing members of the IASC Board. However, the IFAC has provided a continuing place for IASB as an observer in its governance arrangements. It is considered important for the new IASB to work hard to maintain and foster these international relationships.

THE IASC STANDARD ON AGRICULTURE (AIS 41)

The Standard on Agriculture is an important one, although it deals with specialized transactions and was not part of the core set of standards. Financial support for the work on this project was originally provided by The World Bank.

The fact that the IASC had been working on this project for over six years indicates the difficulty of the issues, particularly in deciding on the relative emphases to be given to fair-value-based measurements as opposed to cost-based measurements of agricultural assets. IAS 41 prescribes the accounting treatment, financial statement presentation, and disclosures related to agricultural activity, a matter not covered in any other International Accounting Standard.

For the purpose of this Standard, agricultural activity is considered to be the management by an enterprise engaged in the biological transformation of living animals or plants (biological assets):

*   For sale.
*   Into agricultural produce.
*   Into additional biological assets.

IAS 41 requires measurement at fair value less estimated point-of-sale costs from initial recognition of biological assets up to harvest, other than when fair value cannot be measured reliably on initial recognition. A change in fair value less estimated point-of-sale costs should be included in net profit or loss for the period in which it arises.

IAS 41 *does not* deal with processing of agricultural produce after harvest. Processing grapes into wine for sale, for example, is generally accounted for under IAS 2, *Inventories.*

There is a presumption that fair value can be measured reliably for a biological asset. That presumption can be rebutted only on initial recognition for a biological asset for which market-determined prices or values are not available and for which alternative estimates of fair value are determined to be clearly unreliable. In such a case, IAS 41 requires an enterprise to measure that biological asset at its cost less any accumulated depreciation and any accumulated impairment losses.

Once the fair value of such a biological asset becomes reliably measurable, an enterprise should measure it at its fair value less estimated point-of-sale costs. In all cases, an enterprise should measure agricultural produce at its fair value less estimated point-of-sale costs.

Unique Aspects of Agriculture

The Board concluded that the Standard should require a fair value model for biological assets because of the unique nature and characteristics of agricultural activity. One of these unique characteristics is the management of biological transformation.

The financial statements of enterprises undertaking agricultural activity should reflect the effects of biological transformation, which are represented by fair value changes in biological assets. Under a transaction-based, historical cost accounting model, the effects of biological transformation are not reflected because the patterns of biological transformation often differ significantly in timing from the patterns of cost.

Fair Value Measurement Is Not Always Possible

The Board also concluded that fair value cannot be measured reliably for some biological assets. The questionable reliability of fair value measurement for some and the lack of an active market for other biological assets, in particular for those with a long growth period, poses a problem. In addition, present value of expected net cash flows is often an unreliable measure of fair value because of the necessity of using subjective assumptions. Therefore, the Board decided that there was a need to include a reliability exception for cases in which market-determined prices or values are not available and alternative estimates of fair value are determined to be clearly unreliable.

The Standard is effective for annual financial statements covering periods beginning on or after January 1, 2003. Earlier application is encouraged.

THREE REVISED STANDARDS ISSUED BY THE IASC

Standard setting is an ongoing process, even in the most established standard setting bodies. It is no wonder, then, that the IASC has found it necessary to publish limited revisions to three International Accounting Standards: IAS 12, *Income Taxes,* IAS 19, *Employee Benefits,* and IAS 39, *Financial Instruments: Recognition and Measurement.*

There was no specific topic that needed addressing in each, but a chain reaction set in. The revisions to IAS 39 are accompanied by consequential changes to IAS 27, *Consolidated Financial Statements and Accounting for Investments in Subsidiaries;* IAS 28, *Accounting for Investments in Associates;* IAS 31, *Financial Reporting of Interests in Joint Ventures,* and IAS 32, *Financial Instruments: Disclosure and Presentation,* and to the other two IASs named above.

Specifically, the revisions address the *income tax* consequences of dividends, *pension plan* assets, and technical application issues on *financial instru-*

ments. The large majority of respondents supported the proposed revisions in Exposure Drafts ED66, ED67 and ED68.

The only substantive change to the proposals made in the three Exposure Drafts is that the revised definition of plan assets in IAS 19 is broadly similar to the definition proposed in ED67. However, in response to comments received on ED67, the Board extended the scope of the definition to include certain insurance policies (now described in IAS 19 as qualifying insurance policies) that satisfy the same conditions as other plan assets. These insurance policies have similar economic effects to funds whose assets qualify as plan assets under the definition proposed in ED67.

The limited revisions to the three Standards and other related Standards became operative for annual financial statements covering periods beginning on or after January 1, 2001.

THE IASC CONSIDERS ACCOUNTING BY MINING, AND OIL AND GAS COMPANIES

An issues paper on financial reporting by enterprises in the extractive industries (mining, and oil and gas companies) was developed with the help of a steering committee of experts on the extractive industries.

The aim of the issues paper is to identify the important accounting and disclosure issues relating to exploration and production activities in these industries, and to evaluate the merits of alternative ways of resolving the issues. To provide a focus for commentators, the issues paper sets out the tentative views that the IASC steering committee has developed on some of the most significant issues at this stage of the project.

Among the critical issues are:

- The extent to which the costs of finding, acquiring, and developing reserves should be capitalized.
- The methods of depreciating (amortizing) capitalized costs.
- The degree to which quantities and values of reserves, rather than costs, should affect recognition, measurement, and disclosure.
- The definition and measurement of reserves.

Today, there is a wide divergence in accounting standards and practices between countries and within individual countries. Even in the few countries in which financial reporting standards have been prescribed for the mining or petroleum industries, alternative treatments have been allowed and are commonly used.

Although many companies currently disclose estimated quantities of reserves in the ground, and some disclose estimated values as well, nearly all enterprises use *historical costs,* rather than *values,* as the basis of their accounting.

Two common methods illustrate the wide variety of accounting practices:

1. *The successful efforts method.* Successful efforts accounting is used by most large petroleum enterprises and many small ones, as well as by some mining enterprises. Costs that lead directly to finding reserves are capitalized, while costs that do not lead directly to reserves are charged to expense.

2. *Full-cost method.* Under full-cost accounting, all costs incurred in searching for, acquiring, and developing reserves in a large cost center such as a country or continent are capitalized as part of the cost of whatever reserves have been found. This is the practice, even though a specific cost was incurred in an effort that was clearly a failure.

Full-cost accounting is used by many small to medium-sized petroleum enterprises, but rarely by mining enterprises. Many mining companies use approaches that are somewhere between the successful efforts and the full-cost methods.

There are important accounting differences, not only as to which costs are capitalized, but also as to how they are depreciated, how impairment of capitalized costs is recognized, and how provisions for future site clean-up costs are made.

The extractive industries also have unique accounting issues in such areas as revenue recognition, inventories, and arrangements that allow two or more entities to share the risks of exploring and developing reserves.

Because of widespread interest in the project, the IASC has sent the issues paper to the senior financial officials of nearly 300 extractive industries companies worldwide, with a request that they consider the issues and provide their comments.

IASC GUIDANCE ON FINANCIAL INSTRUMENTS

In July 2001, IASB issued a consolidated document that includes all questions and answers approved in final form by the IAS 39 Implementation Guidance Committee as of July 1, 2001, including a fifth batch of proposed guidance, issued for comment in December 2000. The Q&A's respond to questions submitted by financial statement preparers, auditors, regulators, and others and have been issued to help them and others better understand IAS 39. The objective is to help ensure consistent, knowledgeable application of the Standard.

There is also a publication, available from IASB, containing the current text of IAS 32 and IAS 39, SIC Interpretations related to the accounting for financial instruments, as well as the IAS 39 Implementation Guidance — Questions and Answers.

In November 2001, the Implementation Guidance Committee issued another document which includes the final versions of the fifth batch of 17 Q&A and two illustrative examples. That document replaces portions of the July 2001 compilation. In addition, some of the earlier Q&A's were eliminated, primarily because the issues involved are being addressed in the Board's current project to amend IAS 39. All current Implementation Guidance Q&A's are included in International Accounting Standards — 2002.

IAS 39 significantly affects corporate financial reporting by establishing for the first time a single set of rigorous and consistent principles for recognizing and measuring financial instruments under IASC standards. The IAS 39 implementation guidance issued helps companies, auditors, and financial analysts better understand and apply the requirements in IAS 39, and helps companies implement this new approach to financial instruments consistently and effectively.

IAS 39 introduces a whole new approach to the accounting for trading, investment, and hedging activities involving financial instruments including derivatives. It is IASC's first comprehensive Standard on the subject. IAS 39 became effective for financial statements for financial years beginning on or after January 1, 2001. Therefore, it is not surprising that companies and their auditors have a lot of questions on how best and most effectively to implement IAS 39.

Issues Covered in Implementation Guides

The IAS 39 implementation guidance issued thus far includes a wide variety of difficult and diverse topics:

- The application of IAS 39 to financial reinsurance contracts, credit derivatives, financial guarantee contracts, and commodity contracts.
- Definitions of derivatives and originated loans.
- Accounting for embedded derivatives.
- Accounting for "regular way" transactions.
- Accounting for transfers of financial assets and portions of financial assets (for instance, in securitizations).
- Accounting for transaction costs.
- Fair value measurement considerations.
- Application of the effective interest method.
- Classification of financial assets as held to maturity.
- Impairment issues.
- Hedge accounting issues (such as hedge accounting considerations when interest rate risk is managed on a net basis, and hedging of risk components).

- Disclosures about financial instruments.
- Application of the transition requirements in IAS 39.
- The interaction between IAS 39 and other International Accounting Standards (such as IAS 21 on the effects of changes in foreign exchange rates).

This implementation guidance was prepared by the IASC Staff and approved for issuance by the IAS 39 Implementation Guidance Committee, which was established for this specific purpose by the IASC Board. It should come as no surprise that the members and observers on the IGC are all experts in financial instruments with backgrounds as accounting standard setters, auditors, bankers, and banking and securities regulators.

EXAMPLES OF COOPERATIVE STANDARD SETTING

In several instances, the Financial Accounting Standards Board has worked with the IASC and with other groups to arrive at compatible standards. Among these endeavors are:

- The FASB-IASC simultaneous effort relating to Earnings per Share, FASB 128 and IASC 33.
- The FASB and the Accounting Standards Board (AcSB) of the Canadian Institute of Chartered Accountants developed almost identical Standards on Segment Reporting and Disclosure. The U.S. Standard is FASB 131. The IASC had also worked with these two groups but hesitated to require as much increased disclosure in IAS 14(rev.).
- The United Kingdom's Accounting Standards Board (ASB)-IASC cooperation on their Standards on Impairment of Assets and also on Provisions, Contingent Liabilities and Contingent Assets. This latter co-operative endeavor also brought them much closer to U.S. GAAP (contained in FASB 5, *Accounting for Contingencies.*)

IOSCO IS INSTRUMENTAL IN LAUNCHING CORE STANDARDS

In May 2000, the International Organization of Securities Commissions announced completion of its assessment of the accounting standards issued by IASC and recommended that its members allow multinational issuers to use 30 of the IASC Standards, including their related interpretations. This was with the understanding that they could be supplemented by reconciliation, disclosure, and interpretation where necessary to address outstanding substantive issues at a national or regional level. These are labeled "the IASC 2000 Standards."

IOSCO believes that use of these Standards by multinational enterprises in preparing their financial statements will facilitate cross-border offerings and listings, and will promote the further development of internationally accepted accounting standards.

IOSCO's Technical Committee published a report summarizing its assessment work, noting outstanding issues that members expect to address through supplemental treatments. IOSCO identified outstanding substantive issues relating to the IASC 2000 Standards in a report that includes an analysis of those issues and specifies supplemental treatments that may be required in a particular jurisdiction to address each of the concerns.

Those supplemental treatments are:

- *Reconciliation:* Requiring reconciliation of certain items to show the effect of applying a different accounting method, in contrast with the method applied under IASC standards.

- *Disclosure:* Requiring additional disclosures, either in the presentation of the financial statements or in the footnotes.

- *Interpretation:* Specifying use of a particular alternative provided in an IASC Standard, or a particular interpretation in cases where the IASC Standard is unclear or silent.

In addition, as part of national or regional specific requirements, waivers may be needed relating to particular aspects of an IASC Standard, without requiring that the effect of the accounting method used be reconciled to the effect of applying the IASC method. The use of waivers should be restricted to exceptional circumstances such as issues identified by a domestic regulator when a specific IASC Standard is contrary to domestic or regional regulation.

Future Development of IASs

The practical consequences of IOSCO's decision will take some time to become fully apparent. Almost all countries of the world — the United States, Canada, Hong Kong, and Japan are the main exceptions — already accept IAS for cross-border listings.

They realize that a key factor will be subsequent action taken by the U.S. Securities and Exchange Commission. As is quite clear, if a foreign company submits financial statements in the United States using IAS, it must produce a reconciliation of its statements to GAAP.

The SEC published a Concept Release in February 2000 seeking comments about the possibility of greater acceptance of IAS. When the comment period ended, the SEC staff began analyzing the comments and considering their next steps. Quoting the IASC, "The United States is currently going through a period of political transition." Evidently, the international organization does not care to hazard a guess as to what that might mean.

It was pointed out that the SEC took a leading role in IOSCO's work in analyzing the core standards, and agreed with the IOSCO resolution. The wording of the resolution and the assessment of the work that has been done in IASC encourages them to expect the United States to move gradually to greater acceptance of IAS Standards. At the same time, it is realistic to expect that the SEC and FASB will continue for some time to require the disclosure of additional information by companies using international standards.

IOSCO realizes that a body of accounting standards like the IASC Standards must continue to evolve in order to address existing and emerging issues. IOSCO's recommendation assumes that it will continue to be involved in the IASC work and structure and that the IASC will continue to develop its body of standards and interpretations.

IOSCO expects to survey its membership to determine the extent to which members have taken steps to permit incoming multinational issuers to use the IASC 2000 Standards, subject to the supplemental treatments described above. At the same time, IOSCO expects to continue to work with the IASC, and will determine the extent to which IOSCO's outstanding substantive issues, including proposals for future projects, have been addressed appropriately.

INTERNATIONALIZATION OF THE U.S. SECURITIES MARKETS

Over the last few years, the number of foreign companies accessing the U.S. public markets has increased dramatically. As of December 31, 2000, there were more than 1,310 foreign companies from 59 countries filing periodic reports with the Securities and Exchange Commission.

Foreign Issuers in the U.S. Market

Foreign companies raising funds from the public, or having their securities traded on a U.S. national exchange, or the NASDAQ Stock Market, are subject to the registration requirements of the Securities Act and the registration and reporting requirements of the Exchange Act. The SEC provides a separate integrated disclosure system for foreign private issuers that provides a number of accommodations to foreign practices and policies. These include:

- Interim reporting on the basis of home country and stock exchange practice, rather than quarterly reports.

- Exemption from the proxy rules and the insider reporting and short swing profit recovery provisions of Section 16.
- Aggregate executive compensation disclosure rather than individual disclosure, if so permitted in an issuer's home country.
- Acceptance of three International Accounting Standards (IASs) relating to:

  a. Cash flow statements (IAS 7).

  b. Business combinations (IAS 22).

  c. Operations in hyperinflationary economies (IAS 21).

- Offering document financial statements updated principally on a semiannual, rather than a quarterly basis.
- An exemption from Exchange Act registration for foreign private issuers that have not engaged in a U.S. public offering, or whose securities are not traded on a national exchange or the NASDAQ Stock Market.

The Commission staff has also implemented procedures to review foreign issuers' disclosure documents on an expedited basis and in draft form, if requested. This helps to facilitate cross-border offerings and listings in light of potentially conflicting home-country schedules and disclosure requirements.

SEC Practice Section of AICPA Changes Rules

Reflecting the importance of audit quality in filings by foreign issuers, the SEC Practice Section (SECPS) of the AICPA changed sections of its membership rules to address SECPS member firms with foreign associated firms that audit SEC registrants. Under the new rules, SECPS members must seek the "adoption of policies and procedures by the international organization or individual foreign associated firms that are consistent with SECPS objectives" for audits of financial statements of SEC registrants. The SECPS member then reports to the AICPA the name and country of any foreign associated firms that demonstrates compliance with that objective. The new rules also establish minimum procedures to be performed by a knowledgeable reviewer with respect to documents to be filed with the Commission.

Interaction with the IASC

The SEC has been working with the IASC through the International Organization of Securities Commissions since 1987 to develop the set of accounting standards for cross-border offerings and listings. The Commission has always maintained that the standards should:

- Include a core set of accounting pronouncements that constitute a comprehensive, generally accepted basis of accounting.
- Be of high quality; in other words they must result in comparability and transparency.
- Provide for full disclosure.
- Be rigorously interpreted and applied.

Amendments to Disclosure Requirements

In late 1999, the Commission adopted changes to its nonfinancial statement disclosure requirements for foreign private issuers, to conform more closely to the International Disclosure Standards endorsed by IOSCO. The changes were intended to harmonize disclosure requirements on fundamental topics among the securities regulations of various jurisdictions.

For a number of years, the Securities and Exchange Commission has been working with other members of IOSCO to develop a set of International Standards for nonfinancial statement disclosures that could be used in cross-border offerings and listings. The International Disclosure Standards developed by IOSCO reflect a consensus among securities regulators in the major capital markets as to the types of disclosures that should be required for international use. The Standards cover fundamental disclosure topics such as the description of the issuer's business, results of operations and management, and the securities it plans to offer or list.

Changes to the Foreign Integrated Disclosure System

The Commission amended Form 20-F (the basic Exchange Act registration statement and annual report form used by foreign issuers) to incorporate the International Disclosure Standards. The Commission also revised the Securities Act registration forms designated for use by foreign private issuers, and related rules and forms, to reflect the changes in Form 20-F.

The amendments do not change the financial statement reconciliation (to GAAP) requirements for foreign issuers, and the SEC will continue to require disclosure on topics not covered by the International Disclosure Standards, such as disclosures relating to market risk and specialized industries such as banks. Unlike the IOSCO International Disclosure Standards, which were intended to apply only to offerings and listings of common equity securities, and only to listings and transactions for cash, the amendments to Form 20-F apply to all types of offerings and listings and to annual reports.

The Commission also revised the definition of "foreign private issuer," which determines an issuer's eligibility to use certain SEC forms and benefit from certain accommodations under Commission rules. These clarify how issuers should calculate their U.S. ownership.

THE EUROPEAN PARLIAMENT'S CHANGES TO ACCOUNTING DIRECTIVES

In amending a European Commission proposal to update two company law directives designed to introduce the principle of *fair value* accounting, members of the European Parliament voted to include banks and other financial institutions. They are among the most frequent users of derivative financial instruments.

The members believe that applying fair value to them will foster market transparency and market discipline. The Commission's proposal does not include banks and other financial institutions, because they prefer to offer similar proposals for their accounting requirements at a later stage.

The amendments, while broadly endorsing the Commission's proposals, are aimed at clarifying and improving the wording of the text. They also include a number of substantive changes in the amendments. They are intended to clarify which categories of a company, as well as which financial instruments and commodity-based contracts, fair value accounting should be applied to.

On information-related matters, Parliament is aiming for more far-reaching disclosure on derivative financial instruments. However, the intention is to allow exemptions for small companies from additional disclosure on the derivatives. In addition, the idea is that there should be no requirement to provide information if it is insignificant.

The purpose of the proposal is to bring EU legislation into line with the new International Accounting Standards and Financial Reporting Standards particularly IAS 39, *Financial Instruments Recognition and Measurement.* In order to take account of the widespread use of derivative financial instruments such as futures, options, forward contracts, and swaps, the IAS have moved away from the *historical cost* valuation model on which the existing directives are based. "Historical cost" is the price actually paid for an asset or liability; "fair value" is the valuation at today's market value. The proposals were unanimously approved by the EU Council of Ministers at their meeting on May 31, 2001.

THE OECD IS SEEKING CONSENSUS ON THE TAX TREATMENT OF E-COMMERCE

Representatives of the Organization for Economic Cooperation and Development (OECD) member governments are attempting to tackle the perplexing problems of how, when, and where to tax international electronic commerce.

As part of its continuing work on the taxation aspects of electronic commerce, the OECD released a set of reports and technical papers illustrating progress toward implementation of the Ottawa Taxation Framework Conditions. Taken together, these reports represent a major step toward reaching an international consensus on the accounting and taxation treatment of e-commerce.

Since the Conditions were agreed to in late 1998, the OECD, through its Committee on Fiscal Affairs, has followed a work program directed at their implementation. A key element of that work program has been an international dialogue, involving not only OECD member countries, but also the international business community and a number of nonmember economies.

In early 2001, they agreed to several important conclusions and recommendations that could provide greater certainty among businesses and consumers regarding e-commerce. The conclusions and recommendations by the Committee on Fiscal Affairs and the business/government advisory groups, cover three main areas:

1. International direct taxation.
2. Consumption taxes.
3. Tax administration.

Status of Specific Taxation Problems

On income taxes, OECD countries have now reached a broad consensus on the interpretation of existing permanent establishment rules that are fundamental for deciding where profits on the conduct of e-commerce can be taxed. They are now working on clarifying the tax treaty treatment of various types of e-commerce payments on the basis of a report just received from a business/government advisory group set up to examine this issue.

In the area of consumption taxes, OECD countries have made significant progress toward identifying pragmatic ways of achieving the desired result of effective taxation in the specific place of the consumption.

In the area of tax administration, OECD governments have reached agreement on the main administrative challenges and opportunities facing tax administrations, and on the sort of responses that governments need to consider. They are now inviting public comments on their proposals regarding consumption taxes and tax administration.

Officials of the OECD agreed there is much that various tax administrations can and should do to share their experience and expertise internationally, especially in the field of taxpayer service. They emphasize that it is important to maintain efforts to strengthen the emerging international consensus. In so doing, it will provide governments and business with the certainty that they need about how taxation rules should apply to e-commerce.

The Basis of Present Considerations

The Committee's work on e-commerce draws its impetus from the Ottawa Taxation Framework Conditions mentioned earlier. The Conditions are a set of principles about how governments should respond to the tax implications of e-commerce. These principles have since been widely recognized as representing a strong foundation for the Committee's current more detailed work. At a recent meeting in Paris, the Committee restated its commitment to a continuing dialogue with the international business community and non-OECD member economies on these issues, and approved new arrangements for continuing the dialogue.

From this basis, emerging conclusions and recommendations from the Committee on Fiscal Affairs have been made in various areas.

International Direct Tax Issues

Broad consensus was recently achieved on clarification in the Commentary on the OECD Model Tax Convention of the application of the current definition of *permanent establishment* (PE). The clarification states that for accounting and tax purposes:

- A Web site cannot, in itself, constitute a permanent establishment.
- A Web site hosting arrangement typically does not result in a PE for the enterprise that carries on business through that Web site.
- An Internet service provider normally will not constitute a dependent agent of another enterprise to constitute a PE for that enterprise.
- Whereas a place where computer equipment, such as a server, is located *may* in certain circumstances constitute a permanent establishment, this requires that the functions performed at that place be significant as well as an essential or core part of the business activity of the enterprise.

The report of its Technical Advisory Group on Treaty Characterization of E-Commerce Payments (see detailed discussion below) is expected to help the Fiscal Affairs Committee reach an early agreement on how treaty characterization issues should be resolved and how the Commentary on the Model Tax Convention should be clarified in that respect. This clarification will address how payments for e-commerce transactions should be accounted for in relation to tax treaty purposes.

Consumption Tax Issues

The Committee endorsed tentative conclusions in a report from its Working Party on Consumption Taxes, and approved its release for public comment.

The report notes that it is necessary to define the principle of taxation in the place of consumption more clearly, and to identify the collection mechanisms that can best support the practical operation of that principle.

The report proposes Guidelines to define the *place of taxation* for cross-border services and intangible property by the business establishment of the recipient business for business-to-business transactions (B2B), and to the recipient's usual place of residence for business-to-consumer transactions (B2C).

Tax Administration Issues

The Committee agreed to the tentative conclusions and future work topics identified in a report on tax administration aspects of e-commerce, and approved its publication for comment. This report addresses such issues as how tax administrations can ensure effective tax collection in an electronic environment. Attention may need to focus on strengthening this cooperation internationally. The report also identifies a range of initiatives that tax administrations across the world are already taking to improve the quality of service that they provide to taxpayers.

Further Work and Future Process

The Committee recognizes that a great deal of additional work remains to be done in several fields. The release of discussion papers is an important part of that process. Principal features of its work program include:

- On direct taxes, work should continue in the areas of:
  - Issues associated with the accounting for profits of a server PE.
  - Refinement of the *place of effective management* concept in determining residence for taxation purposes.
  - Further evaluation of the adequacy of the current treaty rules in the context of electronic commerce, taking into account possible alternatives and the possible clarification or modification of the existing rules.
- On consumption taxes, work should continue on:
  - The feasibility of technology-based collection mechanisms.
  - Simplification opportunities.
  - Means of promoting more effective international administrative co-operation.
- On tax administration issues, the Committee should:
  - Work to strengthen the compliance tools available to tax administrations.
  - Share *best practice* developed worldwide.

—Promote further taxpayer service initiatives.

- On process, the Committee agreed on the need to continue the dialogue with business and nonmembers, through a reinforcement of the current Technical Advisory Group (TAG) process and other initiatives to encourage cooperative international debate.

Report by TAG on Treaty Characterization

The Technical Advisory Group on Treaty Characterization, which was set up in the context of the OECD work on taxation and e-commerce, released its final report early in 2000. The report explored how various types of payments for e-commerce transactions should be accounted for in applying the tax treaties.

The report, which was unanimously approved by TAG members, deals with the determination of which provisions apply to various types of e-commerce payments, thereby, ultimately determining which country may tax these payments and under what conditions.

It includes analysis, conclusions, and recommendations concerning which treaty provisions apply in particular cases, as well as the TAG's views on how such recommendations should be applied in 28 typical categories of e-commerce transactions. Some of the TAG's principal conclusions and recommendations are:

- Transactions that permit the customer to download digital products electronically for that customer's own use or enjoyment (for instance, when a customer orders software or music from an Internet Web site and that digital product is downloaded from the site), the payment should be accounted for as business profits rather than as a royalty payment.

- E-commerce transactions resulting in know-how payments that constitute royalties are relatively rare. The report provides a number of criteria and examples to help distinguish the provision of *services* from the provision of *know-how.*

- Payments for time-limited use of digital products, or for transactions such as data warehousing *cannot* be considered as payments for the use of (or the right to use) industrial, commercial, or scientific equipment. This is not, therefore, to constitute royalties under some of the conventions.

- When payment is for various elements, but one element is predominant and the others are only ancillary and unimportant, it would be more practical to apply the accounting treatment applicable to the main part to the entire payment.

The recommendations of the report (particularly the suggestions for changes to the Commentary of the OECD Model Tax Convention that it includes) will now be examined by the Committee on Fiscal Affairs with a view to making the appropriate changes quickly to the OECD Model Tax Convention. The Tax Convention was first published in 1963 and has been regularly updated since then. It is the basic reference manual used by both OECD and non-OECD countries for the negotiation, application, and interpretation of bilateral tax treaties to coordinate their direct tax systems.

The TAG was set up in 1999 by the OECD's Committee on Fiscal Affairs with the mandate "to examine the characterization of various types of electronic commerce payments under tax conventions with a view to providing the necessary clarifications." Members of the TAG included tax officials from OECD and non-OECD countries as well as representatives from the business community.

The report follows two previous drafts released by the TAG for public comment in 2000. Those earlier drafts reflected some substantial disagreements among the members of the group. The comments received helped the TAG to resolve the disagreements at its final meeting in November, 2000; thus, the unanimous approval of the final report.

THE IMPORTANCE OF GLOBAL ACCOUNTING STANDARDS

The need for global accounting standards, or at a minimum for less diversity in national standards, became painfully evident in 1998. The economic difficulties that began in Asia and spread to other regions of the world rather graphically demonstrated the interdependencies of different nations in the modern global economy.

It has been suggested that part of the blame should be placed on "accounting" — or lack of it. The IASC felt that international investors lacked confidence in the accounting of the countries where the difficulties originated. They felt that the lack of confidence made capital more expensive than it needed to be and added to the threat of serious worldwide economic recession.

As a result, the IASC is as committed as the SEC and the FASB to the belief that "comparability" and "transparency" are key words in healthy financial markets. They acknowledge that:

- An important emphasis in the demand for global accounting standards is *comparability* among businesses in different countries to serve the demands of international capital markets.
- Accounting standards are needed to bring about greater *transparency* and openness in financial reporting by individual countries and their business corporations and financial institutions.

FASB AND IASB WORK TOWARD CONVERGENCE OF GLOBAL ACCOUNTING STANDARDS

In October 2002, the FASB and the IASB issued a memorandum of under-standing, formalizing their commitment to the convergence of U.S. and international accounting standards. The two standard setting bodies presented the agreement to the chairs of leading national standard setters at a two-day meeting held in London. The agreement between the FASB and IASB represents their latest commitment, following their September joint meeting, to adopt compatible, high-quality solutions to existing and future accounting issues.

The agreement follows the decisions recently reached by both Boards to add a joint, short-term convergence project to their active agendas. This project will require both Boards to use their best efforts to propose changes to U.S. and international accounting standards that reflect common solutions to certain specifically identified differences. Working within each Board's due process procedures, the FASB and IASB expect to issue an Expo-sure Draft to address some, and perhaps all, of those identified differences by the latter part of 2003. The elimination of those differences, together with the commitment by both Boards to eliminate or reduce remaining differences through continued progress on joint projects and coordination of future work programs, improves comparability of financial statements across national jurisdictions.

Both Boards agree that by working together on the short-term conver-gence project—as well as on longer-term issues—the chances of success are greatly improved. They feel that the agreement provides a guide for working together to achieve their common goal and underscores another step in the partnership with national standard setters to reach a truly global set of ac-counting standards. They feel that by drawing on the best of U.S. GAAP, IFRSs, and other national standards, the world's capital markets will have a workable set of global accounting standards that investors can trust.

The European Union

Another important development in the demand for International Ac-counting Standards is taking place in Europe. A key current objective of the European Union has been the development of a single economic market. The introduction of the euro on January 1, 1999, was an important step in that di-rection. The single economic market would almost necessitate a single capital market with companies from the different countries competing for capital on equal terms.

Those putting up the capital must be able to assess the performance of different companies with full comparability. Said comparability is not attainable if different accounting standards are used by different companies — even if they are reporting in a common currency. Iass are the crucial to this process.

From the beginning, rather than establish a separate European Accounting Standards Board, the European Commission (EC) planned to work with the IASC to standardize accounting practices for multinational companies within the European Union. The EC's preferred option for the future development of accounting in the EU was to "oblige" listed companies to follow International Accounting Standards. Other companies would follow national codes within the framework of the European directives. Now they have decided that by 2005 all listed companies must use ISAs and IFRSs.

The European Commission concluded that there are no significant conflicts between the EC Accounting Directives and those International Accounting Standards and interpretations of the Standing Interpretations Committee that are applicable to accounting periods beginning before July 1, 1998.

THE ROLE OF IOSCO

In May 2000, IOSCO announced completion of its assessment of the accounting standards issued by the International Accounting Standards Committee. It recommended that its members allow multinational issuers to use 30 IASC standards, as supplemented by *reconciliation, disclosure,* and *interpretation* where necessary to address outstanding substantive issues at a national or regional level. These are labeled "the IASC 2000 standards."

IOSCO believes that use of these standards by multinational enterprises in preparing their financial statements will facilitate cross-border offerings and listings, and will promote the further development of internationally accepted accounting standards.

The members of IOSCO (including the U.S. Securities and Exchange Commission) undertake their own review process before they accept financial reports prepared in accordance with International Accounting Standards for cross-border listings in their own countries. Many countries have already accepted the complete list of Iass. The other members (including the SEC) are in an advanced stage of the evaluation process.

THE ADOPTION OF IAS 40, INVESTMENT PROPERTY

With the adoption of IAS 40, *Investment Property,* effective as of January 1, 2001, all of the basic core topics listed by IOSCO have now been covered.

IAS 40 concerns investment property held by all enterprises and will not be limited to enterprises whose main activities are in this area. Investment property is property (land or a building — or part of a building — or both) held (by the owner or by the lessee under a finance lease) to earn rentals or for capital appreciation or both. Investment property does not include:

- Property held for use in the production or supply of goods or services or for administrative purposes.
- Property being constructed for third parties.
- Property held for sale in the ordinary course of business.
- An interest held under an operating lease if the interest was a long-term interest acquired in exchange for a large up-front payment.

Under IAS 40, an enterprise must choose either:

- A fair value model in which investment property should be recognized in the income statement; or
- A cost model, the same as the benchmark treatment in IAS 16, Property, Plant, and Equipment. Investment property should be measured at depreciated cost (less any accumulated impairment losses). An enterprise that chooses the cost model should disclose the fair value of its investment property.

The Standard requires an enterprise to apply the model chosen to all its investment property. A change from one model to the other model to the other model should be made only if the change will result in a more appropriate presentation. The standard states that this is highly unlikely to be the case for a change from the fair value model to the cost model.

In exceptional cases, an enterprise that has chosen the fair value model may conclude that it cannot determine the fair value of an investment property. In such cases, the enterprise measures that investment property using the benchmark treatment in IAS 16 until the disposal of the investment property. The residual value of the investment property should be assumed to be zero. The enterprise measures all of its other investment property at fair value.

SELECTED IASC STANDARDS WITH COMPARISONS TO U.S. GAAP

The following are recently adopted international standards, several of which have been prepared in cooperation with the U.S. or other English-speaking standard-setting bodies. Each of them covers an important aspect of accounting that has been uppermost in the minds of concerned standard setters. Each of these discussions pinpoints the relationship between the international standard and the relevant GAAP accounting treatment.

IAS 33, *Earnings per Share*

The objective of the FASB and IASC earnings-per-share standards is to prescribe principles for the determination and presentation of earnings per share that will lead to global harmonization of earnings-per-share measurements and disclosures. To this end, both standard setters have concluded where appropriate two earnings-per-share figures should be presented, namely,

1. Basic Earnings per Share, which is computed by dividing income available to stockholders by the weighted average number of common shares outstanding during the period. Shares issued during the period and shares reacquired during the period should be weighted for the portion of the period they were outstanding.

2. Diluted Earnings per Share, which is computed in a similar manner to basic earnings per share after adjusting the numerator and denominator of the calculation for the effects of all potential dilutive common shares that were outstanding during the period. One difference between FASB 128, *Earnings per Share,* and IAS 33 is a matter of degree. FASB 128 requires disclosure of per-share figures for income from continuing operations on the face of the income statement and for extraordinary items, accounting changes and discontinued operations. The international standard requires only net profit per-share amounts on the face of the income statement but also encourages other disclosures.

   The IASC and FASB also differ in their view of the objective of a diluted earnings-per-share presentation. The IASC views the figures as an early warning to investors of possible reductions in the value of EPS, whereas the FASB sees it as a measure of performance rather than an indicator of the future. However, except for some language differences, the basic provisions of IAS 33 are substantially the same as those of FASB 128. (These provisions are discussed more fully in connection with FASB 128 in Chapter 1 in the main volume).

   It is anticipated that IAS 33 will be adopted by:

* Many countries as a national standard.
* Stock exchanges for listing purposes.
* Corporations with a global stock ownership.

These adoptions will be a significant contribution to facilitating global investing in common stocks.

IAS 34, *Interim Financial Reporting*

IAS 34, *Interim Financial Reporting,* requires companies that prepare interim reports to apply the same accounting recognition and measurement principles used in their last annual statements. This requirement will tend to make interim earnings more volatile for non-U.S. companies that heretofore had followed U.S.-style interim reporting rules. U.S. rulings permit some interim income smoothing recognition and measurement practices. The statement also specifies that measurements in interim financial statements should be made on a financial year-to-date basis.

It does not mandate that interim reports be published in the first place, who should publish them, how often they should be prepared, or how soon they should appear after the end of an interim reporting period, if they are prepared. The IASC decided these matters were better left to the discretion of the national governments, securities regulators, stock exchanges, and accounting organizations. At present, in at least 30 countries, the securities regulators, and stock exchanges do, in fact, require interim reporting. Interim reports are used by investors and creditors to check for any signs of weakness — or strength, for that matter.

IAS 34 applies to recognizing, measuring, and disclosing assets, liabilities, income, and expenses for quarterly, biannual, or any other type of interim report.

The United Kingdom's Accounting Standards Board issued a nonmandatory "best practice" statement on interim reporting that is almost identical to the IASC standard. Both use the discrete method for interim reporting. Under this method, as amplified below, the interim period is treated as an accounting period distinct from the annual period. Incomplete transactions are reported, using the same principles that are used for the annual reports.

This statement will get close scrutiny from many sources, including U.S. investors and creditors with worldwide interests. Interim financial reports issued by foreign companies do not conform to APB 28, *Interim Financial Reporting*. This new standard also differs in a number of significant areas from U.S. GAAP. However, U.S. accountants, investors, and financial advisors are already aware of the fact that the accounting used for interim financial reporting purposes in many countries outside of the U.S. is considerably different from U.S. GAAP. The foreign standards are similar in many respects to IAS 34.

Below is a comparison of a few of the provisions to U.S. GAAP governing interim financial reports included in Accounting Principles Board APB 28. (A discussion of other information relating to U.S. GAAP can be found in Appendix E of the main volume).

Independent Theory.   IAS 34 for the most part adopts the independent theory of interim reporting. This approach regards each interim period as a discrete or "stand-alone" reporting period. That is, the events and transactions within each accounting period are to be reported in the accounting period, regardless of its length. Under the independent view, the results of operations for each interim period should be determined basically in the same manner as if the interim period were an annual accounting period. Under this approach, deferrals, accruals, and estimations at the end of each interim period are determined by following basically the same approach as in the annual reports. Thus, if an expenditure is expensed in the annual statement, it should be expensed in any interim report, regardless of the amount of the expenditure and the relationship to the annual amount or the revenues of other interim periods for that year.

Dependent Approach.   APB 28 generally follows the dependent theory of interim period reporting. This approach regards each interim period as an integral part of the annual period. According to the dependent view, interim financial data are an integral part of the annual period, and it is essential to provide investors with timely information on the progress the entity is making in realizing its annual results of operations. Therefore, the usefulness of interim data rests on the predictive relationship that it has to the annual report. Thus, each interim period should be regarded as an integral part of the annual period rather than a discrete period standing on its own.

Under this approach, deferrals, accruals, and estimations at the end of each interim period are affected by predictions about the results of operations for the remainder of the year. Thus, for example, a portion of an estimated annual expenditure that might be expensed for the entire annual period might be accrued or deferred at the end of an interim period as management allocates the estimated annual expense between interim periods on a basis that reflects time, sales volume, or production activity.

Other Differences.   If fully aware of the important differences between the two alternative interim financial reporting approaches, the user of the financial reports should be able to make an intelligent analysis of the information presented. Some of those differences are presented below:

Dependent/Independent.   Because the dependent approach gives accounting flexibility in managing interim earnings to minimize any possibility that the figures might give a misleading picture of the company's current and future performance, company management probably prefers it.

Some users believe that the dependent approach properly applied gives a better indication of a company's annual results, earnings volatility, and risks when the company is geared to such things as seasonal ups and downs of irregular sales, income and expenses. Here the independent approach may result in interim financial reports that overstate the level of risk and volatility associated with the company's actual annual earnings picture.

On the other hand, there are others who are quite sure that the independent approach produces a clearer and more timely picture of coming events in a company's financial prospects.

Mandated/Suggested.   The new Statement does not require companies complying with IAS in their annual reports to publish interim financial reports.

The IASC, however, has indicated that it intends to strongly encourage governments, security regulators, stock exchanges, international bodies, and accounting standard setters to require companies whose debt or equity securities are publicly traded to provide interim financial reports that conform to IAS 34 principles. The IASC will also encourage publicly traded companies to provide interim reports complying with the Statement's principles at least at the end of the first six months of their financial year.

U.S. GAAP does not mandate publication of interim financial reports; however, the Securities and Exchange Commission and the stock exchanges do require listed companies to publish them for the first three quarters of the fiscal year.

When interim financial reports are published, both IAS 34 and U.S. practice require that they include:

- Condensed balance sheet.
- Condensed income statement.
- Condensed cash flow statement.
- Footnote disclosures focusing on changes since the last annual report in accounting principles or estimates, unusual events, trends, and turning points.

Costs.   According to APB 28, costs and expenses that are not allocated or associated directly with product and service revenues may be expensed as incurred or allocated among interim periods based on an estimate of time expired, benefit received, or other activity associated with the period.

IAS 34 requires costs that are incurred unevenly during a company's financial year be anticipated or deferred for interim reporting only if it is appropriate to anticipate or defer those costs at the end of the financial year. An example of costs that often fall into this category are periodic major maintenance or retooling projects.

Comparability.   In the final analysis, even though the interim financial statements may look alike, the operating results for the period under the IASC proposal of a discrete approach and the U.S. GAAP integral approach will not be comparable because of the different concepts. At the same time, comparison of operating results among U.S. companies is not always possible because of discretionary accounting differences permitted for certain items under APB 28.

IAS 35, *Discontinuing Operations*

This Standard's objectives are to establish a basis for segregating information about a major operation that an enterprise is discontinuing from information about its continuing operations and to specify minimum disclosures about a discontinuing operation.

IAS 35 is a presentation and disclosure Standard that focuses on how to present a discontinuing operation in an enterprise's financial statements and what information to disclose. It does not establish any new principles for deciding when and how to recognize and measure the income, expenses, cash flows, and changes to assets and liabilities relating to a discontinuing operation. Instead, it requires that enterprises follow the recognition and measurement principles in other International Accounting Standards.

Definition of a Discontinuing Operation. A discontinuing operation is considered in IAS 35 to be a component of an enterprise:

• That the enterprise, pursuant to a single plan, is:
  —Disposing of substantially in its entirety,
  —Disposing of piecemeal, or
  —Terminating through abandonment.
• That represents a separate major line of business or geographical area of operations.
• That can be distinguished operationally and for financial reporting purposes.

Thus, a discontinuing operation is a relatively large component of an enterprise—such as a business or geographical segment under IAS 14, *Segment Reporting*—that the enterprise, pursuant to a single plan, is disposing of substantially in its entirety or is terminating through abandonment or piecemeal sale.

The new Standard requires that disclosures about a discontinuing operation begin earlier, after the *earlier* of the following:

• An enterprise has entered into an agreement to sell substantially all of the assets of the discontinuing operation.
• The board of directors or other similar governing body has both approved and announced a detailed plan for discontinuance.

Disclosure Requirements. Required disclosures include:

• Description of the discontinuing operation.
• The business or geographical segment(s) in which it is reported in accordance with IAS 14, *Segment Reporting*.
• The date that the plan for discontinuance was announced.
• The timing of expected completion (date or period), if known or determinable.

- The carrying amounts of the total assets and the total liabilities to be disposed of.

- The amounts of revenue, expenses, and pretax profit or loss from ordinary activities attributable to the discontinuing operation during that specific reporting period, and the related income tax expense.

- The amount of any gain or loss that is recognized on the disposal of assets or settlement of liabilities attributable to the discontinuing operation, and related income tax expense.

- The net cash flows attributable to the operating, investing, and financing activities of the discontinuing operation.

- The net selling prices received or expected from the sale of those net assets for which the enterprise has entered into one or more binding sale agreements, and the expected timing thereof, and the carrying amounts of those net assets.

Further Considerations. Financial statements for periods after initial disclosure must update those disclosures, including a description of any significant changes in the amount or timing of cash flows relating to the assets and liabilities to be disposed of or settled and the causes of those changes.

The disclosures would be made if a plan for disposal is approved and publicly announced after the end of an enterprise's financial reporting period but before the financial statements for that period are approved. The disclosures continue until completion of the disposal.

To improve the ability of users of financial statements to make projections, comparative information for prior periods presented in financial statements prepared after initial disclosure must be restated to segregate the continuing and discontinuing assets, liabilities, income, expenses, and cash flows.

Comparison to U.S. GAAP. IAS 35 brings another of IASC's accounting standards closer to U.S. GAAP in that the IASC's standards now actually include a discontinuing operation standard—similar in many respects to the comparable U.S. GAAP standard, Accounting Principles Board Opinion 30 (APB 30).

However, as in most instances, this standard does vary slightly from GAAP. Two examples follow:

1. APB 30 requires the results of discontinuing operations to be reported on the face of the financial statements while IAS 35 only recommends this approach to disclosure.

2. Whereas IASC emphasizes the timeliness of its required initial disclosure event, APB's requirement would very probably occur earlier than IAS 35's requirement. The initial disclosure event specified in IAS 35 is a

binding sales agreement or board of director's approval of a *detailed discontinuing operations plan* and a formal announcement of that plan. On the other hand, APB 30 specifies that the initial disclosure event is the date on which management having authority to approve the discontinuance commits to a formal plan to dispose of a segment of the business.

More Uniform Approach. Because many developing economies (as well as other more advanced ones) do not have specific guidance relating to discontinuing operations accounting, it is probable that the issuance of IAS 35 will inspire a number of them to adopt it outright or to develop their own national standard that will closely follow the requirements of IAS 35. Regardless, a more uniform approach to reporting discontinuing operations should result. As an additional inducement to use the principles of this Standard, appendices to IAS 35 provide illustrative disclosures and guidance on how prior-period information should be restated to conform to the presentation requirements of IAS 35.

IAS 36, Impairment of Assets

International Accounting Standard 36, *Impairment of Assets,* prescribes the accounting and disclosure requirements specifically for impairment of:

*   Goodwill.
*   Intangible assets and property.
*   Plant and equipment.

The Standard includes requirements for identifying an impaired asset, measuring its recoverable amount, recognizing or reversing any resulting impairment loss, and disclosing information on impairment losses or reversals of impairment losses.

It prescribes how an enterprise should test its assets for impairment; that is:

*   The procedures that an enterprise should apply to ensure that its assets are not overstated in the financial statements.
*   How an enterprise should assess the amount to be recovered from an asset (the "recoverable amount").
*   When an enterprise should account for an impairment loss identified by this assessment.

The Standard does *not* cover accounting and disclosure requirements for:

*   Inventories.
*   Deferred tax assets.

- Assets arising from construction contracts.
- Assets arising from employee benefits.
- Most financial assets.

Requirements of IAS 36. According to this IAS, an impairment loss should be recognized whenever the recoverable amount of an asset is less than its carrying amount (sometimes called "book value"). The Standard spells out in detail the procedures to follow when this occurs:

1. The recoverable amount of an asset is defined as the higher of:

   a. Net selling price as measured by the amount obtainable from the sale of the asset in an arm's length transaction between knowledgeable, willing parties, less the cost of disposal.

   b. Value in use as measured by the present value of the asset's estimated future cash flows including disposable cash flows, if any, expected to arise from its continuing use and eventual disposal. The discount rate should be a pretax rate that reflects current market assessments of the time value of money and the risks specific to the asset.

2. An impairment loss should be recognized as an expense in the income statement for assets carried at cost and treated as a revaluation decrease for assets carried at revalued amount.

3. An impairment loss should be reversed and income recognized when there has been a *change* in the estimates used to determine an asset's recoverable amount after the last impairment loss was recognized.

4. The recoverable amount of an asset should be estimated whenever there is an indication that the asset may be impaired. IAS 36 includes a list of indicators of impairment to be considered at each balance sheet date. In some cases, the IAS applicable to an asset may include requirements for additional reviews.

5. In determining value in use, an enterprise should use:

   a. Cash flow projections based on reasonable and supportable assumptions that reflect the asset in its current condition and represent management's best estimate of the set of economic conditions that will exist over the remaining useful life of the asset.

   b. Estimates of future cash flows should include all estimated future cash inflows and cash outflows except for cash flows from financing activities and income tax receipts and payments.

   c. A pretax discount rate that reflects current market assessments of the time value of money and the risks specific to the asset. The discount rate should not reflect risks for which the future cash flows have been adjusted.

6. If an asset does not generate cash inflows that are largely independent from the cash inflows from other assets, an enterprise should determine the recoverable amount of the cash-generating unit to which the asset belongs. IAS 36 provides explicit directions concerning these cash-generating units:

   a. "Cash-generating unit" refers to the smallest identifiable group of assets that generates cash inflows which are largely independent of the cash inflows from other assets or group of assets.

   b. The requirements for recognizing and reversing impairment losses for a cash-generating unit are the same as those for an individual asset.

   c. The concept of cash-generating units should often be used in testing assets for impairment because, in many cases, assets work together rather than in isolation.

   d. In addition, IAS 36 provides information on how to identify the cash-generating unit to which an asset belongs and further requirements on how to measure an impairment loss for a cash-generating unit and then allocate the loss between the assets of the unit.

7. Reversal of impairment losses also comes in for extensive consideration:

   a. An impairment loss recognized in prior years should be reversed if, and only if, there has been a change in the estimates used to determine recoverable amount since the last impairment loss was recognized.

   b. An impairment loss should only be reversed to the extent the reversal does not increase the carrying amount of the asset above the carrying amount that would have been determined for the asset (net of amortization or depreciation) had no impairment loss been recognized.

   c. An impairment loss for *goodwill* should be reversed only if the specific external event that caused the recognition of the impairment loss reverses.

   d. A reversal of an impairment loss should be recognized as income in the income statement for assets carried at cost and treated as a revaluation increase for assets carried at revalued amount.

8. When impairment losses are recognized or reversed, an enterprise should disclose certain information by *class of assets* and by *reportable segments*. Further disclosure is required if impairment losses recognized or reversed are *material* to the financial statements of the reporting enterprise as a whole.

Upon first adoption of IAS 36, its requirements should be applied *prospectively* only; that is, prior periods will *not* be restated.

IASC-UK Cooperation. IAS 36 differs materially in a number of instances from U.S. GAAP and the asset impairment rules of a number of other countries. On the other hand, there are aspects of the international standard that are closer to the provisions of other established national standards.

For example, in developing IAS 36, proposals of the Accounting Standard Board (ASB) in the United Kingdom for a Financial Reporting Standard on impairment of assets were closely monitored by the international body. The ASB and the IASC shared the same objectives for their project, and many of their views regarding requirements coincided. Therefore, the resulting standards are very similar.

Furthermore, IAS 36 provides a standard approach to the recognition, measurement, and disclosure of asset impairments by non-U.S. companies that use IAS in financial statements and furnishes a model for the many developing economies that have not yet adopted an asset impairment standard of their own but look often to IASC for guidance.

The IASC considers this an important step forward from the requirements and guidance for impairment losses that were previously included in its Standards. It points out that IAS 36 provides more details on how to perform an impairment test and it eliminates certain alternatives, such as the option not to use discounting in measuring recoverable amount. (The "options" in many of the older IASs have been particularly worrisome to the SEC, the FASB, and other standard-setting bodies.)

Differences from GAAP.   As mentioned above several significant differences between IAS 36 and U.S. GAAP are specified in FASB 121, *Accounting for the Impairment of Long-Lived Assets and for Long-Lived Assets to Be Disposed Of.*

Differences between the two Standards include:

- Probably most significantly, FASB 121 *does not permit reversal* of asset impairment losses as does IAS 36 — along with much of the rest of the accounting world. (It might be pointed out here that there seems to be little global consensus yet about how to account for asset impairment. Some countries have rulings similar to GAAP, others to the new IAS, others to the old IAS. Still others have standards relating to assessment of recoverability, not valuation; many have no standard at all on impairment. On the other hand, many of the emerging nations will undoubtedly adopt IAS 36.)

- GAAP requires a *quantitative test* of asset impairment before the measurement and recognition of an asset impairment loss is necessitated. This involves figuring the expected cumulative net cash flows from continuing use of the asset, not including interest and not to be discounted less than the asset's carrying amount. IAS 36 does not include this type of test.

- IAS 36 does not distinguish between assets to be held and used and assets to be disposed of when measuring impairment loss; FASB 121 has different impairment loss measurement approaches for the two categories.
  - —FASB 121's measurement of the impairment loss of an asset *to be used* is the difference between the asset's carrying amount and its fair value.
  - —FASB 121 measurement of the impairment loss of an asset *to be disposed of* is the asset's carrying amount less its net realizable value.
  - —IAS 36's measurement of *either* impairment loss is the asset's carrying amount less the higher of its value in use or its net realizable value (fair value minus disposal costs).
- FASB 121 relies on *management judgment* to determine the appropriate future cash flow period and cash flows to determine the equivalent of IAS 36's value in use. Unless management can justify otherwise, IAS 36 limits the maximum future cash flow period to five years and specifies the growth rate in cash flows.

IAS 37, Provisions, Contingent Liabilities, and Contingent Assets

IAS 37, *Provisions, Contingent Liabilities, and Contingent Assets* requires that:

- Provisions should be recognized in the balance sheet only when:
  - —An enterprise has a present obligation (either legal or constructive) as a result of a past event;
  - —More likely than not a transfer of economic benefits will be required to settle the obligation;
  - —The amount of the obligation can be measured reliably.
- Provisions should be measured in the balance sheet at the best estimate of the expenditure required to settle the present obligation at the balance sheet date. This is the amount that an enterprise would rationally pay to settle the obligation, or to transfer it to a third party, at that date. When measuring provisions, an enterprise should take into account any risks and uncertainties. However, uncertainty does not justify the creation of excessive provisions or a deliberate overstatement of liabilities — in other words, the "big bath."

  An enterprise should discount a provision where the effect of the time value of money is material and should take future events, such as changes in the law and technological changes, into account where there is sufficient objective evidence that they will occur.
- The amount of a provision should not be reduced by gains from the expected disposal of assets (even if the expected disposal is closely linked

to the event giving rise to the provision) or by expected reimbursements—from insurance contracts, indemnity clauses, suppliers' warranties and the like. When it is virtually certain the reimbursement will be received if the enterprise settles the obligation, the reimbursement should be recognized as a separate asset.

- A provision should be used only for expenditures for which the provision was originally recognized and should be reversed if an outflow of resources is no longer probable.

IAS 37 sets out three specific applications of these general requirements:

1. A provision *should not be recognized* for future operating losses.
2. A provision *should be recognized* for an onerous contract in which the unavoidable costs of meeting the obligations under the contract are greater than the expected economic benefits.
3. A provision for restructuring costs *should be recognized only* when an enterprise has a detailed formal plan for the restructuring and has raised a valid expectation in those affected that it will carry out the restructuring by starting to implement that plan or announcing its main features to those affected by it; for this purpose, a management or board decision is not enough.

A restructuring provision should exclude costs—such as retraining or relocating continuing staff, marketing or investment in new systems and distribution networks—that are not necessarily entailed by the restructuring or that are not associated with the enterprise's ongoing activities.

IAS 37 replaces part of IAS 10, *Contingencies and Events Occurring After the Balance Sheet Date.* It prohibits the recognition of contingent liabilities and contingent assets. An enterprise should disclose a contingent liability, unless the possibility of an outflow of resources embodying economic benefits is remote, and disclose a contingent asset if an inflow of economic benefits is probable.

UK-IASC Cooperative Effort. Here again, the IASC and the UK's Accounting Standards Board worked in close conjunction to develop virtually identical accounting standards. Their aim is to eliminate many of the questionable accounting practices that have been developing.

One of the most obvious is the "big bath" mentioned and included in the "hocus pocus" practices that the SEC feels has been sullying the financial reporting process here—as well as globally. (The ploy is to report excessive liabilities currently to make future profits look even rosier at the time the liabilities are actually being incurred.)

Global Aspects. On the global front, the standards should help to lessen the diversity of provision recognition and measurement practices that have evolved along with varying accounting regulations and tax treatment of provisions. Not only do these standards cut down on the welter of provisions that were previously provided for in financial statements prepared according to UK and IAS principles, but they also move much closer to U.S. GAAP (contained in FASB 5, *Accounting for Contingencies*).

Some technical differences between GAAP and the two standards are slight enough that they should pose no problem in doing comparative valuations of U.S. and non-U.S. companies. Because provisions can significantly affect a company's balance sheet and net income, reducing the divergence in the handling of "provisions" should be considered an important step in harmonization of global accounting practices, particularly when considering the fact that many countries that have no established procedure for handling provisions and contingencies—or very haphazard ones—will now adopt IAS 37.

IAS 38, *Intangible Assets*

IAS 38 applies to all intangible assets that are not specifically handled in other IASs. Included in the lists of things it does deal with are the accounting for expenditures on advertising, training, start-up activities, research and development activities (R&D), mortgage servicing rights, customer lists, licensing agreements, motion picture patents, and copyrights. It also covers expenditures for computer software that is an integral part of a tangible asset.

The Standard does *not* apply to intangible assets covered by other IASs; financial instruments; mineral rights and expenditures for the exploration, development, and extraction of minerals, oil, natural gas—nonregenerative resources; insurance contracts.

Among those intangible assets covered by another IAS are deferred tax assets, intangible assets held for sale in the ordinary course of business, leases, employee benefits, and goodwill arising from a business transaction.

IAS 38 includes transitional provisions that clarify when the Standard should be applied retrospectively and when it should be applied prospectively.

Requirements of IAS 38. The basic features of IAS 38 include:

- An intangible asset should be recognized initially, at cost, in the financial statement whether it has been acquired externally or generated internally, if, and only if:
  - It is probable that the future economic benefits attributable to the asset will flow to the enterprise;
  - Cost of the asset can be measured reliably;

— The asset falls within the classification of an *intangible* asset; that is, it is *an identifiable nonmonetary asset without physical substance held for use in the production or supply of goods or services, for rental to others, or for administrative purposes.*

- If an intangible item does not meet both the definition and the criteria for the recognition of an intangible asset, IAS 38 requires the expenditure on this item to be recognized as an *expense* when it is incurred. An enterprise is not permitted to include this expenditure in the cost of an intangible asset at a later date.

- Therefore, it becomes evident from the recognition criteria that all expenditures on research should be recognized as an expense. The same treatment applies to start-up costs, training costs, and advertising costs. IAS 38 also specifically prohibits the recognition as assets of internally generated goodwill, brands, mastheads, publishing titles, customer lists and such. However, as mentioned previously, occasionally developmental expenditure may result in the recognition of an intangible asset — some internally developed computer software, for example.

- In accounting for a business combination that is an acquisition, IAS 38 works in combination with IAS 22, *Business Combinations*. This reinforces the stipulation that if an intangible item does not meet both the *definition* and the *criteria* for the recognition as an intangible asset, the expenditure for this item, which was included in the cost of acquisition, should form part of the amount attributed to goodwill at the date of acquisition.

    Therefore, according to this Standard, purchased R&D-in-process should not be recognized as an expense immediately at the date of acquisition, but it should be recognized as part of the goodwill recognized at the date of acquisition and amortized under IAS 22 (rev.), unless it meets the criteria for separate recognition as an intangible asset.

    IAS 22 (rev.) provides that if there is sufficient evidence that the useful life of goodwill will exceed 20 years, an enterprise should amortize the goodwill over its estimated useful life and:

    — Test goodwill for impairment at least annually in accordance with IAS 36, *Impairment of Assets.*

    — Disclose the reasoning behind the presumption in the initial recognition that the useful life of goodwill would not exceed 20 years, and specify the factor(s) that were significant later in determining the useful life of goodwill.

    IAS 22 (rev.) does not permit an enterprise to assign an infinite useful life to goodwill.

- Requires that after initial recognition in the financial statement, an intangible asset be measured under either the *benchmark treatment* or the allowed *alternative treatment.*

— The benchmark treatment is historical cost less any amortization and impairment losses. It is consistent with the GAAP approach.

— The allowed alternative treatment is the revalued amount based on fair value minus any subsequent amortization and impairment losses. However, this treatment is permitted if, and only if, fair value can be determined by reference to an active market for the intangible asset — which is fairly unlikely for *intangible* assets.

The Standard defines fair value of an asset as the amount for which that asset could be exchanged between knowledgeable, willing parties in an arm's-length transaction.

Comparison to GAAP. IAS 38 and the comparable GAAP are similar in many respects. There are some major differences, but even here the FASB and the SEC are looking into revisions in some areas. Current differences include:

- Here again, an international standard differs from U.S. GAAP on the revaluation issue: IAS 38 permits revaluation; GAAP does not.

- GAAP requires that an intangible asset's amortization period not exceed forty years. IAS 38 specifies a maximum twenty-year amortization period. This is rebuttable if a longer amortization period can be justified. (The FASB has now voted to cut to twenty years the write-off time for goodwill from an acquisition.)

- GAAP does not require an active market-based valuation for internally generated intangible assets; IAS does.

- Except for computer software development, GAAP does not permit capitalization of development costs. On the other hand, IAS 38 requires capitalization of development costs in certain cases.

IAS 39, *Financial Instruments: Recognition and Measurement*

In March, 1999, IASC announced that it had published a comprehensive standard on accounting for financial instruments after nine years' effort and four public comment documents. This new Standard, IAS 39, *Financial Instruments: Recognition and Measurement,* will take effect for annual financial statements covering periods beginning on or after January 1, 2001. Earlier application is permitted as of the beginning of a fiscal year that ends after March 15,1999. Retrospective application is not permitted.

Financial instruments include conventional financial assets and liabilities, such as cash, trade receivables and payables, investments in debt and equity securities, and notes, bonds, and loans payable. Financial instruments also include derivatives such as futures, forwards, swaps, and option contracts.

Background. IAS 39 has been in development by IASC since 1989. Its "final" form was preceded by exposure drafts in 1991, 1994, and 1998 and by a steering committee discussion paper in 1997. In 1996, IASC adopted *Financial Instruments: Disclosure and Presentation* (IAS 32) pending completion of a standard on recognition and measurement. IAS 39 expands those disclosures and resolves the accounting questions, including the important area of accounting for hedging transactions.

IASC officials emphasized their belief that IAS 39 fills the biggest void in global accounting standards. They pointed out that of their 104 member countries only the United States has adopted a truly comprehensive standard on recognition and measurement of financial instruments and hedge accounting (FASB 133).

Need for Greater Uniformity. With the phenomenal growth of global trading (and the equally amazing growth of imaginative derivatives, which are often not recognized in the financial statements), IASC suggests that investors sometimes get very unwelcome surprises when losses surface.

The IASC is aware that current accounting practices for financial instruments vary widely around the world, with the result being noncomparability and investor confusion. Even when financial assets such as investments have been recognized on the balance sheet, some companies have measured them at cost, others at lower of cost or market, and still others at fair value.

Further, in the absence of hedge accounting standards, companies often have postponed recognizing any changes in the fair values of financial instruments or, if recognized, companies have deferred the profit-or-loss effects of such changes in the balance sheet. IAS 39 addresses these and other shortcomings of current practice.

Many developing economies are adopting the International Accounting Standards outright or using them as a basis for developing their own national standards. It is probable that not only they, but also many of the developed economies, will progress to more comprehensive accounting standards for financial instruments, including derivatives. After all, both the FASB and the IASC have spent years going over the ground trying to find an effective solution to satisfy all segments of the business and financial world.

IAS 39 does not go as far in accounting for certain financial instruments as U.S. GAAP, but it does move the international standards closer. It should also reduce the global diversity of financial instrument accounting practices, particularly those dealing with debt and equity security instruments, derivatives, and hedges.

Principal Requirements. IAS 39 requires that all financial assets and all financial liabilities, including all derivatives, be recognized on the balance sheet. This means that derivatives can no longer be off-balance-sheet items.

Initially, financial assets and liabilities will be measured at cost, including transaction costs. After initial recognition, most financial assets must be remeasured at fair value; however, the following will be carried at amortized cost subject to a test for impairment:

- Loans and receivables originated by the enterprise and not held for trading.
- Other fixed maturity investments, such as debt securities and mandatorily redeemable preferred shares, that the enterprise intends and is able to hold to maturity.
- Financial assets whose fair value cannot be reliably measured (limited to some equity instruments with no quoted market price and some derivatives that are linked to and must be settled by delivery of such unquoted equity instruments).

After acquisition, most liabilities will be measured at original recorded amount less principal repayments and amortization. Only derivatives and liabilities held for trading (such as short sales of securities) will be remeasured to fair value.

To record the complete amount of periodic unrealized fair value changes an enterprise will have a single, enterprise-wide option to either:

- Recognize the entire amount in income; or
- Recognize in income only those changes in fair value relating to financial assets and liabilities held for trading, with the value changes for nontrading instruments reported in equity until the financial asset is sold, at which time the realized gain or loss is reported in net profit or loss. For this purpose, derivatives are always deemed held for trading unless they are part of a hedging relationship that qualifies for hedge accounting.

Hedge Accounting. The IASC considers hedging, for accounting purposes, as designating the change in value of a derivative, or in limited circumstances a nonderivative financial instrument, as an offset, in whole or in part, to the change in fair value or cash flows of a hedged item. A hedged item can be an asset, liability, firm commitment, or forecasted future transaction that is exposed to risk of change in value or changes in future cash flows. Hedge accounting recognizes the offsetting effects on net profit or loss symmetrically.

Thus, hedge accounting is permitted under IAS 39 in certain circumstances, provided that the hedging relationship is *clearly defined, measurable, and actually effective.*

IAS 39, like FASB 133, recognizes and defines three types of hedges although they are not identical:

1. Fair value hedge: a hedge of the exposure to changes in the fair value of a recognized asset or liability (such as a hedge of exposure to changes in

the fair value of fixed rate debt as a result of changes in interest rates). To the extent that the hedge is effective, the gain or loss from remeasuring the hedging instrument at fair value is recognized immediately in net profit or loss.

At the same time, the gain or loss on the hedged item adjusts the carrying amount of the hedged item and is recognized immediately in net profit or loss.

2. Cash flow hedge: a hedge of the exposure to variability in cash flows attributable to a recognized asset or liability (such as all or some future interest payments on variable rate debt) or a forecasted transaction (such as an anticipated purchase or sale). A hedge of an unrecognized firm commitment to buy or sell an asset at a fixed price in the enterprise's reporting currency is accounted for as a cash flow hedge even though it has a fair value exposure. To the extent that the gain or loss on the effective portion of the hedging instrument is recognized initially, it is recorded directly in equity. Subsequently, that amount is included in net profit or loss in the same period or periods during which the hedged item affects net profit or loss (for example, through cost of sales, depreciation, or amortization). For hedges of forecasted transactions, the gain or loss on the hedging instrument will adjust the basis (carrying amount) of the acquired asset or liability.

3. A hedge of a net investment in a foreign entity (as defined in IAS 21, *The Effects of Changes in Foreign Exchange Rates*): These are accounted for as cash flow hedges.

As we have seen above, hedge accounting is permitted when the hedging relationship is clearly defined, measurable, and actually effective. The enterprise must designate a specific hedging instrument as a hedge of a change in value or cash flow of a specific hedged item, rather than as a hedge of an overall net balance sheet position. However, the approximate income statement effect of hedge accounting for an overall net position can be achieved, in some cases, by designating part of one of the underlying items as the hedged position.

Derecognition.   In addition, IAS 39 establishes conditions for determining when control over a financial asset or liability has been transferred to another party. For financial assets a transfer normally would be accounted for as a sale (derecognized) when:

- The transferee has the right to sell or pledge the asset.
- The transferor does not have the right to reacquire the transferred assets unless either the asset is readily obtainable in the market or the reacquisition price is fair value at the time of reacquisition.

With respect to derecognition of liabilities, the debtor must be legally released from primary responsibility for all or part of the liability either judicially or by the creditor. If part of a financial asset or liability is sold or extinguished, the carrying amount is split based on relative fair values. If fair values are not determinable, a cost recovery approach to profit recognition is taken.

Additional Disclosure Requirements. IAS 39 moves international requirements a big step in the direction of greater transparency. The principal disclosure requirements for financial instruments include:

- Description of methods and assumptions used in estimating fair values.
- Disclosure of whether purchases of financial assets are accounted for at trade date or settlement date.
- Description of the enterprise's financial risk management objectives and policies.
- For each category of hedge: a description of the hedge; which financial instruments are designated as hedging instruments; and the nature of the risks being hedged.
- Disclosure of significant items of income and expense and gains and losses resulting from financial assets and financial liabilities, and whether they are included in net profit or loss or as a separate component of equity and, if in equity, a reconciliation of movements in and out of equity;
- Explanation of details of securitization and repurchase agreements.
- Description of the nature, effect, and reasons for reclassifications of financial assets from amortized cost to fair value.
- Explanation of the nature and amount of any impairment loss or reversal of an impairment loss.

A Stop-Gap Solution. Even though IAS 39 goes a long way toward fair value accounting, the IASC considers it only a partial step. The Board decided not to require fair value measurement for the originated loans and receivables or for held-to-maturity investments at this time for three reasons:

1. Too drastic a change from current practice would be required in many jurisdictions.
2. The existence of portfolio linkage of those assets, in many industries, to liabilities that, under IAS 39, will continue to be measured at their amortized original amount. Banks, for example, say that they manage their depositor liabilities in tandem with their portfolios of mortgage and commercial loans.

3. Some question the relevance of fair values for financial assets intended to be held until maturity, particularly if fair value changes enter into measuring net profit or loss.

The resulting standard should probably be considered a stop-gap measure published to meet the deadline the IASC had set to submit the core set of standards to IOSCO. As noted, it also serves, at least to a certain extent, to answer the urgent need in many countries for a comprehensive financial instruments standard. Although it is similar in many respects to U.S. GAAP, IAS 39 needs more work to raise it to the level of quality the IASC seeks in its standards. (As a matter of fact, there is still considerable debate about whether FASB 133 is the final word on financial instrument accounting and disclosure in this country.)

INTERNATIONAL ACCOUNTING STANDARDS

Following is a list of the International Accounting Standards currently in force or issued recently and not yet effective. Basically, they are the core group of international standards necessary for cross-border filings. Where an IAS has been superseded by a subsequent International Accounting Standard, it is not listed.

IAS 1, *Presentation of Financial Statements*

IAS 2, *Inventories*

IAS 7, *Cash Flow Statements*

IAS 8, *Net Profit or Loss for the Period, Fundamental Errors and Changes in Accounting Policies*

IAS 10, *Events After the Balance Sheet Date*

IAS 11, *Construction Contracts*

IAS 12, *Income Taxes*

IAS 14, *Segment Reporting*

IAS 15, *Information Reflecting the Effects of Changing Prices*

IAS 16, *Property, Plant and Equipment*

IAS 17, *Leases*

IAS 18, *Revenue*

IAS 19, *Employee Benefits*

IAS 20, *Accounting for Government Grants and Disclosure of Government Assistance*

IAS 21, *The Effects of Changes in Foreign Exchange Rates*

IAS 22, *Business Combinations*

IAS 23, *Borrowing Costs*

IAS 24, *Related Party Disclosures*

IAS 26, *Accounting and Reporting by Retirement Benefit Plans*

IAS 27, *Consolidated Financial Statements and Accounting for Investments in Subsidiaries*

IAS 28, *Accounting for Investments in Associates*

IAS 29, *Financial Reporting in Hyperinflationary Economies*

IAS 30, *Disclosures in the Financial Statements of Banks and Similar Financial Institutions*

IAS 31, *Financial Reporting of Interests in Joint Ventures*

IAS 32, *Financial Instruments: Disclosure and Presentation*

IAS 33, *Earnings per Share*

IAS 34, *Interim Financial Reporting*

IAS 35, *Discontinuing Operations*

IAS 36, *Impairment of Assets*

IAS 37, *Provisions, Contingent Liabilities and Contingent Assets*

IAS 38, *Intangible Assets*

IAS 39, *Financial Instruments: Recognition and Measurement*

IAS 40, *Investment Property*

IAS 41, *Agriculture*

Chapter 6

The International Federation of Accountants

CONTENTS

The North Atlantic Treaty Organization (NATO) announced in August 2002 that it is adopting the International Public Sector Accounting Standards (IPSASs) developed by the International Federation of Accountants' (IFAC's) Public Sector Committee for its financial statements starting January 1, 2006.

NATO also reported that most of the 14 NATO entities are adopting IPSASs even sooner than 2006. They may begin using them in January 2003 or 2004. There appears to be a groundswell of movement toward international accounting and auditing standards by diverse groups worldwide.

IPSASs Set Standards for Governments and Public Sector Bodies

IPSASs set out the requirements for financial reporting by governments and other public sector organizations with the ultimate objective of enhancing the accountability and financial management of governments worldwide. The Public Sector Committee receives funding from:

1. The World Bank.
2. United Nations Development Program.
3. Asian Development Bank.
4. International Monetary Fund.

Thus far, the Committee has developed 20 IPSASs as part of its *comprehensive* Standards Project to assist governments in reporting comparable, relevant, and understandable financial information.

The Organization for Economic Cooperation and Development (OECD) has adopted IFAC's International Public Sector Accounting Standards for its own financial reporting. Its 2000 financial statements were audited against these standards. IFAC feels that the adoption of the standards will strengthen the accountability and transparency of NATO financial statements and that other entities around the world will be encouraged to adopt IPSASs.

Working Group on NATO Accounting Standards

NATO's adoption of IPSASs was based on a recommendation from a Working Group on NATO Accounting Standards that was charged with developing a comprehensive set of NATO accounting principles and standards covering all transactions and activities conducted by the Alliance. The primary objective was to harmonize accounting standards and reporting formalities across NATO. The Working Group reviewed existing accounting standards promulgated by nations and other international organizations and ultimately recommended IPSASs. The next step will be to see that the standards are actually utilized and enforced.

PSC Proposes New Standard on Impairment of Public Sector Assets

The International Federation of Accountants has released a new exposure draft (ED) of an International Public Sector Accounting Standard (IPSAS) dealing with the impairment of public sector assets, including assets that are not held for cash-generating purposes. Developed by IFAC's Public Sector Committee (PSC) in conjunction with the GASB ED 23, *Impairment of Assets*, complements IPSAS 17, *Property, Plant and Equipment*, and strengthens and enhances the guidance on financial reporting of these assets.

ED 23 proposes requirements for the identification, recognition, measurement, reversal and disclosure of an impairment loss in general purpose financial statements of public sector entities. Guidance in the ED will also provide useful information about an asset's value in use and changes in that value as input for asset management and resource allocation purposes.

Also featured in the ED are appendices with examples of indicators of impairment and the measurement of impairment loss. Additionally, it includes the PSC's basis for conclusion on key issues and a comparison of the proposed requirements of this ED with International Accounting Standard (IAS) 36, *Impairment of Assets*, on which it is based.

New Handbook of International Public Sector Accounting Standards

The 2003 edition of the IFAC's *Handbook of International Public Sector Accounting Standards* published in March is now available in print and electronic formats. The print version also includes a CD-ROM. This edition features IPSASs 1 through 20, along with a glossary of terms, summary of occasional papers and studies, and a selected bibliography. All guidance has been developed by IFAC's Public Sector Committee (PSC) with input from various stakeholders.

The 2003 edition includes the following newer IPSASs as well as the older standards, which are included at the end of this chapter:

- IPSAS 13 — *Leases.* This standard prescribes for both lessees and lessors the appropriate accounting policies and disclosures to apply in relation to finance and operating leases. It includes guidance on the classification of leases, disclosures to be made in the financial statements of lessees and lessors, and accounting for sale and leaseback transactions.

- IPSAS 14 — *Events After the Reporting Date.* This standard prescribes when an entity should adjust its financial statements for events that occur after the reporting date and the disclosures that it should make about other "non-adjusting" events that occur after the reporting date.

- IPSAS 15 — *Financial Instruments: Disclosure and Presentation.* This standard prescribes how financial instruments are to be classified and identifies disclosures to be made in general purpose financial statements.

- IPSAS 16 — *Investment Property.* This standard prescribes requirements for accounting for investment property, including the initial and subsequent measurement and disclosure of such property by governments and their agencies.

- IPSAS 17 — *Property, Plant and Equipment.* This standard prescribes requirements for the initial recognition and measurement of property, plant and equipment. It also deals with subsequent measurement, depreciation, and disclosures about these assets. The standard provides a transitional period to support the orderly implementation of its requirements and allows but does not require heritage assets to be recognized in general-purpose financial statements.

- IPSAS 18 — *Segment Reporting.* This standard establishes principles for reporting financial information about distinguishable activities of a government or other public sector entity appropriate for:
  - Evaluating the entity's past performance in achieving its objectives.
  - Identifying the resources allocated to support the major activities of the entity.
  - Making decisions about the future allocation of resources.

- IPSAS 19 — *Provisions, Contingent Liabilities, and Contingent Assets.* The objective of this standard is to define provisions, contingent liabilities, and contingent assets and to identify the circumstances in which provisions should be recognized, how they should be measured, and the disclosures that should be made about them. The Standard also requires that certain information be disclosed about contingent liabilities and contingent assets in the notes to the financial statements to enable users to understand their nature, timing, and amount.

- IPSAS 20 — *Related Party Disclosures.* The objective of this Standard is to require the disclosure of the existence of related party relationships where control exists and the disclosure of information about transactions between the entity and its related parties in certain circumstances. This information is required for accountability purposes and to facilitate a better understanding of the financial position and performance of the reporting entity. The principal issues in disclosing information about related parties are identifying which parties control or significantly influence the reporting entity and determining what information should be disclosed about transactions with those parties.

These IPSASs are to be applied when the accrual basis of accounting is adopted. In addition to the IPSASs included in the handbook, the PSC has also developed a cash-basis IPSAS entitled *Financial Reporting under the Cash Basis of Accounting*. All standards have been developed to improve the quality of financial reporting in the public sector worldwide. An important goal is to achieve convergence of these standards where possible. (A brief synopsis of the 12 earlier IPSASs is given at the end of this chapter.)

IASB and PSC Cooperate to Translate Standards

Furthering its efforts to improve financial reporting by governments worldwide, IFAC's Public Sector Committee works with the International Accounting Standards Board (IASB) to translate the *accrual-basis IPSASs* into languages other than English. These IPSASs are based on International Accounting Standards (IASs) and International Financial Accounting Standards (IFRSs) to the extent that the requirements of those IASs and IFRSs are applicable to the public sector.

The PSC has commissioned the translation of the first 18 IPSASs into French and Spanish through the IASB process. The translated IPSASs were to be available during the first half of 2003. The IPSASs may also be translated into other languages through this cooperative process as resources permit. A number of national organizations are also involved in translating IPSASs into their own languages. The PSC encourages professional bodies and other organizations contemplating translation of IPSASs to consider application of the IASB process to their translation.

Study to Assist Public Sector Entities' Transition from Cash to Accrual Basis

The Public Sector Committee has also released Study 14, *Transition to the Accrual Basis of Accounting: Guidance for Governments and Government Entities*. This new study identifies key issues to be addressed in the transfer from the cash to the accrual basis of accounting and alternative approaches that can be adopted when implementing the accrual basis in an efficient and effective manner in the public sector.

It also identifies key requirements of IPSASs and other relevant sources of guidance to assist in the transition from the cash basis to the accrual basis. The Committee believes that governments and governmental entities will find Study 14 a useful tool in dealing with complex issues necessary to implement an accrual system. IFAC refers to the study as a "living document" that will be updated periodically as further IPSASs are issued, and additional implementation issues and experiences are identified.

The new study contributes to the ongoing body of guidance being developed by the Public Sector Committee to enhance the accountability and financial management of governments worldwide.

IFAC AND INTERNATIONAL REGULATORS PROPOSE REFORMS TO STRENGTHEN AUDIT QUALITY

The IFAC, the international accountancy profession, and international regulators, are spearheading reforms to improve the quality of standards and practices in auditing and assurance worldwide and to achieve global convergence of high quality standards. Their focus is on strengthening the international auditing and assurance standards process to bolster public confidence in the work of auditors and in the financial reporting process.

The reforms are being developed by the International Federation of Accountants (IFAC) and international regulators with input from IFAC member organizations, regional accountancy organizations and the profession at large. The plans were finalized in late October 2003, IFAC's Board presented the proposals to its Council for approval in November 2003.

The objective of the reforms, which are expected to be implemented in early 2004, is to help ensure that IFAC's standard-setting activities reflect the public interest and are consistent with the priorities of the international regulatory community. Key aspects of the reform proposals include:

- The development of a more transparent standard-setting process, particularly with respect to audit and assurance standards.
- The provision for greater public and regulatory input into that process.
- The establishment of a Public Interest Oversight Board (PIOB) to oversee IFAC's public-interest activities. (Members of the PIOB are to be selected by the regulatory community.)

Regulatory and other international groups involved in the development of the proposals include:

- The International Organization for Securities Commissions (IOSCO).
- The Basel Committee on Banking Supervision.
- The European Commission.

- The World Bank.
- The International Association of Insurance Supervisors.
- The Financial Stability Forum (FSF).

The IOSCO, which played a major role in the IASB's development of the core group of International Accounting Standards, reported that it "strongly supports IFAC's efforts" to reform its public-interest activities, including the formation of a Public Interest Oversight Board.

The Financial Stability Forum also indicated its support of the reform proposals, which they view as a positive step in ensuring that the international auditing standard-setting process is responsive to the public interest.

New Groups Being Formed

The Public Interest Oversight Board is to consist of 10 members and will focus on IFAC standard-setting activities related to audit and assurance services, independence and other ethics standards. It will also oversee the education standard-setting process and IFAC's proposed member body Compliance Program. The PIOB will decide other areas that might fall within the scope of its oversight after consulting with the Monitoring Group (MG) and the IFAC Leadership Group (ILG). The composition of the PIOB will be selected by the MG from members of the organizations within the MG or their representatives.

The Monitoring Group will be comprised of international regulators and related organizations including representatives of those listed above. The MG will update the PIOB regarding significant events in the regulatory environment, and among other things, will be the vehicle for dialogue between regulators and the international accountancy profession.

IFAC Leadership Group includes the IFAC President, Deputy President, Chief Executive, the Chairs of the IAASB, the Transnational Auditors Committee, the Forum of Firms, and up to four other members designated by the IFAC Board. It will work with the MG and address issues related to the regulation of the profession.

Additional public input into the standard setting process will be obtained through expanding the role of Consultative Advisory Groups in the standard-setting processes. Members will provide input into the technical activities of each area at a time when the role of the groups is being augmented and strengthened. The proposals are also aimed at formalizing ongoing collaboration between regulators and IFAC to ensure effective reform.

ESTABLISHMENT OF FORUM OF FIRMS

Twenty-three international accountancy firms met in London in January 2001 to develop a Global Quality Standard for firms conducting transnational audits. The intention was to ensure consistent, high-quality auditing practices worldwide as a means of protecting the interests of cross-border investors and other economic decision-makers. Their efforts were aimed at promoting global financial market stability. The IFAC sponsored the meeting, and the firms operate as a new section of IFAC known as the Forum of Firms.

The launch of the Forum of Firms is a significant step in implementing the IFAC's plan to strengthen its role as the global standard-setting, self-regulatory, and representational body for the profession's audit and assurance-related services. It is hoped that commitment to the obligations of membership in the Forum will raise the standard of the international practice of auditing and will better serve the interests of the users of the profession's services.

Globalization of business and commerce has *highlighted the inadequacy of financial reporting and auditing in accordance with purely national standards.* Decision makers need assurance that the financial information on which they base their decisions is transparent, consistent, comprehensive, and comparable across national boundaries. Through their commitment to a Global Quality Standard, audit firms that are members of the Forum of Firms should be able to provide this assurance.

STRUCTURE AND REQUIREMENTS OF THE FORUM OF FIRMS

Membership in the Forum of Firms is open to any firm that has been, or is interested in, accepting transnational audit appointments, provided the firm:

1. Agrees to conform to the Forum's Global Quality Standard.
2. Agrees to subject its assurance work to periodic external quality assurance reviews.

It would be safe to assume that the Forum's Global Quality Standard is likely to require:

1. Having audit policies and a methodology for conducting transnational audits in accordance with International Standards of Auditing.
2. Compliance with the IFAC Code of Ethics.
3. Training programs to keep partners and staff up to date on international developments in financial reporting.
4. Maintaining quality control standards and conducting regular quality assurance reviews to monitor compliance with the firm's policies and methodology.

The creation of the Forum of Firms is one prong of a four-pronged program to restructure and strengthen IFAC. The other three aspects of the program are:

1. The introduction of a program for monitoring the compliance of IFAC member bodies with IFAC standards.
2. The strengthening of the processes and broadening of the membership of the International Auditing Practices Committee, which sets International Standards on Auditing.
3. The establishment of an International Public Oversight Board to oversee the activities of IFAC and the Forum of Firms that affect the public interest.

Constitution of the Forum of Firms Approved

Forum of Firms membership consists of firms that (1) perform audits of financial statements that may be used across national borders, and (2) as mentioned, voluntarily agree to meet certain requirements. Commitment to the obligations of membership in the Forum of Firms should contribute to raising the standards of the international practice of auditing in the interest of users of the profession's services.

IFAC Board's approval of the Forum Constitution demonstrates the group's ongoing commitment to promoting consistent and high quality standards of financial reporting and auditing practices worldwide, they believe. Having approved the Constitution, the next major step is to agree on a framework and guidelines for the Forum's quality assurance process.

There are currently 23 provisional members of the Forum of Firms, including the largest accounting firms. They will be admitted to full membership upon demonstrating adherence to the Forum's Quality Standard through satisfactory completion of the quality assurance requirement.

Structure of the Forum

The Forum conducts its business primarily through the Transnational Auditors Committee, an IFAC committee whose members have been nominated by the members of the Forum. As suggested earlier, a Public Oversight Board (POB) will oversee the public interest activities and related governance and infrastructure of IFAC, particularly in the areas of audit standard setting, ethics, membership obligations and quality assurance. The Public Oversight Board will be independent of the profession.

ED on Guidelines for Performing and Reporting on Global Peer Reviews

The Transnational Auditors Committee (TAC) is an executive committee of IFAC dedicated to representing and meeting the needs of the members of the Forum. It is a key component of the international self-regulatory regime adopted by IFAC and plays a major role in encouraging member firms to meet high standards in the international practice of auditing.

Role and Responsibilities

The Transnational Auditor's Committee will:

1. Develop, maintain, and administer a global peer review program to assess the consistency of the policies and practices of members of the Forum of Firms with the Forum's Quality Standard.
2. Encourage the adoption of internationally recognized standards of accounting and auditing.
3. Regularly review issues relevant to auditors with transnational clients and provide supplementary guidance of interest to those firms.
4. Propose observers to participate on other key IFAC committees and work closely with other IFAC committees on matters of interest to Forum members.
5. Supervise the provision of additional technical material regarding the specifics of transnational work necessary to supplement the guidance already issued by IFAC.

TAC has created a Global Peer Review Subcommittee to develop the procedures and oversee the process of global peer review for members of the Forum of Firms.

THE IFAD AND ITS VISION

The IFAC strengthening program fits into the broader initiative to improve the quality of financial reporting and auditing around the world that is being implemented under the auspices of the International Forum on Accountancy Development (IFAD). This organization brings together more than 30 international public and private organizations, including those representing the accounting profession, regulators, standard-setters, development banks and agencies, governments, and users and preparers of financial information.

IFAD was first presented with a "vision" for improving financial reporting and auditing on a worldwide basis in June 1999. IFAD participants endorsed the initiative at their meeting in October 1999. After 18 months of consensus-building and planning, it is now taking concrete form. IFAC considers the agreement to move ahead on the Forum of Firms to be a significant milestone.

THE IFAC JOINS THE XBRL CONSORTIUM

IFAC is a member of the consortium of organizations that are actively contributing resources and funding to ensure the success of XBRL. XBRL stands for eXtensible Business Reporting Language. More than 140 companies and professional organizations representing all sectors of global business have joined forces to develop XBRL. The purpose is the preparation and exchange of business reports and data. The initial goal of XBRL is to provide an XML-based framework that the global business information supply chain will use to create, exchange, and analyze financial reporting information including, but not limited to, general ledger information, regulatory filings such as annual and quarterly statements, audit schedules and tax schedules.

XBRL, which is freely licensed, will facilitate the automatically exchanged and reliable extraction of financial information among various software applications anywhere in the world. The XBRL Specification and the first taxonomy for financial reporting of commercial and industrial companies under U.S. GAAP was released on July 31, 2000. This was a major milestone for the XBRL framework since it allows for the creation of XML-based financial statements using XBRL.

Value of XBRL

The XML-based language automatically and transparently tags each segment of computerized business information with an identification code or marker. These markers remain with the information regardless of how the information is formatted or rearranged by a browser or within software applications.

Before XBRL, no generally accepted format for reporting business data existed. The labor-intensive task of entering and reentering data into computer applications results in substantial costs and the all-too-likely risk of data entry errors. The use of XBRL streamlines this process, potentially lowering costs while helping to ensure the integrity and quality of the data.

With XBRL, once financial information is created and formatted the first time, the data can be rendered in any form; for example:

- A printed financial statement.
- An HTML document.
- A regulatory filing document.
- A raw HML file.
- Credit reports.
- Loan applications.

All of these applications can be created without manually keying information in a second time or reformatting the data.

XBRL does not change existing accounting standards, nor does it require companies to disclose additional information. Instead, it simply enhances the accessibility and usability of the financial information that companies are required to report, according to IFAC.

XBRL Leads to Better Dissemination of Information

By providing easier access to accurate company financial data and more efficient analysis capabilities, XBRL will add value for anyone who creates or accesses an organization's business data. Ultimately, XBRL benefits all users in the financial information supply chain:

- Public and private companies.
- The accounting profession.
- Regulators.
- Analysts.
- The investment community.
- Capital markets.
- Lenders.
- Key third parties — software developers and data aggregators.

IFAC believes that by providing accurate and reliable information, XBRL gives industry leaders access to better information available. Ultimately, it will enable company management to more quickly access information stored in different places within the organization and to move that information both within the company and externally to their shareholders.

With less time spent on translation and data entry, financial advisors and investors, large and small, can devote more time to analysis and can perhaps screen more companies for investment opportunities. This can benefit those companies in the investment community that typically might not make it onto the investor's radar screen.

XBRL should help financial services companies to collect and update information about borrowers, automate reports to regulators and distribute or collect information related to loan portfolio sales and purchases.

Accountancy institutes worldwide consider the development of XBRL as a natural next step in the clarification and development of the fundamental language of business and a vital tool for enhancing the access and breadth of financial information available to the investing public. Additionally, XBRL will help to position accountants as valued knowledge providers and financial advisors for their clients or firms. By helping businesses leverage their use of emerging technologies such as XBRL, accountants can expand their professional opportunities and value in the marketplace, IFAC contends.

THE INTERNATIONAL AUDITING AND ASSURANCE STANDARDS BOARD (IAASB)

The Handbook of International Auditing, Assurance, and Ethics Pronouncements contains all standards and practice statements issued by this "new" Board, the IAASB and its predecessor, the International Auditing Practices Committee. At the same time, December 31, 2002, the *IFAC Code of Ethics for Professional Accountants* was issued by IFAC's Ethics Committee. From the amount of new releases and approvals, it would appear that updated editions might be needed frequently.

New Practice Statement and EDs

At its meeting in March 2003, the IAASB approved for release an International Accounting Practice Statement (IAPS) providing guidance to auditors when reporting on compliance with International Financial Reporting Standards (IFRSs) and two exposure drafts regarding assurance engagements and audits of small businesses. Titles and descriptions of the new and proposed pronouncements follow:

- IAPS 1014, *Reporting by Auditors on Compliance with International Financial Reporting Standards (IFRSs)* —Examples have arisen of entities stating that their financial statements have been prepared in accordance with IFRSs when, in fact, they have not complied with *all* the requirements that IFRSs impose. This practice statement provides guidance on the auditor's responsibilities when management comments on the extent to which financial statements comply with IFRSs, when there is not full compliance. It supplements guidance provided in International Standard on Auditing (ISA) 700, *The Auditor's Report on Financial Statements,* that is being revised.
- An Exposure Draft including a proposed International *Framework for Assurance Engagements* and a proposed International Standard on Assurance Engagements (ISAE) 2000, *Assurance Engagements on Subject Matters Other Than Historical Financial Information,* to replace ISAE 100, *Assurance Engagements,* when it has been finalized.
  The proposed Framework defines and describes the elements of an assurance engagement and identifies those engagements to which ISAs and

ISAEs apply. The proposed ISAE provides guidance to practitioners for the performance of assurance engagements on those subject matters other than historical financial information (which are covered by ISAs) and where no specific ISAEs exist.

- An Exposure Draft entitled *The Special Considerations in the Audit of Small Entities, Proposed Amendment to International Auditing Practice Statement 1005.* Developed with the input of IFAC's Ethics Committee and Small and Medium Practices (SMP) Task Force, this ED presents guidance on how audits of the financial statements of small entities differ from audits of the financial statements of other entities. Specifically, it revises the current IAPS 1005 to take account of ISAs issued from March 1999 through March 2003. The IAASB agreed that new ISAs issued subsequent to March 2003 would, whenever necessary, address SMP considerations.

IAASB Issues ED on Firm Quality Control Practices

In June 2003, in its ongoing efforts to ensure high-quality performance by the world's auditors, the IAASB issued an Exposure Draft of a proposed International Standard on Quality Control (ISQC) 1, *Quality Control for Audit, Assurance, and Related Services Practices,* and a proposed revised International Standard on Auditing (ISA) 220, *Quality Control for Audit Engagements.*

The proposed standards clarify the overall quality control responsibilities and related activities at both firm and engagement levels. The aim is to enhance the engagement quality in the public interest.

The proposed ISQC 1 requires a firm to establish a system of quality control designed to provide it with reasonable assurance that the firm and its personnel comply with professional standards and applicable regulatory and legal requirements. It contains new proposed basic principles and procedures regarding leadership and responsibilities within the firm. This requires that the CEO (or equivalent) of the firm have ultimate responsibility for the firm's system of quality control. Other areas addressed in the ED include:

- Ethics.
- Partner rotation.
- Acceptance and continuance of client relationships.
- Engagement quality control review.
- Monitoring.

ISQC 1 represents the first in a series of International Quality Control Standards. The ultimate goal of the project is to establish quality control standards for all engagements falling within the scope of IAASB engagement standards.

Proposed ISA 220 Revision. The proposed revised ISA 220 establishes basic principles and essential procedures and provides guidance on quality control procedures for audit engagements. These include requirements for an engagement quality control reviewer to perform an objective evaluation of the compliance with applicable professional standards. Guidance is specifically provided on leadership responsibilities, ethics, engagement performance, engagement quality control review, and monitoring.

It is proposed that the new guidance become effective January 1, 2005.

An International Standard on Auditing

The Standard on audit reports now requires the auditor to state clearly the financial reporting framework being used to prepare financial statements. IFAC's International Auditing Practices Committee recommended these revisions to the ISA 700, *The Auditor's Report on Financial Statements,* so that users may better understand the context under which the auditor's opinion is expressed.

Globalization of markets has meant that financial statements are increasingly used by foreign investors and analysts, hence clear labeling of the particular accounting and auditing frameworks is essential.

The IAPC previously recommended that the auditor's report identify which country's accounting principles have been used in audited financial statements where that is not evident.

This requirement is now mandatory. The changes to the Standard will became effective for audits of financial statements for periods ending on or after September 30, 2002.

Audit Planning ED Includes New Guidance

The IAASB has approved the release of an exposure draft of proposed ISA 300, *Planning the Audit,* complementing their proposed guidance on audit risk issued in October 2002. It includes basic principles and essential procedures on the considerations and activities applicable to planning an audit of financial statements. In particular, it provides new guidance on matters the auditor should consider prior to performing significant planning activities:

- Client acceptance and retention.
- Ethical requirements including independence and communications with prior auditors.
- Terms of the audit engagement.

The ED also incorporates more specific guidance regarding planning considerations in initial audits and includes a discussion of the planning considerations related to the direction, supervision and review of the work of engagement team members.

An ISA on Auditing Fair Value Measurements Is Announced

In August 2002, to address the increasing number of complex accounting pronouncements containing measurement and disclosure provisions based on fair value, IFAC's International Auditing and Assurance Standards Board (IAASB) announced development of a new International Standard on Auditing entitled *Auditing Fair Value Measurements and Disclosures.* ISA 545 addresses audit considerations relating to the valuation, measurement, presentation and disclosure for material assets, liabilities and specific components of equity presented or disclosed at fair value in financial statements. Specifically, the ISA provides information on:

1. Understanding the entity's process for determining fair value measurements and disclosures and relevant control procedures.
2. Assessing the appropriateness of fair value measurements and disclosures.
3. Using the work of an expert.
4. Testing the entity's fair value measurements and disclosures.
5. Evaluating the results of audit procedures.
6. Management's process for determining fair value and management representations.
7. Communication with those charged with governance.

The appendix to the ISA discusses fair value measurements and disclosures under different financial reporting frameworks.

The organization emphasizes that it is important that auditors obtain sufficient audit evidence that fair value measurements and disclosures are in accordance with the entity's identified financial reporting framework as changes in fair value measurements that occur over time may be treated in different ways under different financial reporting frameworks.

This ISA is effective for audits of financial statements for periods ending on or after December 31, 2003. Recognizing the important need for guidance in this area, the United States used this ISA as its basis in issuing an Exposure Draft on the same subject within the United States.

IAASB's Proposed ISA Expands Guidance for Fraud Detection

The International Auditing and Assurance Standards Board (IAASB) of IFAC is attempting to come to grips with one of the most important issues facing auditors today: responsibility for detecting fraud. The IAASB approved the release of an exposure draft (ED) of an International Standard of Auditing

(ISA) titled *The Auditor's Responsibility to Consider Fraud in an Audit of Financial Statements* (ISA 240).

This ED sets out the auditor's responsibility to consider fraud in an audit of financial statements. It also explains that the primary responsibility for the prevention and detection of fraud rests with *both those charged with governance and management of the entity* and describes the responsibilities of these parties.

It also alerts auditors to risks of material misstatement due to fraud they may encounter in the conduct of an audit and requires the auditor to assess the risks of material misstatement due to fraud and to respond to the assessed risk.

The new proposed ISA requires the auditor to respond to the presumed risk of improper revenue recognition and the risk of management override of controls. This response includes:

- Testing the appropriateness of journal entries.
- Reviewing the accounting estimates for biases.
- Obtaining an understanding of the business rationale of significant transactions that are outside of the normal course of business for the entity.
- Emphasizing the importance of auditor communications with management and those charged with governance.
- Considering the necessity of auditor communications to regulatory and enforcement authorities.

The IAASB point out that this new ED is designed to help reduce the incidents of financial statement fraud by outlining the responsibilities of all those involved in the financial reporting process and by encouraging auditors to act with *increased professional skepticism*. Until this ED is adopted, the guidance discussed below is still in effect.

Guidance on Fraud

In March 2001, the International Auditing Practices Committee approved two new documents: an updated International Standard on Auditing on fraud and error, and a new International Auditing Practice Statement on auditing derivatives.

The ISA, *The Auditor's Responsibility to Consider Fraud and Error in an Audit of Financial Statements,* updates and expands previous IAPC guidance. It applies to audits of financial periods ending on or after June 30, 2002. The Standard:

1. Emphasizes that when planning and performing an audit procedure, the auditor should consider the risk of material misstatements in the financial statements resulting from fraud and error.

2. Emphasizes the distinction between management fraud and employee fraud.
3. Expands the discussion of fraudulent financial reporting.
4. Includes guidance on the need to obtain management's assessment of the risk of fraud.
5. Clarifies the discussion of the inherent limitations of an audit's ability to detect fraud.

Guidance on Derivatives

The IAPS, *Auditing Derivative Financial Instruments,* provides guidance to the auditor in planning and performing auditing procedures for assertions about derivative financial instruments. The focus of the practice statement is on auditing derivatives held by end users, including banks and other financial sector entities when they are the users.

In addition to addressing auditor responsibilities with respect to assertions about derivatives, the statement also addresses:

1. Responsibility of management and those charged with governance.
2. The key financial risks.
3. Risk assessment and internal control, including the role of internal auditing.
4. Various types of substantive procedures and when they should be used.

Guidance on Assurance Services

The changing information needs of businesses and consumers are resulting in increased demands for the audit to extend beyond the traditional attest function into assurance services. The IFAC, through its International Auditing Practices Committee, is taking a leadership role in supporting the accountant as a provider of these services by developing standards and guidance in areas where the opinion of the independent auditor can add value and credibility to the information provided by directors and management.

ISA 100, *Assurance Engagements,* established basic principles and essential procedures for professional accountants in public practice who perform audit-level assurance engagements on a range of subject matters far broader than financial statements. With the recent publication of the findings from the IAASB commissioned research on the determination and communication of levels of assurance other than high, the IAASB has started to revise ISA 100 to include basic principles and essential procedures for review-level assurance engagements.

Under the current project plan, ISA 100 will be split into two documents:

a *Framework for Assurance Engagements* that sets out the underlying concepts, definitions, and elements of an assurance engagement; and ISAE 2000, *Assurance Engagements,* which establishes the basic principles and essential procedures for, and provides guidance to, the performance of assurance engagements on subject matters other than historic financial information.

This project is particularly important in today's environment as demand for such services continues to grow. It will provide a comprehensive framework for the development of future assurance standards on specific subject matters or topics. An Exposure Draft of a revised ISA 100 and ISAE 2000 was expected to be released by the middle of 2003.

MANAGEMENT ACCOUNTANTS AND THEIR VALUE TO ORGANIZATIONS

A major study released by IFAC's Financial and Management Accounting Committee in June 2002, presents a global, best-practice perspective on management accounting. Contemporary management accounting is an integral part of the management process focused on the effective use of resources in ongoing value creation by organizations. The study highlights the competences related to best practice in management accounting and the competences required of those taking key roles in this field of management.

Entitled *Competency Profiles for Management Accounting Practice and Practitioners,* the study builds on competency standards developed by IFAC member bodies and expands on the groundbreaking International Management Accounting Practice Statement 1, *Management Accounting Concepts.*

The study elaborates competency standards and related assessment methodologies for both management accounting practice and management accounting practitioners. The competency standards are illustrated by profiling contemporary issues related to:

1. Management practices in organizations.
2. Membership of professional associations.
3. Preparatory and continuing education associated with management practice and professional membership.

Those Toward Whom the Study Is Directed

Those who can benefit from the study and the benchmark competency standards it illustrates include:

1. Organizations seeking to move toward best practice in management accounting.

2. Professional accountants seeking to focus their work or develop their careers in the sphere of management accounting.
3. Educators, as they seek to focus and develop curricula that will contribute to the preparation of persons seeking to work in this domain of management.
4. IFAC member bodies in establishing required competences and profiling the developmental needs of their members in this sphere of management.

Study 12 provides both a benchmark and a resource for the development of practice in a range of contexts around the world. Beyond this, it is likely to open up and stimulate discussion internationally about a critical and distinctive dimension of management work.

Management Accountancy Faces a Changing Environment

A publication issued in April 2001 by the Financial and Management Accounting Committee (FMAC) presents a global perspective on the transformation of the accounting profession to a management profession. The study, entitled *A Profession Transforming: From Accounting to Management,* investigates both the causes and effects of the movement by presenting the perspectives and experiences of a dozen professional associations from around the world.

One goal of the publication is to bring to the surface the problems and solutions professional associations of accountants face in trying to understand and cope with the changes. It takes a look at the impact of the past decade of change on both the present and the future.

Such information can be useful to a wide group, including educators preparing the next generation of accountants, employers of management accountants, and professional associations that serve an increasing number of members not employed in public practice.

Currently, IFAC membership totals approximately 2.5 million accountants. More than 60% of them are employed in business. This percentage is rising steadily. The study is important for many of them who are coping with a new and still developing business environment. IFAC points out that the changed environment is one that requires new skills, increasing flexibility, and an unprecedented ability to manage change.

The study also points out that two parallel movements seem to be driving change in the accounting profession:

1. A movement to reform corporate governance as the underpinning of global capital markets, with consequent changes in financial reporting, auditing standards, and processes for institutional oversight and assurance.
2. A less visible but equally strong movement for accounting work to be absorbed into the management process of organizations. This development

not only alters the competencies expected of practitioners but also makes such work accessible to those who are not accountants.

Features of the study include:

1. Twelve distinct perspectives on the changes in the profession. They were contributed by twelve professional associations in Australia, Canada, Italy, Malaysia, the UK, and U.S. chapters.
2. An introductory chapter summarizes key trends, and highlights threats and opportunities facing the management accounting profession and the associations that serve it. This overview also points out how the associations are attempting to meet the challenges.

CODE OF ETHICS FEATURES NEW INDEPENDENCE RULES

IFAC released its updated, *Code of Ethics for Professional Accountants,* featuring new rules on independence. This international Code is intended to serve as a model on which to base national ethical guidance for accountants. The Code includes principles that are applicable to all professional accountants and distinguishes between those that affect professional accountants in public practice and those that are applicable to other accountants employed in business and industry.

Although the accountancy profession throughout the world operates in an environment with different cultures and regulatory requirements, it is vital that all accountants share a commitment to a strong code of ethics. The IFAC Code states the fundamental principles that should be observed by professional accountants to meet their responsibility in protecting the public's interests.

The Ethics Committee suggests the following reasons for the need to update the independence rules:

1. Changes in the global economy.
2. Technology developments.
3. The expanding services performed by the accountancy profession.

The new rules of independence provide:

1. A conceptual framework that focuses on the factors that poses a threat to independence for all assurance engagements.
2. The safeguards that auditors should put in place to preserve their independence.
3. Examples of situations on how the conceptual approach to independence are to be applied to specific circumstances and relationships.

High-quality standards are the fundamental underpinnings of the world's financial markets, IFAC believes.

Reasons for Revisions to Guidance

IFAC's Ethics Committee issued an Exposure Draft to revise the independence statement in *Proposed Changes to the Code of Ethics for Professional Accountants*. It clarifies certain points made in the initial ED, issued in June 2000, and expands the guidance on circumstances creating threats to independence. It establishes a framework for independence requirements for assurance engagements that, if adopted, will be the international standard on which national standards should be based. Accordingly, no member body or firm would be allowed to apply less stringent standards than those stated in the revised ED.

The initial June 2000 Exposure Draft proposed a move to a conceptual framework approach that would require the identification and evaluation of threats to independence, and the application of safeguards to reduce any threats to an acceptable level. Respondents were strongly supportive of this approach and suggested that additional examples be added. The revised Statement includes such examples.

It also expands the group of people who may create threats to independence. As with the June exposure draft, immediate and close family members may create threats to independence; however, the revised Statement also discusses threats to independence that may be created by individuals who are not part of the assurance team. This includes other partners and professional staff within the firm, and the firm itself.

EDUCATION COMMITTEE RELEASES EDS AND GUIDELINE

Working to advance accounting education programs worldwide, particularly in areas where it will assist economic development, IFAC develops International Education Standards that address prequalification education and the continuing professional development of professional accountants and IFAC's Education Committee released exposure drafts of seven standards and one guideline in July 2002.

The overall goal of the proposed standards is to produce competent professional accountants. The global profession is moving toward a common base of standards in accounting, auditing, public sector accounting and ethics and is "raising the bar" in the quality and consistent application of procedures around the world. The acceptance of the need to harmonize technical and practice standards globally has never been more pronounced, the Education Committee believes. However, they add that the global profession will not properly achieve this higher application of standards without a set of robust, codified education standards. Education must be the starting point. Without robustness in education, the achievement of higher compliance with technical and practice standards will flounder.

Revised ED on Content of Professional Education Programs

The Education Committee of the IFAC issued an Exposure Draft revising requirements in the proposed International Education Standard (IES), *Content of Professional Education Programs.* (All of the EDs are briefly described below.)

An earlier ED on this topic, issued in June 2002, prescribed the primary content of professional education programs for professional accountants in three major areas:

1. Organizational and business knowledge.
2. Information technology knowledge.
3. Accounting, finance, and related knowledge.

It also suggested subject matters to be included in each of these areas. The revised Exposure Draft includes modifications to these subject matters and indicates that they are, in fact, mandatory.

During the exposure period, the Education Committee received and considered a number of valuable comments, many of which focused on issues regarding the weightings and relative importance of the three key subject areas. As a result, the Education Committee decided to revise the standard to express the subject areas more clearly and to make these mandatory for all institutions involved in the development of professional education programs for accountants.

The Committee believes that ultimately, such a change can lead to greater convergence in the professional education programs for accountants worldwide. However, the depth of coverage in each subject area may vary, depending on the needs of IFAC member organizations and restrictions imposed by national regulatory authorities.

IFAC RELEASES NEW INTERNATIONAL EDUCATION STANDARDS FOR PROFESSIONAL ACCOUNTANTS

IFAC released six International Education Standards (IESs) in October 2003 that establish the global benchmarks for education and development for professional accountants. The standards are a critical component of IFAC's overall efforts to ensure high quality performance by professional accountants worldwide.

Developed by IFAC's Education Committee, the standards are designed to achieve quality and consistency in global accounting education. They prescribe the essential elements of education to become a professional accountant and the ongoing education requirements necessary to remain competent. All IFAC member bodies are expected to comply with the standards effective January 1, 2005. The IESs are as follows:

- IES 1, *Entry Requirements to a Program of Professional Accounting Education,* prescribes entry requirements for candidates beginning the qualifying process for becoming professional accountants.

- IES 2, *Content of Professional Accounting Education Programs,* prescribes the professional education candidates require to qualify as professional accountants.

- IES 3, *Professional Skills,* prescribe the personal and professional skills candidates must have to qualify as professional accountants.

- IES 4, *Professional Values, Ethics and Attitudes,* prescribes the professional values and ethics that professional accountants need to acquire during their programs of education and practical experience. The aim of this standard is to ensure that candidates for membership of an IFAC member body are equipped with the appropriate professional values and ethics to function as professional accountants.

- IES 5, *Practical Experience Requirements,* prescribes the practical experience and training IFAC member bodies should require their members to obtain to qualify as professional accountants. The aim of this standard is to ensure that candidates for members of an IFAC member body have acquired the practical experience considered appropriate at the time of qualification to function as competent professional accountants.

- IES 6, *Assessment of Professional Capabilities and Competence,* prescribes the requirement for a process of assessment of a candidate_s professional competence before admission to the profession.

An introduction and framework have been issued with the standards. These documents explain the scope of issues covered in the standards and the ways they may be applied to the education programs of IFAC member bodies.

IFAC explains that the standards provide important assistance to IFAC member bodies, which are generally responsible for either establishing or implementing education standards and requirements at the national level. They are also designed to assist those responsible for accounting education to develop the skills and strategies professional accountants require. Another proposed standard on continuing professional development is being re-exposed for comment.

Updated Guidance on Competence-Based Education

One of the most significant issues facing the international accountancy profession, accountancy organizations, and academic institutions is ensuring that prospective professional accountants have the requisite skills and knowledge to meet the challenges they will face. IFAC's Education Committee published a paper on this issue in March 2003, entitled *Towards Competent Professional Accountants*. The paper provides advice to professional bodies planning to adopt a competence-based education and training program. It identifies the objectives of the competence-based approach, defines competence, and describes different types of statements of competence.

The Committee believes that many major employers and the larger accounting bodies are sophisticated users of competence-based approaches to accounting education. This paper was issued to provide an excellent benchmark for them to compare against. It should also provide worthwhile guidance to those embarking on competence-based approaches for the first time.

Historically, there have been two types of competence-based approaches to accounting education:

1. The *functional analysis* approach, favored in Australia, New Zealand, and the UK, emphasizes performance outcomes of the education and training process.
2. The *capabilities* approach adopted by the U.S., focuses on aspects such as the knowledge, skills and professional values necessary to achieve potential competence as a professional accountant. The Education Committee paper explains how the strengths of the two approaches can be blended into a unified approach.

It encourages professional bodies and other organizations responsible for the training of accountants to link accounting curricula more closely with workplace requirements to help ensure that the knowledge and capabilities required of professional accountants remains relevant.

Towards Competent Professional Accountants builds on two previous documents issued by the Education Committee. *Competence-Based Approaches to the Professional Preparation of Accountants,* a discussion paper issued in 1998, and the 2001 Exposure Draft, *Competence-Based Approaches to the Preparation and Work of Accountants. Towards Competent Professional Accountants* reflects comments received from employers of professional accountants, academics, and accountancy organizations during the exposure period and updates the previous discussion papers.

Addressing Accountant Competencies

The paper mentioned above, issued in May 2001, addresses an issue fundamental to the development of the accountancy profession: How does one define and achieve professional accountancy competency? The paper, *Competence-Based Approaches to the Preparation and Work of the Professional Accountant,* explores the topic of accountant competency, providing an analysis of approaches used by various accountancy institutes around the world.

The IFAC emphasizes that the goal of accounting education and experience must be to produce competent professional accountants capable of making positive contributions over their lifetimes to the profession and society in which they work.

Accountancy bodies are coming under increasing pressure to show the public that their members are, and remain, competent. A competence-based approach to education is vital to ensuring and demonstrating that accountants possess the knowledge, skills, and professional values necessary to carry out their responsibilities.

The discussion paper seeks to:

1. Define "competence" and "capabilities."
2. Provide guidance to accountancy membership bodies on their role in developing competence and capabilities.
3. Assess various methods.

This discussion paper draws together these views within a single framework. Traditionally there have been two rather different approaches to competence:

1. Some studies have emphasized outcomes — accountants performing roles and tasks in the workplace to a defined standard.
2. Other studies have placed more emphasis on inputs contributed by the education and training process — knowledge, skills, and abilities.

IT MONITORING GUIDELINES ON RISK

Managing Information Technology Monitoring, a guideline published by IFAC, provides information to help executives, including accountants, financial controllers, auditors, business managers, and others involved in IT decision making, better understand the principles and practices required to monitor the use of IT effectively within their organizations. It appears that IFAC is doing a very good job of helping all of the above-named executives keep pace with the fast-moving ins and outs of information technology.

IT monitoring is important because of the complexity and risks involved in those activities. The IT Governance Board, along with the Information Systems and Audit and Control Association (ISACA), were instrumental in developing this guidance. The chairman of the Board pointed out that IT monitoring is fundamental to IT governance and part of management's responsibility. It is necessary whenever IT is used within an organization. This includes planning, organization, acquisition, implementation, delivery, and support.

IT monitoring covers:

1. How IT sustains the business with operational processes and risk and control systems.
2. Whether IT complies with business strategy, standards and policy.
3. How IT improves the business with technology, process and organizational changes.
4. How IT supports enterprise growth through process knowledge and quality service.

The guideline describes the monitoring tools available to assist management in carrying out these IT monitoring responsibilities and to support effective IT governance. While recognizing that monitoring of IT is unique to an organizational environment, the guideline suggests some generic approaches that may be applied.

IT Monitoring is the sixth guideline in a series developed by IFAC's Information Technology Committee for management of small, medium-sized and large enterprises. The other guidelines in the series are:

1. Managing Security of Information.
2. Managing IT Planning for Business Impact.
3. Acquisition of Information Technology.
4. Implementation of Information Technology Solutions.
5. IT Service Delivery and Support.

IFAC ISSUES NEW PAPER ON E-BUSINESS

A paper issued by IFAC presents certain risk management aspects of e-business relevant to accounting and financial reporting from a managerial perspective. It is entitled, *E-Business and the Accountant: Risk Management for Accounting Systems in an E-Business Environment.*

Directed to the management of organizations, including accountants, *E-Business and the Accountant* points out how e-business changes the way business is conducted and that e-business consequently introduces new risks that enterprises may need to address by implementing a technology infrastructure and controls to mitigate those risks. The paper points out that e-business and its technological environment will have a significant impact on accounting systems and the evidence available to support business transactions, which in turn will lead to changes in the accounting records maintained and accounting procedures followed.

"How To" for E-Business Accounting

The document notes that accountants and auditors may be faced with new challenges and therefore may need to apply new techniques in an e-business environment, such as the development of accounting systems based on the business processes employed, to ensure that transactions:

1. Are appropriately recorded.
2. Are in compliance with local and international legislation and regulations.
3. Meet current and evolving accounting standards and guidance.

To help minimize risks in relation to these issues, the paper provides a useful framework of concepts with which accountants and others can analyze e-business from an accounting point of view. It includes:

1. Best practice guidelines on e-business accounting principles and criteria.
2. Accounting information security.
3. Accounting information processing.
4. Criteria for a functioning accounting system.

IFAC MOVES AGAINST MONEY LAUNDERING

At the new year, 2002, IFAC urged the world's accountants to participate in efforts to combat money laundering. IFAC's Board approved the release of a white paper on anti-money laundering for dissemination to its 156 member organizations and their 2.4 million accountants and is widely disseminating the document through its Web site.

The paper explores the role of all accountants—whether they act as independent auditors, accountants in management positions, or in any other professional capacity—in ongoing public- and private-sector efforts to safeguard against money laundering. It also is designed to highlight potential indications of money laundering and to increase awareness of how professional obligations with respect to money laundering relate to and interact with corruption and transparency, privacy and consumer protection and the professional services provided by accountants. The paper draws attention to numerous risks that could lead to or reveal money-laundering situations and provides best practices to help accountants address those risks.

Accountants Asked to Play Larger Role in Detection

The IFAC emphasized the fact that, until relatively recently, the battle against money laundering and related financial crime was the exclusive domain of law enforcement. Approximately 15 years ago, forensic accountants started to join forces with law enforcement to contribute their skills in detecting possible money-laundering activity buried in the books and records of victimized financial institutions.

Specifically, since 9/11, and the U.S. Patriot Act, even the general public in this country is well aware of money laundering per se and as a method of funneling money to terrorists in particular. However, this awareness is not limited to the American public. Governments and businesses worldwide increasingly look to the accounting profession to:

1. Aid in their monitoring and detection efforts.
2. Establish and strengthen controls and safeguards against money laundering.
3. Identify its perpetrators since they are in a good position to do so.
4. Identify the perpetrators' accomplices in organized financial crime when they become aware of them.

This white paper is part of a series of IFAC initiatives to assist the world's accountants in protecting the public interest as well as their own. In recent years, IFAC has strengthened its standard-setting role with International Standards on Auditing and Public Sector Accounting Standards. It is also in the process of establishing a global self-regulatory regime for the international profession.

SMALL AND MEDIUM-SIZED PRACTICES (SMPS) AND ENTERPRISES (SMES)

IFAC leadership decided to undertake research into the needs of SMPs and explore member bodies' initiatives to meet these needs. Such research will then guide IFAC in determining its role with respect to SMPs.

Additionally, they supported IFAC's role in further exploring how it could best support the SME sector. IFAC has already established an SME Task Force, which specifically focuses on the needs of this constituency. Moreover, some of IFAC's committees, most notably the Information Technology and Financial and Management Accounting Committees, have issued guidance in recent months designed to be of assistance to the management of SMEs.

IFAC is not alone in its plans to aid this sector of the economic world. The Global Corporate Governance Forum (GCGF), a multidonor facility founded by the World Bank and the Organization for Economic Development (OECD) is also interested in his sector. The GCGF's purpose is to promote global, regional, and local initiatives aimed at improving the institutional framework and practices of corporate governance of middle- and low-income countries in the context of broader economic reform programs.

New IT Guidance for SMPs and SMEs

IFAC released two new guidance documents in April 2003 to assist small and medium-sized accounting practices and enterprises in managing and operating their computer systems. They are entitled *Controlling Computers in Business: Backup, Archive and Restore,* and *Controlling Computers in Business: Physical Security.*

This new series of information technology guidance was published under the direction of IFAC's Small and Medium Practices Task Force. The task force selected these topics after receiving input from IFAC's member organizations that such guidance would be useful in the global marketplace. The SMP Task Force believes that, to benefit from their investments in computers and information systems, SMPs and SMEs must devote time to systems management and control issues. This new guidance is designed to provide practical help for SMP and SME managers in identifying and resolving potential problems and risks associated with computers.

Each of the booklets features a series of notes that provide information on specific computer control issues, including definition of key terms, costs and benefits, and risks and practicalities. A best practices checklist is also included with each note. The series was first produced by the Institute of Chartered Accountants of Scotland (ICAS). The majority of the research and drafting of these publications was undertaken by a Big Four accounting firm.

IFAC'S TASK FORCES

From time to time, IFAC's Council appoints special task forces to address significant issues that warrant focused attention. Currently, there are two task forces:

1. IFAC Task Force on Rebuilding Public Confidence in Financial Reporting (Credibility Task Force)
2. Small and Medium Practices Task Force

Web Site Includes Information on Corporate Governance

IFAC introduced an Internet resource center for the public in March 2003 entitled: *Viewpoints: Governance, Accountability and the Public Trust.* This section on the IFAC web site has been developed to support IFAC's Task Force on Rebuilding Credibility in Financial Reporting. The task force is charged with identifying and analyzing the causes of the loss of credibility in financial reporting. It is considering alternative courses of action to restore credibility. The final report will include recommendations on principles of best practices in the areas of financial reporting, corporate governance, corporate disclosure, and auditor performance.

In carrying out its work, the task force is considering:

- The large volume of work already undertaken by IFAC member bodies and others at a national level in addressing the loss of credibility.
- Cross-national variation in the extent of the loss of credibility and its causes.
- The emerging patterns of convergence in such areas as financial reporting and corporate governance.

Categories Deal with Varied Areas. As part of its ongoing work, the task force has assembled numerous materials on various aspects of governance and financial reporting from around the world. This information is posted on the web site as a service to IFAC member bodies and their members, those involved in governance processes, and investors and other stakeholders interested in obtaining additional information on this topic. The information is posted in six categories:

1. *Global perspectives.* Information on a wide range of governance issues categorized by country.
2. *Public policy and regulation.* Statements and positions submitted by regulatory and policy-making bodies from around the world.
3. *The governance process.* Roles and Responsibilities—Papers and speeches on the roles of corporate management, boards of directors, audit committees, and auditors and others involved in the governance process.
4. *Financial reporting.* Research and other materials on the financial reporting model and specific principles and rules.
5. *Auditing issues.* Papers and commentaries on the changing role of auditors and key audit issues, such as scope of services, will be found in this section.
6. *Ethics.* Best practices for codes of ethics for professional accountants and commentaries on ethics in business.

Small and Medium Practices Task Force

The Small and Medium Practices Task Force investigates ways in which IFAC can respond to the needs of members operating in small and medium-sized practices and small and medium-sized enterprises. The Task Force studies issues relevant to SMPs, develops papers on topics of global concern, and provides input on the work of other IFAC committees where appropriate. It also plans to set out proposals for IFAC's future involvement in the SMP/SME area for presentation to the IFAC Board.

The Task Force issued a study, *An Assessment of International Needs and Analysis of the Activities Offered within Seven Member Bodies* to address the needs of SMPs and provide recommendations for action at the international level. The report includes descriptions of current national initiatives based on an analysis of programs and initiatives currently in place in IFAC member organizations in Canada, India, Italy, Israel, the UK, and the U.S.:

- Service to members, including such things as educational courses and training, marketing support, technical aids, web-related services, and networking support.
- Participation of SMPs in standard setting, including their presence on standard-setting committees and on governing bodies of the profession.
- Innovative service areas that can help SMPs grow their businesses and meet expanding client needs.
- Advocacy and alliances, including contacts with public authorities, governmental agencies, and regulators; advertising and promotion; and placement services.

THE HISTORY OF THE IFAC

Founded in 1977, the International Federation of Accountants (IFAC) with headquarters in New York, now consists of 155 national accountancy bodies from 113 countries with 2.4 million members in public practice, education, government service, industry, and commerce.

IFAC seems not to command the notice in the business press that the International Accounting Standards Committee receives, and decidedly not that of the SEC, FASB and GASB in this country.

IFAC AND IASC RELATIONSHIP

By 1982, it became obvious to the leadership of IFAC and the International Accounting Standards Committee, located in London, that their particular bailiwicks needed to be clearly established in order to avoid confusion concerning their respective roles. It was agreed that the IASC should be the sole international body to set *financial accounting and reporting standards.*

At the same time, IASC agreed to IFAC's role as the worldwide *organization for the accountancy profession.*

The Board of IFAC considered the following to be among their most important tasks:

1. Develop auditing initiatives.
2. Develop guidance and standards relating to education, ethics, management accounting, information technology and the public sector.
3. Give consideration to professional issues such as accountant's liability and the liberalization of professional services.
4. Act as primary spokesman on professional accountancy issues.

TWO SEPARATE INTERNATIONAL ORGANIZATIONS

IFAC emphasizes that the international accountancy profession could be considered to have two primary standard-setting bodies: IFAC and the IASC.

Associate members of IFAC are national organizations whose members work in a support role to the accountancy professions and newly formed accountancy bodies that have not yet met the full membership criteria.

Affiliate members of IFAC are international organizations that represent a particular area of interest or a group of professionals who frequently interact with accountants.

There is considerable mutual support for one another's objectives. IFAC member bodies, in addition to their responsibility to promote and use IFAC guidance, are committed to promote and implement IASC pronouncements. There is also regular contact and coordination between the two organizations at the leadership level.

This arrangement has worked for the last 15 years or so. In addition, both organizations appear to believe that it provides, on the one hand, the necessary degree of independence for the IASC Board to set accounting standards but also ensures the commitment of the accountancy profession in helping to see that these standards are actually implemented in international practice.

INFORMATION TECHNOLOGY COMMITTEE (ITC)

This group is charged with keeping the worldwide accounting community abreast of the latest developments and applications relating to information technology (IT). It encourages member bodies to keep up-to-date on available hardware and software and the relationship between IT and the accounting profession.

At a recent international meeting, the committee focused on the use of IT in developing countries and approved a research program and budget. Research will involve determination of the current usage of IT in these countries and identification of the type and level of assistance which would be appropriate in developing economies.

The IFAC *Handbook of International Information Technology Guidelines* includes five Information Technology Guidelines developed by IFAC's IT Committee: *Technology Planning for Business Impact; Managing Information Technology Planning for Business Impact; Managing Security of Information; Acquiring Information Technology;* and *IT Delivery and Support.*

ACCOUNTANCY'S FIGHT AGAINST CORRUPTION

IFAC has published a discussion paper, *The Accountancy Profession and the Fight Against Corruption,* aimed at promoting debate at the national and global levels on the issue of corruption. The paper points out that while there is corruption worldwide, both public and private, it is more pervasive in some places than others.

The paper suggests that corruption has a negative impact on everyone:

1. Economic development is hampered.
2. Investors lose confidence.
3. Entrepreneurs suffer increased costs of doing business and face higher risks.
4. Country credit ratings drop.
5. Professionals, businesspersons, and government officials lose credibility.

Society at large becomes quite cynical. And the impact could be felt most deeply in developing and emerging countries where a resulting drop in aid and investment can certainly have a significant impact on economic development, and create social hardships for peoples attempting to build a better life.

Legal and Governmental Support

The IFAC may be tilting at windmills, but the organization feels that combating corruption must be carried on by all and at all levels of society. They call for a commitment by governments and the existence of a solid framework of laws, regulations, control systems and disciplinary measures that proscribe corrupt acts and prescribe strong penalties for those found guilty of them, as well as adequate protection for whistle blowers.

Just what is the accountant's role in all of this? The profession cannot carry on this battle alone but, as an integral part of society and a major player in the business world, IFAC believes it must be and is ready to play its part if there is appropriate infrastructure and public support.

The Many Faces of Corruption

Bribery, fraud, illegal payments, money laundering, smuggling and as many other forms as criminal minds may devise, IFAC finds lurking everywhere. The paper points out that often corruption takes place not only involving money, but also involving special favors or influence. Economic growth, globalization and new developments in technology provide a changing scenario in which corrupt individuals devise ever-changing forms of corruption. Thus, it concludes, it is impossible to provide an all-purpose rule book on how to contain corruption. The problem is too complex — and never-ending — but the fight must go on.

Coordinated Responsibilities

IFAC concedes that in the business world, management has a critical role in the battle against corruption. It is the management of an organization that will set the parameters by developing and enforcing systems of proper corporate governance. In the public sector, similar governance codes have been or need to be developed.

Since accountants have long been commended for high integrity, objectivity and service to the public interest, IFAC feels that their key internal positions in the public and private sectors, as well as their external responsibilities as auditors or advisors, make them essential in the efforts to reduce corruption.

In addition, the paper cites other aids to tightening the reins on corruption:

1. Most national organizations of accountants, as well as the International Federation of Accountants, have developed standards that are designed to combat corruption.
2. Ethics codes, which apply to all accountants, be they in public practice, business, industry or government, require them to follow the highest standards of objectivity and professional care.
3. Auditing standards alert practitioners to the possibility of fraud and require them to document such possibility in planning audits and to report their findings to management.
4. Codes of corporate governance and appropriate financial and other internal controls should ensure that those accountants in business or in government are aware of their responsibilities to report corruption in a similar manner.

IFAC Proposals

But where is all of this background leading? IFAC states its wish to contribute to the global and national debates which it believes should be developed to ensure that the fight against corruption moves forward. To this end:

1. It has developed the paper on corruption to raise awareness of the issues and contribute to the debate.
2. It is proposing to its member bodies that they:
   a. Develop programs that build collaborative relationships with legislative and regulatory authorities, the legal profession, and other groups interested in strengthening the framework for good governance, transparency, and accountability, as well as the legal framework, so as to minimize corrupt practices, propose solutions based on model legislation and regulations introduced in other countries, and point out where swift action may be required.
   b. Work with government to ensure that the requisite definition of corruption is in place, the legislation proscribing corrupt acts is prepared and appropriate means of protection are developed for those who may "blow the whistle."
   c. Initiate education programs for accountants and the public to create awareness of the detrimental effects of corruption, thereby motivating public action toward its elimination, through press articles, seminars, continuing professional education courses, and speeches by leaders of the profession.
   d. Encourage the national media to make corruption a public issue by devoting attention to the types and hazards of corrupt activities, publication of studies of the harm caused by corruption, and the various steps that can be taken to prevent or expose such harm.
   e. Provide assistance including technical support, to national and international organizations fighting corruption by publicizing their activities, offering assistance in their research, and promoting their proposals.
   f. Encourage practicing firms, their clients and governments to adopt codes of conduct setting the "tone at the top" by establishing sound principles of corporate governance that expressly prohibit corrupt activity, and that provide the benefits flowing from the implementation of internal control systems that help expose corrupt activities.
   g. Encourage audit committees expressly to consider whether appropriate policies are in place to prohibit corrupt acts and to require that any such act be reported to them.

h. Promote a tax system that is efficient and equitable so as to discourage the disparity and burden that leads to corruption, and that does not allow corrupt payments to be deductible from income for tax purposes.

3. It will use its influence with organizations such as the World Bank, the IMF, the Organisation of Economic Coordination & Development (OECD) and the United Nations to encourage the development of proper legislation in all member states.

4. It will establish and maintain links with organizations such as Transparency International and the Financial Action Task Force to ensure that the profession is represented in their governing councils and periodic conferences as a means to increase its profile in the fight against corruption.

In the Final Analysis

The organization calls upon the individual accountant to carry out his or her responsibility in the anticorruption campaign. Professional skepticism is necessary when establishing business relationships, and in the review of transactions between related parties, especially when they appear to have questionable business sense. Corrupt entities and individuals must realize that accountants constitute a barrier against corruption. Above all, each individual accountant must ensure that his or her own behavior reflects an unswerving commitment to truth and honesty in financial reporting.

INTERNATIONAL PUBLIC SECTOR ACCOUNTING STANDARDS— ACCRUAL ACCOUNTING

The PSC has now issued 18 IPSASs. These authoritative international financial reporting standards for governments represent a significant step toward strengthening financial reporting by governments around the world.

The first 12 standards are briefed below. The newer 6 are discussed at the beginning of the chapter.

- IPSAS 1—*Presentation of Financial Statements.* This standard sets out the overall considerations for the presentation of financial statements, guidance for the structure of those statements and minimum requirements for their content under the accrual basis of accounting.
- IPSAS 2—*Cash Flow Statements.* This standard requires the provision of information about the changes in cash and cash equivalents during the period from operating, investing and financing activities.
- IPSAS 3—*Net Surplus or Deficit for the Period, Fundamental Errors and Changes in Accounting Policies.* This standard specifies the accounting

treatment for changes in accounting estimates, changes in accounting policies, and the correction of fundamental errors; defines extraordinary items; and requires the separate disclosure of certain items in the financial statements.

- IPSAS 4 — *The Effect of Changes in Foreign Exchange Rates.* This standard deals with accounting for foreign currency transactions and foreign operations. IPSAS 4 sets out the requirements for determining which exchange rate to use for the recognition of certain transactions and balances, and how to recognize in the financial statements the financial effect of changes in exchange rates.

- IPSAS 5 — *Borrowing Costs.* This standard prescribes the accounting treatment for borrowing costs and requires either the immediate expensing of borrowing costs or, as an allowed alternative treatment, the capitalization of borrowing costs that are directly attributable to the acquisition, construction, or production of a qualifying asset.

- IPSAS 6 — *Consolidated Financial Statements and Accounting for Controlled Entities.* This standard requires all controlling entities to prepare consolidated financial statements that consolidate all controlled entities on a line-by-line basis. The standard also contains a detailed discussion of the concept of control, as it applies in the public sector, and guidance on determining whether control exists for financial reporting purposes.

- IPSAS 7 — *Accounting for Investments in Associates.* This standard requires all investments in associates to be accounted for in the consolidated financial statements using the equity method of accounting. However, when the investment is acquired and held exclusively with a view to its disposal in the near future, the cost method is required.

- IPSAS 8 — *Financial Reporting of Interests in Joint Ventures.* This standard requires proportionate consolidation to be adopted as the benchmark treatment for accounting for such joint ventures entered into by public sector entities. However, IPSAS 8 also permits, as an alternative, joint ventures to be accounted for using the equity method of accounting.

- IPSAS 9 — *Revenue from Exchange Transactions.* This standard establishes the conditions for the recognition of revenue arising from exchange transactions, requires such revenue to be measured at the fair value of the consideration received or receivable, and includes disclosure requirements.

- IPSAS 10 — *Financial Reporting in Hyperinflationary Economies.* This standard describes the characteristics of a hyperinflationary economy and requires financial statements of entities that operate in such economies to be restated.

- IPSAS 11 — *Construction Contracts.* This standard defines construction contracts, establishes requirements for the recognition of revenues and expenses arising from such contracts, and identifies certain disclosure requirements.

- IPSAS 12—*Inventories.* This standard defines inventories, establishes measurement requirements for inventories (including those inventories held for distribution at no or nominal charge) under the historical cost system and includes disclosure requirements.

Chapter 7

The Sarbanes-Oxley Act of 2002

CONTENTS

Many of the provisions of the Sarbanes-Oxley Act are direct attacks on strategies used by corporate officials—selling company stock during black-out periods, insider trading, supporting "tame" analysts to tout their stock, and shredding documents. This legislation is a concentrated effort to restore the investor's faith in the stock market.

PEERING INTO THE FUTURE

Under pressure from accounting scandals at Enron, Congress reached an agreement with lightning speed on legislation to overhaul the rules governing the accounting profession. With the time constraint of the August congressional recess forcing their hand, House and Senate members hammered out a compromise on reform legislation in less than a week and reached an accord on July 24, 2002. The compromise called for the creation of an independent Accounting Oversight Board governed by the Securities and Exchange Commission (SEC).

Despite pressure to tone down the language and requirements of the Sarbanes-sponsored Senate bill, which placed stringent limits on the consulting services that audit firms can provide to public company audit clients, the strictures prevailed. Moreover, the act included House measures on stiffer criminal penalties for corporate crimes.

Adoption of the legislation marked a drastic shift for the accounting profession, which has, thus far, been self-regulated. The legislation makes control of the accounting profession similar to that of the brokerage industry's regulation under the National Association of Securities Dealers (NASD).

The bill places a federal government bureaucracy at the helm of accounting regulation. It is hoped that this new oversight structure will renew the faith the public had in auditors and the financial statements that they helped prepare. On the other hand, it will take a little while to see how closely the SEC and the Oversight Board itself follow the dictates of the law.

The American Institute of Certified Public Accountants (AICPA) noted that the changes demanded by the legislation would be dramatic and challenging for the accounting profession. The AICPA has pledged to work cooperatively with firms engaged in conducting public company audits in adapting to changes mandated by the new legislation. One immediate problem facing the AICPA is the appropriate role of its SEC Practice Section, within the framework of the new oversight board. At this juncture, it is a little difficult to foresee fully just what the role of the AICPA, Financial Accounting Standards Board (FASB), and other professional and standard-setting organizations may be.

An official of the SEC, speaking before a group of accountants at the end of January 2003, remarked that the past two weeks had been ". . . the busiest two weeks of rulemaking in the history of the Commission." He stated his belief that to restore the honor and credibility of the accounting profession, all participants must focus on one thing—doing what is best for investors.

FOCUSING ON INVESTORS

Several of the initiatives under way at the SEC addressed the issue of focusing on investors. Much of this activity was generated by the passage of the Sarbanes-Oxley Act. In that time, the Commission adopted nine final rules implementing both the legislative mandates of the Act and, in some cases, additional reforms that the Commission and Commission staff deemed necessary to advance the interests of investors. Those rules relate to:

1. CEO and CFO certifications.
2. Pro forma financial information.
3. Codes of ethics for senior executives.
4. Financial experts on audit committees.
5. Trading during pension fund blackout periods.
6. Disclosure of material off-balance-sheet transactions.
7. Retention of audit records.
8. Independence standards for public company auditors.
9. Standards of conduct for attorneys.

Importance to the Accounting Profession

Three of these initiatives undertaken by the SEC that are believed to have the potential for having the most significant effect upon the accounting profession are:

1. The establishment of the Public Company Accounting Oversight Board.
2. The adoption of new independence standards for public company auditors.
3. The efforts under way to improve the accounting standard-setting process and bring about international convergence of accounting standards.

The list of rules noted above indicates that the Act requires significant reform in all aspects of financial reporting and the disclosure system. The status of both registrants and auditors has been changed drastically. Other members of the capital market system, including investment bankers, analysts, and attorneys will now also operate under new and more stringent regulation.

Sarbanes-Oxley More Than a List of Specifics

Details of the Act follow, but the Commission considers that the underlying themes are relatively simple, straightforward, and intended to restore market credibility. They include some old-fashioned truths about life in general as well as warnings for avoiding trouble in the corporate world:

- Each person must accept responsibility for his or her own behavior.
- Being an accomplice to, or ignoring, a bad deed may be the same as doing the bad deed.
- Those who carry out bad deeds shall be punished.
- Appearance counts.

TYPES OF SERVICES CONSIDERED UNLAWFUL

The big accomplishment was to bring to fruition what the SEC and FASB had been trying to accomplish (with little success) before all the scandals came to light. Accounting firms are now barred from providing:

1. Bookkeeping or other services related to the accounting records or financial statements of public company audit clients.
2. Financial information systems design and implementation services.
3. Appraisal or valuation services, fairness opinions, or contribution-in-kind reports.
4. Actuarial services.
5. Internal audit outsourcing services.
6. Management functions or human resources.
7. Broker or dealer, investment advisor, or investment banking services.
8. Legal services and expert services unrelated to the audit.
9. Any other service that the Board determines, by regulation, is impermissible.

However, the Board does have the power to grant exceptions. Under certain conditions, some services may be performed if prior approval has been sought and granted. A similar measure in the House bill would have barred only consulting on system implementation and internal audits for audit clients. There are those who feel that Congress did not need to set hard and fast rules regarding independence and non-audit services. Some knowledgeable commenters consider those are matters better attended to by an expert regulatory body. On the other hand, if such matters are actually spelled out, obfuscation might not prevail.

The final legislation took the tougher measures proposed by the House on penalties for corporate crimes. A new securities fraud section was established to handle white-collar crime. Conviction carries a maximum penalty of a 25-year prison term, and penalties for mail and wire fraud are increased to 20 years.

THE PUBLIC COMPANY ACCOUNTING OVERSIGHT BOARD

The Oversight Board has the power to:

1. Establish auditing.
2. Set up quality control.
3. Draft ethics and independence standards for public company auditors.
4. Investigate and discipline accountants.
5. Apply oversight of foreign firms that audit the financial statements of companies under U.S. securities laws.

Because the measure was passed so quickly and powered by such emotional fervor, there may be even more need for "technical corrections" than the many which are necessary for even the most routine legislation. However, until then, qualifications for, and constraints governing, Board membership include the following:

1. The Board is made up of five financially literate members who are appointed for five-year terms.
2. Two of the members must be or have been CPAs.
3. The remaining three *must not be and cannot have been* CPAs.
4. The Chair may be held by one of the CPA members, provided that he or she has not been engaged as a practicing CPA for five years.
5. The Board's members are to serve on a full-time basis.
6. No member may, concurrent with service on the Board, share in any of the profits of, or receive payments from, a public accounting firm, other than "fixed continuing payments," such as retirement payments.
7. Members of the Board are appointed by the SEC after consultation with the Chairman of the Federal Reserve Board and the Secretary of the Treasury.
8. Members may be removed by the SEC "for good cause."

Responsibilities of the Board Related to Auditing Standards

The Oversight Board is expected to:

1. Cooperate on an ongoing basis with designated professional groups of accountants and any advisory groups convened in connection with setting auditing standards. Although the Board can, to the extent that it deems appropriate, adopt standards proposed by those groups, the *Board will have authority to amend, modify, repeal, and reject any standards suggested by the groups.* The Board is to report on these standard-setting activities to the Commission annually.

2. Require registered public accounting firms to "prepare, and maintain for a period of not less than seven years, audit work papers, and other information related to any audit report, in sufficient detail to support the conclusions reached in such report."

3. Require a second partner in public accounting firms to review and approve audit reports that registered accounting firms must adopt related to quality control standards.

4. Adopt an audit standard to implement the internal control review required by the act. This standard must require that the auditor evaluate whether the internal control structure and procedures include records that:

   a. Accurately and fairly reflect the transactions of the issuer.

   b. Provide reasonable assurance that the transactions are recorded in a manner that will permit the preparation of financial statements in accordance with GAAP.

   c. Include a description of any material weaknesses in the internal controls of the particular firm.

Mandatory Registration and Other Oversight Functions

The Board will be responsible for:

1. Registering public accounting firms. In order to audit a public company, a public accounting firm must register with the Board. The Board is empowered to collect a registration fee and an annual fee from each registered public accounting firm in amounts that are "sufficient" to recover the costs of processing and reviewing applications and annual reports.

   The Board is required to establish a reasonable annual accounting support fee in an amount necessary or appropriate to maintain the Board. This fee will be assessed on issuers only.

The registration requirement also applies to foreign accounting firms that audit a U.S. company. This would include foreign firms that perform some audit work, such as in a foreign subsidiary of a U.S. company that is relied on by the primary auditor.

2. Establishing (or adopting, by rule) auditing, quality control, ethics, independence, and other *standards* relating to the preparation of audit reports for issuers.

3. Conducting inspections of accounting firms. Annual quality reviews (inspections) must be conducted for firms that audit more than 100 issues; all other inspections must be conducted every three years. The SEC or the Board may order a special inspection of any firm at any time.

4. Conducting investigations and disciplinary proceedings and imposing appropriate sanctions. All documents and information prepared or received by the Board are treated as confidential and privileged as an evidentiary matter in any proceeding in any federal or state court or administrative agency, unless they are presented in connection with a public proceeding or released in connection with a disciplinary action. However, all such documents and information can be made available to the SEC, the U.S. Attorney General, and other federal and appropriate state agencies. Disciplinary hearings will be closed unless the Board orders that they be public, for good cause, and with the consent of the parties. Sanctions can be imposed by the Board upon a firm if it fails to supervise, within reason, any associated person with regard to auditing or quality control standards, or otherwise. No sanctions report will be made available to the public unless and until stays pending appeal have been lifted.

5. Performing such other duties or functions as necessary or appropriate.

6. Enforcing compliance with the act, the rules of the Board, professional standards, and the securities laws relating to the preparation and issuance of audit reports and the obligations and liabilities of accountants with respect to them.

7. Setting the budget and managing the operations of the Board and the staff of the Board.

SEC OVERSIGHT OF THE OVERSIGHT BOARD

The Securities and Exchange Commission:

1. Has oversight and enforcement authority over the Board.

2. Can give the Board additional responsibilities, other than those specified in the Act.

3. May require the Board to keep certain records.

4. Has the power to inspect the Board itself, in the same manner as it can with regard to self-regulatory organizations, such as the NASD.
5. Is to treat the Board as if it were a registered securities association; that is, a self-regulatory organization.
6. Requires that the Board file proposed rules and rule changes with the SEC and may approve, reject, or amend such rules.
7. Requires that the Board notify the SEC of pending investigations involving potential violations of the securities laws and coordinate its investigation with the SEC Division of Enforcement, as necessary, to protect an ongoing SEC investigation.
8. May, by order, censure or impose limitations on the activities, functions, and operations of the Board if it finds that the Board has violated the act or the securities laws. The same applies if the Board has failed to ensure the compliance of accounting firms, with applicable rules, without reasonable justification.
9. Requires that the Board must notify the SEC when it imposes any "final sanction" on any accounting firm or associated person. The Board's findings and sanctions are subject to review by the SEC. The SEC may enhance, modify, cancel, reduce, or require remission of such sanction.

ACCOUNTING STANDARDS

The SEC is authorized to recognize, as generally accepted, any accounting principles established by a standard-setting body that meets the bill's criteria, which include requirements that the body:

1. Be a private entity.
2. Be governed by a board of trustees (or equivalent body), the majority of whom are not, nor have been, associated with a public accounting firm for the past two years.
3. Be funded in a manner similar to the Board.
4. Have adopted procedures to ensure prompt consideration of changes to accounting principles by a majority vote.
5. Consider, when adopting standards, the need to keep them current and the extent to which international convergence of standards is necessary or appropriate.

PUBLIC COMPANY AUDIT COMMITTEES

The audit committee of the issuers plays an important part in overseeing many of the provisions of the Sarbanes-Oxley Act.

Qualifications and Responsibilities

Each member of the audit committee must be a member of the board of directors of the issuer and otherwise be independent. "Independent" is defined as not receiving (other than for service on the board) any consulting, advisory, or other compensatory fee from the issuer. In addition, no member may be an "affiliated" person of the issuer or of any of his or her subsidiaries. However, the SEC may make exemptions for certain individuals *on a case-by-case basis.* The SEC is expected to announce rules to require issuers to disclose whether at least one member of its audit committee is a "financial expert."

Each issuer must provide appropriate funding to the audit committee to allow the committee to carry out its responsibilities. The audit committee of an issuer, in turn, is directly responsible for the appointment, compensation, and oversight of the work of any registered public accounting firm employed by that issuer. The audit committee must also establish procedures for receiving, retaining, and handling complaints received by the issuer regarding accounting, internal controls, and auditing. In addition, the committee must engage independent counsel or other advisors that it determines necessary to carry out its duties.

Auditor Reports to Audit Committees

The accounting firm must report to the audit committee all critical accounting policies and practices to be used and any alternative disclosures and treatments of financial information within GAAP that have been discussed with management, along with the ramifications of their use and the treatment preferred by the firm. Other nonaudit services, including tax services, require preapproval by the audit committee on a case-by-case basis and must be disclosed to investors in periodic reports.

MANAGEMENT ASSESSMENT OF INTERNAL CONTROLS

The Sarbanes-Oxley Act requires that each annual report of an issuer contain an internal control report, which is to state the responsibility of management for establishing and maintaining an adequate internal control structure and procedures for financial reporting. It also must contain an assessment, as of the end of the issuer's fiscal year, of the effectiveness of the internal control structure and procedures of the issuer for financial reporting. Each issuer's auditor must attest to, and report on, the assessment made by the management of the issuer. An attestation made under this section must be in accordance with standards for attestation engagements issued or adopted by the Board. An attestation engagement may not be the subject of a separate engagement.

The legislation directs the SEC to require each issuer to disclose whether it has adopted a code of ethics for its senior financial officers and the contents of that code. It directs the SEC to revise its regulations concerning prompt disclosure on Form 8-K to require immediate disclosure "of any change in, or waiver of," an issuer's code of ethics.

FINANCIAL REPORT REQUIREMENTS IN THE ACT

Nothing is more important to a business entity, large or small, its creditors, investors, even its employees and rank-and-file officers and directors than a true and honest financial report. When ranking officers do not play by the rules (however flawed the rules) and skew that report to their own advantage, all and sundry suffer in the final analysis.

Much of the Sarbanes-Oxley Act is drafted to attempt to improve the quality and reliability of these reports.

Each financial report must be prepared in accordance with GAAP and must "reflect all material correcting adjustments . . . that have been identified by a registered accounting firm. . . ." In addition, each annual and quarterly financial report is required to disclose all material off-balance-sheet transactions and any other relationships with unconsolidated entities that may have a material current or future effect on the financial condition of the issuer.

The SEC is expected to issue rules providing that pro forma financial information must be presented in such a manner that it does not contain an untrue statement or omit a material fact that, by its omission, would make the pro forma financial information misleading.

Officer and Director Penalties. If an issuer is required to prepare a restatement owing to *material noncompliance* with financial reporting requirements, the chief executive officer and the chief financial officer are required to reimburse the issuer for any bonus or other incentive- or equity-based compensation received during the 12 months following the issuance or filing of the non-compliant document. They must also reimburse the issuer for any profits realized from the sale of securities of the issuer during that period.

In any action brought by the SEC for violation of the securities laws, federal courts are authorized to "grant any equitable relief that may be appropriate or necessary *for the benefit of investors.*"

Improper Influence on Conduct of Audits. It shall be unlawful for any officer or director of an issuer to take any action to fraudulently influence, coerce, manipulate, or mislead any auditor engaged in the performance of an audit for the purpose of rendering the financial statements materially misleading.

Corporate Responsibility for Financial Reports.   The CEO and CFO of each issuer are ordered to prepare a statement to accompany the audit report to certify the "appropriateness of the financial statements and disclosures contained in the periodic report, and that those financial statements and disclosures fairly present, in all material respects, the operations and financial condition of the issuer." A violation of this section must be knowing and intentional to give rise to liability.

SEC INVOLVEMENT IN THE ACT

Not only is a new Board created by the Sarbanes-Oxley Act, but the Securities and Exchange Commission is given control of it, additional oversight assignments, study problems, and added funds and laborpower to accomplish the job. Throughout this chapter, the SEC figures prominently in new and revised rules and regulations. Following are some additional areas of the Commission's role in the new legislation. Among the provisions is a section that empowers the SEC to prohibit a person from serving as an officer or director of a public company if the person has committed securities fraud. This, and many of the other measures, would seem to be iteration of provisions that have been in place, but they need to be emphasized.

Study and Report on Special-Purpose Entities.   The Commission is to study off-balance-sheet disclosures to determine (1) the extent of such transactions (including assets, liabilities, leases, losses and the use of special purpose entities) and (2) whether generally accepted accounting rules result in financial statements of issuers reflecting the economics of such off-balance-sheet transactions to investors in a transparent fashion. The Commission is to make a report containing its recommendations to Congress.

Miscellaneous Assignments.   Various sections of the legislation include the requirements placed on firms and their officers and the specifically assigned oversight tasks to the Commission. Among them are:

1. A direction that the SEC require each issuer to disclose whether it has adopted a code of ethics for its senior financial officers and the contents of that code. The SEC is also directed to revise its regulations concerning prompt disclosure on Form 8-K that requires immediate disclosure of any change in, or waiver of, an issuer's code of ethics.

2. The expectation that the SEC will issue rules providing that pro forma financial information must be presented in such a manner that it does not contain an untrue statement or omit to state a *material fact* that, by its omission, would make the pro forma financial information misleading.

(Many firms that have rather straightforward financial reports have managed to produce questionable pro forma information and have defined materiality rather loosely.)

Officer and Director Penalties. The SEC is empowered to issue an order to prohibit, conditionally or unconditionally, permanently or temporarily, any person who has violated section 10(b) of the 1934 Act from acting as an officer or director of an issuer if the SEC has found that such person's conduct demonstrates unfitness to serve as an officer or director of any such issuer:

(Section 10: It shall be unlawful for any person, directly or indirectly, by the use of any means or instrumentality of interstate commerce or of the mails, or of any facility of any national securities exchange—[b] To use or employ, in connection with the purchase or sale of any security registered on a national securities exchange or any security not so registered, or any securities-based swap agreement (as defined in section in the Gramm-Leach-Bliley Act), any manipulative or deceptive device or contrivance in contravention of such rules and regulations as the Commission may prescribe as necessary or appropriate in the public interest or for the protection of investors.)

Appearance and Practice Before the Commission. The SEC may censure any person or temporarily bar or deny any person the right to appear or practice before the SEC if the person does not possess the requisite qualifications to represent others, lacks character or integrity, or has willfully violated federal securities laws.

Rules of Professional Responsibility for Attorneys. The SEC is required to establish rules setting minimum standards for professional conduct for attorneys practicing before it.

Study and Report. The SEC is ordered to conduct a study of "securities professionals" (public accountants, public accounting firms, investment bankers, investment advisors, brokers, dealers, and attorneys) who have been found to have aided and abetted a violation of federal securities laws.

Temporary Freeze Authority. The SEC is authorized to freeze an extraordinary payment to any director, officer, partner, controlling person, agent, or employee of a company during an investigation of possible violations of securities laws.

Increased Budget for Additional Laborpower. SEC appropriations for 2003 are increased to $776,000,000, compared to the $469,000,000 that was in the budget request. Of these funds, $98 million is to be used to hire an additional 200 employees to provide enhanced oversight of auditors and audit services required by the federal securities laws. This should also enhance the commission's general investigation and enforcement capabilities.

MEASURES RELATING TO CORPORATE OFFICERS

Because many of the problems facing corporations and the stock market at present result from actions by ranking corporate officers, a number of provisions in this legislation deal directly with corporate governance and related matters:

1. *Prohibition of insider trades during pension fund black-out periods.* The Act prohibits the purchase or sale of stock by officers and directors and other insiders during black-out periods. Any profits resulting from sales in violation of this section "shall inure to and be recoverable by the issuer." If the issuer fails to bring suit or prosecute diligently, a suit to recover such profit may be instituted by "the owner of any security of the issuer."

2. *Prohibition of personal loans to executives.* Generally, it will be unlawful for an issuer to extend credit to any director or executive officer. Consumer credit companies may make home improvement and consumer credit loans and issue credit cards to its directors and executive officers, if it is done in the *ordinary course of business* on the same terms and conditions made to the general public.

3. *Timely disclosures.* Issuers must disclose information on material changes in the financial condition or operations of the issuer on a rapid and current basis. Directors, officers, and 10 percent owners must report designated transactions by the end of the second business day following the day on which the transaction was executed.

4. *Conflicts of interest.* The CEO, Controller, CFO, Chief Accounting Officer, or person in an equivalent position cannot have been employed by the company's audit firm during the one-year period proceeding the audit.

5. *Audit partner rotation.* The lead audit or coordinating partner and the reviewing partner must rotate off of the audit every 5 years.

6. *Tampering with an official proceeding.* The Act makes it a crime for any person to corruptly alter, destroy, mutilate, or conceal any document with the intent to impair the object's integrity or availability for use in an official proceeding or to otherwise obstruct, influence or impede any official proceeding. Perpetrators are liable for up to 20 years in prison and a fine.

7. *Sense of congress regarding corporate tax returns.* It is the sense of Congress that the federal income tax return of a corporation should be signed by the chief executive officer of such corporation.

Treatment of Securities Analysts by Registered Securities Associations

National Securities Exchanges and registered securities associations must adopt conflict-of-interest rules for research analysts who recommend equities in research reports.

GAO Studies

The Government Accounting Office (GAO) has also been assigned a part in the new legislations. Its task is to conduct two studies. The first is a study regarding the consolidation of public accounting firms since 1989, including the present and future impact of the consolidation and the solutions to any problems discovered. The second is a study of the potential effects of requiring the mandatory rotation of audit firms for publicly traded corporations.

Amendments to the Sarbanes Senate Bill

Rather than rely on other laws to punish those who dispose of evidence, shred documents, and otherwise attempt to impede investigations, Congress has spelled out the crime and punishment in amendments to the Sarbanes-Oxley Act.

The Corporate and Criminal Fraud Accountability Act of 2002

It is a felony to knowingly destroy or create documents to "impede, obstruct or influence" any existing or contemplated federal investigation. Auditors are required to maintain all audit or review work papers for five years.

The statute of limitations on securities fraud claims is extended to the earlier of five years from the fraud or two years after the fraud was discovered, from three years and one year, respectively.

Employees of issuers and accounting firms are extended whistle-blower protection that would prohibit the employer from taking certain actions against employees who lawfully disclose private employer information to, among others, parties in a judicial proceeding involving a fraud claim. Whistle-blowers are also granted a remedy of special damages and attorney's fees.

A new crime for securities fraud has penalties of fines and up to 10 years of imprisonment.

White-Collar Crime Penalty Enhancement Act of 2002

The provisions include a long list of penalties that have increased the time of imprisonment and amount of fines for specified crimes as follows:

1. The maximum penalty for mail and wire fraud is increased from 5 to 10 years.
2. Tampering with a record or otherwise impeding any official proceeding is classified as a crime.
3. The SEC is given authority to seek a court freeze of extraordinary payments to directors, officers, partners, controlling persons, and agents of employees.
4. The U.S. Sentencing Commission is to review sentencing guidelines for securities and accounting fraud.
5. The SEC may prohibit anyone convicted of securities fraud from being an officer or director of any publicly traded company.
6. Financial Statements filed with the SEC must be certified by the CEO and CFO.
7. The certification must state that the financial statements and disclosures fully comply with provisions of the Securities Exchange Act and that they fairly present, in all material respects, the operations and financial condition of the issuer.
8. Maximum penalties for willful and knowing violations of this section are a fine of not more than $500,000 and/or imprisonment of up to five years.

ALL ACCOUNTANTS NEED TO BE AWARE OF PROVISIONS

Nonpublic companies' Cpas also need to study the implications of the act. Many of the reforms should probably be considered best practices that will result in new regulations by federal and state agencies.

Unquestionably, this act dramatically affects the entire accounting profession. It impacts not just the largest accounting firms, but also any CPA actively working as an auditor of, or for, a publicly traded company or any CPA working in the financial management area of a public company. In fact, the trickle-down or cascade effect will certainly mean that every accountant should be familiar with the new requirements in the field.

ACTIONS RESULTING FROM SARBANES-OXLEY

The SEC released a policy statement in April 2003 reaffirming the Financial Accounting Standards Board as a Designated Private-Sector Standard Setter. The Commission determined that the FASB and its parent organization, the

Financial Accounting Foundation (FAF), satisfy the criteria in section 108 of The Sarbanes-Oxley Act of 2002 and, accordingly, FASB's financial accounting and reporting standards are recognized as "generally accepted" for purposes of the federal securities laws. As a result, registrants are required to continue to comply with those standards in preparing financial statements filed with the Commission, unless the Commission directs otherwise. The determination is premised on an expectation that the FASB, and any organization affiliated with it, will address the issues set forth in this statement and any future amendments to this statement, and will continue to serve investors and protect the public interest.

This policy statement updates the SEC's Accounting Series Release 150, issued on December 20, 1973, which expressed the Commission's intent to continue to look to the private sector for leadership in establishing and improving accounting principles and standards through the FASB with the expectation that the body's conclusions will promote the interests of investors.

SEC's Relationship with the FASB

The federal securities laws set forth the Commission's broad authority and responsibility to prescribe the methods to be followed in the preparation of accounts and the form and content of financial statements to be filed under those laws, as well as its responsibility to ensure that investors are furnished with other information necessary for investment decisions. To assist it in meeting this responsibility, the Commission historically has looked to private sector standard-setting bodies designated by the accounting profession to develop accounting principles and standards. At the time of the FASB's formation in 1973, the Commission reexamined its policy and formally recognized pronouncements of the FASB that establish and amend accounting principles and standards as "authoritative" in the absence of any contrary determination by the Commission. The SEC concluded at that time that the expertise and resources the private sector could offer to the process of setting accounting standards would be beneficial to investors.

The Sarbanes-Oxley Act amends section 19 of the Securities Act of 1933 to establish criteria that must be met in order for the work product of an accounting standard-setting body to be recognized as "generally accepted." A new subsection indicates that, in carrying out its authority under the Securities Exchange Act of 1934, the Commission may recognize as "generally accepted" for purposes of the federal securities laws any accounting principles established by a standard-setting body that:

- Is organized as a private entity.
- Has, for administrative and operational purposes, a board of trustees serving in the public interest, the majority of whom are not, concurrent

with their service on such board, and have not been during the two-year period preceding such service, associated persons of any registered public accounting firm.

- Is funded as provided by the Sarbanes-Oxley Act.
- Has adopted procedures to ensure prompt consideration, by majority vote of its members, of changes to accounting principles necessary to reflect emerging accounting issues and changing business practices.
- Considers, in adopting accounting principles, the need to keep standards current in order to reflect changes in the business environment, the extent to which international convergence on high-quality accounting standards is necessary or appropriate in the public interest and for the protection of investors.

Representatives of the FASB and FAF requested that "[t]he FASB . . . continue to be the designated organization in the private sector for establishing standards of financial accounting and reporting." In reaffirming the FASB's position, the SEC pointed out that the Act does not restrict the Commission's ability to develop accounting principles on its own, nor does it limit the number of private-sector bodies the Commission may recognize.

Qualification and Recognition of the FASB

In assessing compliance with the provisions of section 108, the SEC evaluated the organizational structure, operations, and procedures of both the FAF and the FASB.

The FAF is composed of independent trustees and is responsible for overseeing, funding, and appointing members of the Board, as well as selecting members of an advisory body. The Commission was informed that the majority of the FAF trustees is not, and has not been during the two-year period preceding their service on the FAF, associated with a public accounting firm. Based on their past relationship with the FAF, the SEC believes that the FAF serves the public interest. Accordingly, the FAF meets the applicable criteria in section 108 of the Sarbanes-Oxley Act for the board of trustees of a recognized private sector accounting standard setter.

The Board is responsible for promulgating financial accounting and reporting standards. It currently has seven members who have expertise in accounting and financial reporting. Members generally are appointed for five-year terms and can be reappointed to one additional term. Board members are full-time employees of the FAF.

Commission Oversight of FASB Activities

Whereas the SEC consistently has looked to the private sector to set accounting standards, the securities laws, including the Sarbanes-Oxley Act, clearly provide the SEC with authority to set accounting standards for public companies and other entities that file financial statements with the Commission. In addition, recognition of standards set by a private sector standard-setting body as "generally accepted" is only appropriate under section 108 of the Sarbanes-Oxley Act if, among other things, the Commission determines that the private-sector body "has the capacity to assist the Commission in fulfilling the requirements of . . . the Securities Exchange Act . . . because, at a minimum, the standard setting body is capable of improving the accuracy and effectiveness of financial reporting and the protection of investors under the securities laws." As previously noted, section 108 also emphasizes the Commission's responsibility to determine that the standard-setting body:

- Has "procedures to ensure prompt consideration . . . of changes to accounting principles necessary to reflect emerging accounting issues and changing business practices."
- Considers the need to amend standards "to reflect changes in the business environment."
- Considers, to the extent necessary or appropriate, international convergence of accounting standards.

Given the Commission's responsibilities under the securities laws and specific responsibilities under the Sarbanes-Oxley Act to make findings regarding the procedures, capabilities, activities, and results of any designated accounting standards-setting body, the SEC believes that:

- The FAF and FASB should give the SEC timely notice of, and discuss with it, the FAF's intention to appoint a new member of the FAF or FASB. The FAF makes the final determinations regarding the selection of FASB and FAF members. However, to fulfill its statutory responsibilities, the SEC provides the FAF with its views, and expects that they will continue to be taken into consideration in making the final selection. The SEC, FAF, and FASB share the belief that the qualifications and appropriateness of each member of the FAF and the FASB are critical if the FASB is to continue to be a premier private sector standards-setting body.
- The FASB, in its role of "assist[ing] the Commission in fulfilling the requirements of the Securities Exchange Act," should provide timely guidance to public companies, accounting firms, regulators, and others on accounting issues that the Commission considers to be of immediate significance to investors. The Commission and its staff, however, do not prohibit the FASB from also addressing other topics and do not dictate the direction or outcome of specific FASB projects so long as the conclusions reached by the FASB are *in the interest of investor protection*.

The SEC staff will continue to refer issues to the FASB or one of its affiliated organizations when those issues may call for new, amendments to, or formal interpretations of, accounting standards. The FASB is expected to address such issues in a timely manner. On occasions when the FASB determines that consideration of the issue is inadvisable or that the issue cannot be resolved within the time frame acceptable to the SEC, it is expected that the Board will notify the Commission or its staff promptly, provide its views regarding an appropriate resolution of the issue, and work with the Commission to ensure the protection of investors from misleading or inadequate accounting or disclosures.

One such affiliated organization is the Emerging Issues Task Force (EITF), which comprises approximately 13 members who serve, generally without compensation, on a part-time basis. EITF members are partners in large, medium-sized, and small accounting firms; business executives; financial analysts and other users of financial statements; and academics. Upon ratification of an EITF consensus by the FASB, the consensus is published as part of the EITF's minutes and may be relied upon by SEC registrants and others in the preparation of financial statements that purport to conform to generally accepted accounting principles.

- Because the SEC and FASB share the common goal of providing investors with the disclosure of meaningful financial information, the Commission anticipates continuation of the collegial working relationship with the FASB. It expects that, when requested to do so, the FASB will make information and staff reasonably available to facilitate the understanding and implementation of a particular FASB standard.

The SEC and its staff intend to work with the FAF and the FASB to ensure that proper oversight procedures and policies are in place to allow the SEC to assess whether the FASB continues to meet the characteristics of an accounting standard setter that are discussed in the Sarbanes-Oxley Act.

Key FASB Initiatives

As noted earlier, the SEC has treated FASB accounting standards as authoritative since 1973. In order for U.S. accounting standards to remain relevant and to continue to improve, however, the Commission expects the FASB to:

- Consider, in adopting accounting principles, the extent to which international convergence on high-quality accounting standards is necessary or appropriate in the public interest and for the protection of investors, including consideration of moving toward greater reliance on principles-based accounting standards (rather than specifics) whenever it is reasonable to do so. The SEC expects that, during its deliberations of any accounting issue, the FASB will carefully consider international accounting and financial reporting standards that cover that same issue. This has been done in the past and increasingly so in recent years as it becomes clear that it is, indeed, a global economy.

- Take reasonable steps to continue to improve the timeliness with which it completes its projects while satisfying appropriate public notice and comment requirements.
- Continue to be objective in its decision making and to weigh carefully the views of its constituents and the expected benefits and perceived costs of each standard.

FASB's Independence

Although effective oversight of the FASB's activities is necessary in order for the Commission to carry out its responsibilities under the securities laws, the SEC continues to recognize the importance of the FASB's independence. Therefore, the Commission's determination is that the FASB should continue its role as the preeminent accounting standard setter in the private sector. In performing this role, the SEC feels that the Board must use independent judgment in setting standards and should not be constrained in its exploration and discussion of issues. This is necessary to ensure that the standards developed are free from bias and have the maximum credibility in the business and investing communities.

Conclusion of the Commission

Based on available information, the SEC has reached several conclusions. The organizational structure, operating activities, and procedures of the FAF and FASB were deemed to meet the criteria in section 108 of the Sarbanes-Oxley Act. As mentioned, one of the statutory criteria is that the recognized accounting body be funded as provided in section 109 of the Act. These funding provisions replace the FAF's funding responsibilities; the FAF will continue to be responsible for the fee requests, including establishing the FASB's budget for review by the Commission each year. The SEC stated that it is providing the endorsement of the FASB so that it can begin to work with the Public Company Accounting Oversight Board to implement these funding mechanisms. The recognition of the FASB by the SEC is in anticipation of, and with the expectation that, this funding will be forthcoming in the near term. There has been a great deal of discussion concerning the source of this funding.

The FASB has the capacity to assist the Commission in fulfilling the requirements of the Securities Act of 1933 and of the Securities Exchange Act of

1934 and is capable of improving both the accuracy and effectiveness of financial reporting and the protection of investors under the securities laws. The FASB does not act alone, but receives input relating to standard setting and interpretation from, among other sources, a standing advisory body, the Financial Accounting Standards Advisory Council (FASAC), which is composed of members from the accounting and business communities, academia, and professional organizations. All share an interest in fostering quality financial reporting and disclosure. FASAC's primary mission is to advise the FASB on its projects and agenda. In addition, the FASB has established a User Advisory Council (UAC) to assist the FASB in raising awareness of how investors and investment professionals, equity and credit analysts, and rating agencies use financial information. The FASB has recruited more than 40 professionals, representing a variety of investment and analytical disciplines, to participate on the UAC. Council meetings will concentrate on major Board projects that could significantly change financial information currently available to users. Early meetings have covered a range of issues including accounting for financial instruments, revenue recognition, and pension accounting.

The standards set by the FASB should be recognized as "generally accepted" under section 108 of the Sarbanes-Oxley Act. (At the same time, the Sarbanes-Oxley Act states, "Nothing in this Act, . . . shall be construed to impair or limit the authority of the Commission to establish accounting principles or standards for purposes of enforcement of the securities laws.")

As required under the securities laws, including the Sarbanes-Oxley Act, the Commission will monitor the FASB's procedures, qualifications, capabilities, activities, and results, as well as the FAF's and FASB's ongoing compliance with the expectations and views expressed in this policy statement.

The SEC will issue an appropriate revision of this policy statement if it determines that the FAF or FASB no longer meets the statutory criteria or expectations discussed in the policy statement, or if it is otherwise necessary or appropriate to do so. The occasions when the Commission has not accepted a particular FASB standard have been extremely rare because of its past and continuing recognition and support of the Board's independence. The Commission and its staff do not prohibit the FASB from addressing a particular topic and do not dictate the direction or outcome of specific FASB projects provided that the conclusions reached by the FASB are in the interest of investor protection.

SEC Adopts Attorney Conduct Rule under Sarbanes-Oxley Act

In January 2003, the SEC adopted final rules to implement section 307 of the Sarbanes-Oxley Act by setting "standards of professional conduct for attorneys appearing and practicing before the Commission in any way in the representation of issuers."

In addition, the Commission approved an extension of the comment period on the "noisy withdrawal" provisions of the original proposed rule and publication for comment of an alternative proposal to it. There was much concern expressed regarding the effects of the original "noisy withdrawal" proposal. The American Bar Association was particularly concerned about several issues, including the client confidentiality aspects of the provisions.

On November 6, 2002, the Commission voted to propose the new standards of professional conduct. That proposal more specifically defined the role and activities of a lawyer who is *appearing and practicing before the Commission* in the representation of an issuer. Attorneys were required to report evidence of a material violation "up the ladder" within an issuer. In addition, under certain circumstances, these provisions permitted or required attorneys to effect a so-called "noisy withdrawal"—that is, to withdraw from representing an issuer and notify the Commission that they have withdrawn for professional reasons.

Provisions of the Rule

The rules adopted by the Commission:

- Require an attorney to report evidence of a material violation, determined according to an objective standard, "up the ladder" within the issuer to the chief legal counsel or the chief executive officer of the company or the equivalent.
- Require an attorney, if the chief legal counsel or the chief executive officer of the company does not respond appropriately to the evidence, to report the evidence to the audit committee, another committee of independent directors, or the full board of directors.
- Clarify that the rules cover attorneys who are providing legal services to an issuer, who have an attorney-client relationship with the issuer, and who are aware that documents they are preparing or assisting in preparing will be filed with or submitted to the Commission.
- Provide that foreign attorneys who are not admitted in the United States and who do not advise clients regarding U.S. law would *not* be covered by the rule, whereas foreign attorneys who provide legal advice regarding U.S. law would be covered to the extent they are appearing and practicing before the Commission unless they provide that advice in conjunction with U.S. counsel.
- Allow an issuer to establish a "qualified legal compliance committee" (QLCC) as an alternative procedure for reporting evidence of a material

violation. Such a QLCC would consist of at least one member of the issuer's audit committee (or an equivalent committee of independent directors) and two or more independent board members, and would have the responsibility, among other things, to recommend that an issuer implement an appropriate response to evidence of a material violation. One way in which an attorney could satisfy the rule's reporting obligation is by reporting evidence of a material violation to the issuer's QLCC.

- Allow an attorney, without the consent of an issuer client, to reveal confidential information related to his or her representation to the extent the attorney reasonably believes it is necessary in order to:

  —Prevent the issuer from committing a material violation likely to cause substantial financial injury to the financial interests or property of the issuer or investors.

  —Prevent the issuer from committing an illegal act.

  —Rectify the consequences of a material violation or illegal act in which the attorney's services have been used.

- State that these Commission rules govern in the event the rules conflict with state law, but will not preempt the ability of a state to impose *more rigorous* obligations on attorneys that are not counter to the SEC rules.

- Affirmatively state that the rules do not create a private cause of action and that authority to enforce compliance with the rules is vested exclusively with the Commission.

Definition Modified

Further, the final rules modify the definition of the term "evidence of a material violation," which defines the trigger for an attorney's obligation to report up the ladder within an issuer's ranks. The revised definition confirms that the SEC intends an *objective* triggering standard, rather than a *subjective* one.

This "trigger" must involve credible evidence, based on which it would be unreasonable, under the circumstances, for a prudent and competent attorney not to conclude that it is reasonably likely that a material violation *has occurred, is ongoing, or is about to occur.*

Decision on "Noisy Withdrawal" Postponed

The SEC voted to extend for 60 days the comment period on the "noisy withdrawal" and related provisions originally proposed. Given the significance and complexity of the issues involved, including the implications of a reporting out requirement on the relationship between issuers and their counsel, the Commission decided to continue to seek comment and give thoughtful consideration to these issues.

The Commission also voted to propose an alternative to "noisy withdrawal" that would require attorney withdrawal but would require an issuer, rather than an attorney, to publicly disclose the attorney's withdrawal or written notice that the attorney did not receive an appropriate response to a report of a material violation.

Specifically, an issuer that has received notice of an attorney's withdrawal would be required to report the notice and the circumstances related thereto on form 8-K, 20-F, or 40-F, as applicable, within two days of receiving the attorney's notice. Accordingly, the proposal includes proposed amendments to forms 8-K, 20-F, and 40-F to require issuers to report an attorney's written notice under the proposed rule. The proposing release also will seek comment on whether there are circumstances in which an issuer should be permitted not to disclose an attorney's written notice.

The proposed rules would also permit an attorney (if an issuer has not complied with the disclosure requirement) to inform the Commission that the attorney has withdrawn from representing the issuer or provided the issuer with notice that the attorney has not received an appropriate response to a report of a material violation.

Effective Date

The final rules will become effective 180 days after publication in the Federal Register to provide issuers, attorneys, and law firms sufficient time to put in place procedures to comply with their requirements, and to allow the Commission the opportunity to consider the adoption of the proposed noisy withdrawal provision or the alternative disclosure procedure.

Chapter 8

Public Company Accounting Oversight Board

CONTENTS

Under the Sarbanes-Oxley Act, the Public Company Accounting Oversight Board (PCAOB) has been charged with the responsibility for all aspects of supervision of auditors who serve public clients, subject to the Securities and Exchange Commission's (SEC's) oversight. With the auditing profession's image in tatters and investors' confidence almost nonexistent, the goal of the Board is to improve the quality of the independent audit in an attempt to restore the investors' faith in the system.

For whatever reasons, the self-regulatory system did not work; therefore, there will, henceforth, be close supervision and regulation from without. The Oversight Board's statutory responsibilities include:

- Registering CPAs and public accounting firms that prepare audit reports for public companies. This was required to be within 180 days of the

Commission's determination that the Oversight Board was operational (April 25, 2003).

* Establishing auditing, quality control, ethics, and independence standards for auditors and audit firms.
* Conducting inspections, investigations, and disciplinary proceedings of public accounting firms and their associated persons that work on public companies.
* Enforcing compliance with the rules of the Oversight Board and professional standards.

SEC staff members outlined many of the problems facing this new group. They pointed out that the Sarbanes-Oxley Act actually contains detailed guidance describing Congressional intent on *how* the Oversight Board should carry out these responsibilities. The Act also provides the Oversight Board with the flexibility to make additional changes, if appropriate, subject to the Commission's oversight.

Under the Act, registrants will involuntarily fund both the Oversight Board and the FASB. The accountants and the accounting firms that serve public companies will also be required to chip in. The Commission and its staff will continue to oversee the FASB; that is, the FASB will not be under the umbrella of the Oversight Board, although registrants may ultimately receive a single bill for the funding of the two operations.

VARIED RESPONSIBILITIES ASSIGNED TO THE PCAOB

The Sarbanes-Oxley Act established the Public Company Accounting Oversight Board, to be organized as a nonprofit corporation, with SEC administration and oversight. The PCAOB's mission is to oversee the audits of public companies and related matters. Its more specific tasks as described in the Act include:

* *Auditor registration.* All auditors of public companies must register with the PCAOB, identify public audit clients, identify all accountants associated with those clients, list fees earned for audit and nonaudit services, explain their audit quality control procedures, and identify all criminal, civil, administrative, and disciplinary proceedings against the firm or any of its associated persons in connection with an audit.
* *Inspection of CPA firms.* The PCAOB must inspect all CPA firms that audit public companies to assess compliance with the law, SEC regulations, rules established by the PCAOB, and professional standards. Firms that audit more than 100 public companies will be inspected annu-

ally. Firms that audit 100 or fewer public companies must be inspected at least once every three years. If violations are found, the PCAOB must take disciplinary action.

- *Audit, quality control, ethics, and independence standards.* The PCAOB must adopt audit, quality control, ethics, and independence standards. In doing so, the PCAOB may look to standards established by recognized professional organizations such as the AICPA.

- *Quality control.* The PCAOB's quality control standards must require that registered firms properly supervise all work, monitor compliance with ethics and independence rules, and establish internal systems for consultation, professional development, and client acceptance and retention.

- *Restrictions on services to audit clients.* The Act restricts consulting work that auditors can do for their audit clients. The PCAOB may enumerate additional prohibited services to those covered in the Act.

FINAL RULES FOR INSPECTIONS

Following through with the responsibility for the inspection of CPA firms, the PCAOB adopted final rules relating to inspections of registered public accounting firms in October 2003. These rules will not take effect unless approved by the Securities and Exchange Commission.

Section 104(a) of the Sarbanes-Oxley Act directs the Board to conduct a continuing program of inspections to assess the degree to which each registered public accounting firm and its associated persons are complying with the Act, the Board's and the Commission's rules, and professional standards in connection with audits, audit reports, and related matters involving U.S. public companies.

Consistent with the Act, the Board's rules subject registered public accounting firms to such regular and special inspections as the Board may from time to time conduct. The rules establish a schedule for regular inspections that is consistent with Section 104(b)(1) of the Act, including annual inspections for firms that do the largest volume of audit work and at least triennial inspections for other firms that do some volume of audit work. Special inspections are not subject to a schedule and would be conducted as necessary or appropriate to address issues that come to the Board's attention.

The rules also implement the authority and responsibility that the Act gives the Board to report information indicating possible violations of law or professional standards to:

- The Securities and Exchange Commission.
- Appropriate state regulatory authorities.
- Other regulators and law enforcement authorities.

The rules also implement the Board's authority to commence its own investigation or disciplinary proceeding based on such information.

In addition, they set forth a process by which a firm may submit written comments on a draft inspection report before the Board issues a final inspection report. The firm's response to the draft inspection report would be attached to and made part of the final inspection report. Further, the rules implement the Act's requirement that portions of a final inspection report that deal with criticisms or potential defects in a firm's quality control systems may be made public *only* if the firm fails to address those matters to the Board's satisfaction within 12 months after the issuance of the final inspection report. The Board may, at any time, publish general reports concerning the procedures, findings, and results of its various inspections. These reports may include discussion of criticisms of, or potential defects in, quality control systems of any firm or firms that were the subject of a Board inspection. These published reports, however, would not identify the firm or firms to which the criticisms relate, or at which the defects were found, unless the information had previously been made public pursuant to the Board's rules or other lawful means.

DECISIONS, DECISIONS

One thing the Board did in early stages was to study the current self-regulatory system to assess both its strengths and weaknesses. It began by studying the past activities and effectiveness of all aspects of the self-regulatory system, including the functions of the:

- AICPA SEC Practice Section including the peer review, discipline, and quality control functions.
- Auditing Standards Board.
- Transition Oversight Staff.

Why the profession's self-regulatory system failed is open to question, but many of the more obvious structural deficiencies have been addressed in the development of the Oversight Board itself. The Act either explicitly or implicitly addresses issues such as independent funding, the ability to gather information during investigations, and accountability of the oversight function.

More Questions Than Answers in the Early Stages

Implementation of a quality inspection program may be the Oversight Board's most pressing and, possibly, most vital challenge. The Act provides that the largest firms must be inspected each year and other firms every third year, but questions remain as to who should be reviewed; how thorough the inspection should be; when it should occur; how timing of a review might be influenced by the IRS and SEC calendars; how many partners in what size firm should be reviewed each time the firm is reviewed; what functions will be reviewed; and what the inspection is hoping to (or hoping not to) discover.

It is obvious that this aspect of the Board's responsibilities could very quickly become overwhelming, as the Board must decide who will perform the required inspections; whether to contract some inspections out; where to find experts to handle such issues as computer auditing, independence, client acceptance and continuance, technical accounting consultations, and auditing fair value estimates; and how to address the expertise needed in specific businesses and industries.

Once inspections and reviews have been completed, the Board must determine what remedial actions should be taken if inspections indicate deficient auditing. It must also determine the form of report that will be submitted to the SEC as well as how the inspection process will be affected by other new Commission rules applicable to particular types of firms.

Peer reviews obviously have never been an overwhelming success, but the Oversight Board's staff hopes to gain perspective on what the review process, in general, should accomplish. In other words, how much of that knowledge and experience gained in the peer review process can be incorporated into the new oversight review process, how important the expertise of the reviewer or inspector is in evaluating specific industries or businesses, and how to deal with situations in which state regulatory requirements require firm-on-firm peer reviews.

Some Early Questions Being Answered

Some of these questions were answered, pending SEC approval, when the final inspection rules, *Inspections of Registered Public Accounting Firms,* were announced in October 2003. These rules establish a procedural framework for the PCAOB's inspection program as directed under Section 104(a) of the Sarbanes-Oxley Act. The rules provide for:

- Annual inspections for firms issuing audit reports for more than 100 issuers during the prior calendar year.
- Triennial inspections for firms that issued or played a substantial role in the preparation of audit reports for 1 to 100 issuers during any of the three prior calendar years.
- Special inspections to be conducted as necessary.
- Reporting information of possible violations of law or professional standards to the SEC, state regulatory authorities, and other regulators and law enforcement authorities.
- A process by which a firm may submit written comments on a draft inspection report prior to issuance of a final inspection report.

- A portion of the final inspection report related to criticisms or potential defects of a firm's quality control system to be made public if not resolved with the PCAOB within 12 months of the report's issuance.
- Issuance of general reports discussing criticisms or potential defects of a firm's quality control system that do not identify the firm unless the information was previously made public.

AUDIT STANDARD-SETTING

With regard to standard setting, the first question was whether the Board would set its own standards or adopt standards recommended by an advisory group. Regardless of that decision, any new rules would require SEC approval. Effectively ending the era of self-regulation for the public accounting and auditing industry, the PCAOB unanimously voted to review the existing auditing standards and to write new ones. This, in effect, replaces the Auditing Standards Board (ASB) of the American Institute of Certified Public Accountants (AICPA) as the highest authority for standard-setting guidance of public companies. The Sarbanes-Oxley Act had allowed the PCAOB the option of delegating that authority to an industry group such as the ASB, but the PCAOB decided to accept the responsibility of developing its own guidance. Accounting, investment, and financial experts will be asked to assist in developing the new auditing standards.

In the interim—or transition period—the SEC issued an order that the adoption of interim professional standards be consistent with the requirements of the Act and the federal securities laws. These interim professional standards were considered necessary for use in connection with the audits of public companies and for the protection of investors.

Under the Sarbanes-Oxley Act, the PCAOB's duties include the establishment of auditing, quality control, ethics, independence, and other standards relating to public company audits. In connection with this standard-setting responsibility, section 103 of the Act provides that the PCAOB may adopt any portion of any statement of auditing standards or other professional standards that the PCAOB determines satisfy the requirements of the Act and that were proposed by one or more professional groups of accountants as initial or transitional standards, to the extent the PCAOB determines necessary. This section of the Act also provides that any such initial or transitional standards must be separately approved by the Commission at the time it makes the determination required by the Act, without regard to the procedures that otherwise would apply to Commission approval of PCAOB rules.

The PCAOB has determined that it is necessary in the public interest to adopt initial or transitional professional standards. In this connection, the PCAOB has advised the Commission that it has adopted the following rules setting forth interim, or transitional, standards that the PCAOB finds satisfy the requirements of the Act:

- **Rule 3200T, Interim Auditing Standards.** In connection with the preparation or issuance of any audit report, a registered public accounting firm and its associated persons must comply with generally accepted auditing standards, as described in the AICPA Auditing Standards Board's (ASB's) Statement of Auditing Standards (SAS) 95 (AU 150) and as in existence on April 16, 2003.

  Public accounting firms were not required to be registered with the Board until October 23, 2003. The Board intended that the Interim Auditing Standards apply to public accounting firms that would be required to be registered after the mandatory registration date and to associated persons of those firms, as if those firms had already registered.

- **Rule 3300T, Interim Attestation Standards.** In connection with an engagement described in the ASB's Statements on Standards for Attestation Engagements (SSAE), and related to the preparation or issuance of audit reports for issuers, a registered public accounting firm and its associated persons must comply with these standards and related interpretations and Statements of Position in existence on April 16, 2003.

- **Rule 3400T, Interim Quality Control Standards.** A registered public accounting firm and its associated persons should comply with quality control standards as described in the ASB's Statements on Quality Control Standards (SQCSs) and in existence on April 16, 2003, and with the AICPA SEC Practice Section's Requirements of Membership in existence on April 16, 2003.

- **Rule 3500T, Interim Ethics Standards.** In connection with the preparation or issuance of any audit report, a registered public accounting firm and its associated persons are to comply with ethics standards as described in the AICPA's Code of Professional Conduct Rule 102 and interpretations and rulings in existence on April 16, 2003.

- **Rule 3600T, Interim Independence Standards.** In connection with the preparation or issuance of any audit report, a registered public accounting firm and its associated persons are required to comply with independence standards as described in the AICPA's Code of Professional Conduct Rule 101 and interpretations and rulings in existence on April 16, 2003, as well as with Standards 1, 2, and 3 and Interpretations 99-1, 00-1, and 00-2 of the Independence Standards Board. (The Board's Interim Independence Standards do not supersede the Commission's auditor independence rules. Therefore, to the extent that a provision of the Commission's rule is more restrictive or less restrictive than the Board's Interim Independence Standards, a registered public accounting firm must comply with the more restrictive rule.)

Each of the interim standards described would remain in effect until modified or superseded either by PCAOB action approved by the Commission as pro-

vided in the Act or by Commission action pursuant to its independent authority under the federal securities laws and those rules and regulations.

EXPOSURE DRAFT ON AUDITING INTERNAL CONTROL

The PCAOB has begun its audit standard-setting activities with the proposed
public company auditing standard, *An Audit of Internal Control over Financial
Reporting Performed in Conjunction with an Audit of Financial Statements.*
This addresses both the work that is required to audit internal control over
financial reporting and the relationship of that audit to the audit of the financial statements. The integrated audit results in two audit opinions.

If approved, this standard will be the standard referred to in Sections 404
and 103 of the Sarbanes-Oxley Act. The proposed standard requires:

- The auditor to communicate in writing significant deficiencies and material weaknesses to the company's audit committee.
- The auditor to communicate in writing internal control deficiencies to the
company's management and notify the audit committee that such communication has been made.
- The auditor to evaluate factors related to whether the audit committee is
effective.

The proposed standard also identifies a number of circumstances that would be
considered significant deficiencies and a strong indicator of a material weakness. The proposed effective date is for fiscal years ending on or after June 15,
2004, for accelerated filers (seasoned U.S. companies with public float exceeding $75 million). Other companies, foreign private issuers, and companies with
only registered debt securities have until fiscal years ending on or after April 15,
2005. To be effective, the SEC must approve the final standard.

PCAOB PROPOSES RULES TO COLLECT FEES TO FUND BUDGET

The Sarbanes-Oxley Act established the Board as a nonprofit corporation. The
Board was formed to oversee the audits of public companies that are subject to
the securities laws, and related matters, in order to protect the interests of investors and further the public interest in the preparation of informative, accurate, and independent audit reports for companies whose securities are sold to,
and held by and for, public investors. As such, the Board is subject to, and has
all the powers conferred upon a nonprofit corporation by, the District of
Columbia Nonprofit Corporation Act.

Section 109 of the Sarbanes-Oxley Act provides that funds to cover the

Board's annual budget (less registration and annual fees paid by public accounting firms) are to be collected from public companies (i.e., "issuers," as defined in the Act). The amount due from such companies is referred to in the Act as the Board's "accounting support fee." (The Big Four and other major firms will also pay hefty fees—those referred to above as "registration and annual fees"—to be regulated by the PCAOB.)

The Board decided to apply a similar sliding-scale fee structure to corporations registered with the SEC. The schedule discussed below could require some large-capitalization companies to pay as much as $1 million in annual fees.

The 2003 operating budget approved by the Board projected $68 million in revenues for the year to come from the "accounting support fees" paid by corporations. The Oversight Board's budget expects that 97 percent of SEC registrants will pay these bills.

The initial registration fees collected from audit firms was not included in the Board's 2003 budget, because the exact fee structure had not yet been determined. Those fees go toward reducing the accounting support fee for 2004 budget expenses.

The government supplied more than 15 million to the PCAOB to cover the Board's startup costs. According to Board members, they intended to repay the advances in full during their first year of operation.

The biggest line item in the PCAOB's 2003 budget was payroll, with $28.9 million slotted for salaries, benefits, and payroll taxes. This reflected the Board's hiring plans, which called for the agency to grow from initial personnel of eight in January 2003 to 216 by the end of the year.

The Board has adopted five proposed rules relating to public company funding of the Board's operations, plus certain definitions to implement section 109 of the Sarbanes-Oxley Act.

Details of the Schedule of Fees for Accounting Support

The Board's proposed rules provide for the equitable allocation, assessment, and collection of the fees from public companies. The fee is payable by two classes of issuers:

1. Publicly traded companies with average, monthly U.S. equity market capitalization during the preceding year, based on all classes of common stock, of greater than $25 million. (This is the threshold figure for small business issuers.)
2. Investment companies with average, monthly U.S. equity market capitalizations (or net asset values) of greater than $250 million. In recognition of the structure of investment companies and the relatively less complex nature of investment company audits (as compared to oper-

ating company audits), investment companies would be assessed at a lower rate.

All other issuers, including the following, would be allocated shares of zero:

- Those not required to file audited financial statements with the Commission.
- Employee stock purchase, savings, and similar plans.
- Bankrupt issuers that file modified reports.

Computation of Accounting Support Fee and Allocation

Once each year, the Board will compute the accounting support fee. This fee will equal the sum that the Board has arrived at to cover the proposed budget for that year, as approved by the Commission, less the amount of registration and annual fees received during the prior year from public accounting firms.

In establishing rules for the allocation of the accounting support fee, the Board was guided by two major principles required by section 109 of the Act. Generally, the accounting support fee must be allocated in a manner that reflects the proportionate size of issuers, and within that framework, the accounting support fee must be allocated in an equitable manner. These two principles are related in that, at least as a general matter, the size of issuer serves as an indication of the complexity of an audit, which could be an equitable measure on which to base allocation of the accounting support fee.

With respect to the measurability of issuers' proportionate size, the Board faces certain limitations. To explain, first, although section 109 provides a formula based on equity market capitalization by which to measure the proportionate size of issuers, market data may not be reliable or even regularly available with respect to some issuers, including:

- Issuers whose securities are not traded on an exchange or quoted on NASDAQ.
- Issuers whose securities are otherwise illiquid.
- Certain investment companies, such as unit investment trusts and insurance company separate accounts.
- Issuers whose only publicly traded securities are debt securities do not have equity market capitalization.

Second, to the extent that there are issuers, as that term is defined in the Act, that are not required to file audited financial statements, it may not be equitable to allocate any share of the accounting support fee to them. Further, although most investment companies file annual audited financial statements, the assets of many of those companies consist of investments in issuers who will have themselves been allocated shares of the accounting support fee.

In order to allocate the accounting support fee among issuers in a manner that reflects the overarching principles and the inherent limitations of available data, the Board's proposed rules divide issuers into four classes:

1. All issuers whose average, monthly U.S. equity market capitalization during the preceding calendar year, based on all classes of common stock, is greater than $25 million and whose share price on a monthly, or more frequent, basis is publicly available. (*Equity Issuers class*)

2. Registered investment companies and issuers who have elected to be regulated as business development companies whose average, monthly market capitalization (or net asset value), during the preceding calendar year, is greater than $250 million and whose share price (or net asset value) on a monthly, or more frequent, basis is publicly available. (*Investment Company Issuers class*)

   As discussed below, the allocation formula scales down market capitalization (or, in the case of investment companies whose securities are not traded on an exchange or quoted on NASDAQ, net asset value) of investment companies by 90 percent, such that a $250 million investment company would be allocated a share equal to that of a $25 million operating company.

3. All issuers who, as of the date the accounting support fee is calculated under SEC Rule 7100,:

   a. Have a basis, under a Commission rule or pursuant to other action of the Commission or its staff, not to file audited financial statements,

   b. Are employee stock purchase, savings, and similar plans—interests that constitute securities registered under the Securities Act of 1933— as amended, or

   c. Are subject to the jurisdiction of a bankruptcy court and satisfy the modified reporting requirements of Commission Staff Legal Bulletin 2. (*Issuers Permitted Not to File Audited Financial Statements and Bankrupt Issuers That File Modified Reports class*)

4. All other issuers (i.e., issuers who do not fall into classes 1, 2, or 3 (*All Other Issuers class*)

A company's status as an issuer (or as an investment company, business development company, issuer excused from filing audited financial statements, or bankrupt issuer) will be determined as of the date on which the amount of the annual accounting support fee is set. Companies that are not issuers on that date will not be required to pay any fee during that year.

The accounting support fee will be allocated among the issuers in the four classes in the following manner. Each company in the Equity Issuer and Investment Company Issuer classes will be allocated an amount equal to the accounting support fee, multiplied by a fraction. The numerator of the fraction will be the issuer's average, monthly market capitalization during the preceding calendar year. The denominator will be the sum of the average, monthly market capitalizations of all Equity and Investment Company Issuers. For purposes of this allocation, however, the market capitalization of an investment company issuer will be 10 percent of the investment company's market capitalization or net asset value. All issuers in the other two classes—issuers permitted not to file and all other issuers—will be allocated a share of zero. Issuers will be required to pay their allocated shares of the accounting support fee, rounded to the nearest hundred. Accordingly, issuers whose shares of the accounting support fee are less than $50 will have their shares rounded to zero and will not be assessed a fee.

REGISTRATION REQUIRED OF ALL PUBLIC FIRMS

The PCAOB has adopted a registration system for public accounting firms, including non-U.S. firms. The Sarbanes-Oxley Act of 2002 made it unlawful to play a substantial role in preparing or issuing an audit report on a public company without being registered with the PCAOB. Foreign auditors have been given an additional six months to comply with the new guidelines.

The Board fixed upon an all-electronic Web-based registration system. Domestic firms that audit U.S. companies were given until approximately October 24, 2003, to complete the registration process; foreign firms, until April 26, 2004.

This additional time should give the non-U.S. auditors an opportunity to determine how any of these rules might affect their home-country and international rules as well as allowing U.S. regulators to resolve compliance concerns raised by the auditors and government officials. PCAOB members view this as one of the most controversial matters facing the Board. They agree that they must be prepared to work with their foreign counterparts to find ways to accomplish the oversight goals and protect investors' interests without subjecting foreign firms to unnecessary burdens or conflicting requirements. They believe the 180-day deferral of foreign firm registration affords an opportunity to explore ways of accomplishing that goal with non-U.S. accounting oversight bodies. Regardless, the Sarbanes-Oxley accounting reform law left the PCAOB with no justification for exempting non-U.S. firms.

The Board agrees for the need to avoid unnecessary administrative burdens on public accounting firms arising from the oversight of multiple jurisdictions, but it also believes that, regardless of where they are located, all auditors who participate in the preparation or issuance of audit reports for U.S. issuers should be governed by the same rules and oversight requirements. Early objections, which threatened to become rancorous, rapidly dissipated in the light of yet another prominent non-U.S. firm and its top officials being exposed as equally capable as their U.S. counterparts of malfeasance and corporate skullduggery.

Some Specifics

The Board did make a concession for foreign audit firms that find themselves subject to home-country legal restrictions that prohibit them from disclosing information sought by the PCAOB. In response to concerns raised by non-U.S. accountants during a meeting with PCAOB members early in the formation process, the Board agreed to allow accountants to withhold information if they could document that disclosure would violate non-U.S. laws.

The Board's new registration rules—which are still subject to approval by the Securities and Exchange Commission—also include provisions that:

- Entitle accounting firms to a hearing before the PCAOB if the Board determines that the registration application is inaccurate or incomplete.
- Confirm that the information in these registration applications will be made publicly available as soon as practicable after the Board approves or rejects them.
- Allow both foreign and domestic firms to request confidential treatment of any portion of an application that contains nonpublic personal or proprietary information.
- Eliminate a controversial requirement in the proposed version of the rule that would have required accounting firms to provide additional financial information about their revenue source.
- Narrow the types of criminal, civil, and administrative proceedings that accounting firms must disclose in their registration applications.

CONCERNS OVER FOREIGN COMPANY REGISTRATION

As late as mid-October 2003, European representatives were trying to reach a compromise relating to the mutual supervision of accountants. Although they were given a later date to comply with the U.S. rules, foreign accounting firms that audit U.S. companies must comply with the new accounting oversight board's registration process. The European Union still does not like the idea, but a compromise that will placate both sides may be possible. On the other hand, any firm that affects the financial status of U.S. companies must be overseen by the PCAOB, or the Board will be defeated almost before it is up and operating.

As noted above, the PCAOB mandates that European firms that audit U.S. public companies be registered. One European representative agreed that European firms could register with the U.S. accounting oversight board if the two sides reach an agreement on enforcement.

In late October, the PCAOB released a briefing paper that describes the broad parameters of the Board's approach to the oversight of non-U.S. accounting firms. In the briefing paper are the Board's plans for oversight of non-U.S. registered public accounting firms, based on cooperation with appropriate non-U.S. auditor oversight authorities. This cooperative approach would allow the Board to fulfill its responsibilities to protect the interests of investors and to further the public interest, in keeping with the statutory authority granted to the Board. Plans outlined in the briefing paper include:

- A framework to permit varying degrees of reliance on a firm's home country system of inspections, based on a sliding scale depending upon the strength of the particular country's system.
- Modification of the registration form to permit, where applicable, the inclusion of certain information about a non-U.S. firm's home country oversight system to facilitate coordination between the two systems.
- A 90-day extension of the Board's deadline for non-U.S. firm registration in order to allow sufficient time for the Board to have final rules in place, as well as to permit non-U.S. firms additional time to understand and prepare for registration.

BOARD SETS CRITERIA FOR ADVISORY GROUP

The PCAOB has adopted a rule relating to the formation of advisory groups under section 103 of the Sarbanes-Oxley Act. The rules were submitted to the Securities and Exchange Commission for approval. Pursuant to section 107 of the Act, Board rules do not take effect unless approved by the Commission.

In order to obtain the advice of a broad range of experts, the Board will form a Standing Advisory Group (SAG), which may be divided into subgroups by the Board if needed for specialized advice. The Board may also establish one or more ad hoc task forces to assist the staff with various specialized responsibilities—the drafting of technical language, among other things.

First Advisory Group Formed

In line with the rule that provides that the Board may form such advisory groups to assist in carrying out its responsibilities, the Board adopted Rule 3700 on the formation of its first advisory group.

Advisory groups must be composed of individuals with expertise in a variety of fields, including accounting, auditing, corporate finance and corporate governance, investing in public companies, and other areas that the Board deems relevant to one or more of the auditing or professional practice standards. The rule also provides that members of any advisory group are selected by the Board based upon nominations, including self-nominations, received from any person or organization. Membership in an advisory group is personal to the member, and the duties and responsibilities of the member cannot be delegated to others. Further, the rule provides for members to be subject to the provisions of the Board's Ethics Code.

Ground Rules for the Standing Advisory Group

The Board voted to issue a Release discussing nominations and qualifications of members, terms and conditions of membership, the conduct of meetings, and other matters related to its use of a Standing Advisory Group. The Board contemplates that the SAG will initially have approximately 25 members. The SAG will be composed of individuals with a variety of backgrounds, including practicing auditors, preparers of financial statements, investors (both individual and institutional), and others (e.g., from academia and state accounting regulators). In order to achieve this diversity, the Board expects that no one field of expertise will predominate among the SAG membership. Although SAG members may be employed or otherwise affiliated with particular organizations, the Board expects SAG members to serve in their individual capacities and not to serve as representatives of particular interests, groups, or employers.

In determining appointments to the SAG, the Board intends to solicit nominations, including self-nominations. In evaluating nominations for the SAG, the Board will seek individuals with an interest in the quality of the audits of public companies.

Unless the appointment is revoked for cause, as determined by the Board, or unless the SAG member voluntarily resigns, SAG membership will be for a term of two years; provided, however, that approximately 50 percent of the initial members will be appointed for a three-year term to ensure continuity. Members will not be limited in the number of terms they may serve.

In addition to requiring compliance with certain provisions of the Board's Ethics Code, the Board requires as conditions of membership that SAG members:

- Act in the public interest in their individual capacities.
- Withdraw or recuse themselves from certain matters that pose potential conflicts.

- Attend meetings and dedicate 50 to 100 hours per year (and more if needed) to SAG service on a voluntary basis.

The SAG will hold at least two open meetings a year (and may have more). Any final decisions on recommendations to the Board are made at open meetings. Presentation of SAG recommendations are made to the Board at open meetings of the Board.

Role of the SAG

The role of the SAG will be to assist the Board in reviewing existing Standards, in evaluating proposed Standards recommended by Board staff, Board-formed technical task forces, or others, and recommending to the Board new or amended Standards. The role of the SAG will not ordinarily include technical drafting (which will be performed by the Board's staff, with the assistance of ad hoc task forces, when necessary). Instead, the Board will look to the SAG to provide advice and insight concerning:

- The need to formulate new Standards.
- The advisability of changing or amending existing Standards.
- The possible impact of proposed new or changed Standards.
- Participation in the standards-setting process.

Meetings and Board Relations

The Board decided that the first Chair of the SAG, also acting as general liaison to the Board, will be the Board's Chief Auditor and Director of Professional Standards. He or she will be a nonvoting member of the Group. The Board will approve the agenda for all annual, semiannual, or quarterly SAG meetings. Agenda items may also be added when the Board determines that the assistance of the SAG is required in response to emerging issues or problems.

The SAG will hold annual and semiannual meetings to discuss the agenda presented to them on the annual standards-setting process and related matters. Both meetings will be open to the public. Meetings of the SAG may also be held, at the direction of the Board or the Chair, during the intervening quarters. At the direction of the Chair, monthly meetings of the SAG may be held by video or teleconference.

Final decisions on recommendations to the Board and related activities will be conducted at the annual, semiannual, or other open meetings of the SAG. The meetings held in the quarters between the annual and semiannual meeting, if any, and monthly meetings will not generally be open to the public.

If so directed by the Chair of the SAG, the Group may convene hearings, roundtable discussions, or other fact-finding activities designed to assist them in the development of recommendations to the Board. Because the Board expects the SAG to make decisions in an efficient manner, the Group need not defer decisions on recommendations for the annual or semiannual open meetings. They may make decisions on recommendations at any meeting, so long as it is open to the public in some manner, including, at the direction of the Chair, telephonically.

Chapter 9

Auditor Independence and the Audit Committee

CONTENTS

The new Public Company Accounting Oversight Board (PCAOB) is just one important step toward restoring investor confidence in auditors and, more generally, in the capital markets. The new rules regarding independence standards for public company auditors that the Securities and Exchange Commission (SEC) adopted in January 2003 are viewed by the agency as another important step.

The Commission points out that with the accusatory headlines pointing at the accounting profession, it is perceived as no longer acting in a manner that puts investors first. Whether that assertion is true or not really does not matter anymore, according to the SEC. The perception is so strong in the minds of so many people that it has been affecting business activities, investment decisions, and the markets.

IMPORTANCE OF AUDIT COMMITTEE EMPHASIZED BY NEW RULINGS

New rules have been adopted that are aimed at addressing an auditor's independence for the registrant it audits *in both fact and appearance.* The independence and importance of the independent auditor and audit committee were forcibly emphasized again when the Commission adopted rules in April 2003, directing the national securities exchanges and national securities associations (self-regulatory organizations) to prohibit the listing of any security of an issuer that is not in compliance with the audit committee requirements established by The Sarbanes-Oxley Act of 2002. These rules and amendments implement the requirements of the Securities Exchange Act of 1934, as added by section 301 of the Sarbanes-Oxley Act.

REQUIREMENTS FOR AUDIT COMMITTEE

Under these rules, national securities exchanges and national securities associations are prohibited from listing any security of an issuer that is not in compliance with the following requirements:

- Each member of the audit committee of the issuer must be independent, according to the specified criteria in section 10A(m).
- The audit committee must be directly responsible for the appointment, compensation, retention, and oversight of the work of any registered public accounting firm engaged for the purpose of preparing or issuing an audit report or performing other audit, review, or attest services for the issuer, and the registered public accounting firm must report directly to the audit committee.
- The audit committee must establish procedures for the receipt, retention, and treatment of complaints regarding accounting, internal accounting controls, or auditing matters, including procedures for the confidential,

anonymous submission by employees of concerns regarding questionable accounting or auditing matters.

- The audit committee must have the authority to engage independent counsel and other advisors, as it determines necessary to carry out its duties.
- The issuer must provide appropriate funding for the audit committee.

Criteria for Committee Members

The rules established two criteria for audit committee member independence:

1. Audit committee members must be barred from accepting any consulting, advisory, or compensatory fee from the issuer or any subsidiary, other than in the member's capacity as a member of the Board or any Board committee.
2. An audit committee member must not be an affiliated person of the issuer or any subsidiary apart from capacity as a member of the Board or any Board committee.

Specific Rules for Foreign Issuers

The rules apply to both domestic and foreign listed issuers. It is important to note that, based on significant input from, and dialogue with, foreign regulators and foreign issuers and their advisers, several provisions, applicable only to foreign private issuers, have been included that seek to address the special circumstances of particular foreign jurisdictions. These provisions include:

- Allowing nonmanagement employees to serve as audit committee members, consistent with "co-determination" and similar requirements in some countries.
- Permitting shareholders to select or ratify the selection of auditors, also consistent with requirements in many foreign countries.
- Allowing alternative structures, such as boards of auditors, to perform auditor oversight functions where such structures are provided for under local law.
- Addressing the issue of foreign government shareholder representation on audit committees.

The rules also make several updates to the Commission's disclosure requirements regarding audit committees, including updates to the audit committee financial expert disclosure requirements for foreign private issuers.

The release also provides guidance on the provision of nonaudit services by foreign accounting firms, including the treatment of legal services and tax advice. The SEC also stands ready to work with other regulatory bodies on these issues.

The Commission established two sets of implementation dates for listed issuers. Generally, listed issuers are required to comply with the new listing rules by the date of their first annual shareholders meetings after January 15, 2004, but in any event no later than October 31, 2004. Foreign private issuers and small business issuers are required to comply by July 31, 2005.

STRICTER REQUIREMENTS REGARDING AUDITOR INDEPENDENCE

The SEC adopted amendments to its existing requirements regarding auditor independence to enhance the independence of accountants who audit and review financial statements and prepare attestation reports filed with the SEC. The final rules emphasize the critical role played by audit committees in the financial reporting process and the unique position of audit committees in ensuring auditor independence.

Consistent with the directions in the Sarbanes-Oxley Act, the SEC adopted rules to:

- Revise the Commission's regulations related to the nonaudit services that, if provided to an audit client, would impair an accounting firm's independence.

- Require an issuer's audit committee to preapprove all audit and nonaudit services provided to the issuer by the auditor of an issuer's financial statements.

- Prohibit certain partners on the audit engagement team from providing audit services to the issuer for more than five or seven consecutive years, depending on the partner's involvement in the audit, except that certain small accounting firms may be exempted from this requirement. The rules provide that firms with fewer than five audit clients and fewer than ten partners may be exempt from the partner rotation and compensation provisions, provided each of these engagements is subject to a special review by the PCAOB at least every three years.

- Prohibit an accounting firm from auditing an issuer's financial statements if certain members of management of that issuer had been members of the accounting firm's audit engagement team within the one-year period preceding the commencement of audit procedures.

- Require that the auditor of an issuer's financial statements report certain matters to the issuer's audit committee, including "critical" accounting policies used by the issuer.

- Require disclosures to investors of information related to audit and nonaudit services provided by, and fees paid to, the auditor of the issuer's financial statements.

- In addition, an accountant would not be independent from an audit client if the audit partner received compensation based on selling engagements to that client for services other than audit, review, and attest services.

These rules also have an impact on foreign accounting firms that conduct audits of foreign subsidiaries and affiliates of U.S. issuers as well as of foreign private issuers. Many of the modifications to the proposed rules, such as those limiting the scope of partner rotation and personnel subject to the "cooling off period," have the added benefit of addressing particular concerns raised about the international implications of these requirements. Additional time is being afforded to foreign accounting firms with respect to compliance with rotation requirements. Guidance on the provision of nonaudit services by foreign accounting firms, including the treatment of legal services and tax services is provided in the final rule.

Transition Period Provided

The effective date was May 6, 2003; however, a transition period was also provided. If the following relationships did not impair the accountant's independence under preexisting requirements of the Commission, the Independence Standards Board, or the accounting profession in the United States, an accountant's independence is not deemed to be impaired:

- By employment relationships described that commenced at the issuer prior to May 6, 2003.
- By certain compensation earned or received during the accounting firm's fiscal year that includes May 6, 2003.
- Until May 6, 2004, by the provision of certain services described *provided* those services are pursuant to contracts in existence on May 6, 2003.
- Until May 6, 2003, by the provision of services that have not been pre-approved by an audit committee as now required.
- Until the first day of the issuer's fiscal year beginning after May 6, 2003, by a "lead" partner and other audit partner (other than the "concurring" partner) providing services in excess of those permitted under section 210.2-01(c)(6).
- Until the first day of the issuer's fiscal year beginning after May 6, 2004, by a "concurring" partner providing services in excess of those permitted under section 210.2-01(c)(6).

BACKGROUND FOR AMENDMENTS TO AUDITOR INDEPENDENCE

Title II of the Sarbanes-Oxley Act, entitled "Auditor Independence," required the Commission to adopt, by January 26, 2003, final rules under which certain nonaudit services are prohibited, conflict of interest standards are strengthened, auditor partner rotation and second partner review requirements are also strengthened, and the relationship between the independent auditor and the audit committee are clarified and enhanced.

These rules are amendments to current SEC rules regarding auditor independence. The final rules advance the SEC's policy goal of protecting the millions of people who invest in securities markets in reliance on financial statements that are prepared by public companies and other issuers and that, as required by Congress, are audited by independent auditors. The final rules were an attempt at striking a reasonable balance among commenters' differing views about the proposals while achieving the Commission's public policy goals.

As directed by the Sarbanes-Oxley Act, the rules focus on key aspects of auditor independence:

- The provision of certain nonaudit services.
- The unique ability and responsibility of the audit committee to insulate the auditor from the pressures that may be exerted by management.
- The potential conflict of interest that can be created when a former member of the audit engagement team accepts a key management position with the audit client.
- The need for effective communication between the auditor and audit committee.

In addition, under the final rules, an accountant would not be independent from an audit client if any audit partner received compensation based directly on selling engagements to that client for services other than audit, review, and attest services.

Additions to the Securities Exchange Act of 1934

Title II of the Sarbanes-Oxley Act adds new subsections (g) through (l) to section 10A of the Securities Exchange Act of 1934 as follows:

- Section 201 adds subsection (g), which specifies that a number of nonaudit services are prohibited. Many of these services were previously prohibited by the Commission's independence standards adopted in November 2000 (with some exceptions and qualifications). The rules amend the Commission's existing rules on auditor independence and clarify the meaning and scope of the prohibited services under the Sarbanes-Oxley Act.
- Section 201 also adds subsection (h), which requires that nonaudit services that are *not* prohibited under the Sarbanes-Oxley Act and the Commission's rules be subject to preapproval by the registrant's audit com-

mittee. These rules specify the requirements for obtaining such pre-approval from the registrant's audit committee.

- Section 202 adds subsection (i), which requires an audit committee to pre-approve allowable nonaudit services and specifies certain exceptions to the requirement to obtain preapproval. These rules specify the requirements of the registrant's audit committee for preapproving nonaudit services by the auditor of the registrant's financial statements.

- Section 203 adds subsection (j), which establishes mandatory rotation of the lead partner and the concurring partner every five years. These rules expand the number of engagement personnel covered by the rotation requirement and clarify the "time out" period.

- Section 204 adds subsection (k), which requires that the auditor report on a timely basis certain information to the audit committee. In particular, the Sarbanes-Oxley Act requires that the auditor report to the audit committee on a timely basis:

  — Alternative accounting treatments that have been discussed with management along with the potential ramifications of using those alternatives.

  — Other written communications provided by the auditor to management, including a schedule of unadjusted audit differences. These rules strengthen the relationship between the audit committee and the auditor.

- Section 206 adds subsection (l), which addresses certain conflict-of-interest provisions. The Sarbanes-Oxley Act prohibits an accounting firm from performing audit services for a registrant if certain key members of management have recently been employed in an audit capacity by the audit firm. These rules clarify which members of management are covered by these conflict-of-interest rules.

- Under the final rules, an accountant would not be independent of an audit client if the audit partner received compensation based on selling engagements to that client for services other than audit, review, and attest services.

As noted above, the rules establish and clarify the important roles and responsibilities of registrant audit committees as well as the registrant's independent accountant.

The SEC also adopted a separate rule under the Exchange Act to implement the Sarbanes-Oxley Act and clarify that the rules implementing Title II of Sarbanes-Oxley not only define conduct that impairs independence but also constitute separate violations under the Exchange Act. In addition, it adopted rules (except for the proxy disclosure changes) as part of Regulation S-X, and placed them among the current auditor independence provisions.

CONFLICTS OF INTEREST RESULTING FROM
EMPLOYMENT RELATIONSHIPS

The Commission's previous rules deem an accounting firm to be not independent with respect to an audit client if a former partner, principal, shareholder,
or professional employee of an accounting firm accepts employment with a
client if he or she has a continuing financial interest in the accounting firm
or is in a position to influence the firm's operations or financial policies. The
2003 rules do not change that existing requirement, but they do add other
restrictions.

"Cooling Off" Period Provided

In line with section 206 of the Sarbanes-Oxley Act, the SEC added a
restriction on employment with audit clients by former employees of the accounting firm. The Act specifies that an accounting firm cannot perform an audit for a registrant if its chief executive officer, controller, chief financial officer,
chief accounting officer, or any person serving in an equivalent position for the
issuer was employed by that registered independent public accounting firm
and *participated in any capacity in the audit* of that issuer during the one-year
period preceding the date of the initiation of the audit.

Admittedly, the passage of time is an additional safeguard to reduce the
perceived loss of independence for the audit firm caused by the acceptance of
employment by specified members of the engagement team with an audit
client. However, the SEC believes that the Act is clear that the cooling off
period should apply more broadly.

The Commission decided that, when the lead partner, the concurring
partner, or any other member of the audit engagement team who provides
more than 10 hours of audit, review, or attest services for the issuer accepts a
position with the issuer in a "financial reporting oversight role" within the one-
year period preceding the commencement of audit procedures for the year that
included employment by the issuer of the former member of the audit engagement team, the accounting firm is not independent with respect to that registrant. The rule applies to all members of the audit engagement team unless
specifically exempted, as discussed later. (The term "financial reporting oversight role" refers to any individual who has direct responsibility for oversight
over those who prepare the registrant's financial statements and related information (e.g., management's discussion and analysis) that are included in filings
with the Commission.)

The Commission recognizes that, in certain instances, there are individuals who meet the definition of engagement team members while spending a
relatively small amount of time on audit-related matters of the issuer. For
example, a staff member may be asked to spend one day of time to observe

inventory. Although the input may have been important to resolving specific aspects of the audit, the staff member likely has not had significant interaction with the audit engagement team or management of the issuer. However, it is likely that those who spent more than a de minimis amount of time on the engagement team *did* participate in a meaningful audit capacity. Because of their roles in the engagement, the lead and concurring partner are *always* considered to have participated in a meaningful audit capacity, regardless of the number of hours spent on the engagement. In order to provide useful guidance, the SEC decided that the rule on conflicts of interest resulting from employment relationships should specify that, other than the lead and concurring partner, an individual must provide more than 10 hours of service during the annual audit period as a member of the engagement team to have participated in an audit capacity.

The rules relating to the cooling off period and to employment relationships entered into between members of the audit engagement team also apply to "any person serving in an equivalent position for the issuer."

Few Exemptions Provided. Because the Sarbanes-Oxley Act and the Commission view the auditor independence issue as being vitally important in the effort to regain investor confidence in the veracity of financial statements, few exceptions to the rules have been permitted. They include:

- Those who provided *10 or fewer hours* of audit, review, or attest services.
- Conflicts that are created through merger or acquisition, unless the employment was taken in contemplation of the combination. The individual or the issuer could not be expected to know that his or her employment decision would result in a conflict. Thus, as long as the audit committee is aware of this conflict, the audit firm would continue to be independent under these rules.
- Emergency or unusual circumstances, which should be invoked very rarely. Because in certain foreign jurisdictions, it may be extremely difficult or costly to comply with these requirements, the Commission decided upon an additional exemption. For a company to avail itself of this exemption, the audit committee must determine that doing so is in the best interests of investors.
- Difficulties when there is, potentially, a different applicable date for each member of the engagement team. For that reason, the final rule adopted a uniform date for all members of the engagement team. For purposes of this rule, audit procedures are deemed to have commenced for the current audit engagement period the day after the prior year's periodic annual report (e.g., Form 10-K, 10-KSB, 20-F, or 40-F) is filed with the Commission. The audit engagement period for the current year is

deemed to conclude the day the current year's periodic annual report (e.g., Form 10-K, 10-KSB, 20-F, or 40-F) is filed with the Commission.

The Sarbanes-Oxley Act specifies that the cooling off period must be one year. Under Commission rules, the prohibition would require the accounting firm to have completed one annual audit subsequent to when an individual was a member of the audit engagement team. As previously discussed, the measurement period is based upon the dates the issuer filed its annual financial information with the Commission.

With respect to investment companies, the employment of a former audit engagement team member in a financial reporting oversight role at any entity in the same investment company complex during the one-year period after the completion of the last audit would impair the independence of the accounting firm with respect to the audit client. The rule was designed to prevent a former audit engagement team member from taking a position in an investment company complex where he or she could influence the preparation of the financial statements or the conduct of the audit.

The rule recognizes that certain positions exist at an entity in the investment company complex that would be considered financial reporting or oversight positions but that have no direct influence in the financial reporting or operations of an investment company in the investment company complex. In these instances, the SEC believes tailoring the focus of this rule will not harm investor interests.

To provide for orderly transition, the rules are effective only for employment relationships with the issuer that commence after the effective date of the rules.

SCOPE OF SERVICES PROVIDED BY AUDITORS

Section 201(a) of the Sarbanes-Oxley Act adds a new section to the Securities Exchange Act of 1934. Except as discussed below, this section states that it is unlawful for a registered public accounting firm that performs an audit of an issuer's financial statements (and any person associated with such a firm) to provide to that issuer, contemporaneously with the audit, any nonaudit services, including the nine categories of services set forth in the Act. In addition, the Act states that any nonaudit service, including tax services, that is not described as a prohibited service can be provided by the auditor without impairing the auditor's independence only if the service has been *preapproved* by the issuer's audit committee. The categories of prohibited nonaudit services included in the Act are:

- Bookkeeping or other services related to the accounting records or financial statements of the audit client.

- Financial information systems design and implementation.
- Appraisal or valuation services, fairness opinions, or contribution-in-kind reports.
- Actuarial services.
- Internal audit outsourcing services.
- Management functions or human resources.
- Broker or dealer, investment adviser, or investment banking services.
- Legal services and expert services unrelated to the audit.
- Any other service that the Board determines, by regulation, is impermissible.

The Commission's principles of independence with respect to services provided by auditors are largely predicated on three basic principles, violations of which would impair the auditor's independence. An auditor cannot:

- Function in the role of management.
- Audit his or her own work.
- Serve in an advocacy role for his or her client.

The Commission adopted rules related to the scope of services that independent accountants *can* provide to their audit clients. In adopting these rules, the Commission is clarifying the scope of the prohibited services. The prohibited services contained in these rules apply only to nonaudit services provided by independent accountants to their audit clients. These rules do not limit the scope of nonaudit services provided by an accounting firm to a nonaudit client. Under the Act, the responsibility falls on the audit committee to preapprove all audit and nonaudit services provided by the accountant.

Bookkeeping or Other Services Related to Financial Statement Preparation

Previously, an auditor's independence was impaired if the auditor provided bookkeeping services to an audit client, except in limited situations, such as in an emergency or where the services are provided in a foreign jurisdiction and certain conditions were met. The current rule continues the prohibition on bookkeeping, but the SEC eliminated the limited situations where bookkeeping services could have been provided under the previous rules.

Citing the principle that an auditor cannot audit his or her own work and maintain his or her independence, the SEC pointed out that when an accounting firm provides bookkeeping services for an audit client, the firm may be put in the position of later auditing the accounting firm's own work. If, during an audit, an accountant must audit the bookkeeping work performed by his or her accounting firm, it is questionable that the accountant could (or that a reasonable investor would believe that the accountant could) remain objective and impartial. If the accountant found an error in the bookkeeping, the accountant could well be under pressure not to raise the issue with the client. Raising the issue could jeopardize the firm's contract with the client for bookkeeping services or result in heightened litigation risk for the firm. In addition, keeping the books is a *management function,* which also is prohibited. Therefore, the SEC determined that all bookkeeping services would cause the auditor to lack independence unless it is reasonable to conclude that the results will not be subject to audit procedures. (This proviso applies to all of the services discussed.) The final rules strongly emphasize the responsibility of the accounting firm in making a determination that these services, if provided, will *not* be subject to audit procedures, as further discussed below.

Definition of Bookkeeping or Other Services Used in SEC Rules.   The rules utilize the previous definition of bookkeeping or other services, which focuses on the provision of services involving:

- Maintaining or preparing the audit client's accounting records.
- Preparing financial statements that are filed with the Commission or the information that forms the basis of financial statements filed with the Commission.
- Preparing or originating source data underlying the audit client's financial statements.

This definition demonstrates that the concept of bookkeeping and other services is well understood in practice. Accountants are sometimes asked to prepare statutory financial statements for foreign companies, and these are not filed with the SEC. Consistent with the Commission's previous rules, an accountant's independence would be impaired where the accountant prepared the statutory financial statements if those statements form the basis of the financial statements that are filed with the Commission. Under these circumstances, an accountant or accounting firm that has prepared the statutory financial statements of an audit client is put in the position of auditing its own work when auditing the resultant U.S. GAAP financial statements.

With respect to the prohibitions on bookkeeping; financial information systems design and implementation; appraisal, valuation, fairness opinions, or contribution-in-kind reports; actuarial services; and internal audit outsourcing, the rules state that the service may not be provided "unless it is reasonable to conclude that the results of these services will not be subject to audit procedures during an audit of the audit client's financial statements."

As proposed, for bookkeeping, appraisal or valuation, and actuarial services, the provision was "where it is reasonably likely that the results of these services will be subject to audit procedures during an audit of the audit client's financial statements," whereas for the other two services, there was no such wording. The Commission added the new wording to all five services to provide consistency in application. In addition, the change from "reasonably likely . . ." to "unless it is reasonable to conclude" is intended to narrow the circumstances in which that condition can be invoked to justify the provision of such services.

Financial Information Systems Design and Implementation

Currently, there are certain information technology services that, if provided to an audit client, impair the accountant's independence. The proposed rules identified information technology services that would impair the auditor's independence.

The Commission adopted rules, consistent with previous rules, that prohibit an accounting firm from providing any service related to the audit client's information system. These rules do not preclude an accounting firm from working on hardware or software systems that are unrelated to the audit client's financial statements or accounting records, as long as those services are pre-approved by the audit committee.

The rule does prohibit the accountant from designing or implementing a hardware or software system that aggregates source data or generates information that is significant to the financial statements taken as a whole. In this context, information would be "significant" if it is reasonably likely to be material to the financial statements of the audit client. Because materiality determinations may not be complete before financial statements are generated, the audit client and accounting firm by necessity will need to evaluate the general nature of the information as well as system output during the period of the audit engagement. An accountant, for example, would not be independent of an audit client for which it designed an integrated Enterprise Resource Planning or similar system, as the system would serve as the basis for the audit client's financial reporting system.

Designing, implementing, or operating systems affecting the financial statements may place the accountant in a management role, or result in the accountant auditing his or her own work or attesting to the effectiveness of internal control systems designed or implemented by that accountant. This prohibition does not, however, preclude the accountant from evaluating the internal controls of a system as it is being designed, implemented, or operated — either as part of an audit or as part of an attest service — and making recommendations to management. Likewise, the accountant would not be precluded from making recommendations on internal control matters to management or other service providers in conjunction with the design and installation of a system by another service provider.

Appraisal or Valuation Services

The SEC's previous independence rules stated that an accountant is deemed to lack independence when providing appraisal or valuation services, fairness opinions, or contribution-in-kind reports for audit clients. However, the previous rules contained certain exemptions that have been eliminated.

Appraisal and valuation services include a process of valuing assets, both tangible and intangible, or liabilities. They include valuing, among other things, in-process research and development, financial instruments, assets and liabilities acquired in a merger, and real estate. Fairness opinions and contribution-in-kind reports are opinions and reports in which the firm provides its opinion on the adequacy of consideration in a transaction. When it is time to audit the financial statements, it is likely that the accountant would review his or her own work, including key assumptions or variables that underlie an entry in the financial statements. Moreover, if the appraisal methodology involves a projection of future results of operations and cash flows, the accountant who prepares the projection may be unable to evaluate skeptically and without bias the accuracy of that valuation or appraisal. Therefore, the rules prohibit the accountant from providing *any* appraisal service, valuation service, or any service involving a fairness opinion or contribution-in-kind report for an audit client.

The rules do not prohibit an accounting firm from providing such services for non-financial reporting (e.g., transfer pricing studies, cost segregation studies, and other tax-only valuations) purposes. Similarly, the rules do not prohibit an accounting firm from utilizing its own valuation specialist to review the work performed by the audit client itself or an independent, third-party specialist employed by the audit client, provided that specialist (and not the specialist used by the accounting firm) provides the technical expertise that its client used in determining the required amounts recorded in the client's financial statements.

In those instances, the accountant will not be auditing his or her own work, because a third party or the audit client is the source of the financial information subject to the audit. In fact, the quality of the audit may be improved where specialists are utilized in such situations.

Because a strict application of these rules related to contribution-in-kind reports may create conflicts in certain foreign jurisdictions, the SEC will continue to work with other regulatory agencies in solving this type of problem.

Actuarial Services

The previous rules generally barred auditors from providing actuarial services related only to insurance company policy reserves and related accounts. However, the SEC believes that when the accountant provides actuarial services for the client, he or she is placed in a position of auditing his or her own work. Accordingly, the current rules prohibit an accountant from providing an audit client any actuarially oriented advisory service involving the determination of amounts recorded in the financial statements and related accounts for the audit client. It is permissible to assist a client in *understanding* the methods, models, assumptions, and inputs used in computing an amount. Nevertheless, the Commission believes that it is appropriate to *advise* the client on the appropriate actuarial methods and assumptions that will be used in the actuarial valuations. It is not appropriate for the accountant to provide the actuarial valuations for the audit client. The rules also provide that the accountant may utilize his or her own actuaries to assist in conducting the audit provided the audit client uses its own actuaries or third-party actuaries to provide management with its actuarial capabilities.

Internal Audit Outsourcing

The previous rules on internal audit outsourcing allowed a company to outsource part of its internal audit function to the independent audit firm subject to certain exemptions. For example, smaller businesses were exempt from the internal audit outsourcing prohibition because there had been concerns about the potentially disproportionate impact on such companies.

Some companies outsource internal audit functions by contracting with an outside source to perform, among other things, all or part of their audits of internal controls. As emphasized by the Committee of Sponsoring Organizations, internal auditors play an important role in evaluating and monitoring a company's internal control system. As a result, some argue that internal auditors are, in effect, part of a company's system of internal accounting control.

Because the external auditor typically will rely, at least to some extent, on the existence of an internal audit function and consider its impact on the internal control system when conducting the audit of the financial statements, the accountant may be placed in the position of auditing his or her firm as part of the internal control system. In other words, if the internal audit function is outsourced to an accountant, the accountant assumes a management responsibility and becomes part of the company's control system.

The rules adopted prohibit the accountant from providing to the audit client internal audit outsourcing services. This prohibition includes any internal audit service that has been outsourced by the audit client and that relates to the audit client's internal accounting controls, financial systems, or financial statements.

When conducting the audit in accordance with generally accepted auditing standards (GAAS) or when providing attest services related to internal controls, the auditor evaluates the company's internal controls and, as a result, may make recommendations for improvements to the controls. Doing so is a part of the accountant's responsibilities under GAAS or applicable attestation standards and therefore does not constitute an internal audit outsourcing engagement.

Along those lines, this prohibition on outsourcing does not preclude engaging the accountant to perform nonrecurring evaluations of discrete items or other programs that are not, in substance, the outsourcing of the internal audit function. For example, the company may engage the accountant, subject to the audit committee preapproval requirements, to conduct "agreed-upon procedures" engagements related to the company's internal controls. It is understood that management takes responsibility for the scope and assertions in those engagements. The prohibition also does not preclude the accountant from performing operational internal audits unrelated to the internal accounting controls, financial systems, or financial statements.

Management Functions

No significant changes were made to the previous rule on management functions. The rules prohibit the accountant from acting, temporarily or permanently, as a director, officer, or employee of an audit client, or performing any decision-making, supervisory, or ongoing monitoring function for the audit client.

However, those types of services in connection with the *assessment* of internal accounting and risk management controls, as well as providing recommendations for improvements, do not impair an accountant's independence. Accountants must gain an understanding of their audit clients' systems of internal controls when conducting an audit in accordance with GAAS. With this insight, accountants often become involved in diagnosing, assessing, and recommending, to audit committees and management, ways in which their audit client's internal controls can be improved or strengthened. The resulting improvements in the audit client's controls not only result in improved financial reporting to investors but also can facilitate the performance of high-quality audits. For these reasons, the rules continue to allow accountants to assess the effectiveness of an audit client's internal controls and to recommend improvements in the design and implementation of internal controls and risk management controls.

Designing and implementing internal accounting and risk management controls is considered to be fundamentally different from obtaining an understanding of the controls and testing the operation of the controls, which is an integral part of any audit of the financial statements of a company. Likewise, design and implementation of these controls involves decision making and therefore is different from *recommending improvements* in the internal accounting and risk management controls of an audit client (which is permissible, if preapproved by the audit committee).

The SEC believes that designing and implementing internal accounting and risk management controls impair the accountant's independence because they place the accountant in the role of management. Conversely, obtaining an understanding of, assessing the effectiveness of, and recommending improvements to the internal accounting and risk management controls are fundamental to the audit process and do not impair the accountant's independence. Furthermore, the accountant may be engaged by the company, subject to the audit committee preapproval requirements, to conduct an agreed-upon procedures engagement related to the company's internal controls or to provide attest services related to the company's internal controls without impairing his or her independence.

Human Resources

The previous rules deemed an accountant to lack independence when performing certain human resources functions. The rules provided that an accountant's independence is impaired with respect to an audit client when the accountant searches for or seeks out prospective candidates for managerial, executive, or director positions; acts as negotiator on the audit client's behalf, such as determining position, status, compensation, fringe benefits, or other conditions of employment; or undertakes reference checks of prospective candidates. Under the current rule, an accountant's independence is also impaired when the accountant engages in psychological testing or other formal testing or evaluation programs, or recommends or advises the audit client to hire a specific candidate for a specific job.

Assisting management in human resource selection or development could place the accountant in the position of having an interest in the success of those employees the accountant has selected, tested, or evaluated.

Broker-Dealer, Investment Adviser, Investment Banking Services

Previous rules deemed an accountant to lack independence when performing brokerage or investment advising services for an audit client. The newer rules add serving as an unregistered broker-dealer to the rules that prohibit serving as a promoter or underwriter, making investment decisions on behalf of the audit client or otherwise having discretionary authority over an audit client's investments, executing a transaction to buy or sell an audit client's investment, or having custody of assets of the audit client. The rule is substantially the same as the Commission's previous rule related to the provision of these types of services to audit clients. However, unregistered broker-dealers are added to the scope of the rules because the nature of the threat to independence is unchanged whether the entity is or is not a registered broker-dealer.

The SEC explains that selling — directly or indirectly — an audit client's securities is incompatible with the accountant's responsibility of assuring the public that the company's financial condition is fairly presented. When an accountant, in any capacity, recommends to anyone (including nonaudit clients) that they buy or sell the securities of an audit client or an affiliate of the audit client, the accountant has an interest in whether those recommendations were correct. That interest could affect the audit of the client whose securities, or whose affiliate's securities, were recommended. These concepts are echoed in the "simple principles" included in the legislative history to the Sarbanes-Oxley Act. In such a situation, if an accountant uncovers an accounting error in a client's financial statements, and the accountant, in an investment adviser capacity, had recommended that client's securities to investment clients, the accountant performing the audit may be reluctant to recommend changes to the client's financial statements if the changes could negatively affect the value of the securities recommended by the accountant to its investment adviser clients.

Broker-dealers often give advice and recommendations on investments and investment strategies. The value of that advice is measured principally by the performance of a customer's securities portfolio. When the customer is an audit client, the accountant has an interest in the value of the audit client's securities portfolio, even as the accountant must determine whether management has properly valued the portfolio as part of an audit. Thus, the accountant would be placed in a position of auditing his or her own work. Furthermore, the accountant is placed in a position of acting as an advocate on behalf of the client.

Legal Services

The previous rule stated that an accountant is deemed to lack independence when he or she provides legal services to an audit client. The SEC believes that a lawyer's core professional obligation is to advance clients' interests. Rules of professional conduct in the U.S. require the lawyer to "represent a client zealously and diligently within the bounds of the law." The lawyer must "take whatever lawful and ethical measures are required to vindicate a client's cause or endeavor. . . . In the exercise of professional judgment, a lawyer should always act in a manner consistent with the best interests of the client."

The Commission maintains that an individual cannot be both a zealous legal advocate for management or the client company, and maintain the objectivity and impartiality that are necessary for an audit. The Supreme Court has also expressed this view. In *United States v. Arthur Young,* the Supreme Court emphasized, "If investors were to view the accountant as an advocate for the corporate client, the value of the audit function itself might well be lost."

The final rule is that an accountant is prohibited from providing to an audit client any service that, under circumstances in which the service is provided, could be provided only by someone licensed, admitted, or otherwise qualified to practice law in the jurisdiction in which the service is provided. There may be implications for some foreign registrants from this rule. For example, in some jurisdictions it is mandatory that someone licensed to practice law perform tax work, and that an accounting firm providing such services, therefore, would be deemed to be providing legal services. As a general matter, SEC rules are not intended to prohibit foreign accounting firms from providing services that an accounting firm in the United States may provide. In determining whether or not a service would impair the accountant's independence solely because the service is labeled a legal service in a foreign jurisdiction, the Commission will consider whether the provision of the service would be prohibited in the United States as well as in the foreign jurisdiction.

Evaluating and determining whether services are permissible may require a comprehensive analysis of the facts and circumstances. The SEC is aware of these issues, and encourages accounting firms and foreign regulators to consult with the SEC staff to address such issues.

Expert Services

The Sarbanes-Oxley Act includes expert services in the list of nonaudit services an accountant is prohibited from performing for an audit client. As discussed earlier, the legislative history related to expert services is focused on the accountant's role when serving in an advocacy capacity.

Clients retain experts to lend authority to their contentions in various proceedings by virtue of the expert's specialized knowledge and experience. In situations involving advocacy, the provision of expert services by the accountant makes the accountant part of the team that has been assembled to advance or defend the client's interests. The appearance of advocacy created by providing such expert services is sufficient to deem the accountant's independence impaired. The prohibition on providing expert services included in this rule covers engagements that are intended to result in the accounting firm's specialized knowledge, experience, and expertise being used to support the audit client's positions in various adversarial proceedings.

The rules now adopted prohibit an accountant from providing expert opinions or other services to an audit client (or the client's legal representative) to advocate that client's interests in litigation and regulatory or administrative proceedings. For example, under this rule an auditor's independence would be impaired if the auditor were engaged to provide forensic accounting services to the audit client's legal representative in connection with the defense of an investigation by the Commission's Division of Enforcement. An accountant's independence likewise would be impaired if the audit client's legal counsel, in order to acquire the requisite expertise, engaged the accountant to provide such services in connection with a litigation, proceeding, or investigation.

The SEC rules do not, however, preclude an audit committee or its legal counsel from engaging the accountant to perform internal investigations or fact-finding engagements. These types of engagements may include, among others, forensic or other fact-finding work that results in the issuance of a report to the audit client. The involvement by the accountant in this capacity generally requires performing procedures that are consistent with, but more detailed or more comprehensive than, those required by GAAS. Performing such procedures *is consistent* with the role of the independent auditor and should improve audit quality. If, subsequent to the completion of such an engagement, a proceeding or investigation is initiated, the accountant may allow its work product to be utilized by the audit client and its legal counsel without impairing the accountant's independence. The accountant, however, may not then provide additional services, but may provide factual accounts or testimony about the work that had previously been performed.

Therefore, the rules do not prohibit an accountant from assisting the audit committee in fulfilling its responsibilities to conduct its own investigation of a potential accounting impropriety. For example, if the audit committee is concerned about the accuracy of the inventory accounts at a subsidiary, it may engage the auditor to conduct a thorough inspection and analysis of the accounts, the physical inventory, and related matters without impairing the auditor's independence.

The auditors already have obligations under the Exchange Act and GAAS to search for fraud that is material to an issuer's financial statements and to make sure the audit committee and others are informed of their findings. Auditors should conduct these procedures whether they become aware of a potential illegal act as a result of audit, review, or attestation procedures or of the audit committee's expressing concerns about a part of the company's financial reporting system. In these situations, the auditor may conduct the procedures, with the approval of the audit committee, and provide the reports that the auditor deems appropriate. If litigation arises while the auditors are conducting such procedures, the SEC would not consider the completion of these procedures to be prohibited, as long as the auditor remains in control of his or her work. The work may not become subject to the direction or influence of legal counsel for the issuer.

Furthermore, under this rule, an accountant's independence is not considered to be impaired when an accountant provides factual accounts or testimony describing work he or she had previously performed. Nor will it be deemed impaired if the individual explains the positions taken or conclusions reached during the performance of any service provided for the audit client.

Tax Services Permitted

Since the Commission issued its auditor independence proposal, there has been considerable debate regarding whether an accountant's provision of tax services for an audit client can impair the accountant's independence. Tax services are unique among nonaudit services for a variety of reasons. Detailed tax laws must be consistently applied, and the Internal Revenue Service has discretion to audit any tax return. In addition, accounting firms have historically provided a broad range of tax services to their audit clients.

The Commission reiterates its long-standing position that an accounting firm can provide tax services to its audit clients without impairing the firm's independence. Accordingly, accountants may continue to provide tax services such as tax compliance, tax planning, and tax advice to audit clients, subject to the normal audit committee preapproval requirements. However, the rules require registrants to *disclose the amount of fees* paid to the accounting firm for tax services. The rules are consistent with the Act, which states that:

> Merely labeling a service as a "tax service" will not necessarily eliminate its potential to impair independence under Rule 2-01(b). Audit committees and accountants should understand that providing certain tax services to an audit client would, or could, in certain circumstances, impair the independence of the accountant. Specifically, accountants would impair their independence by representing an audit client before a tax court, district court, or federal court of claims. In addition, audit committees also should carefully scrutinize the retention of an accountant in a transaction initially recommended by the accountant, the sole business purpose of which may be tax avoidance and the tax treatment of which may be not supported in the Internal Revenue Code and related regulations.

At about the time that these rules were being adopted, the Commission had reason to be concerned about having given auditors *any* right to offer tax services to their audit clients. Some very unorthodox and downright illegal shenanigans between major accounting firms and clients regarding tax shelters were being brought to light. Therefore, audit committees should be doubly careful about their preapproval considerations regarding any tax service being provided.

DEFINITION AND EXTENT OF AUDIT COMMITTEE

The definition of "audit committee" used in the SEC independence rules is the same as that given in section 205 of the Sarbanes-Oxley Act:

> A committee (or equivalent body) established by and amongst the Board of directors of an issuer for the purpose of overseeing the accounting and financial reporting processes of the issuer and audits of the financial statements of the issuer.

The Act further stipulates that if no such committee exists, the audit committee is the entire Board of directors.

The audit committee serves as an important body, acting in the interests of investors to help ensure that the registrant and its accountants fulfill their responsibilities under the securities laws. Because the definition of an audit committee can include the entire Board of directors if no such committee of the Board exists, these rules do not require registrants to establish audit committees. Likewise, the auditor independence rules do not require the committee to be composed of independent members of the Board. Some entities do not have Boards of directors and therefore do not have audit committees. For example, some limited liability companies and limited partnerships that do not have a corporate general partner may not have an oversight body that is the equivalent of an audit committee.

Nevertheless, the Commission is not exempting these entities from the requirements. Such an issuer is expected to scan through each general partner of the successive limited partnerships until a corporate general partner or an individual general partner is reached. With respect to a corporate general partner, the registrant should consider the audit committee of the corporate general partner or to the full Board of directors as fulfilling the role of the audit committee. With respect to an individual general partner, the Commission expects the registrant to consider the individual as fulfilling the role of the audit committee.

The rules, however, do exempt asset-backed issuers and unit investment trusts from this requirement. Because of the nature of the entity, these issuers are subject to substantially different reporting requirements. Most significantly, asset-backed issuers are not required to file financial statements, as are other companies. Similarly, unit investment trusts are not required to provide shareholder reports containing audited financial statements. Such entities are, typically, passively managed pools of assets. Therefore, the requirements related to audit committees in these rules do not apply to such entities.

RETENTION OF RECORDS RELEVANT TO AUDITS

On the same day in January that it approved the above-mentioned rules, the SEC also approved the adoption of Rule 2-06 of Regulation S-X to implement section 802 of the Sarbanes-Oxley Act. This rule requires that accounting firms retain records relevant to the audits or reviews of issuers' and registered investment companies' financial statements, including workpapers and other documents that form the basis of the audit or review and memoranda, correspondence, communications, other documents, and records (including electronic records) that are created, sent, or received in connection with the audit or review and that contain conclusions, opinions, analyses, or financial data related to the audit or review.

These records must be retained for seven years after the auditor concludes the audit or review of the financial statements, instead of the proposed period of five years from the end of the fiscal period in which an audit or review was concluded. This change coordinated the Commission's rule with the expected auditing standards from the PCAOB that are scheduled to require the retention of audit documentation for seven years.

The rule defines the term "workpapers" to be those documents that record the audit or review procedures performed, the evidence obtained, and the conclusions reached by the auditor. The definition recognizes that the PCAOB may establish auditing standards further defining the term.

The rule also spells out a requirement to keep records that either support the auditor's final conclusions or contain information or data, relating to a significant matter, that is inconsistent with the final conclusions of the auditor on that matter or on the audit or review. The rule also states that the documents and records to be retained include, but are not limited to, those documenting consultations on, or resolutions of, differences in professional judgment.

The compliance date for these rules is October 31, 2003.

DISCLOSURE REQUIREMENTS TO IMPLEMENT THE SARBANES-OXLEY ACT

The Commission voted to adopt rules implementing sections 406 and 407 of the Sarbanes-Oxley Act of 2002. These rules require public companies to disclose information about corporate codes of ethics and audit committee financial experts. They require a company subject to the reporting requirements of the Securities Exchange Act of 1934 to include the following two new types of disclosures in their Exchange Act filings:

1. Pursuant to section 407, a company will be required to disclose annually whether it has at least one "audit committee financial expert" on its audit committee. If so, the company is to supply the name of said financial expert and whether he or she is independent of management. If the company does not have an audit committee financial expert, it is required to explain why it has no such expert.

2. Pursuant to section 406, a company is required to disclose annually whether the company has adopted a code of ethics for the company's principal executive officer, principal financial officer, principal accounting officer or controller, or persons performing similar functions. If not, the company is required to explain why it has not. The rules also require a company to disclose on a current basis amendments to, and waivers from, the code of ethics relating to any of those officers.

Audit Committee Financial Experts

The rules expand the proposed definition of the term "financial expert" and also substitute the designation "audit committee financial expert" for "financial expert." The rules define "audit committee financial expert" to mean a person who has the following attributes:

- An understanding of financial statements and generally accepted accounting principles.
- An ability to assess the general application of such principles in connection with the accounting for estimates, accruals, and reserves.
- Experience preparing, auditing, analyzing, or evaluating financial statements that present a breadth and level of complexity of accounting issues that are generally comparable to the breadth and complexity of issues that can reasonably be expected to be raised by the registrant's financial statements, or he or she may have experience actively supervising one or more persons engaged in such activities.
- An understanding of internal controls and procedures for financial reporting.
- An understanding of audit committee functions.

A person can acquire such attributes through any one or more of the following means:

- Education and experience as a principal financial officer, principal accounting officer, controller, public accountant, or auditor or experience in one or more positions that involve the performance of similar functions.
- Experience actively supervising a principal financial officer, principal accounting officer, controller, public accountant, auditor, or person performing similar functions or experience overseeing or assessing the performance of companies or public accountants with respect to the preparation, auditing, or evaluation of financial statements.
- Other relevant experience.

An individual must possess all of the attributes listed in the above definition to qualify as an audit committee financial expert.

The rules also provide a safe harbor to make clear that an audit committee financial expert is not to be deemed an "expert" for any purpose, including for purposes of section 11 of the Securities Act of 1933. The designation of a person as an "audit committee financial expert" does not impose any duties, obligations, or liability on the person that are greater than those imposed on such a person as a member of the audit committee in the absence of such designation, nor does it affect the duties, obligations, or liability of any other member of the audit committee or Board of directors.

Codes of Ethics

Under the rules, a company is required to disclose in its annual report whether it has a code of ethics that applies to the company's principal executive officer, principal financial officer, principal accounting officer or controller, or persons performing similar functions. The rules define a code of ethics as written standards that are reasonably necessary to deter wrongdoing and to promote:

- Honest and ethical conduct, including the ethical handling of actual or apparent conflicts of interest between personal and professional relationships.
- Full, fair, accurate, timely, and understandable disclosure in reports and documents that a company files with, or submits to, the Commission and in other public communications made by the company.
- Compliance with applicable governmental laws, rules, and regulations.
- The prompt internal reporting of code violations to an appropriate person or persons identified in the code.
- Accountability for adherence to the code.

A company is required to make available to the public a copy of its code of ethics, or portion of the code that applies to the company's principal executive officer, principal financial officer, principal accounting officer or controller, or persons performing similar functions. The code of ethics may be made available to the public by filing it as an exhibit to its annual report, providing it on the company's Internet Web site, or as otherwise set forth in the final rule.

A company, other than a foreign private issuer or registered investment company, is also required to disclose any changes to, or waivers of, the code of ethics within five business days, to the extent that the change or waiver applies to the company's principal executive officer or senior financial officers. A company can provide this disclosure on Form 8-K or on its Internet Web site. Foreign private issuers and registered investment companies are required to disclose changes to, and waivers of, such codes of ethics in their periodic reports or on their Internet Web sites.

Companies were required to provide the new disclosures in annual reports for fiscal years ending on or after July 15, 2003. Small business issuers are required to provide the new audit committee financial expert disclosure in annual reports for fiscal years ending on or after December 15, 2003.

THE SEC's 2002 RULES GOVERNING INDEPENDENCE OF AUDITORS

After extensive prodding and action by the SEC, auditor independence and financial disclosure about audit committees came to the foreground in concerns relating to independence and the openness of the auditing and accounting professions.

The rather lengthy lead time, punctuated by considerable negative pressure from Congress (bipartisan and bicameral), the American Institute of Certified Public Accountants (AICPS), three of the Big Five firms and the American Bar Association, to single out only a few, ended with the Security and Exchange Commissioners voting unanimously on November 15, 2000, to adopt new rules that modernize the requirements for auditor independence. Obviously, the measures were too little, too late to protect the investors in Enron. Until additional restrictions and guidelines are officially adopted and put in place, the measures adopted at that time are still in effect.

The three areas covered are:

1. Investments by auditors or their family members in audit clients.
2. Employment relationships between auditors or their family members and audit clients.
3. The third area — the scope of services provided by audit firms to their audit clients — has been superseded by the newer rules delineated above.

The new rules reflect the Commission's consideration of comments received on the rules it proposed in June 2000.

Principal Provisions

Significant features of the new rules include:

1. Reduction of the number of audit firm employees and their family members whose investments in, or employment with, audit clients would impair an auditor's independence.
2. Identification of certain nonaudit services that, if provided to an audit client, would impair an auditor's independence. (The rules do not extend to services provided to nonaudit clients.)
3. Disclosure in their annual proxy statements of certain information about nonaudit services provided by the company's auditors during the last fiscal year.

Four Principles

A preliminary note to the new rules identifies four principles by which to measure an auditor's independence. An accountant is not independent when the accountant:

1. Has a mutual or conflicting interest with the audit client.
2. Audits his or her own firm's work.

3. Functions as management or an employee of the audit client.
4. Acts as an advocate for the audit client.

Financial Relationships

Compared to the previous rules, the newly adopted rules narrow significantly the number of people whose investments trigger independence concerns. Under previous rules, many partners that did not work on the audit of a client, as well as their spouses and families, were restricted from investment in a firm's audit clients. The new rules limit restrictions principally to those who work on the audit or can influence the audit.

Employment Relationships

The employment relationship rules narrow the scope of people within audit firms whose families will be affected by the employment restrictions necessary to maintain independence. The rules also identify the positions in which a person *can* influence the audit client's accounting records or financial statements. These are positions that could impair an auditor's independence if held by a close family member of that auditor.

Business Relationships

Consistent with existing rules, independence will be impaired if the accountant or any covered person has a direct or material indirect business relationship with the audit client, other than providing professional services.

A General Standard for Auditor Independence

This SEC rule is based on the widely endorsed principle that an auditor must be independent both *in fact* and *in appearance*. The new rule specifies that an auditor's independence is impaired either when the accountant is not independent *in fact* or when a "reasonable investor," after considering all relevant facts and circumstances, would conclude that the auditor would not be capable of acting without bias. The reasonable investor standard is a common construct in securities laws.

Affiliate Provisions

When it was first proposed in June 2000, the rule contained a definition of an "affiliate of an accounting firm" that many commenters felt might affect accounting firms' joint ventures with companies that are not their audit clients and the continuation of small firm alliances. These types of relationships traditionally have not been thought to impair an accountant's independence.

After considering these comments, the SEC decided that it would continue to analyze these situations under existing guidance.

An "affiliate of an audit client" continues to be defined as any entity that can significantly influence, or is significantly influenced by, the audit client, provided the equity investment is material to the entity or the audit client. "Significant influence" generally is presumed when the investor owns 20 percent or more of the voting stock of the investee. The significant influence test is used because under GAAP it is the trigger that causes the earnings and losses of one company to be reflected in the financial statements of another company.

Contingent Fee Arrangements

The rules reiterate that an accountant cannot provide any service to an audit client that involves a contingent fee.

Quality Controls

The rules provide a limited exception from independence violations to the accounting firm if certain factors are present:

1. The individual did not know the circumstances giving rise to his or her violation.
2. The violation was corrected promptly once the violation became apparent.
3. The firm has quality controls in place that provide reasonable assurance that the firm and its employees maintain their independence.
4. For the largest public accounting firms, the basic controls must include among others:
   a. Written independence policies and procedures.
   b. Automated systems to identify financial relationships that may impair independence.
   c. Training, internal inspection, and testing.
   d. Disciplinary mechanism for enforcement.

Proxy Disclosure Requirement

Companies must disclose in their annual proxy statements the fees for audit, IT consulting, and all other services provided by their auditors during the last fiscal year.

Companies must also state whether the audit committee has considered whether the provision of the nonaudit services is compatible with maintaining the auditor's independence.

Finally, the registrant is required to disclose the percentage hours worked on the audit engagement by persons other than the accountant's full-time employees, if that figure exceeded 50 percent. This requirement is in answer to recent actions taken by some accounting firms to sell their practices to financial services companies. The partners or employees often, in turn, become employees of the financial services firm. The accounting firm then leases assets, namely auditors, back from those companies to complete audit engagements. In such cases, most of the auditors who work on an audit are employed elsewhere without the public, investors, or the client being aware of the situation.

APPLICATION OF REVISED RULES ON AUDITOR INDEPENDENCE

Since the adoption of the Commission's Revised Rules on Auditor Independence, the SEC staff has received questions regarding the implementation and interpretation of the rules. They encourage these questions and related correspondence regarding auditor independence as they do to all of the rulings which may be difficult to interpret.

Frequently Asked Questions

Publications of staff responses to certain questions received are referred to as Frequently Asked Questions (FAQs). Many of the questions are rather technical, referring to a specific item on a specific schedule. Others have a more general and widespread application and give the preparer a better feel for what the SEC staff is looking for in the reports. Following is a sample of the latter variety.

Question 6
Q: Should the fees billed in prior years be disclosed so investors may compare trends in audit, information technology, and other non-audit fees?

A: The rule does not require comparative disclosures. Registrants may include such information voluntarily.

Question 7
Q: In situations where other auditors are involved in the delivery of services, to what extent should the fees from the other auditors be included in the required fee disclosures?

A: Only the fees billed by the principal accountant need to be disclosed. See Question 8 regarding the definition of "principal accountant." If the principal accountant's billings or expected billings include fees for the work performed by others (such as where the principal accountant hires someone else to perform part of the work), then such fees should be included in the fees disclosed for the principal accountant.

In some foreign jurisdictions, a registrant may be required to have a joint audit requiring both accountants to issue an audit report for the same fiscal year. In these circumstances, fees for each accountant should be separately disclosed as they are both "principal accountants."

Question 8

Q: Does the term "principal accountant" in the ruling include associated or affiliated organizations?

A: Yes. "Principal accountant" has the meaning given to it in the auditing literature. In determining what services rendered by the principal accountant must be disclosed, all entities that comprise the accountant, as defined, should be included. This term includes not only the person or entity who furnishes reports or other documents that the registrant files with the Commission, but also all of the person's or entity's departments, divisions, parents, subsidiaries, and associated entities, including those located outside of the United States.

Question 15

Q: Does the restriction on the independent accountant providing legal services to an audit client apply only to litigation services?

A: No. The Commission's rule provides that an auditor's and firm's independence would be impaired if an auditor provides to its audit client a service for which the person providing the service must be admitted to practice before the courts of a U.S. jurisdiction. This standard includes all legal services. The rule does not apply only to appearance in court or solely to litigators. The only circumstances excluded by the rule are those in which local U.S. law allows certain limited activities without admission to the bar (generally confined to advice concerning the law of foreign jurisdictions).

Additionally, as discussed in the adopting release, some firms may be providing legal services outside of the United States to registrants when those services are not precluded by local law and are routine and ministerial or relate to matters that are not material to the consolidated financial statements. Such services raise serious independence concerns under circumstances other than those meeting at least those minimum criteria.

Question 17

Q: The final rule did not define an affiliate of an accounting firm. Does the lack of a definition signal a change in the Commission's approach to this issue?

A: No. The final rule's definition of an "accounting firm" includes the accounting firm's "associated entities." As noted in the adopting release, the Commission used this phrase to reflect the staff's current practice of addressing these questions in light of all relevant facts and circumstances, and of looking to the factors identified in our previous guidance on this subject. Much of this guidance is cited in footnotes of the adopting release. The staff is available for consultations on this issue.

Question 18

Q: Did the final rule change the Commission's guidance with respect to business relationships?

A: No. The final rule is consistent with the Commission's prior guidance on business relationships. The basic standard of the Commission's prior guidance has now been codified in the rule. In addition, as the adopting release notes, much of the Commission's previous guidance has been retained and continues to apply. For example, joint ventures, limited partnerships, investments in supplier or customer companies, certain leasing interest and sales by the accountant of items other than professional services are examples of business relationships that may impair an accountant's independence.

The SEC further explained its position in a letter to an accounting firm. The Commission stated:

"The Commission has recognized that certain situations, including those in which accountants and their audit clients have joined together in a profit-sharing venture, create a unity of interest between the accountant and client. In such cases, both the revenue accruing to each party . . . and the existence of the relationship itself create a situation in which to some degree the auditor's interest is wedded to that of its client. That interdependence impairs the auditor's independence, irrespective of whether the audit was in fact performed in an objective, critical fashion. Where such a unity of interests exists, there is an appearance that the auditor has lost the objectivity and skepticism necessary to take a critical second look at management's representations in the financial statements. The consequence is a loss of confidence in the integrity of the financial statements."

Question 21

Q: The new rule permits the auditor to continue to provide certain internal audit and financial information systems design and implementation services provided certain criteria are met. Do these criteria for internal audit apply to all internal audit engagements? What are the responsibilities of management pursuant to these criteria?

A: The six criteria for internal audit services apply to all internal audit services the auditor provides to its audit client, including those services related to operational audits or for companies with less than $200 million in assets.

All of the specified criteria must be met for both internal audit and financial information systems design and implementation to ensure that management not only takes responsibility for the services and projects performed by the auditor, but also makes the required management decisions. An audit client that merely signs a letter acknowledging responsibility for the services or project, without actually meeting each of the specified conditions, is not sufficient to ensure the auditor's independence.

WHERE THERE'S A WILL, THERE MAY BE A WAY

Needless to say, all of this activity relating to auditor independence, audit committees, and related financial disclosure did not come about without some very strong impetus. When the public and average investors begin to question truthfulness as well as the usefulness of business "checks and balances," someone will take action.

THE BLUE RIBBON PANEL'S TEN COMMANDMENTS

Although described as "recommendations," the report of the Blue Ribbon Panel on Improving the Effectiveness of Corporate Audit Committees made it quite clear that not only the average investor but also a distinguished group of those "in the know" had questions about the effectiveness of the "independent" audit process. The group comprising the Panel was formed by the New York Stock Exchange (NYSE) and the National Association of Securities Dealers (NASD or NASDAQ) in September 1998, after the SEC Chairman had publicly expressed grave concern about the "independence" of the audit process. During the deliberations of the group consisting of business, accounting, and securities professionals, testimony was provided by two dozen organizations, including the AICPA, the Financial Executives International, the Independence Standards Board, and the Institute of Management Accountants.

The panel's 71-page report listed ten recommendations for strengthening the independence of the audit committee and increasing its importance and effectiveness. These recommendations were:

1. The NYSE and NASD adopt strict definitions of independence for directors serving on audit committees of listed companies.
2. The NYSE and NASD require larger companies to have audit committees composed entirely of independent directors.
3. The NYSE and NASD require larger companies to have "financially literate" directors on their audit committees.
4. The NYSE and NASD require each company to adopt a formal audit committee charter and to review its adequacy annually.
5. The SEC requires each company to disclose in its proxy statement whether it has adopted an audit committee charter as well as other information.

6. Each NYSE and NASD listed company state in the audit committee charter that the outside auditor is ultimately accountable to the board of directors and the audit committee.
7. All NYSE and NASD listed companies ensure their charters mandate that their audit committee does communicate with the outside auditors about independence issues in accordance with Independent Standards Board regulations.
8. Generally accepted auditing rules require that the outside auditor discuss with the audit committee the quality and suitability, not just the acceptability, of the accounting principles used.
9. The SEC require the annual report include a letter from the audit committee clarifying that it has reviewed the audited financial statements with management as well as performed other tasks.
10. The SEC require the outside auditor to perform an interim review under Statement on Auditing Standards (SAS) SAS 71, *Interim Financial Information,* before a company files its form 10-Q.

NEW RULES FOR AUDIT COMMITTEES AND REVIEWS OF INTERIM FINANCIAL STATEMENTS

On December 15, 1999, the Securities and Exchange Commission adopted new rules aimed at improving public disclosure about the functioning of corporate audit committees and enhancing both the reliability and credibility of financial statements of public companies. These SEC rules build upon new rules adopted by the NYSE, the American Stock Exchange (AMEX), and the NASD that govern audit committees of listed companies.

The new rules also coincide with the issuance of Statement of Auditing Standard 90 by the AICPA's Auditing Standards Board. This ASB Standard requires independent auditors to discuss with the audit committee the auditor's judgment about the *quality,* and not just the *acceptability* under generally accepted accounting principles, of the company's own accounting principles as applied in its financial reporting.

Much of this activity results from the grave concern ably and loudly voiced by the SEC (particularly by the Chairman) which, in turn, led to the appointment of the Blue Ribbon Panel on Audit Effectiveness.

SEC Rules Relating to the Interim Statement

The Commission's rules require that:

1. Companies' interim financial statements must be reviewed by independent auditors before they are filed on Forms 10-Q or 10-QSB with the Commission.

2. Companies, other than small business issuers filing on small business forms, must supplement their annual financial information with disclosures of selected quarterly financial data under Item 302(a) of Regulation S-K.

3. Companies must disclose in their proxy statements whether the audit committee reviewed and discussed certain matters relating to:

   a. The ASB's Statements of Auditing Standards 61 concerning the accounting methods used in the financial statements.

   b. The Independence Standard Board's Standard 1 (concerning matters that may affect the auditor's independence) with management and the auditors.

   c. Possible recommendation to the Board that the audited financial statements be included in the Annual Report on Form 10-K or 10-KSB for filings with the Commission.

4. Companies must disclose in their proxy statements whether the audit committee has a written charter, and file a copy of their charter every three years.

5. Companies whose securities are listed on the NYSE or AMEX or are quoted on NASDAQ must disclose certain information in their proxy statements about any audit committee member who is not "independent." All companies must disclose, if they have an audit committee, whether the members are "independent." (Independence is defined in the listing standards of the NYSE, AMEX, and NASD.)

Under the new rules, timely interim auditor reviews were required beginning with the first fiscal quarter ended after March 15, 2000. Compliance with the other new requirements is required in filings after December 15, 2000.

Foreign private issuers are exempt from requirements of the new rules. The new rules include a "safe harbor" for the disclosures.

Blue Ribbon Reminders

In their final report in August, 2000, the Blue Ribbon Panel on Audit Effectiveness recommended that, among other things audit committees:

1. Obtain annual reports from management assessing the company's internal controls.

2. Specify in their charters that the outside auditor is ultimately accountable to the board of directors and audit committee.

3. Inquire about time pressures on the auditor.

4. Preapprove nonaudit services provided by the auditor.

Criteria for Gauging Appropriateness

The Panel, more specifically, provided guidance that an audit committee can use to determine the appropriateness of a service. This guidance includes:

1. Whether the service is being performed principally for the audit committee.
2. The effects of the service, if any, on audit effectiveness, or on the quality and timeliness of the entity's financial reporting process. For example, what is the effect, if any, upon the technology specialists who ordinarily also provide recurring audit support?
3. Whether the service would be performed by audit personnel, and if so, whether it will enhance their knowledge of the entity's business and operations.
4. Whether the role of those performing the service would be inconsistent with the auditor's role (e.g., a role where neutrality, impartiality, and auditor skepticism are likely to be subverted).
5. Whether the audit firm personnel would be assuming a management role or creating a mutual or conflicting interest with management.
6. Whether the auditors, in effect, would be "auditing their own numbers."
7. Whether the project must be started and completed very quickly.
8. Whether the audit firm has unique expertise in the service.
9. The size of the fee(s) for the nonaudit service(s).

Chapter 10
Foreign Currency Translations and Derivative Disclosure

CONTENTS

FASB STATEMENT 52, FOREIGN CURRENCY TRANSLATIONS

FASB 52 covers accounting for the translation of foreign currency statements and the gain and loss on foreign currency transactions. Foreign currency transactions and financial statements of foreign entities include branches, subsidiaries, partnerships and joint ventures, which are consolidated, combined, or reported under the equity method in financial statements prepared in accordance with U.S. generally accepted financial principles.

Why is translation necessary? It is not arithmetically possible to combine, add, or subtract measurements expressed in different currencies. It is necessary, therefore, to translate assets, liabilities, revenues, expenses, gains, and losses that are measured or denominated in a foreign currency.

Definitions

An understanding of this rather complex accounting rule can be aided by becoming familiar with the terms used in the Statement. The following list of definitions will enable the accountant to apply the accounting procedures and methods outlined below.

Attribute — For accounting purposes, the quantifiable element of an item.

Conversion — Exchanging one currency for another.

Currency Exchange Rate — The rate at which one unit of a currency can be exchanged or converted into another currency. For purposes of translation of financial statements, the current exchange rate is the rate at the end of the period covered by the financial statements, or the dates of recognition in the statements for revenues, expenses, gains and losses.

Currency Swap — An exchange between enterprises of the currencies of two different countries with a binding commitment to reverse the exchange of the two currencies at the same rate of exchange on a specified future date.

Current Rate Method — All assets and liabilities are translated at the exchange rate in effect on the balance sheet date. Capital accounts are translated at *historical exchange rates.*

Discount or Premium on a Forward Contract — The foreign currency amount of a contract multiplied by the difference between the contracted forward rate and the spot rate at the date of inception of the contract.

Economic Environment — The nature of the business climate in which an entity *primarily* generates and expends cash.

Entity — In this instance, a party to a transaction which produces a monetary asset or liability denominated in a currency other than its functional currency.

Exchange Rate — The ratio between a unit of one currency and the amount of another currency for which that unit can be exchanged at a particular time. The appropriate exchange rate for the translation of income statement accounts is the rate for the date on which those elements are recognized during the period.

Foreign Currency — A currency other than the functional currency of the entity being referred to. For example, the dollar could be a foreign currency for a foreign entity. Composites of currencies, such as the Special Drawing Rights (SDRs), used to set prices or denominate amounts of loans, etc., have the characteristics of foreign currency for purposes of applying Statement 52.

Foreign Currency Transaction — A transaction in which the terms are denominated in a currency other than an entity's functional currency. Foreign currency transactions arise when an enterprise buys or sells goods or services on credit at prices which are denominated in foreign currency; when an entity borrows or lends funds and the amounts payable or receivable are denominated in foreign currency; acquires or disposes of assets, or incurs or settles liabilities denominated in a foreign currency.

Foreign Currency Translation — Amounts that are expressed in the reporting currency of an enterprise that are denominated in a foreign currency. An example is the translation of the financial statements of a U.S. company from the foreign currency to U.S. dollars.

In the translation of balance sheets, the assets and liabilities are translated at the *current exchange rate,* e.g., rate at the balance sheet date. Income statement items are translated at the *weighted-average exchange rate* for the year.

There are two steps in translating the foreign country's financial statements into U.S. reporting requirements:

1. Conform the foreign country's financial statements to GAAP.
2. Convert the foreign currency into U.S. dollars, the reporting currency.

Foreign Entity — An operation (subsidiary, division, branch, joint venture, etc.) whose financial statements are prepared in a currency other than the currency of the reporting enterprise. The financial statements are combined and accounted for on the equity basis in the financial statements of the reporting enterprise.

Foreign Exchange Contract — An agreement to exchange, at a specified future date, currencies of different countries at a specified rate, which is the *forward rate.*

Functional Currency — The currency of the primary economic environment in which an entity operates; that is, the currency of the environment in which an entity primarily generates and expends cash.

Hedging — An effort by management to minimize the effect of exchange rate fluctuations on reported income, either directly by entering into an exchange contract to buy or sell one currency for another, or indirectly by managing exposed net assets or liabilities' positions by borrowing or billing in dollars rather than the local currency. An agreement to exchange different currencies at a specified future date and at a specified rate is referred to as *the forward rate.*

Highly Inflationary Economy — Economies of countries in which the *cumulative* local inflation rate over a three-year period exceeds approximately 100 per cent, or more.

Historical Exchange Rate — A rate, other than the current or a forward rate, at which a foreign transaction took place.

Inflation — Not defined by specific reference to a commonly quoted economic index. Management can select an appropriate method for measuring inflation. An annual inflation rate of about 20% for three consecutive years would result in a cumulative rate of about 100%.

Intercompany Balance — The foreign currency transactions of the parent, the subsidiary, or both. An intercompany account denominated in the local foreign currency is a foreign currency transaction of the parent. An intercompany account denominated in dollars is a foreign currency transaction of a foreign entity whose functional currency is a currency *other than* the U.S. dollar.

Local Currency — The currency of a particular country.

Measurement — Measurement is the process of measuring transactions denominated in a unit of currency (e.g., purchases payable in British pounds).

Remeasurement — Measurement of the functional currency financial statement amounts in other than the currency in which the transactions are denominated.

Reporting Currency — The currency used by an enterprise in the preparation of its financial statements.

Reporting Enterprise — An entity or group whose financial statements are being referenced. In Statement 52, those financial statements reflect a) the financial statements of one or more foreign operations by combination, consolidation, or equity accounting; b) foreign currency transactions; c) both a) and b).

Self-Contained Operations — Operations which are integrated with the local economic environment, and other operations which are primarily a direct or integral component or extension of a parent company's operations.

Speculative Contracts — A contract that is intended to produce an investment gain (not to hedge a foreign currency exposure).

Spot Rate — An exchange for *immediate delivery* of the currencies exchanged.

Transaction Date — The date at which a transaction, such as a purchase of merchandise or services, is recorded in accounting records in conformity with GAAP. A long-term commitment may have more than one transaction date; for example, the due date of each progress payment under a construction contract is an *anticipated transaction date* credited to shareholders' equity.

Transaction Gain or Loss — Gains or losses from a change in exchange rates between the functional currency and the currency in which a foreign transaction is denominated.

Translation Adjustment — Translation adjustments translate financial statements from the entity's functional currency into the reporting currency. The amount necessary to balance the financial statements after completing the translation process. The amount is charged or credited to shareholder's equity.

Unit of Measure — The currency in which assets, liabilities, revenues, expenses, gains and losses are measured.

Weighted Average Rates — Determined on a monthly basis by an arithmetic average of daily closing rates, and on a quarterly and an annual basis by an arithmetic average of average monthly rates.

Discussion of FASB Statement 52

Statement 52 applies to the financial reports of most companies with foreign operations. The essential requirements of the Statements are:

1. Transaction adjustments arising from consolidating a foreign operation which do not affect cash flows are *not* included in net income. Adjustments

should be disclosed separately and accumulated in a separate classification of the equity section of the balance sheet.

2. Exchange rate changes on a foreign operation which directly affect the parent's cash flows must be included in net income.

3. Hedges of foreign exchange risks are accounted for as hedges without regard to their form.

4. Transaction gains and losses result from exchange rate changes on transactions denominated in currencies other than the functional currency.

5. The balance sheet translation uses the exchange rate prevailing as of the date of the balance sheet.

6. The exchange rate used for revenues, expenses, gains and losses is the rate on the date those items are recognized.

7. Upon sale (or liquidation) of an investment in a foreign entity, the amount accumulated in the equity component is removed and reported as a gain (or loss) on the disposal of the entity.

8. Intercompany transactions of a long-term investment nature are not included in net income.

9. Financial statements for fiscal years before the effective date of this Statement may be restated. If restatements are provided, they must conform to requirements of the Statement.

10. The financial statements of a foreign entity in a highly inflationary economy must be remeasured as if the functional currency were the reporting currency. A "highly inflationary economy" is defined in the Statement to be an economy that has had a cumulative inflation rate of 100%, or more, over a three-year period.

11. If material change in an exchange rate has occurred between year-end and the audit report date, the change should be reported as a subsequent event.

Background.   The rapid expansion of international business activities of U.S. companies and dramatic changes in the world monetary system created the need to reconsider the accounting and reporting for foreign currency translation. In considering this topic, the FASB issued FASB Statement 52, which related to the following four areas:

1. Foreign currency transactions including buying or selling on credit goods or services whose prices are denominated in a foreign currency; i.e., currency other than the currency of the reporting entity's country.

2. Being a party to an unperformed foreign exchange contract.

3. Borrowing or lending funds denominated in a foreign currency.

4. For other reasons, acquiring assets or incurring liabilities denominated in foreign currency.

Statement 52 also applies to a foreign enterprise which reports in its currency in conformity with U.S. generally accepted accounting principles. For example, a French subsidiary of a U.S. parent should translate the foreign currency financial statements of its Italian subsidiary in accordance with Statement 52. The objective of translation is to measure and express in dollars, and in conformity with U.S. generally accepted accounting principles, the assets, liabilities, revenues, or expenses that are measured or denominated in foreign currency. In achieving this objective, translation should remeasure these amounts in dollars without changing accounting principles. For example, if an asset was originally measured in a foreign currency under the historical cost concept, translation should remeasure the carrying amount of the asset in dollars at historical cost, not replacement cost or market value.

The most common foreign currency transactions result from the import or export of goods or services, foreign borrowing or lending, and forward exchange contracts. Import or export transactions can be viewed as being composed of two elements — a sale or purchase and the settlement of the related receivable or payable. Changes in the exchange rate, which occur between the time of sale or purchase and the settlement of the receivable or payable, should not affect the measurement of revenues from exports or the cost of imported goods or services.

Foreign currency statements should be translated based on the exchange rate at the end of the reporting year. Translation gains and losses are presented in the stockholders' equity section. Also important is the accounting treatment of gains and losses resulting from transactions denominated in a foreign currency. These are shown in the current year's income statement.

Because of the proliferation of multinational companies, expanding international trade, business involvement with foreign subsidiaries, and joint ventures, FASB 52 was established, in effect, by popular demand. The stated aims of Statement 52 are to (a) provide information that is generally compatible with the expected effects of a rate change on an enterprise's cash flows and equity, and (b) reflect in consolidated statements the financial results and relationships of the individual consolidated entities as measured in their functional currencies, whether the U.S. dollar or a specified foreign currency, in conformity with U.S. generally accepted accounting principles.

The method adopted to achieve these aims is termed the *functional currency approach* which is the currency of the primary economic environment in which the entity carries on its business; in substance, where it generates and expends cash. The Statement permits a multiple measurement basis in consolidated financial statements (depending upon the country in which the subsidiary operates) because business enterprises made up of a multinational enterprise operate and generate cash flows in diverse economic environments, each with its own functional currency. When an enterprise operates in several of these environments, the results of business transactions are measured in the functional currency of the particular environment. "Measured in the functional currency" has the specific meaning that gains and losses comprising income are determined only in relation to accounts denominated in the functional currency.

Mechanically, the functional currency approach calls for eventual translation of all functional currency assets and liabilities into dollars at the current exchange rate. Under Statement 52, use of the current rate for all accounts resolves both the economically compatible results and operating margins distortions. In the past, these distortions came about with the translation of nonmonetary accounts at historical rates. The volatility of earnings distortions is alleviated by recording the translation adjustments directly into shareholders' equity.

The functional currency approach presumes the following:

1. Many business enterprises operate and generate cash flows in a number of different countries (different economic environments).
2. Each of these operations can usually be identified as operating in a single economic environment: the local environment or the parent company's environment. The currency of the principal economic environment becomes the functional currency for those operations.
3. The enterprise may be committed to a long-term position in a specific economic environment and have no plans to liquidate that position in the foreseeable future.

Because measurements are made in multiple functional currencies, decisions relating to the choice of the functional currency of a specific foreign operation will in all likelihood have a significant effect upon reported income. Even though the management of the business enterprise is entitled to a degree of latitude in its weighing of specific facts, the thinking behind adoption of this Statement is that the functional currency is to be determined based on the true nature of the enterprise and not upon some arbitrary selection which management feels might be of particular advantage to the reporting entity.

Determining the Functional Currency.   Multinational companies are involved with foreign business interests either through transactions or investments in foreign entities operating in a number of different economic environments. Each of these endeavors may be associated with one primary economic environment whose currency then becomes the functional currency for that operation. On the other hand, in a foreign country where the economic and/or political environment is so unstable that a highly inflationary economy is likely, it may be deemed wise to carry on the enterprise with the dollar as the functional currency. If the operations in situations of this nature are remeasured on a dollar basis, further erosion of nonmonetary accounts may be avoided.

When there is a reasonably stable economic situation, the national environment of each operation should be considered as the primary economic environment of the particular operation since national sovereignty is a primary consideration in relation to currency control.

Industry practice, on the other hand, may in some instances be instrumental in the determination of a primary economic environment and functional currency. If it is an industry-wide practice that pricing or other transaction attributes are calculated in a specific currency, such as prices set in dollars on a worldwide basis, that fact may be more of a determinant than local currency considerations.

The actual decisions in determining a functional currency depend to a large extent upon the operating policy adopted by the reporting company. Two broad classes of foreign operations are to be considered:

1. Those in which a foreign currency is the functional currency. This designation will have been made after receiving the facts and determining that this particular aspect of foreign business operations is largely autonomous and confined to a specific foreign economic environment. That is, ordinary operations are not dependent upon the economic environment of the parent company's functional currency, nor does the foreign operation primarily generate or expend the parent's functional currency.

2. When the workaday business of the foreign operation is deemed to be in actuality just an extension of the parent company's operation and dependent upon the economic environment of the parent company, the dollar may be designated as the functional currency. In substance, most transactions can reasonably be in dollars, thus obviating the need for foreign currency translation.

One of the objectives of Statement 52 is to provide information that is generally compatible with the expected economic effects of a rate change on an enterprise's cash flow and equity in a readily understood manner. If a foreign operation's policy is to convert available funds into dollars for current or near-term distribution to the parent, selection of a dollar functional currency may be expedient.

Therefore, reporting for investments expected to be of short-term duration, such as construction or development joint ventures, the dollar should probably be designated the functional currency. If the nature of an investment changes over a period of time, future redetermination of the appropriate functional currency may become necessary. Such redetermination is permissible only when, in actual fact, significant changes in economic facts and/or circumstances have occurred. The operative functional currency cannot be redetermined merely because management has "changed its collective mind." It becomes evident that functional currency determination should be carefully considered with the decision weighted in favor of the long-term picture rather than short-term expectations.

In the event that redetermination is necessary, three procedures should be kept in mind:

1. When the functional currency has been changed, Statement 52 provides that the prior year's financial statement need not be restated for a change in functional currency.
2. When the functional currency change is from the local currency to the dollar, historical costs and exchange rates are to be determined from translated dollar amounts immediately prior to the change.
3. When the functional currency change is from the dollar to the local currency, nonmonetary assets are to be translated at current exchange rates, charging the initial translation adjustment to equity similar to that produced when Statement 52 was adopted.

Translation.   Translation is the process of converting financial statements expressed in one unit of currency to a different unit of currency (the reporting currency). In short, translation as used in Statement 52 is the restatement into the reporting currency (the U.S. dollar) of any/all foreign currency financial statements utilized in preparing the consolidated financial statements of the U.S. parent company.

Thus, the focus for the preparation and subsequent translation of the financial statements of individual components of an organization is, as previously stated, to:

1. Provide information that is generally compatible with the expected economic effects of a rate change on the enterprise's cash flows and equity, and
2. Reflect in consolidated statements the financial results and relationships of the individual consolidated entities as measured in their functional currencies in conformity with U.S. generally accepted accounting principles.

Measurement is the process of stating the monetary value of transactions denominated in a particular unit of currency (e.g., purchases payable in British pounds). These transactions may also be figured in a unit of currency other than that in which they are denominated. This process then becomes remeasurement and is accomplished by assuming that an exchange of currencies will occur at the exchange rate in effect at the time of the remeasurement. As is evident, should the exchange rate fluctuate between the date of the original transaction and the date of the exchange, a foreign exchange gain or loss will result.

The gains or losses so recorded vary little from other trading activities and are, therefore, included in income.

It is important to note that while translations were formerly based on the premise that financial statements of a U.S. enterprise should be measured in a single unit of currency—the U.S. dollar—translation was under FASB 80, *Accounting for Futures Contracts,* a one-step process that included both remeasurement and reporting in dollars. In the newer context of the functional approach, multiple units of measure are permitted so that remeasurement is required only when (1) the accounts of an entity are maintained in a currency other than its own functional currency, or (2) an enterprise is invoiced in a transaction which produces a monetary asset or liability not denominated in its functional currency.

The subsequent translation to dollars under FASB 52 is the second step of a two-step process necessary to prepare U.S. dollar financial statements.

Foreign Currency Transactions.   Foreign currency transactions are those denominated in a currency other than the entity's functional currency. These transactions include:

1. Buying or selling goods priced in a currency other than the entity's functional currency.
2. Borrowing or lending funds (including intercompany balances) denominated in a different currency.
3. Engaging in an unperformed forward exchange contract.

As becomes evident, companies with foreign subsidiaries can readily become engaged in foreign currency transactions which must be considered when financial statements are prepared. But, in addition, companies which have no foreign branches may also in the everyday course of business become involved in foreign currency transactions.

Regardless of whether the company is entirely domestic-based or not at the transaction date, each resulting asset, liability, revenue, expense, gain, or loss not already denominated in the entity's functional currency must be so measured and recorded. At the close of each subsequent accounting period, all unsettled monetary balances are to be remeasured using the exchange rates in effect on the balance-sheet date. Gains and losses from remeasuring or settling foreign currency transactions are accounted for as current income.

FASB Statement 107, *Disclosure about Fair Value of Financial Instruments*

Statement 107, *Disclosure About Fair Value of Financial Instruments,* defines fair value to mean the amount at which a financial instrument could be exchanged in a current transaction between willing parties, other than a forced or liquidation sale.

The rule is a broad approach to help issuers of financial statements understand what is required of them in meeting the newer, improved disclosure requirements, as well as to help minimize the costs of providing that information. Of course, the reasoning behind the stipulations in this Statement is to ensure a clearer, better defined picture of the fair value of financial instruments than has been provided in the past. This truer picture of an entity's financial activities should be of value to creditors, current and potential investors, and others in making informed decisions concerning granting credit to, investing in, or investigating more thoroughly, a particular entity.

Other impetus for enactment of this rule comes from a desire to provide another useful indicator of the solvency of a financial institution. A recent report issued by the U.S. Treasury Department has suggested that further market value information about various financial institutions could be of aid in regulatory supervision.

Since in many instances generally accepted accounting principles already necessitate disclosure, the term *fair value* use in FASB 107 in no way supersedes or modifies the set of figures obtained using *current value, mark-to-market,* or simply *market value.* It is simply an attempt to get more accurate information about financial instruments—both their assets and liabilities whether on or off the balance sheet—available for easy access.

For the purposes of this Statement, a financial instrument is cash, an ownership interest in an entity, or a contract that imposes on one entity a contractual obligation to deliver cash or another financial instrument to a second entity, or to exchange other financial instruments on potentially unfavorable terms with the second entity. The agreement gives the second entity a contractual right to receive cash or another financial instrument from the first entity, or to exchange other financial instruments on potentially favorable terms with the first entity.

If available, open-market prices are the best and easiest to obtain a measure of fair value of financial instruments. If quoted market prices or other established values are not available, estimates of fair value can be based on the quoted market price of a financial instrument with similar characteristics. Estimates can also be based on valuation techniques, such as the present value of estimated future cash flows using a discount rate commensurate with the risks involved, or using option pricing models. If it is not practicable to estimate the fair value of a particular financial instrument, reasons why it is not practicable must be thoroughly explained.

In all instances, descriptive material must be included detailing the method(s) and the basis for assumptions utilized in arriving at a stated fair value or in the failure to do so. In any event, failure to do so is not to be considered final. A continuing effort to arrive at a practicable (without incurring excessive cost) fair value should be carried out. Because the Board realizes that the cost of attempting to compute fair value in some instances would become excessive, certain types of financial instruments have been excepted from the requirements of Statement 107. These are:

1. Extinguished debt and assets held in trust in connection with a defeasance of that debt.
2. Insurance contracts, other than financial guarantees and investment contracts.
3. Lease contracts as defined in FASB Statement 13.
4. Warrant obligations and rights.
5. Unconditional purchase obligations.
6. Investments accounted for under the equity method.
7. Minority interests in consolidated subsidiaries.
8. Equity investments in consolidated subsidiaries.
9. Equity instruments issued by the entity and classified in stockholders' equity in the statement of financial position.
10. Obligations of employers and plans for pension benefits, other post-retirement benefits including health care and life insurance benefits, employee stock option, and stock purchase plans.

FASB STATEMENT 133, ACCOUNTING FOR DERIVATIVE INSTRUMENTS AND HEDGING ACTIVITIES

The derivatives standard was adopted by a unanimous vote on June 1, 1998, after more than 10 years of painstaking effort by the FASB. Unquestionably, this Standard will be one of the most far-reaching accounting standards yet produced. It will also be the one that has raised the most hue and cry in every segment of the economy.

The FASB repeatedly made it clear that they would not back down on certain requirements, regardless of "special interest" objections. The Board pointed out that trillions of dollars' worth of derivative transactions are occurring in the marketplace and they believe "investors have little, if any, information about them." They believe that the new Standard will give the investor further information about an entity so that they can make more knowledgeable decisions.

The U.S. Senate, the House of Representatives, the Federal Reserve, the American Bankers Association, and assorted others entered the fray over derivatives with very little success. On the other hand, the Board had modified some of the earlier positions in response to user requests, as in the Chicago Board of Trade's concern about some of the provisions relating to hedging.

One of the most important concessions was to the projected timing of the effective date. The Standard was to have become effective June 15, 1999. This meant that for calendar-year companies it would be effective January 1, 2000. Many segments had complained that the extra time and money being expended on trying to solve Y2K problems, coping with a new derivatives Standard of such proposed magnitude by December 15, 1998, was expecting too much.

FASB Statement 137, *Accounting for Derivative Instruments and Hedging Activities—Deferral of the Effective Date of FASB Statement 133*—delayed for a year the required application of FASB 133 to June 15, 2000. However, entities that had already issued interim or annual financial statements according to the requirements of Statement 133 could not return to their previous method of accounting for derivatives or hedging activities.

FASB 137 did not change any of the requirements; it merely postponed the inevitable to give the issuers additional time to cope with Y2K considerations and digest the ramifications of the new requirements.

The FASB also appointed a special task force to aid with implementation issues on derivatives. Among the comments received from users were many related to the complicated provisions of the proposed Standard—admittedly covering very complicated financial instruments. The Board agreed with the constituents that it should be prepared to provide assistance and guidance on a timely basis: thus, the task force. The task force continues to help in identifying implementation issues and recommending conclusions to the Board.

ED Modified Somewhat, Not Substantially

FASB Standard 133 retained most of the provisions that were issued in the ED of September, 1997. All derivatives are to be reported as assets or liabilities in financial statements at their fair value. New approaches to hedge accounting are outlined. As a result, more detailed, useful disclosures of derivatives, hedging activities, and related accounting practices should furnish the investor, creditor, and user with a better picture of an entity's true financial condition. In effect, the new derivative accounting practices should then reveal the economic realities of derivative transactions to the financial statement reader.

The requirements to record all derivatives on the face of the balance sheet at fair value, and some of the new hedge accounting requirements, may very well increase the assets reported by some companies and change their return on assets. On the other hand, the result may be an increase of the liabilities reported by some companies, resulting in a change in their liabilities-to-owners'equity ratio.

Hedge Accounting

Under certain conditions, the new derivative Standard will permit management to designate a derivative as one of the following hedges — a fair value, cash flow, or foreign exchange hedge.

1. A *fair value hedge* is a hedge of the exposure to changes in the fair value of an asset or liability recognized on the balance sheet or of a firm commitment. The exposure to change must be attributable to a specific risk.
   For this type of hedge, the gain or loss is recognized in current income. This amount is offset by the gain or loss in the fair value of the hedged item. The carrying amount is adjusted to reflect the fair value gain or loss. If the hedge is working as it is intended, the adjustment to the carrying amount of the hedged item recognized in income will equal the offsetting gain or loss on the hedging derivative and there will be no net effect on earnings. If the hedge, on the other hand, is not operating as it should, earnings will be affected to the extent that the hedge is ineffective. Assessment of effectiveness is required.

2. A *cash flow hedge* is a hedge of an exposure to variability in the cash flows of an asset or liability recognized on the balance sheet, or of a forecasted transaction, that is attributable to a particular risk. Forecasted transactions include forecasted sales and purchases for which no firm commitment has been made, and interest payments on variable rate debt reported as a liability.
   The effective part of a gain or loss on a derivative designated as a cash flow hedge is initially recognized in owners' equity as part of other comprehensive income and then in earnings in the same period in which the hedged forecasted transaction affects earnings. The ineffective aspect of the gain or loss is recognized in earnings.

3. A *foreign currency exposure hedge* is a hedge of the foreign currency exposure of:
   a. A firm commitment which is a foreign currency fair value hedge.
   b. An available-for-sale debt security, a foreign currency fair value hedge.
   c. A foreign currency-denominated forecasted transaction which is a foreign currency cash flow hedge.
   d. A net investment in a foreign operation.
   The gain or loss on a derivative or nonderivative financial instrument designated as a foreign currency hedge is accounted for depending upon its designations as a fair value or cash flow hedge in the same way as outlined above for those types of hedges.

Thus, the gain or loss on a derivative financial instrument designated and qualifying as a foreign currency hedging instrument is to be accounted for as follows:

a. The gain or loss on the hedging instrument in a hedge of a firm commitment is to be recognized in current earnings along with the loss or gain on the hedged firm commitment.

b. The gain or loss on the hedging derivative in a hedge of an available-for-sale security is to be recognized in current earnings along with the loss or gain on the hedged available-for-sale security.

c. In general, the effective aspect of the gain or loss on the hedging instrument in a hedge of a foreign-currency denominated forecasted transaction is to be reported as a component of other comprehensive income, outside of earnings. It is to be recognized in earnings in the same period or periods during which the hedged forecasted transaction affects earnings. The ineffective aspect of the gain or loss on the hedging instrument and any other remaining gain or loss on the hedging instrument is to be recognized in current earnings.

d. The foreign currency transaction gain or loss on the hedging instrument in a hedge of a net investment in a foreign operation is to be reported in other comprehensive income as part of the cumulative translation adjustment. The remainder of the gain or loss on the hedging instrument is to be recognized in current earnings.

Derivatives

A derivative is a financial instrument or other contract with several distinguishing characteristics:

1. It has one or more *underlyings* and one or more *notional amounts* or payment provisions or both. Those terms determine the amount of the settlement or settlements, and in some cases, whether or not a settlement is required.

2. It requires no initial net investment or one that is smaller than would be required for other types of contracts expected to have a similar response to changes in market factors.

3. The terms require or permit net settlement; it can readily be settled net by a means outside the contract, or it provides for delivery of an asset that puts the recipient in a position not substantially different from net settlement.

An "underlying" may be one of a number of variables that is applied to the notional amount to determine the cash flows or other exchanges required by the contract—a commodity price, a per-share price, an interest rate, a foreign exchange rate, or some other variable.

"Notional amount" refers to an amount of money, a number of shares, a number of bushels, pounds, or whatever can be dreamed up to create a more exotic derivative. A contract with these characteristics is a derivative instrument according to the Statement if, by the terms at its inception or upon the occurrence of a specified event, the entire contract meets the conditions delineated above.

FASB 133 specifically states that the following transactions do not constitute derivatives for the purpose of this Statement:

1. Regular security trades.
2. Normal purchases and sales.
3. Contingent consideration from a business combination.
4. Traditional life insurance contracts.
5. Traditional property and casualty contracts.
6. Most financial guarantee contracts.

The new Statement also points out that some contracts may be accounted for as derivatives by the holder but not by the user. These would include:

1. Contracts that are both indexed to the entity's own stock and classified in stockholders' equity on their balance sheets.
2. Contracts issued in connection with stock-based compensation arrangements covered in FASB 123, *Accounting for Stock-Based Compensation.*

How FASB 133 Affects Other Accounting Literature

FASB 133 supersedes and amends several other Statements. It supersedes:

1. FASB 80, *Accounting for Futures Contracts.*
2. FASB 105, *Disclosure of Information About Financial Instruments with Off-Balance-Sheet Risk and Financial Instruments with Concentrations of Credit Risk.*
3. FASB 119, *Disclosure About Derivative Financial Instruments and Fair Value of Financial Instruments.*

It amends:

1. FASB 52, *Foreign Currency Translation,* to permit special accounting for a hedge of a foreign currency forecasted transaction with a derivative.
2. FASB 107, *Disclosures About Fair Value of Financial Instruments,* to include in Statement 107 the disclosure provisions about concentrations of credit risk from FASB 105.

FASB 133 also nullifies or modifies the consensuses reached in a number of issued addressed by the Emerging Issues Task Force.

Application to Not-for-Profit Organizations

Since the Statement applies to all entities, not-for-profit organizations should recognize the change in fair value of all derivatives as a change in net assets in the period of change. In a fair value hedge, the changes in the fair value of the hedged item attributable to the risk being hedged also are recognized.

However, because of the format of their statement of financial performance, not-for-profit organizations may *not* apply special hedge accounting for derivatives used to hedge forecasted transactions. In addition, FASB 133 does not consider how a not-for-profit organization should determine the components of an operating measure if one is presented.

Another Amendment

The Financial Accounting Standards Board issued Statement 138, *Accounting for Certain Derivative Instruments and Certain Hedging Activities — an Amendment of FASB Statement 133* in June, 2000. The Statement addresses a limited number of issues causing implementation difficulties for a large number of entities getting ready to apply Statement 133.

The Board points out that FASB 133, *Accounting for Derivative Instruments and Hedging Activities,* establishes accounting and reporting standards for derivative instruments, including certain derivative instruments embedded in other contracts, (collectively referred to as derivatives) and for hedging activities. Because of difficulties in application and interpretations, the Statement amends FASB 133 so that:

1. The normal purchases and normal sales exception is expanded.
2. The specific risks that can be identified as the hedged risk are redefined so that in a hedge of interest rate risk, the risk of changes in a benchmark interest rate would be the hedged risk.
3. Recognized foreign-currency-denominated debt instruments may be the hedged item in fair value hedges or cash flow hedges.
4. Intercompany derivatives may be designated as the hedging instruments in cash flow hedges of foreign currency risk in the consolidated financial statements even if those intercompany derivatives are offset by unrelated third-party contracts on a net basis.

Certain Board decisions based on recommendations of the Derivatives Implementation Group (DIG) to clarify Statement 133 also have been incorporated in the Statement. The Statement 138 is the result of the Board's decision, after listening to its constituents, to address a limited number of issues using the following criteria:

1. Implementation difficulties would be eased for a large number of entities.
2. There would be no conflict with or modifications to the basic model of Statement 133.
3. There would be no delay in the effective date of Statement 133.

And Yet Another Amendment!

And yet another amendment to FASB 133! Like the GASB and its efforts to make sure that everyone affected understands the workings of GASB 34 (the major overhauling of state and local accounting procedures), the FASB is trying to solve all questions raised in relation to derivatives and FASB 133.

An exposure draft, *Amendment of Statement 133 on Derivative Instruments and Hedging Activities,* has been approved to amend the definition of a derivative in paragraph 6 of FASB 133. The ED would also consider various decisions made as part of the Derivatives Implementation Group process.

The proposal resolves issues raised in connection with an implementation issue "Application of Statement 133 to Beneficial Interests in Securitized Financial Assets." Resolution would require that beneficial interests that do not qualify for the exception in paragraph 14 of Statement 133 (as amended) be evaluated. The evaluation would be to determine whether those beneficial interests in securitized financial assets (such as the interests in securitized credit card receivables) meet the amended definition of a derivative in paragraph 6 of Statement 133.

The Board concluded that other changes proposed in implementation issues are in conflict with Statement 133. In particular, an issue regarding "initial net investment," which provides proposed guidance that conflicts with the definition of a derivative. After considering alternatives for resolving this conflict, the Board decided to amend the Statement.

The Board agreed that the changes required by the ED would improve financial reporting by requiring that contracts with comparable characteristics be accounted for similarly. In particular, it should clarify under what circumstances a contract (either an option-based contract or a non-option-based contract) with an initial net investment would meet the characteristic of a derivative discussed in paragraph 6. The change would result in more consistent reporting of contracts as either derivatives or hybrid instruments.

The proposed effective date for the accounting change is the first day of the first fiscal period beginning after November 15, 2002, which, for calendar year-end companies, will be January 1, 2003.

FASB Statement 149 Amends and Clarifies Guidance on Derivatives

The FASB issued Statement No. 149, *Amendment of Statement 133 on Derivative Instruments and Hedging Activities,* amending and clarifying accounting for derivatives, including certain derivative instruments embedded in other contracts, and for hedging activities under Statement 133 in April 2003.

The new guidance amends Statement 133 for decisions made:

- As part of the Derivatives Implementation Group process that effectively requires amendments to Statement 133.
- In connection with other Board projects dealing with financial instruments.
- Regarding implementation issues raised in relation to the application of the definition of a derivative. This is particularly in regard to the meaning of an underlying instrument and the characteristics of a derivative that contains financing components. The language now conforms to that used in the definition of an underlying in FASB Interpretation 45, *Guarantor's Accounting and Disclosure Requirements for Guarantees, Including Indirect Guarantees of Indebtedness of Others*

The amendments set forth in FASB 149 improve financial reporting by requiring that contracts with comparable characteristics be accounted for similarly. It clarifies under what circumstances a contract with an initial net investment meets the characteristic of a derivative described in Statement 133. In addition, it clarifies *when* a derivative contains a financing component that calls for special reporting in the statement of cash flows.

Statement 149 also amends certain other existing pronouncements. Those changes will result in more consistent reporting of contracts that are derivatives in their entirety or that contain embedded derivatives that warrant separate accounting.

Effective Dates

This Statement was effective for contracts entered into or modified after June 30, 2003, except as stated below and for hedging relationships designated after June 30, 2003. The guidance should be applied prospectively.

The provisions of this Statement that relate to Statement 133 Implementation Issues effective for fiscal quarters beginning prior to June 15, 2003, should continue to be applied in accordance with their respective effective dates. In addition, certain provisions relating to forward purchases or sales of *when-issued* securities or other securities that do not yet exist, should be applied to existing contracts as well as new contracts entered into after June 30, 2003.

TECHNICAL BULLETIN TO IMPROVE DISCLOSURES ABOUT DERIVATIVES

In an effort to improve disclosures about the risks associated with derivative contracts, the GASB issued accounting guidance in June 2003 that provides more consistent and comprehensive reporting by state and local governments. The Technical Bulletin, *Disclosure Requirements for Derivatives Not Presented at Fair Value on the Statement of Net Assets,* is designed to increase the public's understanding of the significance of derivatives to a government's net assets and to provide key information about the potential effects on future cash flows. It will also provide the users of financial statements with better information about the risks assumed in derivative contracts. Derivatives are often used by governments as a means to potentially reduce borrowing costs. Although derivatives may support financing needs, the lower costs come with additional risks. The objectives and terms of derivative contracts, their risks, and the fair value of the contracts had generally not been specified in financial reports.

This Technical Bulletin is designed to increase the public's understanding of the significance of derivatives to a government's financial position and provide key information about their potential effects on future cash flows.

The GASB pointed out that even estimating the notional amounts of outstanding derivatives in this market is difficult based on information that has been readily available. Estimates of notional value range from $200 billion to $400 billion. Under this guidance, state and local governments are *required* to disclose such information.

One GASB official agreed that its own research indicated that it often has been difficult to understand how governments have been accounting for derivatives. These disclosures should clear up the mystery surrounding the transactions. It should now be possible to see what a government has done, why it has done it, the fair value of the derivative, and the risks that have been assumed. Governments will be required to disclose information in their financial statements about risks that relate to credit, interest rates, basis, termination dates, rollovers and, market access.

While state and local governments use an array of increasingly complex derivative instruments to manage debt and investments, they may, at the same time, be assuming significant risks. Governments are expected to communicate those risks to financial statement users and the public. The proposed Technical Bulletin's purpose is to clarify existing accounting guidance so that more consistent disclosures can be made across all governments.

The GASB is aware of the fact that the market for derivative instruments has expanded for state and local governments, which find themselves in a dismal budgetary environment. Some derivative contracts may pose substantial risks; therefore, the Board's aim is to help officials better explain those risks in their financial statements.

This Technical Bulletin requires that governments disclose the derivative's:

- Objectives.
- Terms.
- Fair value.
- Risks.

The proposed accounting guidance requires the governments to disclose in their financial statements what is faced in:

- Credit risk.
- Interest rate risk.
- Basis risk.
- Termination risk.
- Rollover risk.
- Market access risk.

This Technical Bulletin became effective for periods ending after June 15, 2003.

Chapter 11

Equity Strategies

CONTENTS

Because of the more widespread nature of investment by clients, the CPA/ personal financial specialist (PFS) must learn and know about equities and debt. In the 1950s, only wealthy people owned stocks and bonds. Now, all clients seem to have investments. For the CPA, there is a sea of licensing possibilities that are available on both a state and federal level to address these needs.

Many aspects of the license process have been made confusing as more and more investment titles have been created. The fate of AICPA special designations has been decided at least for the time being. In October 2003, the group's Governing Council voted to retain the three designations—the Personal Financial Specialist, Certified Information Technology Professional, and the Accredited in Business Valuation—in addition to earmarking $16 million in funding for them. They also approved a resolution by the Board to kill an annual review of the credentials, but agreed that the designations become self-supporting by specific dates, and attract a minimum number of credential holders.

The vote came on the final day of the Council's fall meeting in New Orleans and followed six months of exploring whether to keep the specialties within the AICPA organization.

The PFS must hit the break-even target on July 31, 2006, while the CITP and the ABV must reach that goal by July 31, 2008. At their break-even dates the PFS must have 3,600 holders, while the ABV and CITP must have 2,700 and 1,700, respectively. Currently there are 3,188 PFS holders, while the ABV and CITP have 1,536 and 527, respectively.

In its resolution, the Board offered funding recommendations for Personal Financial Planning ($4.6 million in excess of revenues through 2006), Information Technology ($5.6 million in excess of revenues through 2008), and Business Valuation/Forensic & Litigations Services ($5.75 million in excess of revenues through 2008). The Council adopted these recommendations.

Council also agreed with the Board's determination that retention strategies should not include a national branding campaign because of the cost and effort necessary to achieve that level of recognition. Rather, the AICPA has agreed to develop marketing tools to aid the credential holders in promoting the designations in their local markets.

The National Accreditation Commission (NAC), which oversees the credential programs, has decided that credential holders will receive annual statements on each designation as a quasi-progress report and that the commission would coordinate with the executive committee for each designation to map out implementation and marketing strategies.

The AICPA will develop a variety of resources to help credential-holding practitioners provide services to their clients and employers. The NAC will coordinate its activities with the executive committees of each underlying discipline to achieve an integrated approach to help members succeed in their specialty areas.

The National Association of Securities Dealers (NASD) administers all licenses for the Securities and Exchange Commission (SEC). However, even if the CPA elects not to pursue a PFS designation or any of the various financial services licenses, he or she had best be familiar with stocks, bonds, and their corresponding mutual funds—if only from the standpoint of self-defense!

What the Different Types of Stock Investments Offer

When the CPA/PFS discusses the types of stock investments that are available to the client, he or she must first look at what can be done for the client—the professional must define results. Results in the stock arena are measured in three ways: growth, income, and total return.

To make the best choice for the client, the CPA/PFS must know what these three goals mean and what they have to offer the client as an investor. Each offers something different:

- Growth increases net worth.
- Income is cash flow to the shareholder.
- Total return is a combination of both growth and income.

Examining each type of investor and providing an example of each may help matching a particular investor with the appropriate stocks.

The Growth Investor

Growth investors typically are those with an ongoing need to increase their net worth and are willing to accept some risk and volatility to accomplish this goal. A growth-oriented investor tends to be either middle class or wealthy. If the investor is wealthy, watching growth stocks is an enjoyable experience. If an investor is of moderate means, seeing a measurable increase year after year in net worth is exhilarating. However, the median investor must be more circumspect in choosing stock, because money is often illiquid and cannot be easily replaced. These investors should look back to when they had very little and should continue looking forward to when they will need a lot. The CPA/PFS needs to help median investors keep their feet firmly on the ground. They have little margin for error, especially when their time considerations are factored into the equation.

Growth stocks are what equity investments are all about. When they perform well, the world is seen through the snappiest rose-tinted glasses. For example, Mary Sue is an administrative manager working at a large computer sales company and makes $35,000 per year. She receives $10,000 per year from her widowed mother to put away for her children's education and often is able to supplement that with a portion of her annual bonus of $5,000 to $15,000. What kind of stocks should she buy for her children? Growth stocks. They have no need for current income, as they are students in school, but their needs for college are almost limitless. Mary Sue's plan of action should be to research and select industries she feels will provide real growth during her children's school years and start a portfolio of the industry leaders in her chosen groups.

She can consider as many industry groups as she wants, define her parameters, and start narrowing down her choices. With several good candidates, she then chooses stocks and proceeds to invest her money. She does not have to make perfect choices, but she should look for some research consensus about her selections.

The Income Investor

An income stock is not as glamorous as a growth stock, but it performs a noble function. It is very kind to one's standard of living because it generates a usable cash flow, cushions downturns in growth stocks, and provides a supplement to fixed income investments that neither increase dividends as earnings increase nor have a particularly high yield.

Aunt Sally is a representative income stock investor. During the Carter era, she was happy to roll over short- and intermediate-term fixed income instruments, such as Certificates of Deposit and Treasury Bills, but now the yield advantage of those investments is ancient history. Sally must turn to stocks because the inflation of the ensuing years has eroded the purchasing power of her remaining fixed income investments and she simply has to have more cash flow. For a number of reasons, stocks with big dividends are the answer. She is not happy about buying stock, but the advantages from an income standpoint far outweigh the risks.

The following are reasons for moving to a stock income portfolio:

- Income stocks pay higher yields than comparable fixed income investments because stock investments are more risky than bond investments — the yields are higher because there is no set rate or income for a set rate of time.

- Historically, successful income stocks tend to increase their dividends — a real plus for the income investor. As time and inflation marches on, the investor receives more and more dividends, which hopefully keep pace with her need for more income.

- The growth component inherent in stock investing cannot be ignored — if the value of the stocks appreciate, and should the need arise, some of the stock can be liquidated to generate cash for Sally. Her profits can then be used to pay her obligations.

The Total Return Investor

Total return stocks are the best of both worlds — growth increases net worth and income generates cash flow to supplement other income. It is prototypical money management because the growth and income stocks complement each other and are a balancing factor that is required by many investors. Most people have both net worth and income-sensitive concerns.

Phil is looking forward to retirement in several years. He has almost enough to live on happily in retirement, but he is worried about having to dip into his principle later in life. He is more than a little concerned about the future of Social Security, and whether his pension plan, which does not have cost-of-living adjustments, will be sufficient for future living expenses. Phil needs everything stock investment has to offer — growth and income.

Phil can afford to be moderately aggressive because he is well established for life. But he has to watch his balance. If he generates some decent dividend income before he needs it, he can use his cash flow to address his upcoming requirements later in life. He needs help in seeking out the highest-quality total return stocks the industry provides and starting to build positions in them now.

DETERMINING AN INVESTMENT PROFILE HELPS INVESTORS MAKE THE RIGHT CHOICES

Different personalities and incomes have different profiles. The extent to which clients are comfortable with risk cannot be overstated. The more clients and their CPA/PFSs learn about stocks, the more comfortable they can be with volatility when facing the long-term horizon. The more concerned a person is with risk, the more cautiously a person should ease into stock investment. Starting out, investments should be the most conservative, household name, investment grade stocks. As stock investors learn more about the market and are more comfortable with its volatility, they can expand their horizons. They can naturally progress to more risk-oriented investments, so they can realize a suitable return on their investments.

For the more savvy investors who know their own profile and their own needs well, the learning process has not ceased. They just simply have to look for more sophisticated strategies and techniques to accomplish their goals. Warren Buffet is the premier stock investor in history. Who thinks he is done learning? Not a chance — there are always ways to grow in this field.

FITTING STOCKS INTO AN INVESTMENT PLAN

The clients are all in different places with different goals for their financial plan, but the roads to success for everyone are actually very similar. Stocks fit all but the most conservative, short-term, risk-adverse investment profiles. For some, stocks are not an option until certain criteria related to debt and other financial obligations are met. But, once they are met, stocks are the best and sometimes the only way to reach their goals.

How does the CPA/PFS fit stock into an investment plan? Simply put, he or she calculates how much discretionary cash the clients have—what do they have, what do they owe, how much can they invest? It is always best to pay off all consumer debt first and then figure how much and for what purpose the clients wish to invest. This will require some financial planning on their part. Some generalizations about stock investing are true:

- The youthful investor has a strong growth bias. It is often easy to be too conservative with college savings plans and allow the seriousness of the task to inhibit the aggressiveness necessary to achieve the goal of making enough money.
- The middle-aged investor is often total return oriented. This is not only because of a more conservative bias toward some income, but also because the type of stocks middle-aged investors conventionally need and select are often total return stocks. Why? Cash must be generated, but a growing portfolio for the future is needed, too. The last three years have created a new generation of total return investors because so much equity has been lost.
- The mature investor overwhelming gravitates toward income stocks. The retired investor rarely reflects an aggressive growth profile because most wealth accumulation was accomplished during peak earnings years. This investor is more concerned with safety of principle and earning a decent, rather than spectacular, return on investments. Volatility is often very unsettling to mature investors, as it is reminiscent of the stock market crash of 1929 and the Great Depression.

Direct Investment Puts the Investor in Charge

Many people want to be the masters of their own fates. Direct investment allows people to rely upon everything they know about themselves and their world. Hunches, research, tips—are all figured in here.

For example, a mother actively involved with her four children's spending begins to notice a pattern in their consumer trends. She starts buying stocks in the various companies that provide the consumer goods that her children and their friends have shown the most loyalty to over their childhood years. She determines for herself the industry groups, companies, and weightings for each stock in the family portfolio.

Managed Accounts Let Investors Tap Experienced Advisors

Managed accounts help the investor stay in the driver's seat, but they will have—and need—an expert traveler to help on the trip. The CPA/PFS and the client can control the overall strategy, the investment parameters, the buying and selling level, and the asset allocation through the guidelines established for the manager. The professional and client tell the managers what they want and the manager will do it for them. Managed accounts are for people who have neither the time nor drive to acquire the knowledge needed to make a portfolio, but who can afford an advisor who will accomplish all this for them. Together, the CPA/PFS, client, and money manager can make a great team.

Mutual Funds Provide Diversity and Simplicity

Diversity is achieved through investing in many types of stock funds with many types of stocks in them. Simplicity is achieved with ease of investment and ease of understanding. Mutual funds take much of the work out of investing in stocks. The investors have one end of the stock spectrum to the other end of the stock spectrum all growing and playing in a system of checks and balances as the fund families compete for the investment dollar. They attempt to keep pace with whatever index their fund is pegged to — all the CPA/PFS has to do is select a fund, have the client provide a lump sum of money to start the position, continue to contribute money to this fund, if successful, and watch it grow. A merry-go-round to some, but to others, it is the only way to go. Managed money and mutual funds are the vehicle of choice if the client choses not to own individual stocks.

Index Funds Offer Proven Results

The CPA/PFS and client may know the indexes of stocks better than the stocks themselves. Furthermore, they may better know the indexes than the various mutual funds and their families. Everyone knows them as the Dow Jones Industrials, the S&P 500, the Value Line Index, and a host of other proprietary performance measurements. Almost any index (domestic and foreign) that anyone can name has a corresponding index fund available for retail investment. The returns on these funds are the returns on the indexes because the funds perfectly (less management fees) mirror the performance of the indexes they duplicate. Like conventional managed mutual funds, but even more so, the index funds take pressure off the investor because they not only remove stock picking from the investor area of responsibility but also the task of fund picking. All the investor does is pick an index and commit money — it is as simple as that. Indexes are good choices for both novice and experienced investors because their benefits for the investor are clear:

- They are "no brainer" investments.
- They have immense diversification.
- The costs of most index products are minimal.

- For some, index funds comprise the investor's plan of action for asset al-location — and asset allocation can be the key to an investor's success.

CHOOSING STOCK INVESTMENT STRATEGIES THAT WORK FOR THE CLIENT

There are many ways to invest in the stock market. What will be significant is the strategy that works for the client's personality and needs of the time. For-tunately, stock investment strategies that work well are plentiful. Clients will undoubtedly change their strategy as time changes their investment outlook. Knowing investment options and using these strategic tools will make invest-ing more interesting and financially rewarding for the client.

Investing for Appreciation: Building a Nest Egg

The first and most common strategy is growth investing. It offers the glis-tening opportunity of building a nest egg. Growth moves in mysterious ways. Even in the best of times and strongest of markets, many excellent stock fund managers underperform the benchmark stock indexes they are measured against. In contrast, it is much easier for bond fund managers to perform in the vicinity of their benchmarks. Bonds are much easier to successfully manage because there are fewer variables in the debt universe than there are in the eq-uity universe. Equity managers are stock pickers by choice, and it is hoped the CPA/PFS and their clients are doing it by choice, too.

Imagine that a client just read in the paper about a new company that cre-ated a running shoe sole that will last for years. The client is a runner and knows that no running shoe lasts longer than 300 miles, so the prospect of buying some of these shoes is very exciting. As a CPA/PFS, the immediate thought is that the client might be able to get in early on what might have enormous im-plications not only for running shoes, but for footwear per se. The first thing is to determine whether the shoe manufacturer is a publicly held company. Once the professional has done that, and discovered that the public can actually own the stock, the research process starts preparatory to investing in the company:

1. The CPA/PFS finds out what brokerage firms, if any, cover the stock.
2. The CPA/PFS calls and asks for copies of any available research reports.
3. The CPA/PFS reads the reports and, if they are positive, calls the share-holder relations area of the company and requests public data available on the company — quarterly and annual reports, balance sheets, financial statements, and publicity releases.

Once the CPA/PFS has digested all of this, and it appears to be a positive step, it is time to determine how much money the client is comfortable committing to the stock and then purchasing it.

Growth starts with ownership in a business that succeeds. What helps a business succeed? Following are some universal concepts of startups that become successful businesses and therefore growth stocks:

- There is a market for the product that the company sells. The existence of a product does not necessarily mean there is a market for that product.
- The product truthfully and successfully meets the needs of a ready market. The existence of a market does not necessarily mean there is a product for that market.
- The product is produced by a well-managed company, and the company provides an environment and opportunity for success for its employees and its product. The performance of the technical tasks necessary to the development of a product is totally different from the performance necessary for running a successful company. Managers are managers; inventors are inventors; salespeople are salespeople. It is necessary to determine whether the stock choice has strong divisions of power to support the overall excellence of the product.
- The company must be capable of functioning in the 21st century: management is not only personnel oriented but also now systems and processor oriented.

What does all this mean to the CPA/PFS as an advisor and the client as a stock investor? It means each can devote common sense to stock choices and become capable fundamental analysts. Fundamental analysts study, assess, and judge the overall strength of a company from every informational point of view imaginable. Although few in the public may ever be able to analyze figures that well, many can use instinctive judgments based on experience, learning, and observation.

A client comes to the CPA/PFS with a hot stock tip. What should the CPA/PFS do?

1. Check the performance of the stock—its past, its perceived future.
2. Check the company for strength and stability in today's market.
3. Check plans for the future. Does this stock have a plan and a place in tomorrow's market?
4. Determine need. A strong need is the fuel for success.
5. Determine competition—is something else out there to compare it to?

The growth goal is to hit home runs. The growth stock investor wants to increase money as quickly as possible. Although people often say they would be content with "a sustained period of growth with inflation-adjusted returns somewhat above Treasury rates," they are really often impatient. The CPA/PFS must never lose sight of the client's true goals.

Aggressive Investing: More Risk, More Potential

By looking at the most aggressive form of equity investment, venture capital (which is oriented toward seed money in various stages of an uncreated company's development), the CPA/PFS can gain a picture of what to look for in any type of stock. Stocks are often classed as investment grade, good quality, speculative, or high risk. Venture capital is in the high-risk category. The client initially may never think of plunking down hard-earned capital for a venture capital investment, but as the portfolio expands and securities knowledge grows, it is not uncommon for a client to discover the benefits of aggressive growth.

Angel investing is business startup financing. There are investment services throughout the United States that help match companies and investors in various equity projects in various stages of development. For example, Uncle Ed Jones has just invented a substance that will keep guns in storage clean and rust-free for years in any climate or environment. Hunters and target shooters throughout the county buy his goop and his family quickly realizes he has a niche product that is a telemarketing dream — cheap, easy to make, and appeals to lots of people. What to do now? None of them has either the capital or the expertise necessary to market Gun Goop. Where do they go and what do they do to set the wheels in motion? There are venture capital placement and financing services in every major city in the United States. Uncle Ed and the family find a silent partner and are on their way to becoming the gun collector's answer to rust and storage problems. If the company continues to succeed because of excellent management, marketing, and sales, a public offering may materialize.

Everyone would like to be part of an investment early in its growth cycle. However, startups are by definition the birth of a company; they are also long-term commitments that might go nowhere. Ideally, an equity investor selects companies that are building for a successful future, with a goal of having a good profit run for years.

What is there in these private capital activities that helps the CPA/PFS learn more about stock picking tasks? As the most selective investors in the world, venture capitalists look for the following qualities in a company, and so should CPAs/PFSs and their clients:

- The company's products have a broad, general appeal.
- The management teams are experienced in their company's product area. Regardless of the quality of the product, if the company fails, so will the stock.
- Today's technology is capable of handling the company's current needs and those of the intermediate future. Inventory and distribution are essential elements of business.

- There are excellent reasons for the consumer to buy the company's products. The cost is reasonable and the product is reliable.

- The company's revenues exceed expenses, and expenses are production generated. Value, not creative management, sells the product; it has been approved by the appropriate government agencies, and it can stand on its own as a successful product.

- The product is what started the company and the product remains the powerful source of revenue for the company, as opposed to creative number crunching.

Is it risky? Yes, of course. However, if the CPA/PFS is research oriented with an knowledge of marketing trends and opportunities, companies and economics, this may dramatically increase net worth for the clients.

Stock Investing for Income: Returns Investors Can Use Today

For the investor facing a conventional retirement dependent upon a combination of corporate or government pensions, Social Security, IRAs and 401(k)s, and personal savings, investing for income becomes increasingly significant as time passes.

From an asset allocation standpoint, the closer a person is to retirement, the larger cash flow needs may become. Cash flow, as previously stated, mitigates many of the unappealing aspects of stock investment.

Before discussing income stock investments, it is important to point out that some income-oriented stock investments can be less risky and safer investments than corporate bonds. Not only may the underlying credit rating services' opinions be higher, but with the potential of rising income from increased stock dividends, they pay better.

Investors often fail to understand that an income flow changes the longer-term appreciation pattern of stock investing into one of immediate rewards and gratification. Stocks that pay dividends pay them every quarter. Stocks, of course, lack a maturity, and the dividend can be reduced, so they do not have a stated fixed interest payment, as with bills, notes, or bonds. This is not necessarily a detriment. Investors often take smaller than expected fixed income interest payments because they are afraid to assume holding periods with maturities dictated by longer-term debt securities. However, that is a mistake — bills, notes, and bonds are fully as liquid as stocks and can be very volatile, especially in the longer maturities. Investors have a mind-set about fixed income investments that is totally foreign to the stock arena. The benefit to investors is that they can create a regular income stream that has the distinct possibility of increasing significantly in value as the years go by.

Dividend income flows are usually measured in two ways: they are (1) stated as a function of cash flow (the amount of dollars and cents of income that goes directly into the hands of the shareholder), or (2) as a dividend yield, which is a percentage expression of the current amount of the dividend in cash divided by the current value of the underlying stock that pays the dividend.

For example, the shareholder can earn a 4 percent yield at the time of investment in XYZ. He or she can expect this to continue indefinitely, with a reasonable expectation of having that dividend increased if the company prospers and the board of directors continue to care about satisfying its existing income-oriented shareholders and trying to attract new investors.

The board of directors of XYZ determines the whether, how much, and when of dividend payments. Particularly in the blue chip arena, dividend issues can be a major source of board and shareholder focus. To the board, dividend payments are often reflective of the board's ability to generate earnings and willingness to distribute some of these earnings to the shareholders. To the shareholders, dividends represent a tangible manifestation of their ownership of the stock of XYZ. If the stock increases in value, they are of course pleased; but their ability to do much with this increase in value is very limited unless they sell XYZ. This is certainly a poor way to reward XYZ and its board for going up in value.

Stock dividends are a continuing inducement every 13 weeks to continue to own XYZ — the clearest validation to stockholders of their investment ownership in the company.

A less tangible, but certainly important, benefit of dividend cash flow is that it tends to stabilize the price of a stock in a down market. Many times, a stock declining in value bottoms out, not because investors are no longer selling it, but because new investors are buying it for the cash flow. This is particularly the case with very large capitalization stocks that have a historically secure dividend with a regular record of increasing (or, at least, not reducing) these dividends. Knowledgeable investors are very aware of the bargains created when stocks decline in value that have not missed or reduced their dividends in decades or have increased their dividend payouts regularly for decades. These stocks generally bounce off 52-week lows or sharp market-related declines very quickly.

What this all means to an investor is that it is important to understand income stock investing. Income stock investing exemplifies cash flow management, the answer to almost every financial issue. The benefits to the investors are as many as they have uses for cash flow. Whether used to buy bread, reinvest in more securities, or give to a favorite charity, stock dividends are an immediate benefit of investing that anyone can appreciate.

Speculative Investments: Taking a Chance with Excess Funds

These stocks pay no dividends, often earn very little money, and can be depended upon to seesaw in price with mind-numbing regularity. However, as they trade through ranges of higher highs and, as is hoped, higher lows, the investor can benefit from rapidly accelerating price appreciation that could never be realized in more staid, blue chip growth, income, or total return stocks. Speculation often has a negative connotation, but the fact remains that a great deal of wealth in this country was created by investing in speculative growth companies. The U.S. government and Internal Revenue Service are fully cognizant of the value of this type of investing. They encourage it by the favorable tax treatment of stock gains.

At the other end of the spectrum are speculative recovery situations in blue chip fallen angels. The domestic automotive industry, domestic computer hardware industry, and international money center bank stocks are examples of industry groups that have seen primary constituents collapse over the years. However, phoenix-like, they have sprung from their own ashes to achieve extraordinary levels of return for their steely nerved value investors.

The most popular speculative stocks are the lower-priced, over-the-counter "story" stocks. They are often perceived by their investors as undiscovered gems that will become the blue chip index stocks of the future. They usually have no solid track record of earnings, products, or performance, but they are as long on expectations as they are short on results. They usually have a need to generate cash flow and have no idea from whence it will appear. Nevertheless, sometimes, they develop a product that changes the world.

Many types of aggressively traded speculative and high-risk vehicles are usually unprofitable. Whereas for some, penny stock, option, futures, and hard asset trading may be genuinely appealing, unless these investments are traded under expertly managed conditions, it is likely the retail speculator will lose every cent invested. As a confirmation of this cautionary statement, it is difficult for the conventional retail client to gain approval from a wire house, discount, or bank brokerage firm to trade these vehicles. However, the primary benefit to the investor is that these securities and others contained in high-risk managed money portfolios do sometimes generate enormous trading profits. The road can be extraordinarily bumpy, but there are widely available, fully audited, remarkably profitable portfolios for the CPA/PFS to investigate should these techniques and strategies have appeal to a client. For the investor who is predisposed toward extreme risk and volatility, the return that can be earned on these investments may dramatically enhance the cumulative return of the total portfolio.

To conclude, when analyzing high-risk investments, the distinction between speculation and gambling may seem nonexistent. However, there is a genuine difference between the two. Speculation involves a measurement of risk and reward parameters, whereas gambling is often a chance, random event based on luck. Speculation is attractive to investors because some of the largest capitalization stocks in existence were recently speculative stocks with names familiar to basically no one.

The investor is trying to become someone who puts money into investments that will earn a reasonable and regular return consistent with that investment. Over the long term, investors look to both appreciation and income to resolve financial issues. The mind-set a speculator must cultivate with speculative investments is a totally short-term view that revolves around actively trading securities. The benefits to the securities investor are abundantly clear — quick profits. Although the risks are more immediate and apparent than with long-term investments, the truth is that the potential rewards are enough to overcome any objections for some people.

Successfully Coping with Market Fluctuations

Risk concerns become most stressful when the client addresses the area of market timing. Ideally, investors want to invest money in the stock market and receive an excellent return on their investment commensurate with their risk-to-reward profiles. Market timing is the notion that an investor buys at the trough of a down cycle in price. This way, the investor earns more than by simply buying when there is money to invest. The equity investor of today attempts to identify when the market is at its peak, but no one can truly do this. A successful investor is aware of various techniques and patterns that provoke a course of action when markets fluctuate excessively and threaten to undermine the most determined investor's confidence.

Study after study shows that market timing works only in hindsight; the long-term investor usually makes money, regardless of timing. From an asset allocation standpoint, what is important is that the investor is invested. The key is to own stock, but, how does one cope with market fluctuations?

Historically, bear markets have been brief. Until the last three years, corrections have been sharp and of a relatively brief duration. The worst nightmare is to invest at a peak, have a sudden correction in the market and prices drop, and have another three-year bear market begin. There is no corrective action the investor can take, but doing nothing is actually doing something. When invested in good-quality growth companies, the client has bought in for the long term. To be proactive in a bear market, the client must continue to invest, as money becomes available or even systematically. This is known as dollar-cost averaging. The virtue of repeated investing at regular intervals is that, if there is a long-term upward trend, in time the investor makes money. If clients are not out for a quick killing in the market, or they have not borrowed on margin to invest, or their immediate livelihood is not predicated on the performance of this investment, time is a friend.

For example, dollar-cost averaging results in buying more shares in down markets and fewer shares in up markets. Volatility is advantageous, because the client would never buy at the lowest lows if securities never changed in value. Indeed, a narrow trading band does not benefit dollar-cost averaging, because the security is trading near its median price.

To illustrate, David buys XYZ stock regardless of its price every month. If he buys $1,000 per month and his stock is $100 per share at the start of the year, goes up to $120 per share, down to $60 per share, and finishes out the year back at $100 per share, what does David accomplish? David can end up with about 10 percent more shares than if the stock traded only up or down $10, because he never would have bought his inexpensive shares. In the long run, David ends up owning many more shares of XYZ.

VALUE AND GROWTH STOCK INVESTING

Both value and growth have strengths and weaknesses. There are no perfect solutions for investment, or there would be only a few investments from which to choose. Fortunately, there are plenty of investments available to earn the client's money. Three basic characteristics of value and growth help summarize their styles:

1. Value focuses on past performance to determine what is undervalued; growth is very forward looking to project anticipated earnings momentum.
2. Value opportunities are created by the predictably bad behavior of investors; growth opportunities depend on corporate management to make the right decisions to fulfill expectations.
3. Value focuses on out-of-favor basic industries that are staples of society; growth looks at glamour industries for explosive returns.

The CPA/PFS can work through stocks' realistic possibility of increase based on these parameters. This exercise will narrow the field and offer direction toward attainable goals as clients choose to buy stock.

Value Stock Investing

A traditional solution for a bear market is for the CPA/PFS to look for relative value every time the investor makes a securities purchase. The difficulty lies in defining "value." The answer is to buy a quality stock that has rising earnings prospects; that is, it is selling at a discount to itself, its industry group, or the market. This applies to individual stocks, groups, or even markets.
Several examples of value investing follow:

- A stock has had bad earnings because of a one-time charge against earnings for a write-off. Ignoring long-term excellent prospects, institutional investors sell the stock and in one week the stock is off 20 percent. The stock is an A rated equity by Standard & Poor's, analysts still like its long-term appreciation potential, and the stock's 2 percent dividend is perceived as secure. For value and fundamental analytical reasons, the CPA/PFS selects it and the client buys it.

- A group of software stocks has lagged the market. Every time the group starts to rally, one of the companies announces bad earnings, has some negative event, or runs afoul of regulatory agencies. Because the CPA/PFS decides the product the group provides is essential to the United States, he or she picks several of the best stocks in the group, and clients buy them.

- A country has settled its differences with its neighbors and a new government has taken power thanks to supervised elections. The new leaders embrace capitalism wholeheartedly and immediately move to privatize (sell to the public through a stock offering) the telephone company of this emerging nation. Clients buy the stock on the offering. They consider the telephone company a proxy for the whole country, whose prospects the CPA/PFS analyzes and likes. The CPA/PFS considers this an index for the country's fledgling market and concludes that it will take off during this period of enlightened rule.

Much can go wrong, which is why there are always contrary convictions. Because there is a case for three hypothetical investments, playing devil's advocate helps explain when not to make these investments. These are the cases for not investing in any of the preceding three choices:

1. The client decides not to buy the stock. The CPA/PFS decides not to endorse the stock because of its 20 percent drop in one week. They are not totally confident of the company's long-term prospects, because no analyst expected this write-off. What bad news will the next announcement bring?

2. The client decides against investing in stocks in this underperforming software group. A chain is only as strong as its weakest link. The CPA/PFS cannot decide whether it is profit margins, management, or the cost of financing, but there is something wrong.

3. The client decides to look at another country for foreign investment. The new government seems open to U.S. involvement, but what if they receive all this cash and nationalizes its telephone company again? Even if the government is stable, emerging markets regularly collaspe and close for months on end.

Investors must constantly evaluate the risk-to-reward parameters of value stocks. If they are engaged in direct investment, they must continually draw conclusions on examples like these. If the clients have managed money or mutual funds, the portfolio manager is responsible for making these decisions.

Growth Stock Investing

If value investing and all it entails seems too demanding, perhaps the investor is better suited to investing for growth. Growth stocks show great earnings momentum. They are concentrated in the glamour stocks that are all household names, rather than in the fallen angels of esoteric industries that are impossible to understand.

Following are some pithy investment ideas for growth stocks:

- Buy USA! In a risk-averse world, the only safe place to invest money is in the United States. Here is where the earnings are. Every other country is subject to high risk, and why assume more risk than the minimum needed to take the investors where they want to go?
- Buy technology! In a post-industrial society, all that matters is information services. Brains are more important than brawn and technology is where the brains are. Who cares about the last three years—it will all work out over time.

Once again, as with value investing, what can go wrong? The answer is plenty. Look at the other side of the coin:

- Buy foreign! Many foreign markets have outperformed the U.S. markets. They will continue to do so as long as they continue to develop at the extraordinary rate of growth they have demonstrated for the past decade.
- Forget about technology! The margins in the high-tech industries have shrunk to such an extent that it is impossible to accurately forecast earnings for any of these companies. The technology area soon will be left with only nine or ten companies. The rest will vanish.

HIGH-QUALITY VERSUS LOW-QUALITY STOCKS

If the investor would rather not juggle value versus growth, another stock strategy is selecting high-quality versus low-quality stocks. Low-quality stocks in theory provide significantly greater returns over time because the investor assumes more risk. Unfortunately, this approach can be disappointing. Sometimes, low-quality stocks, when price/earnings ratios are compared, trade at a premium to quality. Therefore, investors have a good chance of losing significantly more money than they can make because they have paid for the privilege of assuming more risk. That is a lose-lose proposition if ever there was one. If the investors have bought low-quality stock, when the high- and low-quality stocks start to trade in line again, the investors may lose in another way. Their low-quality stocks come back to the mean, in addition to underperforming the good-quality stocks. From a commonsense standpoint, most people cannot address such issues because most people simply do not have several dozen (let alone hundreds) of stock positions. The primary benefit of understanding high-quality versus low-quality stock is to gain an understanding of which types of mutual funds to invest in either inside of or outside of a self-directed retirement plan. Although value and growth questions are not too much of an issue with fund choices, most conservative stock funds are of high quality, and most speculative stock funds are of low quality. When it is time for the CPA/PFS to vote with the client's money, the CPA/PFS and clients must choose the quality with which they feel most comfortable.

SMALL, MIDDLE, AND LARGE CAPITALIZATION STOCKS

The CPA/PFS could take a totally different tack and decide to concentrate on selecting weightings between small, mid, and large capitalization stocks. Such stocks define the size of a company. Small capitalization stocks are stocks of up to $10 billion in size, mid caps are up to $100 billion, and large caps can be as much as $500 billion in value of outstanding shares. The larger the capitalization, the larger the trading volume and the better the liquidity. Larger capitalization stocks have more research and media coverage than do small caps. However, small and mid cap stocks traditionally have greater gain potential. It is possible to make a modest investment and have a sizable windfall profit within a few years' time in these less-well-known stocks.

Small cap stocks have historically outperformed large cap stocks, but for the last few years, large cap stocks have survived better than small cap stocks. Some calculate that the earnings streams of small cap are more dependable than large cap because their revenues are not dependent on foreign countries for income. In some corrections, the entire episode seemed to be generated by foreign markets. However, the thought of concentrating on small cap stocks can be dangerous. The professional knows that most small and mid cap stocks are over-the-counter stocks. The NASDAQ, where these stocks are traded, has suffered drastic losses in the past few years.

SOLUTIONS

Solutions are not simple. After examining value and growth, high-quality versus low-quality, and small, medium, and large capitalization stocks, the CPA/PFSs and their clients may feel overwhelmed. There are pitfalls, but stock investing can be financial rewarding for the clients and their families. Historically, large-company stocks return about 10 percent per year and small company stocks return 12 percent per year. Treasury bills return about 3 percent, long-term bonds about 6 percent. What matters ultimately is that an investor own stock. The CPA/PFS must determine with the client a comfort level with risk and reward parameters and then create a stock investment plan that is consistent with this risk profile. With the help of the CPA/PFS, clients must invest money and leave it invested, periodically add to their portfolio, and consider the long term. All these equity investment approaches work over time to a greater or lesser degree — that is why they exist. The benefits of stock investing ultimately outweigh the risks over an extended time period.

CONTROLLING RISK THROUGH DIVERSIFICATION

What do the institutional money managers responsible for managing multibillion dollar portfolios and funds do with money? The best lessons in the investment world come from success stories. Modern money management, despite many well-publicized fiascoes, is doing a better job of generating profits and managing risk for clients. Investors can learn a lot from what is applicable to the retail stock portfolio. In the past few years, money managers have attempted to "style invest," which is rotating between value and growth. However, the attempt to correctly time switching between value and growth is only marginally less frustrating than trying to define the styles themselves. Understanding what they are trying to do has clear benefits to stock investors because money management issues are a macrocosm of everything individual investors are trying to accomplish.

Style switchers try to invest in the up cycle of whichever style — value or growth — is outperforming the other. For example, if there is a perception that blue chip basic industry stocks have hit their peak, managers switch over to explosive growth, small capitalization, over-the-counter stocks. When value outperforms, growth underperforms — there is a cycle to that performance. There is a reversal and growth outperforms value. The managers then reverse direction and sell their small caps and go back to the large caps. Market timing is anything but neutral — it is totally subjective, because investors are completely dependent on the manager's insights to switch styles. This method is not foolproof. Sometimes the waxing and waning of value and growth only reveals itself in hindsight.

CONSTRUCTING A STOCK PORTFOLIO THAT MAKES SENSE

The CPA/PFS is looking for the accurate equity portion of the client's asset allocation. This is not as difficult as it sounds, because there are standard measurements available. From a securities standpoint, the number of different types of investors is by no means infinite. The investor should look for interlocking relationships between a number of different, conventional financial planning characteristics. The financial planning process can address the issues of stock selection.

The CPA/PFS must initially address age, net worth, income, retirement, and educational needs. The benefit of considering these characteristics for investors is that these considerations force them to quantify their seemingly subjective financial profile into totally objective numbers. Then the CPA/PFS and the clients determine what needs to be done. "What needs to be done" determines the type of stock portfolio the client constructs and the selection of the investments that go into that portfolio.

Furthermore, job stability and tenure, expected inheritances, and counterbalancing of financial needs and desires all affect stock blend. Although there is no need to assume more risk than needed to reach goals, the situation may dictate that the way to achieve these ends is to assume a more aggressive stance than the client might otherwise deem acceptable.

The CPA/PFS as a Star Stock Picker

The keys to success in stock investing are as follows:

1. *Invest for the long haul.* The client as an investor becomes a long-term position builder. Not everyone has the money or the inclination to become involved in a systematic investment plan. But, the CPA/PFS must approximate that system, as it is what works best and makes the most money for the client.

2. *Invest in quality earnings streams.* The CPA/PFS must make the right selection to start building the client's positions. The way to create wealth is to determine the right choices, either of stocks, money managers, or funds, and hold them as long as they show appropriate growth. Stock performance is a direct reflection of earnings growth expectations.

3. *Stay invested.* Clients will see downswings. Given the extreme cyclical nature of investing, they will also have the opportunity to revel in upswings.

4. *Once a decision has been made, run with it.* Stock prices often are a reflection of variables neither the CPA/PFS nor their clients can control. Clients must remember why they bought their shares but be alert to any changes within the company other than the price of the stock.

Investment Rationale

There is a longstanding belief that markets are somehow removed from the economies in which they are located. The adherents to this theory believe that markets behave in a random pattern and are reflective of nothing. This could not be further from the truth. Markets are efficient processors of information and respond to all the information an economy provides them. Critics have complained many times that governments become slaves to their financial markets, but markets clearly reflect investors' opinions of the effectiveness of governments.

Therefore, as an investment professional, CPA/PFSs must accommodate these vagaries into their clients' investment and asset allocation plans. The CPA/PFS cannot respond to upswings and downturns. He or she must remain optimistic that the client's money is where it belongs and have faith in the system that accommodates these markets. The key to success in equity investment is the continued accumulation of quality holdings that become larger and larger positions with a lower and lower cost basis.

How the CPA/PFS and Clients Put It All Together

Professionals cultivate discipline and responsibility. Regardless of whether clients use a simple or complex plan, professionals must cultivate discipline and responsibility. Professional behavior is far more important than style because it has a far greater impact on the clients' long-term performance results. The ways to establish behavior characterized by discipline and responsibility are the following:

1. Complete a financial plan.
2. Establish a clear risk profile.
3. Know the client.
4. Pick a strategy that is suitable for the client.
5. Find research to explain, support, and expand the strategy.
6. Invest the client's money in a few well-chosen stocks.
7. Continue to search for and identify new candidates.
8. Listen to and talk with other professionals, shareholders, and investors, but use them as guides, not leaders.
9. Keep the long-term view in mind.
10. Look for consumer trends that support or refute stock picks.

To maintain professional standing, CPAs/PFSs should be aware that:

- Traders pay a lot of unnecessary brokerage fees, which affects performance negatively.
- Sellers generate capital gains tax liabilities.

- Hot trend followers tend to escalate their risk parameters with each failure and ultimately lose money.
- Strategies that require a lot of time, reading, and computer work are by definition too elaborate for most investors.
- Excessive diversification usually is for giant mutual funds that are regulated by the SEC.

It is impossible to know whether any long-term strategy will continue to be successful, but the strategies examined above have enjoyed historic and present successes. With reasonable diversification, disciplined investment, and a responsible approach to methodology, investors should earn excellent long-term results and achieve all of their long-term goals.

Chapter 12

The Jobs and Growth Tax Relief Reconciliation Act of 2003

CONTENTS

The goal of The Jobs and Growth Tax Relief Reconciliation Act of 2003, which was signed into law May 22, 2003, is to stimulate the economy. The way the law is designed to stimulate the economy is with tax cuts that have two stated purposes: to encourage investing and to encourage spending.

TAX REDUCTIONS

The new bill puts into place the following tax reductions that begin immediately:

- Reduce the actual tax brackets.
- Reduce the marriage penalty.
- Increase the child credit earlier than planned.
- Lower taxes on dividends.
- Lower taxes on capital gains.

Although most Americans will feel the effect of these new tax reductions right away, virtually all of them have none-too-distant expiration clauses that result in their disappearance down the road in several years. Some expire as soon as December 31, 2004, so they are truly short-term measures specifically meant to stimulate the economy, rather than exhaustive, permanent tax revisions. Tax cuts with "Cinderella" or "sunset" provisions are a direct, but not permanent, means of stimulating the economy without incurring huge budget deficits. Details for the five provisions follow.

Reduce Actual Tax Brackets (Tax Rates).   The new tax rates are 25, 28, 33, and 35 percent. These replace the current tax rates of 27, 30, 35, and 38.6 percent.

Reduce the Marriage Penalty.   The basic standard deduction for married taxpayers filing a joint return is two times the basic standard deduction amount for single taxpayers for 2003 and 2004. The new law is then scheduled to phase out after 2004 and revert to the much-maligned present law; therefore, the new law is in effect from January 1, 2003, to January 1, 2005. In 2005, the standard deduction for married taxpayers will fall to 174 percent of the standard for single taxpayers and then gradually increase to double the amount by 2009. For 2003, the standard deduction for single taxpayers remained at $4,750. The standard deduction for married taxpayers will rise to $9,500. Married taxpayers filing a separate return will have the same standard deduction as a single person.

For 2003 and 2004, the 15-percent tax bracket is twice that for joint filers as for single filers. After 2004, the 15-percent tax bracket drops to 180 percent of the maximum taxable income in the same bracket for unmarried taxpayers, as adjusted for inflation.

Increase Child Credits.   The child credit is immediately increased from $600 to $1,000. The credit remains in place for 2003 and 2004. After 2004, the child credit reverts to the current level. The increased amount of $400 will be paid up front to the taxpayer. The taxpayers will be informed July 23, July 30, and August 6 of 2003 of their advance payment amount. The credit, however, is reduced for individuals who make $75,000 and joint filers who make $110,000.

Lower Taxes on Dividends.   Dividends are taxed exactly as ordinary income for the taxpayer. President George W. Bush has tried many times to eliminate this taxation completely. In a compromise, the new law reduces the taxation rate on dividends to 15 percent for taxpayers in the 25-percent bracket and higher and reduces the rate to 5 percent for taxpayers in the 10- and 15-percent brackets. These rates will remain in place through 2007 and drop to zero in 2008, but return to the pre-new act rates in 2009. The dividends are described as those received from domestic and qualified foreign corporations. The tax treatment covers both regular and alternative minimum tax (AMT).

Lower Taxes on Capital Gains.   The law allows capital gains to be taxed at the same rates for the same time periods as dividends. The tax treatment also covers both regular tax and AMT. The definition of "capital gain" as "assets held more than one year" remains the same.

The administration hopes that changing the way dividends and capital gains are taxed will stimulate investment in dividend-paying common stock as an alternative to conventional debt securities. Although they are two very different investments, what is bound to be the case is that publicly held companies will reconsider their dividend policies. Those that pay them may increase them; those that do not pay them may start declaring them. Reducing capital gains taxes will have a profound effect on the way investors look at holding periods because the gap is narrowed between short-term and long-term gains.

ADDITIONAL PROVISIONS

Although little publicity has been attached to anything but individual concerns, the agreement also provides some fiscal relief on a temporary basis to the state governments. There is a $10 billion fund established, divided equally among the states, to be utilized for essential government services. In addition, another $10 billion fund has been set up for Medicaid needs. This provision goes into effect immediately.

Qualified small business stock sales have had their capital gain exclusion revised upward. Currently, 21 percent of an investor's total realized gain from selling or exchanging small business stock is used in the computation of alternative minimum taxable income (AMTI). The new law has only 3.5 percent used in the computation of AMTI.

Last, corporations get a two-week delay on their estimated tax deadline. The deadline is immediately moved from September 15, 2003, to October 1, 2003.

BENEFITS AND DRAWBACKS FOR TAXPAYERS

There are both benefits and drawbacks for taxpayers. The benefits are:

- Reduction in current income tax rates.
- Reduction in capital gains rates on capital assets.
- Reduction in the personal holding company tax rate to 15 percent.

The drawbacks are specific to fewer individuals, to say the least:

- Carryover securities losses are worth less because gains are taxed less.
- Collectible sales, such as of stamps and coins, are still subject to a 28-percent capital gain rate.
- Depreciable real estate with an unrecaptured Section 1250 gain is subject to a 25-percent rate.

Chapter 13

Saving for a Higher Education

CONTENTS

Education-related tax breaks come in three varieties—deductions, credits, and income exclusions—each with its limitations and restrictions. Some can be used together; some are mutually exclusive. Some change incrementally each year; some the government changes arbitrarily. Some are federal; some are state.

Confused? Just imagine what the client is thinking . . . and join the club. Take the state-offered College 529 plans. With more than 40 plans sold nationwide by individual states, they include an ever-changing array of state tax implications, a wide range of fees, and everything from an average portfolio with conservative returns to high-risk mutual fund investments. It's a jungle out there.

Federally, the IRS delineates education-related adjustments to income. The guidelines are fairly clear. However, which to use, when and whether you can use multiple adjustments, is not. This is mostly because each individual and the circumstances are different. That is where the financial advisor earns his or her money.

There are dozens of Internet Web sites that compare and contrast many of these college plans, showing up-to-the minute changes and excellent definitions of each plan. As always, reader beware. Web sites are for educational purposes only and usually present one side of a discussion — it is important to check the credibility of the Web site and it authors.

IRS Changes for 2003

Three important changes are taking place in 2003:

1. The amount of qualified tuition and related expenses allowed in figuring the lifetime learning credit has increased from $5,000 to $10,000. The credit will equal 20 percent of these qualified expenses, with the maximum credit being $2,000.
2. The income ranges for phasing out the student loan interest deduction may be adjusted annually for inflation.
3. There will be no excise tax on excess contributions if the excess and its earnings are withdrawn before the beginning of the sixth month following the year of the contribution.

Employer-Provided Educational Assistance

Employers may provide their workers with as much as $5,250 a year in tax-free educational assistance benefits. This tax benefit now applies to graduate-level courses, as well as undergraduate courses.

Qualified Tuition Programs (QTPs)

Many states now offer programs that allow individuals to prepay a student's tuition or contribute to a higher education savings account. These tax benefits related to such programs also apply to tuition prepayment programs offered by qualifying private educational institutions. As before, payments or contributions to a QTP are not deductible. However, numerous changes in the past two years have increased the tax benefits of distributions from QTPs.

Students receiving tax-free benefits from QTPs will also be allowed to claim the Hope or Lifetime Learning Credits or receive a tax-free distribution from a Coverdell Education Savings Account (ESA), as long as the same expenses are not used for more than one of these benefits.

Taxable distributions not used for qualified higher education expenses are generally subject to an additional 10 percent tax.

Distributions from State-Maintained QTPs

A distribution from a QTP established and maintained by a state (or an agency or instrumentality of the state) can be excluded from income if the amount distributed is used for higher education. Previously, the beneficiary was required to pay tax on any earnings from a QTP unless the earnings were tax free under some other provision of the law.

QTPs Maintained by Educational Institutions

An individual can make contributions to a QTP established and maintained by one or more eligible educational institutions. Any earnings distributed before January 1, 2004, will be taxable. Previously, contributions could be made only to a QTP established and maintained by a state (or an agency or instrumentality of the state).

Rollovers of QTPs to Family Members

For purposes of rollovers, and changes of designated beneficiaries, the definition of family members is expanded to include first cousins of the original beneficiary.

A qualifying family member may become a designated beneficiary, or an amount rolled over to a family member's QTP within 60 days of distribution, without tax consequences.

Rollovers of QTPs without Changing Beneficiary

Amounts in a QTP can be rolled over, tax free, to another QTP set up for the same beneficiary. However, the rollover of credits or other amounts from one QTP to another QTP for the benefit of the same beneficiary cannot apply to more than one transfer within any 12-month period.

Qualified Expenses

Calculation of the amount that is considered reasonable for room and board expenses has been changed. The dollar limits for qualifying room and board expenses for students living off-campus now reflect the qualifying educational institution's published "cost of attendance" amounts. The taxpayer must contact the educational institution for their qualified room and board costs.

Special Needs Beneficiaries

The definition of "qualified higher education expenses" has been expanded to include expenses of a special needs beneficiary that are necessary for that person's enrollment or attendance at an eligible institution.

Coordination with Coverdell ESAs

Someone can make contributions to QTPs and Coverdell ESAs (the new name for Education IRAs) in the same year for the same beneficiary. Previously, contributions could be made to only one program or the other.

COVERDELL ESAs (FORMERLY EDUCATION IRAs)

Coverdell Education Savings Accounts—formerly known as Education IRAs—do not give any immediate tax benefit, but they allow beneficiaries to accrue tax-free earnings for qualifying educational expenses. There have been numerous changes to ESAs in the past two years, including:

- Qualifying educational expenses now include certain elementary and secondary school costs.
- College students who use Coverdell ESA funds may also claim the Hope or Lifetime Learning Credits, as long as the credits are claimed for different expenses than those paid from the ESA funds.
- Although most beneficiaries must use up their ESA accounts before age 30 or transfer them to a qualified relative, there is no longer an age limit for special needs beneficiaries.

Contributions

The most an individual can contribute each year to a Coverdell ESA is $2,000. If taxpayers file a joint return, the amount they can contribute to a Coverdell ESA will be gradually reduced if their modified adjusted gross income (MAGI) is more than $190,000 but less than $220,000. They will not be able to contribute to a Coverdell ESA if their MAGI is $220,000 or more.

The original due date of the contributor's tax return is the deadline for contributions for the current year. For most individuals, that means an April 15th deadline for the previous year.

A beneficiary may have contributions made to both a Coverdell ESA and a state tuition program in the same year.

Qualified Expenses

The definition of qualified education expenses has been expanded to include elementary and secondary education expenses. Qualified elementary and secondary education expenses include expenses for:

- Tuition, fees, academic tutoring, special needs services in the case of a special needs beneficiary, books, supplies, and other equipment incurred in connection with enrollment or attendance as an elementary or secondary school student at a public, private, or religious school.
- Room and board, uniforms, transportation, and supplementary items and services (including extended day programs) that are required or provided by a public, private, or religious school in connection with such enrollment or attendance.
- The purchase of computer technology or equipment or Internet access and related services if such technology, equipment, or services are to be used by the beneficiary and the beneficiary's family during any of the years the beneficiary is in school (not including expenses for computer software designed for sports, games, or hobbies unless the software is predominantly educational in nature).

Special Needs Beneficiaries

The taxpayer can continue to make contributions to a Coverdell ESA for a special needs beneficiary after his or her 18th birthday. A person can also leave assets in a Coverdell ESA set up for a special needs beneficiary after the beneficiary reaches age 30.

Coordination with Hope and Lifetime Learning Credits

A person can claim the Hope or lifetime learning credit in the same year he or she takes a tax-free distribution from a Coverdell ESA, provided the distribution from the Coverdell ESA is not used for the same expenses for which the credit is claimed. Previously, an individual could not claim the Hope or lifetime learning credit if he or she received a tax free withdrawal from a Coverdell ESA and did not waive the tax-free treatment of the withdrawal.

Coordination with Qualified Tuition Programs

The taxpayer can make contributions to Coverdell ESAs and qualified tuition programs in the same year for the same beneficiary. Previously, contributions could be made to only one program or the other.

New Deduction for Higher Education Expense

Beginning in 2002, taxpayers might have been able to deduct qualified tuition and related expenses paid during the year for themselves, their spouse, or a dependent, even if they did not itemize deductions.

Qualified tuition and related expenses are tuition and fees required for enrollment or attendance at an eligible educational institution. They may be paid for the expenses of:

- The taxpayer.
- The taxpayer's spouse.
- A dependent for whom the taxpayer claims an exemption.

Student activity fees and fees for course-related books, supplies, and equipment are included in qualified tuition and related expenses only if the fees must be paid to the institution as a condition of enrollment or attendance.

An eligible educational institution is any college, university, vocational school, or other postsecondary educational institution eligible to participate in a student aid program administered by the Department of Education. This encompasses virtually all accredited, public, nonprofit, and proprietary (privately owned, profit-making) postsecondary institutions. (The particular educational institution should be able to tell the taxpayer if it is an eligible educational institution.)

A person must reduce qualified expenses by the amount of any tax-free educational assistance received. Tax-free educational assistance includes:

- Scholarship.
- Pell grants.
- Employer-provided educational assistance.
- Veterans' educational assistance.
- Any other nontaxable payments (other than gifts, bequests, or inheritances) received for education expenses.

Expenses that are not considered "qualified tuition and related expenses" include the cost of:

- Medical expenses (including student health fees).
- Insurance.
- Room and board.
- Transportation.
- Similar personal, living, or family expenses.

This is true even if the fee must be paid to the institution as a condition of enrollment or attendance.

Qualified tuition and related expenses generally do not include expenses that relate to any course of instruction or other education that involves sports, games, or hobbies, or any noncredit course. However, if the course of instruction or other education is part of the student's degree program, these expenses can qualify.

Maximum Deduction

For tax years beginning in 2002 and 2003, the taxpayer may be able to deduct as much as $3,000 paid for qualified tuition and related expenses as an adjustment to income. For 2004 and 2005, he or she may be able to deduct $4,000.

Income Limits

For tax years beginning in 2002 and 2003, the CPA may deduct as much as $3,000 of qualified tuition and related expenses if the MAGI is not more than $65,000 ($130,000 on a joint return). If the MAGI is more than $65,000 ($130,000 on a joint return), the CPA cannot take the deduction.

For tax years beginning in 2004 and 2005, the taxpayer may deduct as much as $4,000 of qualified tuition and related expenses if the MAGI is not more than $65,000 ($130,000 on a joint return). If the MAGI is more than $65,000 ($130,000 on a joint return) but not more than $80,000 ($160,000 on a joint return), the accountant may deduct up to $2,000 of qualified tuition and related expenses. If the MAGI is more than $80,000 ($160,000 on a joint return), the deduction cannot be taken.

For purposes of this deduction, the MAGI is the adjusted gross income shown on the taxpayer's income tax return plus any foreign earned income exclusion, foreign housing exclusion or deduction, exclusion of income for bona fide residents of American Samoa, and exclusion of income from Puerto Rico.

Coordination with Credits and Other Deductions

The taxpayer cannot deduct any amount for qualified tuition and related expenses for a year if:

- A Hope credit or lifetime learning credit is claimed with respect to expenses of the individual for whom the tuition and related expenses were paid.
- The expense can be deducted under any other provision of the law.

Coordination with Exclusions

The CPA must reduce the qualified tuition and related expenses by:

- Expenses used to figure the amount of interest on qualified U.S. savings bonds that the taxpayer excluded from income because it was used to pay qualified higher education expenses.
- Expenses used to figure the amount of any tax-free withdrawals from a Coverdell ESA.
- Expenses used to figure the portion of any distribution of earnings from a qualified tuition program a person excludes from income because the earnings were used to pay the beneficiary's qualified higher education expenses.

Limits on Eligibility

The student cannot claim the deduction for qualified tuition and related expenses if any of the following applies:

- Another taxpayer is entitled to claim an exemption for that individual as a dependent on his or her return. This is true even if the other taxpayer does not actually claim the exemption.
- The filing status is married filing separate return.
- The student is a nonresident alien and has not elected to be treated as a resident alien for the tax year.

Year of Deduction

Generally, the taxpayer can deduct only those expenses for a year that are in connection with enrollment at an institution of higher education during the same year. However, it is possible to deduct expenses paid in a year if they are for an academic period beginning within the year or during the first three months of the next year.

Student Name and ID Number

To take the deduction, the taxpayer must show on the income tax return the name and taxpayer identification number (usually the Social Security number) of the person for whom the expenses were paid.

Termination

This new deduction is not available for tax years beginning after 2005.

STUDENT LOAN INTEREST DEDUCTION

If the taxpayer pays interest on a student loan, the CPA may be able to deduct the interest as an adjustment to income.

Limit on Deduction Based on MAGI

Beginning in 2002, the amount of the taxpayer's student loan interest deduction will be phased out if the modified adjusted gross income is between $50,000 and $65,000 ($100,000 and $130,000 if a joint return is filed). The individual will not be able to take a student loan interest deduction if the MAGI is $65,000 or more ($130,000 or more if a joint return is filed). For 2001, the deduction was phased out if the MAGI was between $40,000 and $55,000 ($60,000 and $75,000 if a joint return was filed). The CPA could not take a student loan interest deduction if the MAGI was $55,000 or more ($75,000 or more if a joint return was filed).

Prior to 2002, the MAGI for purposes of the student loan interest deduction was the adjusted gross income as shown on the return modified by adding back any:

- Foreign earned income exclusion.
- Foreign housing exclusion or deduction.
- Exclusion of income for bona fide residents of American Samoa.
- Exclusion of income from Puerto Rico.

Beginning in 2002, the taxpayer must also add back any deduction of qualified tuition and related expenses.

TAX-EXEMPT BOND FINANCING FOR QUALIFIED PUBLIC EDUCATIONAL FACILITIES

Beginning in 2002, the private activities for which state and local tax-exempt bonds may be issued will be expanded to include providing qualified public educational facilities.

A qualified public educational facility is any school facility that is:

- Part of a public elementary school or a public secondary school, and
- Owned by a private, for-profit corporation under a public private partnership agreement with a state or local educational agency.

The issuer of the bond should be able to tell the taxpayer whether the bond is tax exempt or not.

EDUCATION-RELATED ADJUSTMENTS TO INCOME

Taxpayers do not have to itemize deductions on Schedule A to claim the three deductions described below. Each is an adjustment to income on the first page of either Form 1040 or 1040A. These deductions are not available on Form 1040EZ.

Tuition and Fees Deduction

Most taxpayers with adjusted gross incomes up to $65,000 ($130,000 on a joint return) may deduct up to $3,000 for tuition and fees paid to attend an accredited college, university, or vocational school. Married couples filing separately and individuals who may be claimed as a dependent may not take this deduction.

A taxpayer may not claim both this deduction and a tax credit for education expenses for the same student in one year. Qualifying expenses from a Coverdell ESA, a qualified tuition program, or an education savings bond must be reduced by any nontaxable earnings.

Student Loan Interest Deduction

Interest on student loans for higher education are deducted whenever paid, regardless of the age of the loan. Prior to 2002, only payments made during the first 60 months of the required repayment term counted. Voluntary payments—for example, those made before the student graduated—did not qualify for the deduction.

This deduction is now available to most taxpayers with incomes up to $65,000, with the deduction amount phasing out as income increases above $50,000. For married couples filing jointly, the phaseout range is from $100,000 to $130,000.

Tax-Free Scholarships

Although scholarships are usually taxable if they carry a future service requirement, tuition, books, and other equipment paid for by the National Health Service Corps Scholarship Program or the Armed Forces Health Professions Scholarship and Financial Assistance Program are no longer taxed. This benefit does not extend to room and board payments under these programs.

Deduction for Educator Expenses

Educators who work at least 900 hours during a school year as a teacher, instructor, counselor, principal, or aide, may deduct up to $250 of qualified out-of-pocket expenses for books and classroom supplies. The deduction is available for those in public or private elementary or secondary schools (including kindergarten). Educators must reduce qualifying expenses by any non-taxable earnings received from Coverdell ESAs, qualified tuition programs, or educational savings bonds.

An eligible educator is one who, for the tax year, is a kindergarten through grade 12 teacher, instructor, counselor, principal, or aide, and who works at least 900 hours during a school year in a school that provides elementary or secondary education, as determined under state law.

Qualified Expenses

These are unreimbursed expenses paid or incurred for books, supplies, computer equipment (including related software and services), other equipment, and supplementary materials used in the classroom. For courses in health and physical education, expenses for supplies are qualified expenses only if they are related to athletics.

To be deductible as an adjustment to income, the qualified expenses must be more than the following amounts for the tax year:

- The interest on qualified U.S. savings bonds the individual excluded from income because the taxpayer paid qualified higher education expenses.
- Any distribution from a qualified tuition program that was excluded from income.
- Any tax-free withdrawals from the taxpayer's Coverdell ESA.

529 EDUCATION FUNDS

More than 40 states offer a variety of 529 plans that have been developed to help families save for college expenses. Many of those states offer 10 or 15 variations of plans within the state itself. Regardless, all plans adhere to 529 basic requirements and therefore the earnings are free of federal taxes. These funds are often exempt from state income taxes — but not always. More and more states are taxing earnings of their residents who save in 529s outside their home states. Although these plans are aimed mostly at parents, other relatives can participate in the saving of up to $100,000 a year without paying federal gift and estate taxes.

Pitfalls to Watch For

Most of the 529 plans fall into one of two categories: either they are plans that financial professionals sell, or they are plans that are sold directly by the state. The majority of plans are sold by financial professionals, and this is no surprise, as it takes a diligent professional to sort through this can of worms. However, in the states' favor, the costs and fees generated by using a financial advisor can offset any benefit earned by the fund. In addition, 529s purchased through financial professionals often have higher management and maintenance fees than plans purchased from the state, with another fee tacked on if the plan is used sooner than anticipated.

Conversely, with the assistance of a financial planner, the client has a better opportunity to make an informed decision. In addition, with recent rule changes, it is much easier to change from one state's plan to another's, without penalty.

Financial planners should advise clients not to make a 529 plan their sole college savings, but just one part of the portfolio.

PREPAID TUITION PLANS

Many states also offer a prepaid tuition plan that permits saving for college via a tax-advantaged investment account. Most prepaid plans are limited to state residents and are not marketed by financial firms, so their scope is not as wide as the 529 tuition provisions arrangements.

Prepaid tuition plans offer major tax benefits. Gains are tax free if they are being used for college tuition. Some states even allow for part of the contribution to be exempt from state income tax. The primary disadvantage is that, although some funds may be used outside of the home state, the funds may not go as far as intended. If a recipient attends a private school, or transfers in to a state university as an out-of-state resident, the funds may not stretch far enough to meet the student's needs. A prepaid tuition plan is just that— prepaid tuition; this money may not be used for housing expenses, books, or supplies. In addition, financial aid may be harder to qualify for, as often scholarships will be reduced based on the amount of money saved within the Prepaid Tuition Plan. Finally, many prepaid programs only have one window of time in which to invest every year.

Chapter 14
Tip Income

CONTENTS

What's the big deal? An estimated $9 billion a year in unreported, untaxed tip income, that's what. Reporting all tip income has always been required by law. When the significant extent to which taxpayers were ignoring the law became evident, the IRS stepped up the emphasis on the requirements for both employee and employer to report tip income.

TIP RATE DETERMINATION/EDUCATION PROGRAM

The Tip Rate Determination/Education Program (TRD/EP) was first promoted in the gaming industry (casino industry) in Las Vegas, Nevada, and has spread to the food and beverage industry. Other industries whose employees receive tips include beauty parlors, barber shops, nail salons, taxi companies, and pizza delivery establishments.

The Tip Rate Determination/Education Program created in 1993 is a national program used in all states. The employer has the option to enter into one of two arrangements under this program: the Tip Rate Determination Agreement (TRDA) or the Tip Reporting Alternative Commitment (TRAC) created in June 1995.

With the introduction of the new programs, four options became available for tip reporting:

1. Tip Rate Determination Agreement.
2. Tip Reporting Alternative Commitment.
3. The status quo—the old basic method following the requirements listed below without any "formal" agreement.
4. Examination of Tip Income Reporting.

Under the Tip Rate Determination/Education Program, the employer may enter into either the TRDA or TRAC arrangement. The Internal Revenue Service (IRS) will assist applicants in understanding and meeting the requirements for participation. Many similarities exist between the two new alternatives, but there are some differences. Following is a descriptive list of the requirements for each, particularly in reference to the food and beverage industry:

TRDA

1. Requires the IRS to work with the establishment to arrive at a tip rate for the various restaurant occupations.
2. Requires the employee to enter into a Tipped Employee Participation Agreement (TEPA) with the employer.
3. Requires the employer to get 75 percent of the employees to sign TEPAs and report at or above the determined rate.
4. Provides that if employees fail to report at or above the determined rate, the employer will provide the names of those employees, their social security numbers, job classification, sales, hours worked, and amount of tips reported.
5. Has no specific education requirement relating to legal responsibility to report tips under the agreement.
6. Participation assures the employer that prior periods will not be examined during the period that the TRDA is in effect.

7. Results in the mailing of a notice and demand to employer for the employer's portion of FICA taxes on unreported tips determined for the six month period used to set the tip rate(s).
8. Prevents employer (only) assessments during the period that the agreement is in effect.

TRAC

1. Does not require that a tip rate be established, but it does require the employer to:
   a. Establish a procedure where a directly tipped employee is provided (no less than monthly) a written statement of charged tips attributed to the employee.
   b. Implement a procedure for the employee to verify or correct any statement of attributed tips.
   c. Adopt a method where an indirectly tipped employee reports his or her tips (no less than monthly). This could include a statement prepared by the employer and verified or corrected by the employee.
   d. Establish a procedure where a written statement is prepared and processed (no less than monthly) reflecting all cash tips attributable to sales of the directly tipped employee.
2. Does not require an agreement between the employee and the employer.
3. Affects all (100 percent) of the employees.
4. Includes a commitment by the employer to educate and reeducate quarterly all directly and indirectly tipped employees and new hires of their statutory requirement to report all tips to their employer.
5. Participation assures the employer that prior periods will not be examined during the period that the agreement is in effect.
6. Prevents employer (only) assessments during the period that the agreement is in effect.
7. Assures that employers comply with all tax reporting, filing, and payment obligations.
8. Requires employers to maintain and make available records to the IRS.
9. Emphasizes that employees earning $20 or more a month in tips must report them to the employer.

In return, the IRS generally will not perform a tip examination on employers complying with the TRAC guidelines. In contrast, an establishment whose employees underreport their tips could be liable for back FICA taxes.

The approach has helped lead to increased tip reporting, but the IRS believes there is still ample room for improvement. In the food and beverage sector alone, tip reporting jumped from $3.9 billion in 1993 to $5.2 billion in 1995 to more than $7 billion in 1998. However, estimates placed the amount of annual tips going to those same workers at $18 billion annually.

TRAC Agreement Revised.   The IRS has been working cooperatively with the restaurant industry in response to industry concerns regarding some aspects of the TRAC program. In late 1999, the IRS took steps to reduce the administrative burdens of restaurant operators by making several changes in the regulations:

1. The IRS will no longer revoke TRAC agreements in cases where employers make a good-faith effort at following the guidelines but employees still fail to report tips. Instead of pursuing the employers in such situations, the IRS will focus on the employees who are not in compliance with tip reporting.

2. Another change involves restaurants with locations in different IRS Districts. Under the new plan, the restaurant's headquarter operations will work directly with their local IRS office on TRAC issues. This streamlined approach will be simpler and more straightforward than the old system, where different locations of a company had to deal with different people in different IRS Districts.

3. The third change involves the expiration date of the TRAC program. Instead of ending in May 2000, the program will now run through May, 2005, with the possibility of its being extended even longer.

About 10,000 companies, representing more than 30,000 locations, have already entered the agreements, and the IRS hopes more will follow in the months ahead as a result of this shifting of more responsibility to the employee.

Instituting the Program

To enter into one of the arrangements, an employer should submit an application letter to the area IRS Chief, Examination/Compliance Division, Attn: Tip Coordinator. The Tip Coordinator can provide a letter format as well as extensive information on the two separate arrangements.

All employers with establishments where tipping is customary should review their operations. Then, if it is determined that there is or has been an underreporting of tips, the employer should apply for one of the two arrangements under the TRD/EP. Employers currently with the TRDA in effect may revoke the arrangement and simultaneously enter into a TRAC.

The particular advantage to the employer who adopts one of these programs is that no subsequent tip examination is imposed as long as terms of the arrangement have been met and all tips have been reported.

EMPLOYER TIP REPORTING ALTERNATIVE COMMITMENT PROGRAM (EMTRAC)

The IRS developed the EmTRAC Agreement program in response to employers in the food and beverage industry who expressed an interest in designing their own TRAC programs. These agreements are available to employers in this industry in which employees receive both cash and charged tips. The EmTRAC program retains many of the provisions of the TRAC agreement, including:

- The employer must establish an educational program that emphasizes that the law requires employees to report to their employer all of their cash and charged tips.
- Education must be furnished immediately for newly hired employees and quarterly for existing employees.
- The employer must establish tip reporting procedures under which a written or electronic statement is prepared and processed on a regular basis (no less than monthly), reflecting all tips for services attributable to each employee.

The employer may have one, or many places of business. For purposes of the program, each place of business is called an establishment. If an employer has more than one establishment, it can choose which establishments to include in its EmTRAC program.

Specific Requirements of the Program

The EmTRAC program provides an employer with considerable latitude in designing its educational program and tip reporting procedures, which the employer may combine. For example, a point-of-sale tip reporting system could meet both of these requirements, because the employee is reminded of the tip reporting requirement at the end of each sale and because the reporting occurs at the end of each sale.

The employer must agree:

- To comply with the requirements for filing all required federal tax returns and paying and depositing all federal taxes.
- To maintain the following records for at least four years after the April 14 following the calendar year to which the records relate:
  —Gross receipts subject to tipping.
  —Charge receipts showing charged tips.

- Upon the request of the IRS, to make the following quarterly totals available, by establishment, for statistical samplings of its establishments:
  - Gross receipts subject to tipping.
  - Charge receipts showing charged tips.
  - Total charged tips.
  - Total tips reported.

The IRS agrees:

- Not to initiate any tip examinations of the employer or an establishment included in the EmTRAC for any period for which the EmTRAC program is in effect, except in relation to a tip examination of one or more employees or former employees of the employer or an establishment.
- To base any section 3121(q) notice and demand issued to the employer or an establishment included in the EmTRAC and relating to any period during which the EmTRAC program is in effect solely on amounts reflected on:
  - Form 4137, *Social Security and Medicare Tax on Unreported Tip Income,* filed by an employee with his or her Form 1040, or
  - Form 885-T, *Adjustment of Social Security Tax on Tip Income Not Reported to Employer,* prepared at the conclusion of an employee tip examination.
- Not to evaluate the employer for compliance with the provisions of its EmTRAC program for the first two calendar quarters for which the EmTRAC program is effective.

Both parties agree that, for purposes of the EmTRAC program, a compliance review is not treated as an examination or an inspection of books of account or records, and an inspection of books of account or records pursuant to a tip examination is not an inspection of books or records for purposes of section 7605(b) of the Code, and is not a prior audit for purposes of section 530 of the Revenue Act of 1978.

The effective date of an EmTRAC program is the first day of the quarter beginning on or after the date the IRS signs an approval letter.

An employer may at any time terminate its EmTRAC program either completely or with respect to one or more establishments. The IRS may terminate its approval with respect to the EmTRAC program or a specific establishment or establishments, only if:

- The IRS determines that the employer or establishment(s) has failed to comply with the required provisions.
- The IRS pursues an administrative or judicial action relating to the employer, an establishment included in the EmTRAC, or any other related party to the employer's EmTRAC program.

Generally, any termination is effective the first day of the first calendar quarter after the terminating party notifies the other party in writing. If the employer has an existing TRAC agreement or TRDA covering one or more establishments included in the employer's EmTRAC program, the existing TRAC agreement or TRDA will terminate with respect to that establishment or those establishments upon the approval of the employer's EmTRAC program.

Procedures for Requesting Approval

The employer must request approval of its EmTRAC program. For this purpose, the Service has developed a pro forma letter that an employer must use to request approval of its EmTRAC program. The letter requests approval of the employer's EmTRAC program and states that the employer will comply with the provisions set forth in the letter and in the information above. A copy of the approval request letter can be obtained by mail by contacting the tip coordinator in any local IRS office or by calling (202) 622-5532.

Procedures for Approving Requests

After receiving the approval request letter, the IRS will review the employer's program. If the program meets the necessary requirements, the IRS will send the employer an approval letter specifying the effective date of the employer's EmTRAC program.

If the IRS determines that the employer's EmTRAC program fails to meet all the requirements, it will contact the employer and offer assistance in working out a program that will meet both the employer's needs and the IRS requirements.

Upon request to the local tip coordinator or the EmTRAC Coordinator, the IRS will assist any employer in establishing, maintaining, or improving its educational program or tip reporting procedures.

The Commissioner of Internal Revenue may terminate all EmTRAC programs at any time following a significant statutory change in the FICA taxation of tips. After December 31, 2005, the Commissioner may terminate prospectively the Tip Rate Determination/Education Program and all EmTRAC programs.

BASIC RULES RELATING TO TIP INCOME REPORTING

The following discussion concerns how tip income is taxed and how it should be reported to the IRS on the federal income tax return. The employees of food and beverage companies are the main subjects of this review; the record keeping rules and other information also apply to other workers who receive tips.

As pointed out earlier, all tips that are received by employees are taxable income and are subject to federal income taxes. Employees must include in gross income all tips received directly from customers, and tips from charge customers paid to the employer, who must pay them to the employee. In addition, cash tips of $20 or more that an employee receives in a month while working for any one employer are subject to withholding of income tax, social security retirement tax, and Medicare tax. The employee should report tips to the employer in order to determine the correct amount of these taxes.

Tips and other pay are used to determine the amount of social security benefits that an employee receives when he or she retires, becomes disabled, or dies. Noncash tips are not counted as wages for social security purposes. Future Social Security Administration (SSA) benefits can be figured correctly only if the SSA has the correct information. To make sure that an employee has received credit for all his or her earnings, the employee should request a statement of earnings from the SSA at least every other year. The SSA will send the person a statement that should be carefully checked to be sure it includes all of the employee's earnings.

Every large food and beverage business must report to the IRS any tips allocated to the employees. Generally, tips must be allocated to be paid by employees when the total tips reported to an employer by employees are less than 8 percent of the establishment's food and beverage sales of that employee. This necessitates the employer and employees keeping accurate records of the employee's tip income.

Daily Tip Record

The employee must keep a daily tip record so he or she can:

1. Report tips accurately to the employer.
2. Report tips accurately on a tax return.
3. Prove tip income if the taxpayer's return is ever questioned.

There are two ways to keep a daily tip record:

1. The employee can keep a daily "tip diary."
2. The employee should keep copies of documents that show the tips, such as restaurant bills and credit card charge slips.

The employee can start record keeping by writing his or her name, the employer's name, and the name of the business if it is different from the employer's name. Each workday, the employee should write and date the following information in a tip diary.

1. Cash tips received directly from customers or other employees.
2. Tips from credit card charge customers that the employer pays the employee.
3. The value of any noncash tips received, such as tickets, passes, or other items of value.
4. The amount of tips the employee paid out to other employees through tip pools, tip splitting, or other arrangements, and the names of the employees to whom tips were paid.

Reporting Tips to the Employer

The employee must report tips to the employer so that:

1. The employer can withhold federal income tax, social security taxes, and Medicare taxes.
2. The employer can report the correct amount of the employee's earnings to the Social Security Administration. This will affect the employee's benefits when the employee retires or becomes disabled, or the family's benefits upon the employee's death.

What Tips to Report

Only cash, check, or credit card tips should be reported to the employer. If the total tips for any one month from any one job are less than $20, they should not be reported to the employer. The value of any noncash tips, such as tickets or passes, is not reported to the employer because the employee does not have to pay social security and Medicare taxes on these tips. The employee will, however, report them on his or her individual tax return. The following information should be written on the report to be given to the employer:

1. Name, address, and social security number.
2. The employer's name, address, and business name if it is different from the employer's name.
3. The month, or the dates of any shorter period, in which the tips are received.
4. The total amount of tips the employee received.

The employee must sign and date the report and give it to the employer. The employee should keep a copy of the report for his or her personal records. The report is to be completed each month and given to the employer by the tenth of the next month.

Employer Records for Tip Allocation

Large food and beverage establishments are required to report certain additional information about tips to the IRS. To make sure that employees are reporting tips correctly, employers must keep records to verify amounts reported by employees. Certain employers must allocate tips if the percentage of tips reported by employees falls below a required minimum percentage of gross sales. To allocate tips means to assign an additional amount as tips to each employee whose reported tips are below the required percentage. The rules apply to premises in which:

1. Food and beverages are provided for consumption on the premises.
2. Tipping is customary.
3. The employer normally employed more than ten people on a typical business day during the preceding calendar year.

Tip allocation rules do not apply to food and beverage establishments where tipping is not customary such as:

1. A cafeteria or fast food restaurant.
2. A restaurant that adds a service charge of 10 percent or more to 95 percent or more of its food and beverage sales.
3. Food and beverage establishments located outside the United States.

The rules apply only if the total amount of tips reported by all tipped employees to the employer is less than 8 percent, or some lower acceptable percentage of the establishment's total food or beverage sales, with some adjustments. If reported tips total less than 8 percent of total sales, the employer must allocate the difference between 8 percent of total sales, or some lower acceptable percentage approved by the IRS, and the amount of tips reported by all tipped employees. The employer will exclude carryout sales, state and local taxes, and sales with a service charge of 10 percent or more when figuring total sales.

Usually, the employer will allocate to all affected employees their share of tips every payroll period. However, the employer should not withhold any taxes from the allocated amount. No allocation will be made to the employee if the employee reports tips at least equal to the employee's share of 8 percent of the establishment's total food and beverage sales.

Penalty for Not Reporting Tips

If the employee does not report tips to his or her employer as required, the employee can be subject to a penalty equal to 50 percent of the social security and Medicare taxes owed. The penalty amount is in addition to the taxes owed. The penalty can be avoided if the employee can show reasonable cause for not reporting the tips to the employer. A statement should be attached to the tax return explaining why the tips were not reported to the employer. If an employee's regular pay is not enough for the employer to withhold all the taxes owed on the regular pay plus reported tips, the employee can give the employer money to pay the rest of the taxes, up to the close of the calendar year.

If the employee does not give the employer enough money, the employer will apply the regular pay and any money given by the employee in the following order:

1. All taxes on the employee's regular pay.
2. Social security and Medicare taxes on the reported tips.
3. Federal, state, and local income taxes on the reported tips.

Any taxes that remain unpaid can be collected by the employer from the employee's next paycheck. If withholding taxes remain uncollected at the end of the year, the employee must make an estimated tax payment. To report these taxes, a return must be filed even if the employee would not otherwise have to file. If the employer could not collect all the social security and Medicare taxes owed on the tips reported to the employer, the uncollected taxes must be shown by the employer on a Form W-2. The employee must then also report these uncollected taxes on his or her return.

Tip Rates

Depending on the Occupational Category and the employer's business practices, tips can be *measured* in different ways.

1. *Actual tips* generally apply to Employees in Occupational Categories (O.C.) where pooling of tips is common. The tips are pooled during a shift and the total is split among the employees of the O.C. who worked the shift.
2. *Tip rates* generally apply to employees in O.C. where pooling of tips is not common. The rate may be a percentage of sales, a dollar amount, or other accurate basis of measurement per hour or shift, a dollar amount per drink served, a dollar amount per working hour, or other accurate measurement.

Methods for Determining Tip Rates

The employer will determine tip rates for the O.C. based on information available to the employer, historical information provided by the IRS representative, and generally accepted accounting principles (GAAP). The rates will specify whether the tips are received as a percentage of sales, a dollar amount per hour or shift, a dollar amount per drink served, a dollar amount per dealing hour in a casino, or on another basis.

Initial Tip Rate

The initial tip rate for each O.C. is shown where pool and split tips methods are used by the employees.

ANNUAL REVIEW

The employer will review annually, on a calender year basis, changes in the tip rates assigned to its O.C. In connection with the review, the employer can review its O.C. The initial rates for each O.C. will apply to the first full calendar year of the review.

Employer Submission

If the employer believes that a revision of one or more rates or O.C. is appropriate, the employer will submit proposed revisions to the IRS representative by September 30. If the employer fails to submit a proposed rate revision by September 30 of the taxable year, the employee will be treated as having submitted the rate in effect for the current year.

Internal Revenue Service Review

The IRS representative will review the proposed rates and notify the employer in writing of the approval or disapproval by November 30. If the IRS representative does not approve one or more proposed rates, the existing rate or rates will be continued until no later than the last day of the following February.

The effective date of revised rates and O.C. will become effective on the later of January 1 of the calendar year, or on the first day of the month following the date the employer and the IRS representative agree upon a revised rate. The IRS representative can examine a participating employee's tip income for any period if an employee reports tips at a rate less than the tip rate for the employee's occupational category.

These amounts must be an additional tax on the employee's tax return. The employee may have uncollected taxes if his or her regular pay was not enough for the employer to withhold all the taxes the taxpayer owed, but did not give the employer enough money to pay the rest of the taxes. The employee must report these uncollected taxes on a return.

ALLOCATED TIPS

Allocated tips are tips that the employer assigned to an employee in addition to the tips the employee reported to the employer for the year. The employer will have done this only if the employee worked in a restaurant, cocktail lounge, or similar business that must allocate tips to employees, and the reported tips were less than the employee's share of 8 percent of food and drink sales. If allocated tips are shown on a return, and if social security and Medicare taxes were not withheld from the allocated tips, these taxes must be reported as additional tax on a return.

Allocation Formula

The allocation can be done either under a formula agreed to by both the employer and the employees or, if they cannot reach an agreement, under a formula prescribed by IRS regulations. The allocation formula in the regulations provides that tip allocations are made only to directly tipped employees. If tips are received directly from customers, the employees are directly tipped employees, even if the tips are turned over to a tip pool. Waiters, waitresses, and bartenders are usually considered directly tipped employees. If tips are not normally received directly from customers, the employee is an indirectly tipped employee. Examples are busboys, service bartenders, and cooks. If an employee receives tips both directly and indirectly through tip splitting or tip pooling, the employee is treated as a directly tipped employee.

If customers of the establishment tip less than 8 percent on average, either the employee or a majority of the directly tipped employees can petition to have the allocation percentage reduced from 8 percent. This petition is made to the IRS representative for the IRS district in which the establishment is located. The percentage cannot be reduced below 2 percent.

A fee is required to have the IRS consider a petition to lower the tip allocation percentage. The fee must be paid by check or money order made out to the Internal Revenue Service. (The user fee amount for 2003 is $275; the IRS representative in the taxpayer's area will know if this amount has changed.)

The employees' petition to lower the allocation percentage must be in writing, and must contain enough information to allow the IRS representative to estimate with reasonable accuracy the establishment's actual tip rate. This information might include the changed tip rate, type of establishment, menu prices, location, hours of operation, amount of self-service required, and whether the customer receives the check from the server or pays the server for the meal. If the employer possesses any relevant information, the employer must provide it to the district upon request of the employees or the IRS representative.

The employees' petition must be consented to by more than one-half of the directly tipped employees working for the establishment at the time the petition is filed. If the petition covers more than one establishment, it must be consented to by more than one-half of the total number of directly tipped employees of the covered establishments. The petition must state the total number of directly tipped employees of the establishment(s) and the number of directly tipped employees consenting to the petition.

The petition may cover two or more establishments if the employees have made a good faith determination that the tip wages are essentially the same and if the establishments are:

1. Owned by the same employer.
2. Essentially the same type of business.
3. In the same Internal Revenue Service region.

A petition that covers two or more establishments must include the names and locations of the establishments and must be sent to the IRS representative for the district in which the greatest number of covered establishments are located. If there is an equal number of covered establishments in two or more districts, the employees can choose which district to petition. Employees who file a petition must promptly notify their employer of the petition. The employer must then promptly furnish the IRS representative with an annual information return form showing the tip income and allocated tips filed for the establishment for the three immediately preceding calendar years.

The employer will report the amount of tips allocated to employees on the employees' Form W-2 separately from wages and reported tips. The employer bases withholding only on wages and reported tips. The employer should not withhold income, social security, and Medicare taxes from the allocated amount. Any incorrectly withheld taxes should be refunded to the employee by the employer.

If an employee leaves a job before the end of the calendar year and requests an early Form W-2, the employer does not have to include a tip allocation on the Form W-2. However, the employer can show the actual allocated amount if it is known, or show an estimated allocation. In January of the following year, the employer most provide Form W-2 if the early Form W-2 showed no allocation and the employer later determined that an allocation was required, or if the estimated allocation shown was wrong by more than 5 percent of the actual allocation.

If an employee does not have adequate records for his or her actual tips, the employee must include the allocated tips shown on the Form W-2 as additional tip income on the tax return. If the employee has records, allocated tips should not be shown on the employee's return. Additional tip income is included only if those records show more tips received than the amount reported to the employer.

SUPREME COURT RULING ON "AGGREGATE METHOD"

In 2002, a 6-3 ruling by the Supreme Court upheld a move by federal tax collectors to force employers to pay the 7.65 percent Social Security tax on all income received by their workers, including tips. The dispute originally arose over the method used to calculate the total tip income, specifically in restaurants.

At some previous time, restaurant owners had been told that they could rely on reports from their servers and bartenders. However, tips were being notoriously underreported as was pointed out in the first paragraph of this chapter.

In the early 1990s, the IRS decided to survey credit card slips to calculate how much waiters and waitresses were actually receiving in tips. From this information, the Service would use the average tip to estimate the total of tips. For example, if customers on average added a 15 percent tip on their credit cards, the IRS would assume that customers tipped 15 percent on all of the restaurant's income, including cash payments. The owner could be assessed back taxes based on this amount.

The restaurant industry objected strenuously, claiming that customers who pay in cash often leave lower tips and that some leave no tip whatsoever. However, the Supreme Court Justices discounted such complaints and upheld the estimates based on credit card receipts as a reasonable way to assess the taxes owed by a restaurant.

In the specific instance, the IRS estimated the tips for 1992 as $368,374, not the $220,845 that the servers had reported. The IRS sent the owner an $11,286 bill for back taxes for 1992 to cover his share of the employee Social Security taxes, known officially as the Federal Insurance Contribution Act (FICA) taxes.

Steps Toward a Decision

A Circuit Court of Appeals judge had then ruled the IRS was not empowered to "slap an employer" with back tax assessments based on "rough and somewhat inflated estimates." However, the U.S. Solicitor General appealed the issue to the Supreme Court. It was pointed out that the amount of reported tips to the IRS rose from $8.5 billion in 1994 to $14.3 billion in 1999 after the tax agency pressed for better compliance. This demonstrated rather graphically that tip income had been greatly underreported.

There is no question but that the restaurant owners can challenge the accuracy of their tax assessments. However, the majority opinion of the Supreme Court stated that their objections do not "show the aggregate estimate method is an unreasonable way of ascertaining unpaid FICA taxes for which the employer is indisputably liable."

Reaction to the Decision

Leaders of the National Restaurant Association, which represents 200,000 eating establishments, denounced the decision and said they would take their fight to Congress. They feel that the ruling may affect all employers, like hotels, casinos and taxi companies whose employees receive tips.

An IRS lawyer stressed that the "aggregate estimate" method (the term given to this system of determining tax owed) has not been widely used so far. Moreover, it was emphasized that it is brought into the picture only when it appears restaurants are underpaying their taxes.

Understandably, the Commissioner for the IRS favored the Supreme Court decision and feels that it upholds the IRS's ability to make sure all Americans pay a fair share of taxes. The IRS plans to continue working cooperatively with the restaurant industry and other industries where tips are common.

With the 6-3 decision in the books, the IRS does not anticipate any particular change in the manner of determining and collecting the taxes on tip income.

Index

ASPEN PUBLISHERS

SOFTWARE LICENSE AGREEMENT FOR ELECTRONIC FILES TO ACCOMPANY
2004 ACCOUNTING DESK BOOK (THE "BOOK").

PLEASE READ THE TERMS AND CONDI-TIONS OF THIS LICENSE AGREEMENT CARE-FULLY BEFORE INSTALLING THE FILES FROM THE CD-ROM.

THE ELECTRONIC FILES ARE COPYRIGHTED AND LICENSED (NOT SOLD). BY INSTALLING THE ELECTRONIC FILES ("THE SOFTWARE"), YOU ARE ACCEPTING AND AGREEING TO THE TERMS OF THIS LICENSE AGREEMENT. IF YOU ARE NOT WILLING TO BE BOUND BY THE TERMS OF THIS LICENSE AGREEMENT, YOU SHOULD REMOVE THE SOFTWARE FROM YOUR COMPUTER AT THIS TIME AND PROMPTLY RETURN THE PACKAGE IN RE-SELLABLE CONDITION AND YOU WILL RE-CEIVE A REFUND OF YOUR MONEY. THIS LICENSE AGREEMENT REPRESENTS THE ENTIRE AGREEMENT CONCERNING THE SOFTWARE BETWEEN YOU AND ASPEN PUB-LISHERS (REFERRED TO AS "LICENSOR"), AND IT SUPERSEDES ANY PRIOR PROPOSAL, REPRESENTATION, OR UNDERSTANDING BETWEEN THE PARTIES.

1. License Grant. Licensor hereby grants to you, and you accept, a nonexclusive license to use the Software, and any computer programs contained therein in ma-chine-readable, object code form only, and the accom-panying User Documentation, only as authorized in this License Agreement. The Software may be used only on a single computer owned, leased, or otherwise controlled by you, or in the event of the inoperability of that computer, on a backup computer selected by you. Neither concurrent use on two or more comput-ers nor use in a local area network or other network is permitted without separate authorization and the pos-sible payment of another license fees. You agree that you will not assign, sublease, transfer, pledge, lease, rent, or share your rights under the License Agreement. You agree that you may not reverse engineer, decom-pile, disassemble, or otherwise adapt, modify, or trans-late the Software.

Upon loading the Software into your computer, you may retain the Software CD-ROM for backup pur-poses. In addition, you may make one copy of the Software on a set of diskettes (or other storage me-dium) for the purpose of backup in the event the Soft-ware files are damaged or destroyed. You may make one copy of any additional User Documentation (such as the README.TXT file or the "About the Com-puter Disc" section of the Book) for backup purposes. Any such copies of the Software or the User Docu-mentation shall include the Licensor's copyright and other proprietary notices. Except as authorized under this paragraph, no copies of the Software or any por-tions thereof may be made by you or any person under your authority or control.

2. Licensor's Rights. You acknowledge and agree that the Software and the User Documentation are propri-etary products of Licensor protected under U.S. copy-right law. You further acknowledge and agree that all right, title, and interest in and to the Software, includ-ing associated intellectual property rights, are and shall remain with Licensor. This License Agreement does not convey to you an interest in or to the Soft-ware, including associated intellectual property rights,

which are and shall remain with Licensor. This Li-cense Agreement does not convey to you an interest in or to the Software, but only a limited right of use rev-ocable in accordance with the terms of this License Agreement.

3. License Fees. The license fees paid by you are paid in consideration of the licenses granted under this License Agreement.

4. Term. This License Agreement is effective upon your installing this software and shall continue until terminated. You may terminate this License Agree-ment at any time by removing all copies of the Soft-ware and returning the CD-ROM to Licensor. Licen-sor may terminate this License Agreement upon the breach by you of any term hereof. Upon such termi-nation by Licensor, you agree to return to Licensor the Software and all copies and portions thereof.

5. Limited Warranty. Licensor warrants, for our benefit alone, for a period of 90 days from the date of commencement of this License Agreement (referred to as the "Warranty Period") that the Program CD-ROM in which the software is contained is free from defects in material and workmanship. If during the Warranty Period, a defect appears in the Program CD-ROM, you may return the Program to Licensor for either replacement or, at Licensor's option, refund of amounts paid by you under this License Agree-ment. You agree that the foregoing constitutes your sole and exclusive remedy for breach by Licensor of any warranties made under this Agreement. EX-CEPT FOR THE WARRANTIES SET FORTH ABOVE, THE PROGRAM CD-ROM, AND THE SOFTWARE CONTAINED THEREIN, ARE LI-CENSED "AS-IS," AND LICENSOR DISCLAIMS ANY AND ALL OTHER WARRANTIES, WHETHER EXPRESS OR IMPLIED, INCLUD-ING, WITHOUT LIMITATION, ANY IMPLIED WARRANTIES OF MERCHANTABILITY OR FITNESS FOR A PARTICULAR PURPOSE.

6. Limitation of Liability. Licensor's cumulative liabil-ity to you or any other party for any loss or damages resulting from any claims, demands, or actions arising out of or relating to this Agreement shall not exceed the license fee paid to Licensor for the use of the Software. IN NO EVENT SHALL LICENSOR BE LIABLE FOR ANY INDIRECT, INCIDENTAL, CONSEQUENTIAL, SPECIAL OR EXEMPLARY DAMAGES (INCLUDING, BUT NOT LIMITED TO, LOSS OF DATA, BUSINESS INTERRUP-TION, OR LOST PROFITS) EVEN IF LICENSOR HAS BEEN ADVISED OF THE POSSIBILITY OF SUCH DAMAGES.

7. Miscellaneous. The License Agreement shall be construed and governed in accordance with the laws of the State of New York. Should any term of this Li-cense Agreement be declared void or unenforceable by any court of competent jurisdiction, such declara-tion shall have no effect on the remaining terms hereof. The failure of either party to enforce any rights granted hereunder or to take action against the other party in the event of any breach hereunder shall not be deemed a waiver by that party as to subsequent enforcement of rights or subsequent actions in the event of future breaches.